Neil

To my friend Mitchell,
with gratitude for giving
me the opportunity to
teach again,

Solly

THE TALE OF THE SCALE

The Tale of the Scale

AN
ODYSSEY
OF INVENTION

———

Solly Angel

OXFORD
UNIVERSITY PRESS

2004

OXFORD
UNIVERSITY PRESS

Oxford New York

Auckland Bangkok Buenos Aires Cape Town Chennai
Dar es Salaam Delhi Hong Kong Istanbul Karachi Kolkata
Kuala Lumpur Madrid Melbourne Mexico City Mumbai Nairobi
São Paulo Shanghai Taipei Tokyo Toronto

Copyright © 2004 by Oxford University Press
Published by Oxford University Press, Inc.
198 Madison Avenue, New York, New York 10016
www.oup.com

Oxford is a registered trademark of Oxford University Press

Library of Congress Cataloging-in-Publication Data
Angel, Solly.
The tale of the scale: an odyssey of invention / Solly Angel.
p. cm.
Includes bibliographical references and index.
ISBN 0-19-515868-7
1. Scales (Weighing instruments).
2. Inventions.
3. Industrial design.
4. Angel, Solly.
I. Title.
TS410.A54 2003
681'.2—dc21
2003048699

Book design and composition by Mark McGarry,
Texas Type & Book Works
Set in Minion

1 3 5 7 9 10 8 6 4 2
Printed in the United States of America on acid-free paper

For Lucinda

Contents

1

Isn't There a Better Way?

The road to Jerusalem was dark and wet. I was ten at the time, sitting in the passenger seat. A partner of my father, a family friend, was driving me back home from somewhere. He had an imposing bulbous nose, laced with purple veins. I avoided staring at it, choosing instead to gaze through the raindrops at the emptiness ahead. We were quiet. There was not much to say. Suddenly, bales of hay from the overloaded truck ahead of us started to tumble onto the road. Our wheels screeched, as one bale squeezed under the car and another landed on the windshield. The car shook to an abrupt stop. The driver turned to me, looked me in the eye, and said: "You see, Solly, either things go according to plan, or there is a story."

———

AUGUST 1986

I have noticed that people have minivisions. They are quite common, in fact, and almost everyone has had them. They involve thinking up something useful and interesting that does not yet exist—some new gadget, for example, or a new service, or a new idea for a book or a movie—and then starting to fantasize about making it happen, taking it to market, so to speak. Most minivisions are soon extinguished, for better or for worse, because conditions—and there are many—are simply not right. Of the many thousands of minivisions that pop into ordinary people's minds every day, only a chosen few are actually ever pursued.

One day in 1986, while the monsoon rains were flooding Bangkok, I had a minivision too. It was not the first one I had and would not be the last one. But that Bangkok minivision of mine was one of those chosen few, and it surely succeeded in seducing me into pursuing it. It was an unlikely siren, not being a particularly brilliant idea or a potential milestone in the history of innovation, nor even remotely related to my field of expertise. My background was in architecture and urban planning, and I had no mechanical skills and no penchant for electronics.

Yet in my minivision, it occurred to me that the portable personal scale—more commonly known as the bathroom scale—could be reinvented so that it would be no more than a quarter inch in thickness and weigh no more than one pound. Then it would be truly portable and one could even carry it around in one's bag on one's travels, like just another accessory. I could see it so clearly in my mind's eye. Wouldn't that be elegant, I mused to myself. Soon enough, these

musings jelled into a plan. *The Tale of the Scale* is the story of how that plan was
carried out. But I am running ahead of myself.

* * *

Before expounding on my minivision, I need to explain what I was doing in
Bangkok of all places in the 1986 rainy season. I came to Bangkok in 1973 actually, only a year or so after acquiring a doctoral degree in urban planning at
Berkeley. A former classmate offered me a one-year teaching assignment at the
Asian Institute of Technology—a regional graduate school of engineering serving South and Southeast Asia—to help start an urban planning program there. I
accepted it reluctantly, mostly out of curiosity. But when the year was up, I found
I could not bring myself to leave. The city (and, more generally, the East) already
had me under its spell. And so I stayed.

As a student of cities, the largest of all man-made objects, I found Bangkok
fascinating—it somehow worked, even flourished, in the absence of any planning at all. I was especially drawn to its slums, the clusters of wooden houses on
stilts scattered throughout the city, along the meandering canals, behind luxurious residential compounds, over the swamps of the Klong Toey port area (Fig. 1),
everywhere. They embodied an absence of formal, studied "architecture"; and
they possessed a fundamental legitimacy born out of necessity—one that con-
formed neither to zoning laws and building codes, nor to the abstractions of
property law.

To me, these dwellings—simple, and often in the shape of work-in-progress—
seemed more like a solution than a problem: They needed to be improved rather

1 *The Port of Klong Toey slum in Bangkok*

than destroyed. But to the Thai government, they were like a cancer infesting the city, malignant growths to be surgically removed. From time to time, the authorities half-heartedly pledged to uproot the slums and replace them with costly apartment blocks—the ultimate symbols of modernity. This was wishful thinking. By my count, a quarter of the population of the city—some one million people—lived in slums, and the awesome budget for housing all of them at the public's expense would never materialize.

Together with a friend, I wrote a polemical article in the *Bangkok Post*, entitled "Seventeen Reasons Why the Housing Problem Can't Be Solved." It suggested that we were looking for solutions in the wrong places while overlooking the obvious. It prepared me for what lay ahead: the awesome task of dismantling an entrenched mode of interpreting the housing problem. How did one go about that? There were so many questions that needed answers. I seemed to have found my calling.

I soon immersed myself in the housing problem. I read whatever I could find on housing, but I found most of it repetitive and unsatisfactory. I explored slum communities throughout Asia until I felt I understood how they came to be and how they functioned. I was humbled by the realization that there was never a limit to the resourcefulness of the poor in managing to take care of their housing needs. They did it as a matter of course, much like birds went about building their nests.

Gradually, with newly acquired Thai friends, I started to work with the poor. In one slum—a Moslem one with a blue mosque at its center—we trained a fire brigade and helped finance and construct a pumphouse and a network of pipes and hydrants. The pump house was located on the canal adjoining the community. Water was to be drawn out of the canal by a pump that was powered by a rebuilt Toyota truck engine. The people made all the critical design decisions.

We later organized some 200 poor families to build a new residential community on the outskirts of Bangkok. We called it Building Together. It was based on utopian principles of self-help and mutual aid. Groups of families—men, women, and children—were engaged in building clusters of houses together during evenings and weekends. It was exciting and fulfilling work, but it was slow. It would have been much faster, and possibly cheaper, to hire a contractor to build those houses. But we were not just building houses, we were building a community and that took time, a long time.

By 1986, having been at the housing problem for some 13 years, I was a familiar face on the housing scene, both in Bangkok and abroad. In August of that year, in the middle of the rainy season, I accepted a one-year consulting contract to work at the heart of the beast—the National Housing Authority itself. I was appointed to head a research team that was to advise the authority on matters of housing policy. I had no other pressing obligations and I was ready to start. The tale of the scale was ready to start too.

* * *

The scale minivision occurred on an afternoon I spent at home—a pink stucco house surrounded by a brick wall, not far from the Royal Palace. The rain that started less than an hour earlier was falling in sheets, the house was engulfed by water, and the water level was rising. It had nowhere to go but up, because all of the streets of Bangkok were under water—a common occurrence during the monsoon season. They had been flooded for days. The city slowed to a crawl. Some, I knew, had a four-hour commute in either direction. But the people I saw wading through the streets—in water up to their thighs—had wider-than-usual smiles on their wet faces. Productivity and efficiency plummeted. It must have felt like the good old days.

The storm lasted barely an hour, and, in an instant, the sky was clear again and the sun was out, pretending nothing had happened. The maid's room in the back of the house was flooded. She walked into the house with a broad smile, leaving her wet footprints on the teak floor, quietly opening all the wooden shutters and letting the light in. "It rains a lot," she said in Thai, by way of making conversation. "It rains a lot," I agreed. The ceiling fans were fervently turning overhead, but with little effect. Humidity was still at 100 percent and so it would be for a while.

I had just arrived back from a month in the States that same day. I felt disoriented, and all I could do was to sit in the living room, doing nothing. My gaze—somewhat frozen with jetlag—now rested on the bathroom scale tucked under the rattan bookshelf.

This scale was essentially a shallow metal box with rounded corners covered by a second metal box turned upside down. The outer box was ten inches square and maybe two inches high, and the whole scale probably weighed some six pounds. The rubber mat on top of the outer box was loose, lying at a skewed angle—the glue that bonded it to the metal was never meant for tropical humidity. At the center of the outer box there was a plastic window, below which there was a circular white dial. When you stepped on the scale, the white dial turned. It indicated what your weight might be—within a few pounds—if you zeroed it regularly, didn't sway too much, and didn't compare it with your weight on other scales.

In the great leap forward that most tools and appliances seemed to have taken of late, this pitiful object had been left behind. "Isn't there a better way?" I asked myself, maybe not for the first time but louder than before. Yes, there is a better way, was the answer. I could already see a new scale in my mind's eye: it would be no more than a quarter inch in thickness—like one of those new electronic calculators that fit into your shirt pocket—and it would weigh no more than a pound. Strangely, I felt that the scale was luring me from its place under the rattan bookshelf, imploring me, almost pleading with me to be redesigned. Why me? I didn't know yet, but I was attracted.

* * *

Questions such as "Isn't there a better way?" "Does it have to be this way?" or "Is this the only way?" are the motors of our ingenuity, the questions from which arise political reforms, scientific discoveries, new inventions, and even new religions. Surely, these are the questions that initiate all deviations from the path of least resistance and from the passive and meek acceptance of our fate. Some may mistakenly think that these questions are only formulated in the West: people in the East are more inclined to accept things as they are, goes the myth, and people in the West question why things are the way they are and then proceed to improve them. This is not so.

Let me give an example. It is said that the Buddha—having observed the inevitable suffering associated with loss, pain, old age, sickness, and death—left his comfortable home in search of a permanent cure for suffering. He must have asked himself "Isn't there a better way?" in some form or another. One day, after studying with numerous ascetics and practicing austerity for some six years, he was sitting in fasting meditation in a cave with five of his friends. As the day wore on, he eventually turned to them and said: "I am hungry and tired, my mind is blurred, and I cannot think. This cannot be the way. I am leaving." His friends implored him to stay and continue to fast, but he left them and went to sit under a tree by a nearby river (Fig. 2).

Having feasted on a tray of delicious food offered him by a woman who had chanced by, he floated the tray on the river, saying to himself: "If this tray floats downstream, I shall return home and leave this futile search behind me. If it floats upstream, I shall sit under this tree and I shall not rise until I find the

2 *The Buddha sitting in meditation after leaving the cave*

cure." The tray floated upstream. By the end of that fateful night he discovered the cure for suffering—he understood what suffering was, what was the cause of suffering, what was the nature of the end of suffering, and what was the way to end suffering. The cure consisted of the systematic and practical training of the mind. It involved no magic, miracles, or divine intervention. He discovered, in other words, an uncharted region of the human mind—and charted a path to it.

The question "Isn't there a better way?" is meant to jar us out of our blind acceptance of things as they are, and to make us conscious of the world around us. An acquaintance—trapped in a bad marriage—once said to me: "I can't afford to ask myself that question, because I am not going to like the answer." How sad. I, for one, could not afford not to ask it. Even if I asked it and then chose to leave things as they are, then I have chosen consciously—I have asked the question and answered it.

When, and under what conditions, does one decide to press for change, to take on a new project, to embark on a journey, to develop a new theory, or to harness oneself to a cause? Can one know when to pursue a hunch and when to dismiss it? Can one know in advance when to engage and when to leave things be? No, in a sense one never does. The kind of certainty one seeks in the proverb "God grant me the equanimity of accepting what cannot be changed, the courage to change what can be changed, and the wisdom to distinguish between the two" does not really exist except in trivial cases. In matters of importance, one cannot know in advance what can be changed and what cannot be changed, what should be accepted and what should be rejected, no matter how wise and how knowledgeable one is.

William Thomson (Lord Kelvin, 1824–1907), to take a famous example, was certainly wise and knowledgeable. It was said of him that during the first half of his distinguished career he seemed incapable of being wrong, while during the second half of his career he seemed incapable of being right: "This seems too extreme a view but Thomson's refusal to accept atoms, his opposition to Darwin's theories, his incorrect speculations as to the age of the Earth and the Sun, and his opposition to Rutherford's ideas of radioactivity, certainly put him on the losing side of many arguments later in his career."

Rutherford himself, "who more than any other man laid bare the structure of the atom," frequently ridiculed those who claimed that the energy locked up in matter could be released. The first chain reaction was started in Chicago a mere five years after he died.

If such wise luminaries could not distinguish between what to challenge and what to leave be, what can we mere mortals hope for? How can we predict the outcome of a new venture correctly? How can we be sure that we are on the right track? How can we protect ourselves from failure?

Fudé I (pronounced ee), an elderly and refined Chinese engineering professor, once asked me, on the way to lunch, what I wanted out of life. "I want to become a bit more mature," I offered. "Don't become too mature, Solly," he said with a grave smile, gently putting his delicate hand on my shoulder. "Mature people never try anything new. They know in advance that everything is more difficult than it seems, and that nothing good ever comes of it." The old gentleman was trying to tell me that seeking assurances and protections from failure simply held one back. In the search for the new, there were none to be had.

Some time later, he cast the decisive "no" vote on my fast-track promotion to full professor at the institute. To my surprise, he came to talk to me about it: "I told them you will get there anyway, so why the hurry?" I could never decide whether he voted that way because of his oncoming senility or because he was following some ancient teaching. Either way, I could never quite manage to hold it against him.

* * *

I must have contemplated that scale on the teak floor with a rather immature frame of mind, entirely oblivious to any risk that lay ahead. The possibility that I could fail or that I was not the right man for the job never occurred to me. I did not feel humbled by my total ignorance, nor did I feel like an outsider. "If I put my mind to it, it will eventually succumb," I told myself, without giving much thought to my limitations, which were many.

My thoughts bounced back and forth between the housing problem and the scale. Compared to cities—so big they can be seen with a naked eye from outer space—the scale was very small. It was more tangible than a policy or a program. I could hold it in my hand. I could design it from scratch, construct it, conduct experiments with it and then redesign it, reconstruct it, and conduct some more experiments with it—something I could never dream of doing with cities.

The pursuit of the scale also promised to be less noble and more whimsical too. Rather than facing a dutiful task—imbued with a social purpose and a sense of working for the greater good—I felt a sense of eager anticipation for a trip I thought I had earned. And the housing field, I knew already, was no molecular biology. In the former, you could disappear for a few years and upon your return you should not be surprised to learn that virtually nothing had changed. In the latter—I am told—you could barely stay abreast of new developments if you kept running on evenings and weekends and never rested.

I already understood then that meaningful changes in housing policy do happen, and that they come about only when their time has arrived. I was intent on pursuing my work at the National Housing Authority with enthusiasm and diligence, because I believed it mattered. But I also sensed the beginnings of an attraction to the new scale quest, coupled with a budding sense of liberation from the burden of the unrelenting seriousness of the housing problem.

Soon thereafter, having donned the mantle of an inventor-to-be, I started to keep a diary, a must—I was told—for all budding inventors. The first entry in my diary, dated 18 August 1986, reads: "Basically the idea is to produce a lightweight thin scale. It should be the size of a *Newsweek* magazine, something you can stick in your suitcase when you travel—a personal scale you could trust—so that you don't have to lose yourself while on vacation—'I went to Paris for two weeks and I put on six pounds. The hotel there had no scale (or the scale they had could not be trusted).'"

Did I think it would change the world? Not really. As I said, I had already been working at changing the world for years, and a respite from it would be welcome. I was ready for a gradual descent from a moral high ground peopled with well-meaning "do-gooders"—priests preaching a liberation theology, inspired community organizers, anarchist architects, charitable aristocrats, and free-thinking public servants—to the plains inhabited by ordinary consumers and producers.

I had come across a simple yet unmet need and an idea for a new and useful object that could help meet that need. This small yet powerful realization was enough for me to take a first step on my journey. At the time, I did not need a better reason beyond my emphatic "yes" to the question "Isn't there a better way?" There was no orderly procedure, no tested method, for me to arrive at that decision anyway.

At Berkeley, I sat in on a Scientific Method course taught by Paul Feyerabend. His blue eyes piercing through the straw-blond hair falling on his forehead, the man used to rave in class. He debunked all method, calling Isaac Newton a manipulator and a teller of half-truths and accusing Niels Bohr of standing imperiously in the way of scientific progress. He presented science as a nasty and disorderly struggle, freeing me—once and for all, it seemed—from the awe that science, scientists, and scientific methods inspired. I quote him here:

> Science is essentially an anarchistic enterprise: theoretical anarchism is more humanitarian and more likely to encourage progress than its law-and-order alternatives. . . . This is shown by an examination of historical episodes and by an abstract analysis of the relation between idea and action. The only principle that does not inhibit progress is *anything goes*. . . . Creation of a thing, and creation plus full understanding of a correct idea of the thing, are very often parts of one and the same indivisible process and cannot be separated without bringing the process to a stop. The process itself is not guided by a well-defined programmes, and cannot be guided by such a programme, for it contains the conditions for the realization of all possible programmes. It is guided rather by a vague urge, by a "passion" (Kierkegaard). The passion gives rise to specific behaviour which in turn creates the circumstances and the ideas necessary for analysing and explaining the process, for making it "rational."

Inventing, I intuitively concluded, need not follow an institutional program, a scientific procedure, or a social agenda. In fact, it need not follow any external mandate whatsoever. After all, even necessity was rarely the mother of invention. Not material necessity anyway. People who have had to attend to meeting their basic necessities rarely had the time or the surplus resources to invent anything. Their lives were so circumscribed that they could never afford to take any risk. Inventing out of dire necessity would have been equivalent to relying on the casino to double their welfare checks.

Inventors, on the other hand, were invariably people whose basic needs were met, who had both the time and the surplus resources on their hands to pursue new agendas, and who had a high tolerance for risk. But if there ever was a necessity that was the mother of invention, it must have been emotional necessity, that fiery and tireless passion that fuels the relentless pursuit of a special kind of peace of mind, a peace of mind that can only be attained through the ultimate reconciliation of two implacable foes—"what is" and "what can be":

> Edison's most famous invention to come out of Menlo Park was the light bulb (Fig. 3). . . . One tough piece was finding the right material for the filament—that little wire inside the light bulb. He filled more than 40,000 pages with notes before he finally had a bulb that withstood a 40-hour test in his laboratory. In 1879, after testing more that 1,600 materials for the right filament, including coconut fiber, fishing line, and even hairs from a friend's beard, Edison and his workers finally figured out what to use for the filament—carbonized bamboo.

I confess that a passion of such intensity did not yet burn in my stomach at the onset of the scale quest. I could never imagine attaining such tenacity and such resilience to frustration. I discovered only much later what the Sufi sage Jalaluddin Rumi (1207–1273) discovered many centuries ago. He understood that it is the ability to heighten necessity—rather than the urge to diminish it—that empowers invention: "New organs of perception come into being as a result of necessity. Therefore, O man, increase your necessity, so that you may increase your perception."

I, for one, felt no heightened sense of necessity during that fateful rainy season in Bangkok. The foremost question on my mind was "Should I or shouldn't I?" and the answer I came up with was a rather liberating and lighthearted "Why not?"

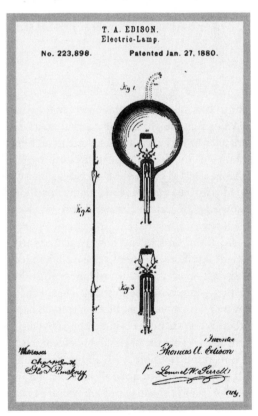

3 *Edison's patent for the electric lamp*

2

What Is Wrong with the Machine?

I have heard: before sonar became operational, at the height of the First World War, the American and British navies had not yet devised a method for detecting German submarines. The U-boats—as they came to be called—could still roam the ocean unmolested, inflicting heavy damage on the allies' supply convoys plowing the Northern Atlantic. At a meeting to explore possible answers to this threat, a frustrated old British admiral had an idea: "Why don't we just empty the ocean? Then we could see those rascals clearly on the ocean floor." When asked: "But how could we empty the ocean, sir?" he gruffly replied: "My staff handles the details."

———

The idea of taking a mental object that exists only in the mind's eye and transforming it into a physical object that exists in the material world had always fascinated me; it is what attracted me to architecture and design in the first place. There was magic in it—turning nothing (no-thing) into a thing. Sad to say, when it came to scales, I was no magician. My thin scale was only a fantasy. I had no idea how to make it work, and no staff to handle the details. In fact, I had no knowledge of scales whatsoever, and no clue about the mechanisms that made them work.

Yes, I did understand how a balance worked. In a balance, an object whose weight is unknown is put in one dish, and its weight is determined by balancing it against objects of known weight in the other dish (Fig. 4). For example, Blind Justice—commonly depicted as a beautiful woman in a flowing robe, her eyes covered with a wide kerchief—holds a balance in one hand and a sword in the other. When Justice is blind, the party with the more weighty argument wins simply by tilting the balance in its favor. Her balance is accurate and unbiased, and its result is visible to all and understood by all, for—as an old legal maxim has it—"Justice must not only be done; it must also be seen to be done."

The balance made use of a physical principle we could all see, but the bathroom scale was a black box whose mechanism was entirely hidden from view. One could only guess what was inside unless one had the nerve to take it apart. I did not possess this kind of courage at the time. I took very few things apart during my childhood, and could never put them back together. My valiant childhood attempt to repair the arm of the expensive record player we had—one of

4 *Weighing with a balance: illustration in the* Egyptian Book of the Dead, *1250 B.C.*

the first that could stack records on top of one another—was a veritable disaster. My father had a repairman called in. He was not at all amused. His injunction: "There are professional people who need to make a living repairing such things. Why don't you leave it to them?"

My father did not own any tools, not even a screwdriver. He never opened the hood of his car. He never even washed his car. "This car should serve me," he would say, "rather than me serving it." And me? I didn't mind washing my car occasionally, but other than that, in things mechanical I took after my father. Yes, over the years I became a bit better with my hands, but I really only mastered one tool—the mat knife or box cutter—with which I excelled at making architectural models out of cardboard and balsawood. Anything mechanical—not to mention electronic—was clearly out of my range.

As far as the scale venture was concerned, I did not consider that as anything but a temporary handicap. No, I did not dare take apart my poor bathroom scale. I rationalized my dread by convincing myself that it would not really teach me anything; that the reason there were no thin scales on the market at the time was simply that existing scales used the wrong principle for measuring weight. Therefore, I quickly surmised, I needed a more exotic weighing principle for my scale, one that common scales did not use. The 18 August 1986 diary entry read: "The principle contemplated here is to contain a liquid between two hard plates. Since the liquid cannot really be compressed, the weight of a person standing on the top plate results in an equal increase in pressure all around. This pressure can then be measured."

That fresh approach presented me with the exciting possibility of building a prototype. Like my father before me, I had no tools, not to mention a basement workshop. I had no basement either; no Bangkok houses ever did. They were all built on mud. But my idea was so simple that it did not require tools, let alone a workshop. That weekend, I went to the Sapan Khwai market nearby and bought two rectangular pieces of quarter-inch plywood, some clear plastic tubing—a quarter-inch in diameter—and some glue. I filled the tubing with water, looped it into a tight and flat spiral between the plates, and glued it all together (Fig. 5).

I left some ten feet of water-filled tubing free and taped it vertically on the living room wall. I planned to measure pressure—albeit rather crudely—by recording the rise of the water in the tubing as a weight was placed on the water-filled spiral.

The testing of this prototype consisted of the maid's—with a questioning look on her face—stepping barefoot onto it. The water level rose quickly, squirted out, and spilled on the teak floor. The remaining water in the tubing kept rising while she stood idly on the scale, occasionally inquiring if it was time for her to step down. When she swayed, the water level rose and fell. When she stood at one corner, the two plywood plates touched each other and the water level fell. When she got off, the water initially settled at some lower level and then continued to fall. It fell a few more inches overnight. This prototype, I concluded, had clearly failed to behave as a scale. Surely, a scale should have been blind to how long the maid stood on it, to where she stood, or to whether she swayed or not. It should have also returned to its initial state when she stepped down and stayed at that state overnight.

It was easy to acknowledge that the spiral-tube prototype did not work as a scale, at least not yet. I clearly needed an improved version that stood a better chance of working. This required some analysis that, much as I wanted to, I

5 *The spiral tube scale prototype, Scale Diary, 18 August 1986*

could not do. It is true that, had it worked, I would not have needed to ask myself why or how it worked. Had it worked, no questions would have needed to be asked. But it did not work. So I had no choice: I needed to find out why before I could move on. I needed an engineer.

In a Parisian square, one misty dawn in 1792, a noisy crowd surrounded a raised platform, where three men—a poet, a merchant, and an engineer—were shortly to be decapitated by guillotine. The poet, asked whether he had a last wish, exclaimed he wanted to sing the Marseillaise to assert his love of freedom, equality, and fraternity. He then peacefully placed his head under the oblique blade. The heavy blade came down, but stopped an inch above his neck. The executioner hoisted the blade up. The poet was set free—the machine, by Revolutionary Decree, was only given one chance. The crowd cheered. The merchant was next. He also asked to sing, sang the same song, and placed his head under the blade like the poet before him. The polished blade came down and again stopped an inch above his neck. He was also set free. The crowd was ecstatic. The engineer was next. Asked whether he had anything to say, he pointed his finger excitedly at the pulleys above the blade and cried: "I know what is wrong with the machine!"

One engineer in Bangkok that I knew well was a tall and lanky Dane called Jens Overgaard—a structural engineer who worked on low-cost housing at the United Nations and lived close by. Jens, by the way, did not take housing as personally as I did. It simply provided him with a very comfortable job as a career international civil servant. And that coveted status allowed him to stay in the tropics in style, while he leisurely pursued his real passion—building and racing sailboats.

Jens was a model bon vivant: he spent his evenings at home with his quiet Vietnamese wife, listening to Charlie Parker, enjoying a good Dominican cigar and a good scotch with rarely a care in the world, and going to bed early. He spent most weekends at the Royal Varuna Yacht Club, where he was a most active and valuable member. I apprised Jens of my project and of the results of my experiment, and he gladly offered a nontechnical explanation of where I went wrong. First, the plastic tubing expanded under pressure, as well as overnight; it did not retain a constant volume, and that affected the water pressure. Second, the top plate was somehow supported from below, which meant that some of the load did not translate into water pressure. It did not just float, as it should have.

There is no question that I am quick on the draw, maybe too quick for my own good. My seventh-grade math teacher—a sarcastic old brute who could lift his wire-rimmed glasses to his forehead simply by twitching his nose—once announced to the class: "And yet again, Angel was the first to give us the wrong answer." Yes, I confess, I do have a strong preference for quick answers—temporary and unsatisfactory as they may be—and little tolerance for keeping unanswered questions on my mind for too long. I would rather have a temporary answer to a question—however bad—than no answer at all.

I understood what Jens told me and drew some immediate conclusions. To begin with, I needed to get rid of the plastic tubing. This called for the construction of a second prototype, one that needed no tubing—just two plates with a thin waterbed in between. I quickly built one. That one failed to behave like a scale too; the thin waterbed kept exploding under pressure. The third and fourth prototypes failed as well. I was in an impossible double bind: If the envelope of the water was soft, it stretched and changed the volume of the water and distorted my measurements. If it was rigid, however, it supported the top plate from below and distorted my measurements as well. What to do?

Over the next two months, I drew innumerable cross sections and stubbornly built several prototypes in close succession. They all failed. The scale diary was filled with dense entries in my minute and upright handwriting, brimming with half-baked ideas yet to be realized, as well as some catchy names for that yet-to-be-invented product. One entry bemoans: "The general feeling of the past few days is that I have hit a wall." Another, written at midnight, takes stock: "This is turning into an obsession. Today, I could not concentrate on my work at the National Housing Authority."

* * *

By that time, the research work at the authority was beginning to gather steam. I was the only *farang*—a foreigner of European descent, that is—on the study team, occasionally supported by the short-term visits of colleagues from the United States. The rest were Thai professionals—mostly architects, planners, and geographers. They all spoke English, and they never felt uneasy working with *farangs*. This was—at least in part, I felt—because their ancestors never had to suffer the humiliation of European colonialism. Highly skilled in diplomacy, they played the British in India against the French in Indochina and acted as a buffer between them. They were never occupied. They appropriated Western ideas and Western technology freely, at their own pace, keeping their fundamental values and their Thai way of life largely intact.

Most Thais thought that *farangs* had no social graces and generally lacked manners. But they expected (and indeed relied on) *farangs* to shake things up occasionally, something they rarely dared do themselves. *Farangs* were more inclined to make a point than to observe minute rules of etiquette. Conflict avoidance—and more generally, the avoidance of anything that would make anyone uncomfortable (especially one's superior) or cause anyone to lose face—was a supreme Thai value. Truth in general, and the quality of research in particular, often suffered as a result, but Thailand was a very peaceful place. A whole year could go by without one's getting involved in a single vocal confrontation.

The study team had a research agenda. We needed to provide an answer to "What is Wrong with the National Housing Authority?" although on paper it was expressed in more technical and less emotive terms. It was an exciting, yet familiar challenge. I was already immersed in the housing question, and well versed in the intricacies of housing research. I understood Thai cities—and Bangkok in particular. I also had a good grasp of the Thai way of doing things, and I discovered—much to my amazement—that I could choose when to behave like a Thai and when like a *farang*. That privilege often came in handy, especially since I had assigned myself the role of proclaiming, where necessary, that the emperor had no clothes, and this without offending anyone. In short, the machinery was humming and I was in my element. I was perched on the frontier of knowledge about housing, looking into the uncharted territory ahead, and doing "cutting edge" work.

* * *

I wish I could say that about my understanding of scales at the time, but my knowledge was less than rudimentary, never mind cutting edge. I sent copies of some of the early pages of the scale diary to my friend Bill Alonso seeking his advice.

Bill was an urban economist by training and, like me, knew next to nothing about scales. He was a favorite professor of mine at Berkeley and a keen student of cities, looking at them from a great distance and able to observe and explain big-picture patterns that were not visible at street level. He was now at Harvard, overfocused on a complex mathematical model of population growth that was of interest to him and to practically no one else. Still, even though he withdrew into a refined and highly abstract world, he was a consummate reader and a most perceptive social commentator. He rarely missed a chance to put a funny spin on matters serious and less serious. He wrote me shortly after receiving the excerpts from the diary:

> I cannot resist making a couple of kibitzes. First, I think that the simplest road must be the dry machine. . . . The dry model would have several sensors distributed over the area so as to catch the weight. Their readings would then be summed to get the total weight. . . . I had a sense, in reading your notes, that you were caught in what might be called the Babbage Trap: frustratingly trying to solve mechanically a problem for which you have the right fundamental ideas but which requires the properties of electronics rather than of fluids or gears or screws. This may be a function of your Thai environment, and your approach might be different if you were in the midst of Silicon Valley. You are not, of course, and that is a comparative disadvantage.

Many years later, I found out what Charles Babbage (1791–1871)—one of the forefathers of the computer—had attempted to do. In 1822, he tried to build what he called a "difference engine"—a mechanical device that could calculate logarithmic tables (Fig. 6).

He abandoned it in midstream and in 1830 tried to build a more advanced "analytical engine"—a mechanical device with thousands and thousands of moving metal parts that could carry out sequential mathematical operations, employing several procedures later used in modern computers. Unfortunately, until his death Babbage never completed any of these machines. This was partly because he was ahead of his time and the technology he required—electronics—did not yet exist. But it was also partly because for some 50 years he would never stop tinkering with his designs: "No sooner would he send a drawing to the machine shop than he would find a better way to perform the task and would order work stopped until he had finished pursuing the new line."

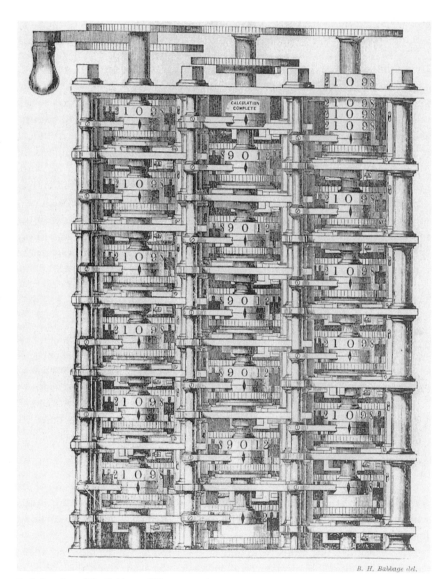

B. H. Babbage del.

6 *A drawing of the Babbage difference engine*

Bill's letter sealed the fate of my wet prototypes. They were clearly a waste of ammunition. I was shooting in the dark at targets I could not see, hoping against hope that I would hit something. I must have somehow internalized the approach to design I was initially exposed to in architecture school—there was no method in it at all. Let me explain.

During our second year at school, for example, we were instructed to design an innovative school building—fundamentally different from anything done before—without bothering to learn what was done before. It was feared that our creative spirits would be dampened and our virgin design intuitions suppressed if we were apprised of what humanity has accomplished thus far in its pursuit of better schools. The goal was to free us completely to explore new and previously unimaginable ideas.

It was a truly modernist agenda. Architectural history was only paid lip service. It was taught with slides often changing at the rate of a century per hour, in dark rooms where almost everyone slept and some occasionally snored. The underlying message of the school was "debunk the past in its entirety, polish the mind into a tabula rasa (blank slate), and start to solve every problem as if you were the first ever to confront it."

I cannot forget the shock I experienced when I brought the cardboard model of my school into the design studio on the appointed day. For the past two weeks, this model had occupied my entire field of vision. Now I saw it gradually become smaller and smaller, disappearing among 60 other models that—for all practical purposes—all looked the same, despite all the frenzied creativity showered on them. I left that architecture school shortly thereafter, in search of someone with a better method, at least some method, for teaching design. One of the lessons I eventually learned was to respect what was done before me, instead of dismissing it altogether. It was now time to apply this lesson.

In October of 1986, I invested $80 in an electronic bathroom scale and brought it to Jens's home—together with my old scale—for him to take apart and explain to me what he saw. I had no choice. How could I innovate without being grounded in what was already known? How could I provide a fresh solution to a problem if I had no idea whether my solution was fresh or not? Having been duly humbled by my wet experiments, I now held these questions foremost in my mind. I had to admit to myself that I needed to take the first small step on the march to the knowledge frontier.

Jens deftly took the scales apart. Both had the same arrangement of metal bars inside them: four metal levers—two long ones and two short ones—transferred the load to a spring located on the central axis of the scale (Fig. 7). In the old scale, the spring turned the white dial as it stretched. In the new electronic one, the spring pulled apart two hinged metal plates as it stretched. "The two plates act as a capacitor," said Jens, "which translates the weight into an electrical signal." I nodded. Now I knew how a bathroom scale worked, even though I knew nothing of capacitors. The arrangement of levers inside was at least one-inch high, I observed, which explained why the scales were not thin. In my scale, there would be no room for levers.

Some two weeks later, I took a second small step: I visited the engineering library at the Asian Institute of Technology to study the literature. My visit to the library was truly a relief. The diary reads: "For the first time, I now have an overview of all the principles for measuring loads and pressures." True, engineering books made for a rather dry reading. But they did excel at categorization—the listing of discrete categories that together provided an embracing "big picture" of a field, no matter how complex and varied it was. I easily found the list I was looking for, and I almost understood what it meant (the bracketed comments are mine):

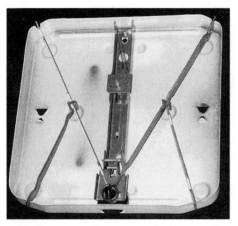

7 *The lever system in a common bathroom scale*

An unknown force [weight is a force] may be measured by the following means: (1) balancing it against the known gravitational force . . . either directly or through a system of levers [this is what the balance held by Blind Justice is doing]; (2) measuring the acceleration of a body . . . [irrelevant, as far as stationary scales are concerned]; (3) balancing it against a magnetic force . . . [also irrelevant]; (4) transducing [read: transforming] the force to a fluid pressure and then measuring the pressure [this is, more or less, the wet scale idea]; and (5) applying the force to some solid elastic member and measuring the resulting deflection [this, I gathered, would be the only dry method available to me].

Engineering—in contrast with architecture or product design—relied on calculation, calculation relied on measurement, and measurement, in turn, relied on instrumentation. Engineers—concerned with the behavior of the physical artifacts they design—have always depended on instruments that measure physical quantities accurately. Since the early 1960s—called to task by the new demands of the space program—they have developed hundreds of new electronic instruments that rely on "sensors."

Sensors (referred to as "transducers" in engineering jargon) rapidly convert physical measurements of all kinds—weight being one of the simplest among them—into an electrical output. Such output can then be converted to a digital display—as in a digital scale, a digital thermometer, or a digital odometer. But it can also be fed into computers, machines, and robots so as to provide them with instant information about the physical world—the feedback they need to decide what to do next. Sensors, in short, are devices that make it possible for machines to see, hear, and touch before taking action.

I was interested, no doubt, but I was also somewhat dismayed to find that I was getting involved in the design of an "instrument." Perceiving the scale as an instrument that relies on sensors was an instructive insight, but it filled me with awe. This may not be as simple as I was hoping. I was no longer dealing with simply giving the bathroom scale a new look and a new elegance, something that I—educated as an architect—could confidently engage in. I was getting involved in the making of a new instrument, venturing into an altogether different discipline. The primary criterion for the success of that instrument was no longer "elegance," but rather "elegance subject to an acceptable level of accuracy" or "accuracy subject to the new requirements of elegance."

This was no longer superficial industrial design, where the form was simply the envelope of the instrument, but could really never question its internal workings. This was rather "function follows form"—the redesign of the internal workings of the instrument itself to meet the formal requirements of elegance and utility, the thin look and the light weight; requirements that could not be met by the available technology.

The most important practical discovery I made in the library that day was that the sensor that measured weight was commonly called a *load cell*. Now, I thought, at least I knew what I needed to look for—load cells. More specifically, I needed to look for thin load cells that could fit into a quarter-inch-thick scale, and I probably needed four of them—one in each corner.

Reading on, I found out that, unfortunately, most load cells were not thin at all, probably because they did not have to be. I did identify, however, at least five kinds of load cells—each one using a different principle and a different technology— that seemed to have a potential for fitting into a very thin scale. Had I been more systematic, I would have become familiar with each one of them and tested them all, and only then would I have selected the most appropriate one. For this, I confess, I had neither the time nor the inclination. I opted for picking load cells off the shelf, at least for now, no matter what principle they employed in sensing weight.

The literature listed several companies in the States that supplied load cells. Without further ado, I decided that I needed to get some, and the sooner the better. The diary reads: "I spent all of Friday morning looking through the Thomas Register of Companies. . . . Found some miniature load cells. . . . I need to send letters to some companies with specifications as to what I want. The problem: they all seem extremely expensive: $200–300 for one unit, and possibly much more. . . . Not much hope."

The Thomas Register was a hard-copy precursor of an Internet search engine. It was a cross-referenced catalog published annually, some three times the size of the *Encyclopedia Britannica*, listing everything that was manufactured in the United States. The load cell that attracted my attention was a "subminiature compression load cell"—a flat steel cylinder with a nipple on top—that had a half-inch diameter and an overall height of 0.15 inches (Fig. 8). The problem: each one cost $495 and I needed four of them.

So now I understood: the engineering problem of making a thin personal scale was probably trivial if cost were no object, because the technology already existed. The cost of making a thin scale—a consumer product, rather than a part of a lunar vehicle—was prohibitive, and that was why there were no thin scales on the market. The sensor I needed must not only be thin, it must also be affordable.

I sent off some 28 letters to load cell manufacturers, including a long wish list of what I thought were reasonable specifications. I got not even one seri- 8 *A subminiature load cell*
ous response. Over the next few months I received only a couple of unhelpful brochures in the mail, nothing more. Since I could not make any progress without real load cells in my hands, I resolved to let go of the scale quest for a while and to concentrate instead on the land and housing markets of Bangkok until my next trip to the States, scheduled for May 1987. I needed to get physically closer to the knowledge frontier before I could make more progress on the scale front.

3

Go West, Young Man!

There is something I don't know
    that I am supposed to know.
I don't know what it is I don't know,
    and yet am supposed to know,
And I feel I look stupid
    if I seem both not to know it
    and not know what it is I don't know . . .
I feel you know what I am supposed to know
but you can't tell me what it is
because you don't know that I don't know what it is.
You may know what I don't know, but not
    that I don't know it,
and I can't tell you. So you will have to tell me everything.

R. D. Laing, *Knots*

————

MAY 1987

The major stop on my American journey was the City of Rolling Hills, California (population 1,900), one of the 35 cities that made up greater Los Angeles. Rolling Hills, like the City of Commerce and the City of Industry a little further east, was a "theme" city—Commerce was designed for commerce, the City of Industry for industry, and Rolling Hills as an equestrian city for horse lovers.

The city consisted largely of expansive hillside lots connected by a network of bridle paths. On each lot stood a rambling ranch house overlooking a striking view. Some of these lovely million-dollar homes—many with wall-to-wall picture windows—were located on rather steep slopes to take full advantage of the majestic ocean views to the west. These were the ones that tended to roll downhill when heavy rains caused mudslides.

Still, the loyal residents proceeded assiduously to repair and rebuild their homes. They dreaded the thought of living in the valleys below, in houses without glorious views, crowded in among all types of undesirables. In fact, to protect the citizens of Rolling Hills from these very undesirables, the city was appropriately "gated"—it was surrounded by a fence and could only be entered through three manned gates, and then only if a bona fide resident was waiting for you. Natural disasters they could face, but strangers? What a frightening thought.

What attracted my gracious host Tommy Heinsheimer—a cerebral, bespectacled urbanite who grew up in Queens and would never dream of mounting a horse—to this place I cannot tell, but he was the mayor of Rolling Hills. Tommy was a brilliant, self-assured, and rather dismissive aerospace engineer. While working in the Mercury space program in the 1960s, he helped design a sensor-based safety instrument that automatically ejected the command module carrying the astronauts if it detected any serious trouble with their *Atlas* rocket as it propelled them through the atmosphere into outer space.

After man landed on the moon, Tommy moved to California to help the aerospace industry absorb large quantities of government funds by proposing ridiculous—yet intriguing—Star Wars projects that were never really meant to work without the further absorption of large quantities of government funds, billions if possible, and hopefully ad infinitum.

This he did for a living, but his heart was really in super-pressurized helium balloons, preferably ones that could circumnavigate the earth. Julie, his wife, forbade him to fly balloons anymore after he was almost killed when the brilliant five-balloon contraption he designed to carry himself (and his rich friend who bankrolled the mission) around the world failed to take off, never mind make it back. He eventually consented to his grounding, but not before setting a national distance record with his *Atmosat* balloon. In addition to tending to her lush garden on the hill, Julie was very active in the affairs of the well-tended botanical gardens a short distance downhill, where sections of the gardens collapsed from time to time into gaping holes—the gardens were, sad to say, located atop a former garbage dump.

* * *

Tommy ridiculed the scale project. "Not exciting enough," he mocked me. "Why not make it measure temperature and pulse as well?" I was disappointed, but could think of little to say in reply except making some deprecating suggestions of my own as to what else it could do. Our conversation trailed off. I had hoped he would lead me to an expert on sensors or to some sensor company he knew and could trust. But he simply refused to become engaged in my quest, let alone give me any useful leads.

He just stood there by the fireplace, aloof yet alert, a rational being, perfectly detached from things of the heart. "I would not spend a dollar of my own money on this if I were you," he advised, "especially not on product development." In his mind, artifacts and gadgets had absolutely nothing personal about them. It did not matter who invented them or who made them, because—if there were a need for them—the market created them anyway, sooner or later. From his disparaging perspective, new technology was nothing to get excited about—it was just a way to make a living. Yes, maybe. But I could not listen to him. By that time, I was already unwilling to simply let go. I needed—or thought I needed—practical help, not preaching.

I had two leads of my own: a company I found in the Thomas Register, Transducer Techniques, that was located in Rancho, California, within driving distance of Rolling Hills; and an old Bangkok hand, also called Tom, who was an electronic engineer and lived in New Hampshire.

I picked up the phone and called Transducer Techniques. Gary Baker, the owner, tried in vain to dissuade me from coming over: "No one ever comes here," he said. "Just send us your drawings and specifications [I had neither] and we will send you an estimate." He confided in me that he hung up on a dozen inventors a month looking for that elusive $1.50 load cell (that was more or less what I was looking for too, although I did not yet know it). But he eventually relented, for some reason, upon learning that I came from Bangkok, never having strayed any further than Mexico himself.

On the appointed day, I drove east, past Los Angeles and then some, into a desert valley surrounded by smooth, barren hills with jagged rocky outcrops on their crowns. Rancho, California, was a quiet, nondescript Anywhere U.S.A. kind of town lining the flat bottom of that valley. Transducer Techniques occupied a five-room place, a door in the wall of a white-stucco building in the new shopping center on Main Street, right behind Sizzler Steak House. This, then, was my introduction to the ex-urban culture of American high-tech—a collection of footloose businesses, large and small, that were free to locate anywhere because long-distance telephones and overnight courier services connected them to all their suppliers, customers, and clients.

Every business in this country was within easy reach, it seemed—no matter how remote—and together they formed one enormous marketplace—cooperating and competing with each other, but no longer insisting on face-to-face contact. Not a small achievement, by any means, and one that gave the country an enormous technological head start over the rest of the world. But if these businesses were really free to locate anywhere, why would they concentrate in California? Was there a geography of invention that explained where they congregated? Was the spirit of invention evenly distributed, or were there places with a higher density of inventors? If there was a map somewhere that showed where inventors were concentrated, I would have liked to see it. At the time, however, I had to just start with a lead and follow it wherever it took me.

My objective in visiting Transducer Techniques was to find out what it was I wanted, something I could not do over the phone. Gary Baker, in jeans and sneakers, introduced me to his son Randy—a kid, barely 20 I figured, in Hawaiian Bermuda shorts, sporting a strange haircut I had never seen before. The two worked together as a father-and-son team—Gary let Randy explain the technology involved and never interrupted him; Randy had good ideas and articulated them very well; and Gary was very proud of Randy and showed it.

Randy took me on a guided tour of the small plant, pointing to several load cells in various states of completion that were being assembled by a few quiet technicians. He patiently explained to me how the load cells worked too, but—

patient as he was—he was still too fast for me. At the time, I must confess, I missed key parts of his explanation, at least partly because I did not listen carefully. The reason I did not listen carefully had to do with my perception of a strict division of labor between the product designer (myself)—who had to worry about how the product looked and how it met the needs of its users—and the product engineer, who had to make it work to the designer's specifications.

In retrospect, not only was this perception—or rather this misconception—wrong, but it turned out to be time consuming and rather costly as well. I really ought to have understood how load cells worked early on—if only to be able to tell the engineers what I wanted, and to understand the constraints imposed on them by the available technology. But, much as I regretted it, my own understanding of how load cells worked was acquired only over a long period of time.

Randy Baker proposed to design a new custom-made load cell that could fit into a quarter-inch scale, similar in shape to the subminiature load cell shown earlier (Fig. 8). He suggested a two-inch-diameter load cell, 0.2-inches thick, to be embedded in the scale platform, flush with its bottom. The load on the cell would be applied from below, through a semispherical button attached to its center, protruding down and acting as a foot. We would, in fact, be measuring the counterweight exerted by the floor on the scale platform, which—according to Newton's third law, the law of action and reaction—is exactly identical to the weight exerted on the platform from above.

If there were to be four load cells embedded in the platform, the weight of a person would be the sum of the weights exerted on all four. Randy could not be sure what the accuracy of such a load cell would be before building and testing some prototypes. The proposed shape and size appealed to me. That was, in fact, what I wanted after all—a thin load cell.

The reason that load cells were expensive, Gary Baker said, was because they required precision parts, precision machining, and precision assembly. He didn't think that I could afford to have them made in the States, but he was excited about the possibility of having my company (assuming I had one) manufacture the load cells in Thailand. Skilled workers there earned $6 a day, and skilled workers in the United States earned 15 to 20 times that amount. "You have a niche there," he said. I, on my part, had never yet thought seriously about manufacturing the scale or any of its components myself, in Thailand or anywhere else. In fact, I had never thought about manufacturing anything. All my thoughts about manufacturing had to do with staying out of it.

* * *

My family has been in manufacturing since 1928, when my grandfather Salomon bought a bankrupt bakery in Jerusalem, made it into his full-time concern, and moved his large family to the apartment above the bakery that came with it. He worked long hours, employing all his younger brothers and later all his sons, with the exception of my father, who became a lawyer. My brother, my sister, and several of my many cousins eventually joined too. Over the years, the bakery moved to an industrial park and filled up with sophisticated machines. Bread was manufactured on automated production lines untouched by human hands. The only remaining manual task was the braiding of four-strand chalahs on Thursday nights, a human activity that could not (yet) be replaced by a machine (Fig. 9).

The Angel Bakery gradually grew into a large industrial concern, geared to supply the entire Israeli army—including its reserves—with its daily bread, in the not-uncommon event of a major war. My early childhood memories are dotted with manufacturing images, accompanied by the sour smell of dough and the intoxicating smell of freshly baked bread.

9 *A braided, four-strand chalah*

When I was five, I already had my first real job: pasting stamps of the bakery's trademark—the tower of David—on oval pieces of shaped dough arranged on crowded metal racks. One of my coworkers was a gentle old man, with a flowing white beard, who I thought looked like God. He appeared more than once in my dreams. Michelangelo apparently had a similar image in mind when he painted the ceiling of the Sistine Chapel in Rome.

I easily mastered the fast pace of that pasting job, my first among many, but I was not at ease—there were distracting shouting matches in the background all too often. I remember my grandfather—a big, mustached man with a cheap unfiltered cigarette hanging permanently from his mouth—shouting and coughing, coughing and shouting, either because not enough bread was produced or because too many loaves remained unsold by the end of the day. One or the other was nearly always the case.

I also remember that Friday family lunch years later, when my uncle Ovad came into the apartment upstairs to announce that the bakery had run out of chalahs, and that there were no chalahs put aside for breaking bread at dinner that evening. My grandfather exploded, as usual, and began heaping abuse on Uncle Ovad. In response, Uncle Ovad picked up the black Bakelite telephone, and hurled it to the tile floor, exploding it into hundreds of pieces.

This act was apparently designed to let my grandfather know, in no uncertain terms, that he, Ovad, was not personally responsible for the chalah incident. My grandfather—never to be outplayed by his offspring—retaliated immediately by faking an almost credible faint and collapsing on the floor, to suggest that sooner or later his very son Ovad was going to make his heart stop beating forever. My grandmother gently sprayed his face with some rosewater, and apparently none of the onlookers, except me, thought it was a particularly memorable event.

Bakers, I concluded very early on, could never be masters of their own lives. The bakery was a relentless taskmaster. On any given day, some machine broke down, usually the one for which spare parts were impossible to get on short notice. The people of Jerusalem, on their part, wanted their fresh bread every morning and were of no mind to accept lame excuses about spare parts. The family had no choice but to keep working, days and nights, resting only on the Sabbath. Passover, when people did not eat bread for seven days, offered no rest either—this was the only time for overhauling the old machines and for installing the new ones.

My mother started to pull me away from the bakery at a very early age, at least in part because she herself did not like the intensity of the family business. But I was not cut out for manufacturing anyway—the shouting bothered me. She must have known that too. I grew up in a home where, as far as I remember, my parents never raised their voices. No wonder I felt so comfortable in Thailand—people very rarely shouted at each other. They preferred smiling, and were somehow able to communicate the entire range of feelings with their smiles.

* * *

I left Transducer Techniques that day rather confused, I must say. I did not quite understand how the load cell Randy had in mind would work, I was not convinced it would work, and I was worried that the cost of manufacturing it in large quantities might still be exorbitant. On the long drive back to Rolling Hills, I also started to nurse a new worry—the electronics for the scale also presented a problem. The high-accuracy voltmeter Randy used—and insisted was a must— was a substantial instrument, the size of a large transistor radio, plugged into the wall. How would I incorporate such bulk into a quarter-inch scale? Neither Randy nor Gary was of any help in the matter. It was out of their orbit, they said, but they could look into it. On the whole, however, I felt that the trip to California was paying off. The diary entry from 8 May 1987 read:

> A telephone call from Gary: Transducer Techniques will produce the prototype sensors for $353 apiece. They can be ready in four weeks. He calculated the manufacturing cost of the sensors based on Thai labor costs, and thinks the results are "inspiring." When I ask whether in his view we should go ahead, he says "Oh yeah, and I'll be able to back up my 'Oh yeah' with numbers when we meet next." This is such an exciting day that I am not able to sleep at all. The whole day was centered on the thought of having to change my life to produce this object. . . . There are many things I don't know yet. There is no particular hurry, but . . . I want to move. If it were not for the Bangkok housing study, I would stay here now.

4

The Enchanting Résumé

MAY 1987–SEPTEMBER 1987

Going ahead with Transducer Techniques made some sense, but it was not to be. In retrospect, maybe I should have ordered four load cells from the Bakers and had them shipped to Bangkok. I could have used them to build and test some thin prototype scales, I suppose. If these load cells worked, whatever that meant, one problem would be solved. But I decided against the whole idea of load cells. It didn't feel right.

During those heady Los Angeles days I was not yet ready to solve one problem at a time. Solving one small design problem at a time is a wonderful privilege, a luxury, certainly a worthy goal to pursue. But it was not something I could engage in when I did not yet have a comprehensive picture of what I was trying to do, and when I did not yet understand the structure of the problem I wanted to solve.

In other words, I did not yet recognize the hierarchy of parts that would make up the scale. Without understanding that hierarchy, there was really no way of knowing at that stage whether load cells were indeed parts in this hierarchy, and no point in assuming that they were. Therefore, I thought, it was too early in the game to buy and test load cells.

The most important lesson that I had learned from my mentor, Christopher Alexander, while an architecture student at Berkeley in the sixties was that truly innovative design involved discarding an old list of parts in favor of a new list that partitioned the form into an entirely new set of components.

Surely, the final form of the truly portable scale—the final answer to the thin-scale problem—would include a finite set of parts connected together seamlessly. They would clearly be different than the set of parts in existing bathroom scales—top plate, bottom plate, a lever system for transferring the loads, a spring, and a dial, for example—but I did not yet know what the new parts would be or how they were to be connected to each other. More specifically, I did not yet know if the thin-scale design really needed four separate load cells, or, if it did, whether there were any special requirements that the forms of these load cells had to meet.

*　*　*

I mentioned earlier that I abandoned my old architecture school—after spending two years there—in search of someone who could teach design. At the time very few universities elicited any name recognition from me, and among those there was no way to choose. I ended up in Berkeley in 1964 after I heard that students walked barefoot on the grass there. That was a good enough criterion, I thought, for selecting a university. By sheer luck, I ran into Alexander, then 28, the author of *Notes on the Synthesis of Form* which came out that year.

Alexander had a degree in mathematics and a doctoral degree in architecture. Rumor had it he was a genius, out to revolutionize the way architecture was practiced by bringing method into design. He was articulate, spoke in plain English, and appealed to reason rather than to an ephemeral artistic sensibility that could not be put into words. He was versed in the physical and social sciences, and drew many of his insights from recent discoveries outside the tired jargon of modern architecture, which he debunked in its entirety. What more could I ask for? I enlisted immediately as a revolutionary foot soldier, resolving to become his top lieutenant in due time.

Only some seven years later did I realize that I had at that moment joined what was to become a sort of a cult, led by a truly charismatic and highly persuasive messianic figure. Alexander demanded absolute loyalty to the "work" from his devotees, a loyalty that required a total and unqualified rejection of modern and contemporary architecture as we have come to know it. We talked and argued ceaselessly, like Talmudic scholars interpreting holy Scriptures. Any insight on our part was welcome, and we were kept on our toes, in wonderful mental shape. Any borrowed wisdom was welcome as well, as long as it came from outside the established world of architecture. It was accepted doctrine that no living architect or writer on architecture had anything of consequence to say.

Our discussions seemed to last forever. No one was allowed to leave until way past dinnertime lest they break the spell by implying that there was something more important in their lives than the work. We parted in the evening only after having arrived at some important insight, a temporary insight though, because the indefatigable Alexander kept communicating with the work at night, coming back the next day with solid reasons to reject the latest insight and start anew.

Still, nothing I can say about the somewhat fanatic aspects of my association with Alexander can diminish the importance of his insights at the time, and the riotous effects that they had on my budding thoughts concerning design. *Notes on the Synthesis of Form* proposed a rather mechanical four-step design method that—although presented as gospel—never caught on, and was abandoned by Alexander himself (as were later timeless truths), not more than two years after its inception.

It was important, however, because it provided a fundamental insight regarding a critical aspect of the creative process, which, in my opinion, is just as relevant today as it was then: one creates an innovative form by inventing a new taxonomy for it. The reader may benefit from the following short exposition of this method, but should refrain from taking it as the letter of the law, focusing instead on its spirit.

First, one identifies an exhaustive list of the functional demands on the form to be designed. It is assumed that the need for a new design arises, most often though not always, from the failure of existing forms to meet the demands exerted on them. In other words, forms maintain their robustness over time by responding effectively to failure. The list is compiled, therefore, by examining, one by one, all the different manifestations of the *absence of fit* between existing specimens of this form and the environments—be they physical or human— into which they are embedded. "We should always expect to see the process of achieving good fit between two entities," writes Alexander, "as a negative process of neutralizing the incongruities, or irritants, or forces, which cause misfit."

How one acquires such a comprehensive list of requirements (or potential sources of failure), how reliable it is, and the relative importance of one requirement vis-à-vis another were never really made clear. There was no question, however, that in a complex design problem—a new town, a robot, a computer chip, or a foreign policy, for example—the number of requirements on such a list could run into the hundreds or thousands.

To solve such a problem, one needs to break down into manageable subproblems that can be solved one at a time, because typically, as any experienced designer will tell you, we can only handle a few design requirements at a time. A classic article by George Miller, entitled "The Magical Number Seven, Plus or Minus Two: Some Limits on Our Capacity for Processing Information," strongly cautions that this number is very small indeed.

Alexander's "method" provides a mechanical way of breaking down a comprehensive list of requirements into smaller and smaller groups of relatively independent groups of requirements that could be handled one group at a time.

The *synthesis of form* consists of attending to small groups of requirements one by one, creating small forms (diagrams, as Alexander called them then, or *patterns,* as they came to be called later) that balance the demands of conflicting requirements. We can then proceed slowly to integrate these forms into larger forms, gradually evolving the new design for the form as a whole. Graphically, as shown in Fig. 10, the overall design program consists of a hierarchy of smaller

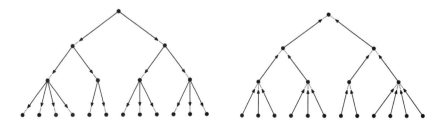

10 *The analysis (left) and the synthesis (right) of form, after Alexander*

and smaller design programs, while the overall design solution consists of a hierarchy of larger and larger forms.

The proposed method in *Notes* never took off. Surely, it was too mechanical, and, as such, too tedious as well. But it was also too ambitious, as it sought to reinvent the wheel, so to speak, time and time again. That aside, I have no doubt that the four-step design method initially outlined in *Notes* was essentially correct. First, debunk existing forms for their failure to meet a comprehensive set of observed and recognizable needs. Second, recognize these needs as demands that can shape a new design problem. Third, break the problem into a new hierarchy of manageable subproblems. Fourth, proceed to invent (or reinvent) a set of new forms by solving each one of these problems independently, giving each new form a name, gradually combining the smaller forms into larger and larger ones and then finally into an efficient, coherent, and sustainable final form. For me, this had been a useful method in architectural design, and later in matters of policy design too. I expected it to be of help in industrial design as well.

In an important way, therefore, Alexander attempted to shift the focus of design from the manipulation of shapes to the invention of new taxonomies, new languages for describing the anatomy, so to speak, of the man-made environment and its artifacts. He understood that design is concerned, above all, with the making of formal distinctions, and that it is words (or names) that create basic distinctions: "In the beginning was the Word, and the Word was with God, and the Word was God." The world is created from chaos by making distinctions, because the making of distinctions transforms chaos into order. Alexander and a number of his disciples, including myself, published a 1,200-page tome in 1977 entitled *A Pattern Language*. It bestowed names on some 253 patterns—or organizing principles—that were to guide, and ultimately humanize and harmonize, the design and construction of towns and buildings.

Given my design education at the foot of the master and my penchant for the breathtakingly new, I assumed that the truly innovative design I was after was going to be so revolutionary that it would require breaking down the scale problem into a new set of parts. In other words, I needed a scale design that did away with load cells altogether. I believed that the thin scale I envisioned required a new conceptual design, a design that needed to be invented from scratch, rather than assembled—like existing commercial and industrial scales, for example—from a small set of off-the-shelf parts.

It was that belief that led me to bet on Harry Jones in Massachusetts, my other lead, rather than on the Bakers at Transducer Techniques. Harry captured my attention when he proposed a complete thin-scale design that did away with load cells altogether. Given my understanding of the way that true innovation came about, how could I resist?

* * *

Three different things made me decide to bet on Harry Jones—that good-natured, reasonable, highly accomplished engineer—rather than on the Bakers.

One, already mentioned, was that Harry proposed a novel thin-scale design that did away with load cells altogether. The second point in his favor was his promise to design and build a prototype of the entire thin scale (electronics included) in his workshop—"soup to nuts," as it were—for what he said would eventually cost less than $10 in mass production. The third was his résumé.

Now that résumé of his was the most impressive one-page résumé I had ever seen, and I do confess it floored me. Harry Jones, Consulting Engineer, it said, had worked with the army, the navy, the air force, NASA, General Electric, and even Raytheon, the company that eventually brought us the telegenic (and as it turned out, pathetically inaccurate) Patriot ground-to-air missiles on CNN during the 1991 Gulf War.

Whether or not Harry was directly involved in the design of the Patriot I never got to know, but guided missile engineering was surely listed in his résumé. His areas of expertise included computer systems, scientific instrumentation, weighing systems, and electro-optics. More specifically, he told me over the phone, he had worked for four years at a very reputable industrial scale company, on the design, development, and production of a 1,000-pound electronic floor scale. To top it all, he now had his own prototype shop, computer systems, and design and drafting facilities.

This heaven-sent man came with a recommendation from a trusted friend, knew everything there was to know about instruments and scales, had worked with *strain gages* (more on that below), and was proficient in electronics. What more could I ask?

I talked to Harry several times on my last day in Los Angeles before flying back to Bangkok. He was soft-spoken, relaxed, and entirely familiar with scale jargon. He already had a conceptual design for the scale, he said, one he had been contemplating for a while, in fact since his days at the scale company. The material for it, he offered, should be a quarter-inch-thick plate of the strongest plastic in existence—Lexan—the bulletproof material that bank tellers and very important people hide behind. A 300-pound person standing on a quarter-inch plate of Lexan barely deflects it, he said. Not only that, Lexan can be reinforced with glass fibers to make it even stronger, and it can be molded into any shape or form.

Jack Welch, the legendary chairman and CEO of General Electric from 1981 to 2000, fell in love with Lexan when he took over the GE Plastics division in 1969:

> When I got the entire plastics operation, which included Lexan, I really believed I had inherited gold. . . . Lexan was a thoroughbred. It was clear as glass and tough as steel. It was flame resistant and lightweight. . . . When we finally got Lexan, I thought we could take on the world and was cocky enough to say so. . . . We added marketing people and began promoting the plastics business as if it were Tide detergent. . . . Dennis McLain, at that time a thirty-game winner with the Detroit Tigers, hurled fastballs at me while I was holding a Lexan plastic sheet in the parking lot of our Detroit office. . . . We took on the big companies and we did well because we could outrun them.

Harry felt very strongly about Lexan, believing, in fact, that it could be a substitute for metal—steel or aluminum—typically used in load cells. He planned to bond strain gages on the Lexan plate itself, he said, eliminating the need for separate load cells altogether.

* * *

What are strain gages and how do they measure weight when you bond them to metal, or, for that matter, to Lexan plastic, as Harry proposed?

Strain gages—like all other sensors—are the interfaces between the physical world and the world of electronics. Their task is to detect a physical quantity—in our case the weight of a person—and to transform it into an electronic quantity—in our case a set of digits on, say, a liquid crystal display. They do so by putting to good use several important discoveries and inventions in close succession. Let me try to explain.

Imagine stretching a column made from any material by loading it. You can do this either by using a universal testing machine (Fig. 11), or by affixing the column to a stationary object from above and attaching a load to it from below.

When heavier and heavier loads are applied to the column, it stretches until it yields and eventually tears in two. Clearly, the thicker the column (and the

stronger the material it is made from) the less it stretches under a given load and the more weight it can sustain before yielding. But all columns, no matter how thick and strong they are, stretch under load just like common springs and rubber bands, even if their elongation cannot be detected by the naked eye.

The ratio of the column's load to its thickness (the area of its cross section) is called the *stress* on the column. In this example, the stress is caused by tension. Alternatively, when a weight is placed on top of a column, the stress is caused by compression. The relative elongation of a column subject to a given stress—the ratio of the added length to the initial length—is called *strain*. It is a positive quantity when the column is lengthened under tension, and a negative one when it is contracted under compression.

Robert Hooke (1635–1702) discovered the key relationship between stress and strain in 1676. Hooke observed that, as long as it is not overstressed, a column under load, like the one in our

11 *A column being stretched by a universal testing machine*

previous example, has an elastic range. The column is elastic in that range in the sense that its deformation under load is not permanent: once the load is removed it returns to its original shape. Hooke's law stated that, within that elastic range, the ratio between the strain and the stress is always a constant number, and that the number is a property of the material itself, which he called its *modulus of elasticity*. Each material has a modulus of elasticity that can be determined once and for all. The modulus for aluminum, for example, was found to be one-third that of steel, implying that an aluminum column will stretch three times as much as an identical steel column subject to the same load.

In a more complex structure than a single square column, stress varies in both quantity and direction in different places in the structure, but in any one location Hooke's law always holds. Structural engineers typically focus their attention on the locations of highest stress concentration in a structure, because this is where failure is most likely to occur. Scale designers also look for locations of highest stress concentration, but for a different reason: these are the best places to measure strains, because, by Hooke's law, the local strains there are also at their maximum; and the higher the strain that can be measured, the higher the accuracy that can be attained.

To take a simple example, imagine a beam projecting horizontally from a wall, fixed rigidly to the wall at one end and subjected to a load pulling down on it at the other end (Fig. 12). The load creates horizontal stresses in the beam that cause it to deflect downward, stretching its top surface (tensile strain) and compressing its bottom surface (compressive strain): "A still more beautiful way of exhibiting the distribution of strain is to use gelatine, into which bubbles of gas have been introduced with the help of sodium bicarbonate. A bar of such gelatine, when bent into a hoop, shows on the one side the bubbles elongated by tension and on the other those shortened by compression."

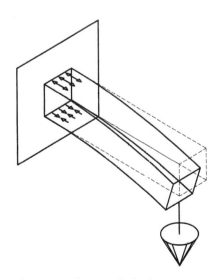

Simple engineering formulas (that will not be reproduced here) show that the highest tensile stress concentration in the projecting beam will be on the top surface of the beam near its fixed end, and that the highest compressive stress concentration will be on the bottom surface of the beam near its fixed end. In fact, the tensile stress on the top of the beam will be equal (and opposite in sign) to the compressive stress on the bottom of the beam exactly below it. And both stresses will be proportional to the

12 *Stresses in a beam under load*

load at the other end of the beam. That implies that if we knew these stresses, we could determine what the load was, and Hooke's law tells us that if we knew the strains there, we could determine the stresses. The question then boils down to how to measure those strains.

The answer to this question requires a basic understanding of electricity. The Yemenite grandmother of an acquaintance of mine used to dangle an electric plug and shake it a few times after she disconnected it from the wall, just to make sure there was no electricity left in it. Electrical current does stop flowing rather instantly once the connection to a power source is severed, but other than that she had the right idea, even though she never mastered reading and writing.

When the positive pole of a battery is connected to the negative pole by a copper wire, the voltage difference between them causes an electrical current to flow through the wire. A copper wire carrying a current is, in fact, analogous to a pipe carrying thick oil: the current is analogous to the rate at which the oil is flowing through the pipe; and the voltage of the battery is analogous to the difference in height between the oil tank and the basin into which it flows. The grandmother, by shaking the plug, was simply taking this analogy at its face value.

Georg Simon Ohm (1789–1854) is credited with discovering that the amount of current flowing through the copper wire will vary in direct proportion to the voltage of the battery. If we double the voltage, the current will double as well. By the same analogy, oil will flow through a given pipe twice as fast if the difference in height between the source and the basin is doubled, which is only to be expected. Ohm's law, formulated in 1825, simply stated that for any given wire, the ratio between the voltage and the current flow is always a constant number, and that the number is a property of the wire—called its *resistance*.

Again, by the same analogy, the electrical resistance in a wire is similar to the friction along a pipe that slows down the flow of oil through it, the friction being a function of the diameter and length of the pipe. Just as shorter and thicker pipes allow oil to flow through them more freely, shorter and thicker wires offer less resistance to an electrical current flowing through them. In Ohm's day, resistance was a newfound electrical property of conductors that could, in principal, be measured.

William Thomson (Lord Kelvin) loved measurement. "When you measure what you are speaking about and express it in numbers," he said, "you know something about it, but when you cannot express it in numbers your knowledge about it is of a meagre and unsatisfactory kind." In his obsessive quest for precise measurement, he discovered in 1856 that when a copper wire of a given length is stretched, its resistance increases in direct proportion to its relative elongation, namely its strain, discussed earlier. Alternatively, if the wire is compressed, its resistance decreases in proportion to its relative contraction. It follows that the change in strain in the wire can be calculated simply by measuring the change in resistance in the wire. This was indeed the key insight that later made possible the creation of strain gages, because it made the connection between a mechanical quantity—strain—and an electrical quantity—resistance.

When a short copper wire (or a set of short parallel wires connected together) is glued tightly to a mechanical element (say, a beam or a column) and that element is loaded, then the strain in the element is identical to the strain in the copper wire(s) at that location. The wire(s) and the column will, in fact, stretch and contract together because of the stiff glue bonding them to each other. We can then measure the change in strain on the surface of the mechanical element at any location simply by measuring the change in resistance in the copper wire(s) bonded in that location.

This was the principle behind the bonded-wire strain gage, invented by Arthur Ruge in 1939 while he was investigating the effects of earthquakes on water towers. Peter Scott Jackson—disgusted with the practical difficulties of using bonded wires in a helicopter project he was working on—pioneered the replacement of Ruge's wires by etching a pattern of parallel wires on a thin foil in 1952, when etching was introduced in printed circuits. "Invention needs two parents," he said, "one anger, the other frustration." One of the more basic applications of the thin-foil strain gage (Fig. 13) has been to measure the weight of objects.

Imagine, for example, attaching a thin-foil strain gage to the top of the projecting beam described earlier (with its wires parallel to the length of the beam) near its fixed end, where the tensile stress—as we noted earlier—is at a maximum. If we then load the beam at its free end, the horizontal stress in the beam will create a strain in the beam; that strain will create an identical strain in the gage; and the strain in the gage will increase its electrical resistance in direct proportion to the load. It follows that if we could measure the added resistance generated in the gage by any given load, then we could determine that load.

To sum up, the strain gage packs the discoveries and inventions described above into one useful device. The gage is bonded to a mechanical element at a specific location. When that element is subject to a load, the load produces a stress at that location. That stress stretches (or compresses) the element and produces a strain. The gage, being bonded rigidly, experiences the same strain. It stretches (or compresses) too, and when it does, its electrical resistance changes

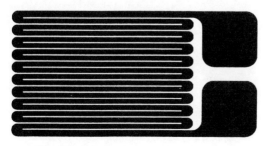

13 *A thin-foil strain gage*

in proportion to the load. That change in resistance can be measured, making it possible to determine the load.

The art of using strain gages in scales involves placing them carefully at locations on a mechanical element where changes in their resistance will be exactly proportional to the load on the element. It also involves designing the mechanical element in such a way that the strain gages will not be subject to any forces or influences other than the load in question. Harry Jones let it be known, in no uncertain terms, that he was a practitioner of this art.

* * *

Harry's idea, he told me over the phone, was to bond strain gages directly to a quarter-inch-thick Lexan plate. In his design, the entire scale plate would become the mechanical element that would deform under load. He thought that eight strain gages would do the trick, two at each corner of the plate. They would be bonded in locations of high stress concentration, one on top of the plate, and one on the bottom of the plate just below it.

He also thought that the electronics could be incorporated into the plate by cutting out two small rectangles—one above and one below the middle—leaving the plate in the shape of an H (Fig. 14). And he was confident—with the customary disclaimers, of course—that with this design we could obtain a high degree of accuracy, of the order of one-tenth of a pound.

That sounded incredible to me. I tried to explain to him that we needed four independent load cells, summarizing my discussions with Gary and Randy Baker. He said there was no need. He had been thinking about this for a long time. It will work, he said, exuding a contagious confidence. I asked him how long it would take and how much it would cost. He said it would take 500 man-hours, 10 50-hour weeks, amounting to $20,000. I said I could afford $10,000 at the most. He said he needed to think about it, hung up, called back, and agreed, promising to send a statement of work to me in Bangkok.

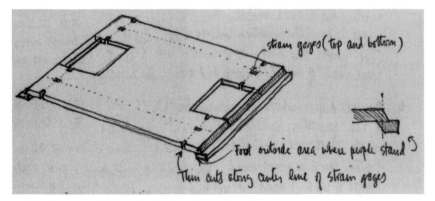

14 *Harry's proposed design, Scale Diary, September 1987*

I surely did not have $10,000. I would have to borrow it. This was no small change either, the kind of small change my father would gamble away twice a week—as far back as I could remember—on five-card-stud poker with his friends. Small-time gambling was taken for granted in my family—poker was considered a part of the children's basic education. But this was, to use my father's words, "a lot worse than poker." Ten thousand dollars was a serious amount of money to gamble away. It was an expensive ticket to a game I wanted to play, one into which only serious players were admitted. Was I a serious enough player?

Before our final talk that day I consulted the *I Ching*—the ancient Chinese oracle known as the *Book of Changes*—seeking its guidance. My old friend John Blofeld—who translated the *I Ching*—once proclaimed, while ordering food at the White Lotus restaurant in Bangkok, that the *I Ching* gave only three kinds of advice—move ahead vigorously, move ahead carefully, and stay right where you are. What kind of advice lay in store for me? The diary entry of 17 May 1987 read: "The first hexagram spoke of thoroughness as a weapon against danger, and told me that overconfidence in the face of risk will lead to trouble. The second hexagram spoke of child folly and its power to start things moving."

I was a great believer in the "child" in me, and it was telling me to start things moving. I was being offered exactly what I was looking for on a silver platter. But I could see the danger too. I had never met the man. I did not really understand what he wanted to do. And I was worried that his design was conceptually wrong. I had to think about this very carefully, and the *I Ching*—having sharpened my understanding of the two forces tearing me apart—was of no further help.

I received the statement of work from Harry a few days after my return to Bangkok. It looked very professional and very convincing, silencing many of my initial doubts. He would design, test, and fabricate a personal scale prototype, a quarter inch in thickness and weighing less than one pound. It would be ready and working two months hence. My brother Joe, at that time baking 600-calorie jumbo muffins in a small bakery in downtown Manhattan, said he could lend me the money. The 1 June 1987 diary entry read: "Midnight: Called Harry Jones and gave him the green light—a new era in my life has just begun!"

* * *

The next three months were dedicated to bringing the Bangkok study to a successful end, and to sharing its findings with all those who cared to listen: the housing situation in the city was improving. The number of new houses built far exceeded the number of new households. The share of the population living in slums declined significantly. Mortgages were easily obtainable. And housing was fast becoming more affordable.

On their part, the self-satisfied officials at the National Housing Authority had to suffer the indignity of realizing that the new houses built by the private sector were cheaper and more plentiful than the highly subsidized housing they were building. Small land-and-house packages sold for as low as $6,000 that year. They took it rather well, I thought, but I could detect their embarrassment, and I hoped that, to prevent future embarrassment, they would constrain their enthusiasm for more public housing in the years to come.

As for me, I was content. Bangkok had now revealed its secrets to me and was no longer the enigma that it was back in 1973. As far as its land and housing were concerned, it was now one of the most studied cities in the developing countries. I was ready to start my exploration of the rest of the world, and—instead of looking for a job—I resolved to let the scale quest show me the way.

5

Specify! Specify!

In the original version of the film *Bedazzled*, a short short-order cook—desperately in love with a tall, plain waitress who looks right through him—sells his soul to the Devil in exchange for seven wishes, hoping to use these wishes to win the heart of the above-mentioned waitress. But every time the poor cook makes a wish—and his wishes become more and more elaborate—he is granted something quite different from what he had in mind. The Devil, shirking all responsibility for the unwanted outcomes, recommends giving more detailed specifications. "But you were nearly there last time," says the Devil. "You just left me one little loophole. I had to take advantage of it. . . . Next time you must *specify*, really spell things out in detail."

Sᴇᴘᴛᴇᴍʙᴇʀ 1987–Oᴄᴛᴏʙᴇʀ 1987

I arrived in New York City at the beginning of September, rented a car, and drove north to New England to meet Harry Jones, Consulting Engineer. Harry's house was a plain one-story ranch house on a wide and very quiet residential street of a small New England town, with broad lawns and high, leafy maple trees. His prototype shop, mentioned in his one-page résumé as "incorporating computer systems, and design and drafting facilities," was a small, crowded room—originally a kid's bedroom, I suppose. There were piles of stuff everywhere, and barely enough room for two people to sit down and talk.

Harry was a short, stocky man, with delicate hands and a clean-shaven, frightened face surrounded by a closely cropped thin beard. His wife, Arlene, was a loud, chain-smoking, obese lady who clearly had him under her spell, partially explaining his startled demeanor when I met him, but only partially, as I soon found out.

Well. To begin with, he was behind schedule—the prototype was far from ready. Second, what he did have—a quarter-inch-thick piece of the legendary Lexan with the contemplated cutouts—was not nearly strong enough under load. He mumbled something about the fibers not being lined up as the reason the Lexan plate was weak, but, as far as I could tell, no matter how the fibers lined up, there was no way that poor plate was going to be strong enough to sustain a person of Arlene's dimensions without bending out of shape.

Most worrisome of all, the poor Lexan—being a plastic after all—was clearly outside its elastic range when loaded with a 100 pounds or more, taking its sweet time to return to its original shape once the load was removed. Plastic, it turned out, was not a material of choice for precision scales.

If that was not bad enough, Harry bought some off-the-shelf electronic circuitry (instead of designing and manufacturing one by himself, as agreed), and it was producing quite a bit of electronic noise, with readings moving up and down several pounds around the desired result and never settling down.

As the leaves kept changing their colors—a mad dance of reds and yellows and pinks and purples, a glorious celebration of their impending death—I came and went for a month, all in all, trying to learn as much as I could, helping Harry with the tests, and making phone calls to suppliers to find out about the availability of parts and their respective costs. The diary entry for 5 September 1987 read:

> Calling in search of parts turns out to be a central activity of inventors, and a most time-consuming one. You start with an 800 number that often hangs up on you, an electronic secretary simply says "Sorry, there are too many calls trying to reach us, please try again later, goodbye" and hangs up. Once you get the national head-quarters, they refer you to their regional distributors, usually the wrong ones, and so on.

The more I called, the more it became clear that the cost of producing the scale along the lines of Harry's design was of the order of $40, and not the promised $10. Why he was so utterly confident it could be produced for $10, I don't know.

As the days passed, more bad news kept coming my way. After the innumerable attempts to reduce the noise in the electronic circuit failed, Harry finally conceded that he needed an amplifier in the circuit, something he apparently thought he could do without. How he thought he could detect minute voltage changes in the strain gages without an amplifier, I had no idea, but what did I know about electronics anyway. It gradually became clear to me, however, just from hanging around and listening to his chatter, that—beyond his mastery of some elementary principles—he did not know much about the electronic circuitry of scales either.

What is more, even when he did hook up an amplifier to the circuit, the prototype scale exhibited large and clearly unacceptable errors. When we placed a 20-pound load in different locations on the scale plate, for example—in what is known as a "cornering" test—we had differences of more than six pounds between one location and another. Six pounds. Other tests had errors of a similar magnitude. This was very discouraging, especially because Harry—under pressure from his ever-present Arlene—was beginning to moan that he had already put in the agreed-upon number of hours and was planning to bring this project to a close in a matter of days. True, he may have put in a lot of time, but we had agreed on a lump-sum contract for finished work, didn't we?

It was then that I had a devastating realization. The diary entry for 12 September 1987 read:

> I just found out that in our letter of agreement, Harry's letter of 18 May 1987, there is no mention of the level of accuracy of the scale. A level of one-tenth of a pound was discussed in our telephone conversation . . . and I don't remember mentioning it in writing. . . . When I said to Harry, "All we have to do now is turn it into a precision instrument," he said, "That would need big bucks."

And so, down the tubes went my $10,000, just like that, while I was left with no "working prototype" of any kind to show for it.

The comic appeal of the film *Bedazzled*—in which the Devil manages to subvert the wishes of his victim, no matter how detailed and specific they are—hinges on the premise that, much as one may insist, a happy outcome can never be fully specified. The Devil, in other words, is in the details. No matter how elaborate the specs, some detail will be left out. A forgotten requirement, an unexpected contingency, or whatever seemed patently obvious and was therefore not mentioned will always allow a seasoned contractor, looking after his own interests, to deliver an unhappy outcome within the parameters of what the client said he or she wanted.

The predicament of the budding inventor seeking professional assistance is especially gruesome in this regard. I confess: I only had a rather vague idea of what I wanted, I did not know how to specify it clearly, and I was easily intimidated into agreeing to something I did not really understand. In truth, I was not the one making the specifications after all, because I was not in command of the language needed to make them. Harry was making them and I was nodding agreement.

But how could I forget to insist on some level of accuracy, or any level of accuracy for that matter? For this rather elementary omission I had no one to blame but myself, but still, as the diary notes, "I couldn't get too depressed about it." I was learning a lot and fast, I reasoned, and that was what mattered. After spending time as Harry's apprentice, I had a much better idea of what accuracy was and how to specify it in the future.

It is no secret that nascent inventors, starting down invention road, are easy prey for swindlers and cheats. Invention promotion firms have been milking inexperienced inventors for years with sweet-sounding promises like, "We think your idea has great market potential"; "Congratulations! We've done a patent search on your idea, and we have some great news—there's nothing like it out there"; "Our company has evaluated your idea, and now wants to make a more in-depth research report." In fact, in 1997 the Federal Trade Commission indicted more than a dozen such companies—companies that had defrauded unsuspecting inventors of more than $90 million in false claims—as part of its Project Mousetrap.

But I thought I was smarter than that. I did not just respond to an advertisement—I contacted the man through my trusted friend Tom, an electrical engineer whom I had known for years who now lived in New Hampshire, not far from Harry's town. Well, it turned out that Tom did not know Harry very well: he just knew of him, had met him a couple of times, and had heard him say something in passing about scales.

To this day I still don't know whether Harry's résumé was real or fabricated, or how he came to work for such a distinguished clientele. He looked honest and well meaning too. He clearly wanted to believe in his fantasies, as if belief was enough to make them happen, and was unwilling to concede that he was, more or less, a hopeless bungler. He needed the work, and he desperately wanted to please his customers, at least as long as it did not compromise his lifelong project of pleasing Arlene. He was a committed "pleaser"; you could see it in his sad, frightened eyes. And he thought nothing of making fancy claims that he could never attain, as long as he felt that he gave them his best shot. So what if he was not much of a shot? He tried, didn't he?

In retrospect, I doubt that I could really have specified a level of accuracy in my contract with him, and then held him to it. Typical development contracts, as I already knew by then, usually contained an escape clause: "While this agreement would not be made unless it was thought that the specifications would be met, it is understood that there is no guarantee on the developer's part to provide more than his best efforts." There was probably no way to insist on any specific performance level in a venture that had so many unknowns. There usually isn't.

In fact, the contractual relationship between someone with an idea—the inventor—and someone who is asked to produce an object that embodies this idea—the developer—is an inherently fuzzy one. Most such contracts, to protect the inventor, require that exchange of information be on a confidential basis. They also specify that "all know-how, improvements, data, drawings, and inventions relating to this invention generated during the period of this development are to be the property of" the inventor. But, as in *Bedazzled*, they do not and cannot guarantee the delivery of what the inventor wants, of what he or she has in mind.

It is for this reason that developing and maintaining an expanding network of trusted and competent professionals is an essential task in the process of invention. During those early New England days, I did not yet have such a network, not even the beginning of one. But I was on my way to building one. Yes, I should have approached Harry Jones more warily. I resolved to make a note of that and move on.

* * *

I was still committed to the notion that the scale plate itself could act as a mechanical element for measuring loads, but I now knew that it had to be stronger, and that the original cutouts in the plate were in the wrong places. Harry agreed with me. He now had a better idea that looked more down-to-earth.

In the absence of a network of trusted professionals, and having no one to turn to, I contracted him yet again right away—for a much smaller sum—to build another prototype. This time, the plate was to be made from a heavy ("we'll worry about making it lighter later") quarter-inch aluminum plate that could withstand 300-pound loads without any visible deflection. He cut some notches into the corners of the plate, again bonded strain gages to the plate itself, and again it did not work. The plate did not deflect much, true, and the test results were not as absurd as in the Lexan model, but they were far from accurate.

I then had yet another plate made of aluminum. It was machined—this time with a grid of ribs and cavities designed to make it lighter—by an old, asocial, German-born machinist in Bridgeport, Connecticut. That machinist got rid of all his employees and was working all alone in his eerie, yet impeccably clean, factory. The new plate he made for me had notches in still different places at the corners of the plate, and Harry bonded strain gages to this plate too. Sad to say, it did not perform any better: it was still inaccurate, and—what was even more worrisome—for all its ribs and cavities, it deflected considerably under load.

Two months of work had gone by, and I had nothing to show for it except for the massive collection of mental postcards of my first glorious Indian summer. But I did come to an important conclusion—the thin plate, the thin load cells, and the thin electronics were, after all, three separable parts. The diary entry for 26 October 1987 reads, "The scale problem now boils down to three separate problems: the plate problem, the load cell problem, and the electronics circuit problem."

I was now convinced that—because they were three discrete problems—they could be solved separately, or at least along parallel tracks, as long as I remained aware at all times of possible interactions between them. For the time being, I did not have a practical solution for any one of these problems, but at least I knew—or thought I knew—what were the three main problems I needed to solve. With this lesson etched in the neuronal circuitry of my mind, I flew back to Bangkok by way of Japan, unsure of the next steps to be taken and open to suggestions.

6

The Secret of the Lightweight Panel

There are two distinct ways you can explore a new city—as a wide-eyed tourist or as someone looking for something—a postage stamp missing from your collection, for example. The first keeps you on well-trodden paths where you can gaze at designated tourist attractions and meet jaded souvenir-shop operators, never making a connection with the city because you don't have a question to ask it. The second allows you to walk down real streets and alleyways into places hidden from view and to converse with real people, because you are after something—that missing stamp you are looking for can get you beyond its façades and into its treasured secrets.

———

OCTOBER 1987–JANUARY 1988

On my way back to Bangkok, I passed through Yokohama, a sprawling industrial city on the eastern shores of Tokyo Bay, centered on its great port, a giant symbol of Japan's resolve to end its historic insularity and trade with the rest of the world. I was there to address a regional conference, organized jointly by the municipality and the United Nations, on the role of government in housing.

On the first of several rainy days of meetings, I argued—in front of a packed auditorium consisting mainly of Japanese government officials, with a sprinkle of familiar faces at Asian housing conferences—that the bulk of the houses built in the developing countries were built despite government and in the face of often-violent resistance by authorities; that the amount of dwelling units provided by government was miniscule in comparison; and that governments were trying to do too much for too few, and ending up doing too little for too many (Fig. 15). The audience clapped politely, and there was a general consensus that my talk was sensible, entertaining, and insightful. Whether it made even one of them examine and mend his or her sorry ways I do not know.

As fate would have it, the organizer of the conference on the part of the UN was none other than my engineer friend Jens Overgaard. In truth, I was much more interested in talking to Jens than to the housing officials and municipal functionaries that surrounded us. Later that evening, after exchanging the necessary politenesses with our hosts and the other conference regulars over cocktails, we ensconced ourselves at the back of the dark bar of the Yokohama Grand Hotel where cigar puffing was allowed.

Jens was admirably laid back, as usual, with not a care in the world despite the fact that he had an international conference on his hands. I related the Harry Jones affair to him in some detail. Then I told him that I had recently realized that the thin-scale problem boiled down to answering three questions: the plate question, the load cell question, and the electronics question. I also explained that the quarter-inch plates we tried in New England were either too heavy or, if not too heavy, too weak to resist deflection under load.

I then asked him the "plate question" that I had posed—in as technical terms as I possibly could—in my diary entry for 26 October 1987, written aboard the Japan Airlines flight to Tokyo: "What material in what configuration will deflect less than one-fifth of an inch with a 300-pound load on a plate measuring approximately seven-by-ten inches, a quarter-inch thick, weighing one pound or less, and costing less than, say, five dollars to make?"

To this he replied simply, "a sandwich structure," and then proceeded to explain to me what he meant, making me happier and happier as he held forth into the night sketching confident lines with his thick fountain pen on the too-absorbent table napkins issued by the bar. What follows is a more elaborate explanation of what he revealed to me that evening, amplified and simplified by what I have managed to learn about the subject since.

15 *Public housing overshadowed by illegal housing in Caracas, Venezuela*

* * *

The sandwich, to begin with, is a generic name for the class of foods that are typically held by hand while eaten, consisting of two slices of bread with sliced meats, cheeses, vegetables, and other condiments wedged between them. It is named after Sir John Montague (1718–1792), the fourth Earl of Sandwich. Legend has it that during a 24-hour stretch at a public gaming table, Sir John, an obsessive gambler, asked that salted beef between two pieces of toasted bread be brought to him, so absorbed in play was he on that long night. The sandwich panel as an engineering structure similarly consists of two thin faces, with a layer of a different kind wedged between them.

As an engineering structure, the scale plate could be considered as a wide rectangular beam, resting freely on four shallow feet at its corners, with the load of the person standing on top of it distributed across it. When such a simply supported beam is weighed down by a person standing on top of it, it deforms into a shallow arch. The top of the beam contracts because it is subject to horizontal compressive stresses, and its bottom expands because it is subject to horizontal tensile stresses. The compressive stresses are highest at the top surface of the beam, and the tensile stresses are highest at the bottom surface. The middle layers of the beam are subject to much lower horizontal stresses. Their chief role is to resist the tendency of the horizontal layers of the beam to slide past each other, a tendency known in engineering parlance as *shear*, which is at a maximum, by the way, in the very middle layer of the beam.

It follows that an efficiently designed beam, made of steel, for example, should not have a rectangular cross section. It should have a concentration of material on its top that can effectively resist compression, another concentration of material on its bottom that can effectively resist tension, and just enough material in its middle layer to resist shear. The most familiar beam of this sort is the I-beam commonly used in building and bridge construction.

Sandwich panels work on the same principle as that of the I-beam. They have two thin surfaces that can resist compression and tension and a core than can resist shear, lend rigidity to the thin surfaces, and prevent them from sliding past each other under load. The twin surfaces can be made of thin metal sheets, fiberglass, or other composite materials that are strong in tension and compression.

The core can be made from parallel ribs (as in ships' hulls, for example), from corrugated materials (as in cardboard boxes), from lightweight organic materials such as balsawood (as in early airplanes), from thin-walled metal or fiber-paper honeycomb (as in commercial jets and the space shuttle), or from hard plastic foams (as in light aircraft, wall and ceiling panels in buildings, and foam-core boards). The core is usually bonded to the two surfaces with a hard adhesive that can also resist shear.

16 *The Mosquito fighter-bomber*

We should not be surprised to find sandwich structures in nature. In fact, our skulls are made from cancellous bones with compact bone tissue in the top and bottom layers and porous, lighter-weight bone tissue in the middle layer. The first use of sandwich structures in man-made artifacts is attributed to the Scottish engineer Sir William Fairbairn (1789–1874), who used it in the design of metal bridge platforms. But the real coming of age of sandwich structures is associated with the development of aircraft in the twentieth century.

During the 1930s, airplanes were still being built with a single metal skin, usually aluminum, reinforced on the inside by a very large number of thin ribs. It was estimated at the time that there were "3,000,000 rivets in a large-sized aircraft and that approximately 50 percent of the total cost of the airframe [was] made up of the cost of fastening together the many pieces that constitute[d] the structure."

But by then, the search for a more efficient, and a lighter-weight, sandwich structure that would eliminate riveting was already gaining steam. The twin-engine de Haviland Mosquito (Fig. 16), for example—the most effective British fighter-bomber during the Second World War—was designed in 1938 entirely of wooden sandwich construction: "The core of the sandwich was made of light-weight balsawood, with skins of heavier and stronger birch plywood glued to either side." It flew its first bombing mission in late 1941.

Balsawood, however, was apt to soak up water and rot. It varied in quality and its supplies were limited—it could only be found in the wild tropical rainforests of Central and South America. It was eventually replaced by metal or impregnated fiber-paper honeycombs (Fig. 17), or by hard foams. The core of the fuselage walls of the Boeing 747 jumbo jet, for example, is primarily a paper honeycomb sandwich—made of a special plastic paper that is dipped in resin to harden it—and "the floors, side-panels, overhead bins and ceiling are also of sandwich construction."

The main reason for the increased use of sandwich construction is that "it has such a high ratio of flexural stiffness to weight." The core of a sandwich structure vastly increases the stiffness of the skins—and thereby their resistance to deflection—by increasing the distance between them without adding a significant amount of weight to the overall structure. A simple calculation shows that if two thin skins bonded together (without any core between them) have a certain stiffness, then adding a core 4 times their individual thickness will increase this stiffness by 12 times, and adding a core 20 times their thickness will increase it by 300 times.

This is a wonderful discovery, for it moves engineering design away from a simple discussion of the optimal shape of a structural element made of a single

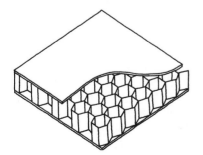

17 *Honeycomb sandwich construction*

material, and into the realm of the appropriate choice of materials to perform specific structural roles within a single structural element. In this sense, the sandwich structure is a variation on composite materials that embed woven or chopped fibers of a high tensile strength in a material of a high compressive strength that can be molded into any desired shape. Fiberglass and fiber-reinforced Lexan are such composite materials, and so is the straw-reinforced clay brick of biblical times: "And Pharaoh commanded the same day the taskmasters of the people, and their officers, saying, Ye shall no more give the people straw to make brick, as heretofore: let them go and gather straw for themselves."

The specific advantage of the sandwich structure is that it is uniquely suited to the construction of lightweight panels that are subjected to bending loads—exactly the structure I was looking for when I crossed the Pacific, and just the one I found out about in that dark bar in Yokohama. Why didn't Jens tell me about all this before, when he knew it all along? Because I didn't ask, that's why.

That discussion with Jens surely energized me. One of the three problems I had posed—the plate problem—was now at least conceptually solved. Applying the sandwich idea to scales was a novel idea, as far as I could see. Now I needed to pursue it further on two separate fronts. First, I had to find out whether I could put this idea into practice and actually produce a sandwich plate that would meet the requirements I had set for myself; namely, be a quarter-inch thick, weigh one pound, and yet be able to sustain a 300-pound person. Second, I wanted to explore whether this was indeed a novel idea, novel enough to be patented. It was not at all clear to me that either a venue could be explored effectively in Bangkok.

* * *

I arrived home in late October only to find that my maid had grown noticeably fatter and lazier during my long absence. The interior of the house had acquired a permanent layer of dark soot that could not be easily removed. Traffic congestion had somehow crossed over from the bearable to the unbearable. And there was yet another paper on housing waiting for me to coauthor. It now demanded intellectual energies I did not have.

It was difficult for me to remember exactly why I came back in the first place, except that this was still home. I had no job here, nor did I want one. Then I realized why I came back: I came in order to leave. I came back to gradually, yet irreversibly, disengage from Thailand. For the first time, after 14 years, I was ready to depart.

On a personal level, I had already become too comfortable, I knew, and I dreaded turning into one of these expatriates around me who could never hack it back home. I was most worried about my mind losing its edge, and I felt that to keep it in shape I needed to practice a higher level of mental gymnastics than the one into which I had settled. The scale conundrum was now pulling me back to the West, and Thailand looked helpless and irrelevant, unable to offer me the cerebral playground I needed. Definitely not the right place for an investigation in high tech, I said to myself.

Surely, Thai industrial plants were on the cutting edge, producing and assembling anything from Mercedes Benz cars to disk drives. Anything could be produced in Thailand, because labor was smart, docile, and cheap. But the invention of new technologies was generally absent—new gadgets and artifacts were simply imported from the West. Thailand already had its unique traditional architecture, its unique customs, and its exquisite cuisine. But new local inventions were, as a rule, few and far between.

The one that stood out, as an exception to the rule, was the omnipresent longtail boat, a flat-bottomed long and thin boat with an engine especially fitted to maneuver in very shallow water (Fig. 18). The engine was a car engine— usually a rebuilt one, without a gearbox or a clutch—mounted in the back of the boat, with a long shaft extruding horizontally from it, at the end of which there was a propeller. Using a lever welded to the engine, the boatman could move the engine in all directions, lifting the propeller out of the water when necessary, or placing it just below the water level and holding it there. This made it possible to navigate quickly (and very noisily) through the shallow canals and rivers—often choked by water hyacinth—that laced the country.

Much as I had always admired the longtail boat, the technology that it employed was too elementary for my project. There was no longer any question in my mind that to pursue the scale project, I would have to head back to the West; to thrust myself into an unpredictable future and a very predictable reduction in the standard of living to which I had become accustomed. That felt quite

18 *A Thai longtail boat*

19 *The Temple of the Golden Pavilion in Kyoto*

right to me, but I was neither ready nor willing to leave Thailand for good. I loved this country and its people too much to simply let go, to just pick up and leave.

I needed a reason to come back, or better yet, a place to come back to again and again. And during those months, I wanted to complete a house I had designed and was having built in Krabi, one of the southern Thai provinces, a house that was going to wait for me. Its design was inspired by the early-fifteenth-century Temple of the Golden Pavilion in Kyoto (Fig. 19), a place that had a strong magnetic attraction for me. And not for me alone: a young student monk, driven mad with jealousy by the restful beauty of that glowing temple, burned it to the ground in 1950, perishing in the blaze.

The house I built sat in front of a coconut grove, right in the middle of a crescent-shaped white beach that faced due west. The coconut grove was surrounded by 500-foot limestone cliffs covered in thick jungle vegetation, cliffs that jutted into the water on both sides of the beach.

The house had only two rooms, a larger one on the ground floor and a smaller one above it. The bedroom upstairs had no walls, only wide windows facing all four directions (Fig. 20). One woke up in the morning to the hoots of the monkeys in the cliffs, or to the shouts "Krabi, Krabi" of the longtail boatmen waiting impatiently for passengers to the nearby provincial town. One took a morning swim before the morning coffee, and then set out to do nothing in the most inefficient way possible, until it became time to watch the wild sunset for a couple of hours (the natural alternative to television), while nursing a cold Singha beer. This house was magical, and it worked its magic on everyone who inhabited it or just passed by to stare or snap a photograph. I felt blessed.

"I can now retire peacefully," I wrote to a friend in late November, "having built at least one beautiful house. I finally paid my debt to architecture. For so many years I dared not touch it, and then it came my way effortlessly. . . . The beach is very peaceful. . . . The sunsets are long and elaborate, and if you are in the water looking at the beach, the houses turn into gold. I was standing there looking and taking it all in, and my head was shaking in disbelief. It was so beautiful, so exquisitely beautiful."

* * *

There was not much else I had to do in Thailand, except for completing the house and making preparations for pulling out my stakes. I did make some parts for a new prototype, putting the sandwich plate idea into practice for the first time, but I quickly discovered that some of the high-tech materials I needed—rigid foam, for example— were not readily available. The new prototype would have to wait for my return to New York.

20 *The house on Railei beach*

As my sojourn in Thailand was drawing to a close, a UN functionary I knew offered me an opportunity to earn some badly needed money. Pietro Garau—a suave, moccasined Italian who would never be caught without a new joke—worked at the UN Center for Human Settlements in Nairobi. He was one of the few people I could count on for occasional work at that time. He wanted to know if I could come to Nairobi for a couple of weeks, on my way back to the States, to help put together a UN policy document on housing. As a way of replenishing my empty coffers, it came in handy. And though my thoughts were fast moving away from housing, I reluctantly accepted.

7

A Single Organizing Principle

Purity of heart is to will one thing.

Søren Kierkegaard

———

Nairobi was an attractive town, about one-tenth the size of greater Tokyo, and much more dangerous to walk around in, especially at night when machete-wielding thugs prowled the streets. It was a very young city, established by the British as a railway supply depot as late as 1899, after which it grew very rapidly. From the air it seemed covered with thick tropical vegetation. Driving through its potholed streets, one was surprised at the number of flowering bushes and trees. Many walls were covered in flaming bougainvilleas in all colors, and the gardens were full of jacaranda and frangipani trees. The weather there was always mild and pleasant too—it was situated right on the equator, but on a plateau more than a mile above sea level.

Nairobi housed several global UN agencies—Pietro Garau's agency, commonly known as UN Habitat, among them—in a modern low-rise complex on the outskirts of town. The foreign international civil servants, and there were quite a few, did not seem to socialize much with the local bourgeoisie. They lived in walled compounds protected by armed guards. They spent their days inviting each other to dinner or sipping long drinks at sports clubs—leftovers from an earlier colonial era—where they largely kept to themselves. And they sent their kids to the international school or to boarding schools abroad.

Pietro, for example, lived with his small family in a seven-acre fenced-off compound in Karen, a rich suburb almost an hour's drive from work, from where the blue Ngong Hills could be seen clearly at the distance. On his way to work in his red duty-free Fiat he passed by several slums; dense collections of tottering one-story shacks, built of roughly sewn wood and covered with rusty corrugated-iron sheets.

My task was to edit a bulky draft of a UN document entitled "The Global Strategy for Shelter for the Year 2000," which was to become the official housing policy of the United Nations. Pietro, to my surprise and without telling me in advance, enlisted yet another person to the task of editing the Strategy document—Steve Mayo, a weighty and convivial urban economist from Arkansas, working on housing out of the World Bank in Washington.

The two of us, meeting for the first time, sat down to talk housing policy. We carried on and on, in what seemed like one long discussion. The drafts we got from Pietro were badly written wish lists that did not add up to anything. Everything was important, and so nothing was really important. Every issue was touched upon, every important word in the housing jargon was mentioned at least once, and the fingerprints of every possible special interest were everywhere. There was a recognizable effort not to leave anyone or anything out. But there was not even a modicum of effort to remove the inconsistencies, or shall I say the contradictions, among the different concerns. And there was no way imaginable to simply integrate these disparate requirements into a seamless single strategy. Having acquainted ourselves with the lists, all we could do was to set them aside and start afresh.

What we needed was one central theme or concept, a *parti,* as it was called in architecture school, a single organizing principle that then incorporated a descending hierarchy of other ideas and still other ideas. There was no doubt in our minds that the Global Strategy had to be one strategy in pursuit of one single objective. "Purity of heart," says the Danish existentialist philosopher Søren Kierkegaard, "is to will one thing."

A well-designed form had an overriding wholeness that resulted from an overriding purpose. Wholeness was what distinguished good design from hodgepodge, and that was why it was impossible to transform wish lists into good design.

Our proposed *parti* was rather simple: the object of housing policy, we argued, was the housing sector as a whole, incorporating all types of housing, all actors in the housing sector, all housing activities, and all housing markets. The overriding singular objective of government in housing was to create and maintain a well-functioning housing sector. It attained this objective by one single strategy: enabling all the stakeholders engaged in housing—be they builders, lenders, or dwellers—to do their work in an efficient, equitable, and sustainable manner.

Our proposed Global Shelter Strategy thus redefined housing policy. Housing policy no longer focused on the miniscule amount of housing projects that the government built, managed, and financed, but rather on the housing sector as a major economic sector. It was premised on the acknowledgment that housing action was best left to builders, developers, banks, civil society groups, and families, and that government would do well if it focused on facilitating their work rather than doing their work for them.

Given this single organizing principle, it was now possible to differentiate the Global Strategy into an orderly hierarchy of government interventions in the housing sector. Now each intervention was not just another intervention, but one that supported that single organizing principle, enriched it, and made possible its effective application. Each particular intervention was now a specific mode of enabling the actors in the housing sector to carry out their respective tasks.

Governments could engage in enabling action in the housing sector by adopting a set of concrete strategies that, employed together, combined into a comprehensive housing policy: bestowing property rights to squatters who built their homes illegally on public lands; giving housing allowances to needy households so that they could buy or rent a place for themselves or improve and expand their existing homes; making mortgages more secure so that commercial banks would get into the mortgage business; building roads that opened up new lands for settlement so that residential land would not be in short supply; improving the water and sewerage networks in poor neighborhoods so as to cut down on waterborne diseases; facilitating the entry of firms and individuals into the construction business; or enacting building codes and subdivision regulations that could be realistically adopted by poor families so that they would not be forced into illegality.

Now, these disparate forms of government intervention in the housing sector were not a hodgepodge, but a comprehensive set of interventions that, together, combined into one integrated program of action. In other words, national housing policy had a set of discrete parts that needed to be developed and implemented one by one—a property rights regime, a housing subsidy regime, a housing finance regime, a regulatory regime, and so on.

Our proposed draft of the Global Shelter Strategy was well received, and a few months later, with minor changes, the General Assembly approved it and sanctioned it as the official housing policy of the United Nations.

* * *

It should not be difficult to see that the design of housing policy was not that different from the design of a house or a thin scale. Good design practice always seemed to involve, in some still loosely defined sense, the pursuit of "one thing," a *parti*, a single organizing principle. This did not necessarily recommend a form that had that property as a particularly practical or useful one. But it transformed it into a form "whose elements," to quote the mathematician Henri Poincaré, "are harmoniously disposed so that the mind without effort can embrace their totality while realizing the details."

Good design, as a product of the human mind, must eventually form an articulated whole. It cannot remain a collection of ideas thrown together without a dominant idea to inform and organize them. To quote Immanuel Kant's comment on "the architectonic of pure reason":

> Under the sway of reason, our knowledge must not remain a rhapsody, but must become a system, because thus alone can the essential objects of reason be supported and advanced. By a system I mean the unity of various kinds of knowledge under one idea. This is the concept given by reason of the form of the whole, in

which concept both the extent of its manifold contents and the place belonging to each part are determined *a priori*. . . . Thus the whole is articulated (*articulatio*), not aggregated (*coacervatio*).

The application of a single organizing principle in architecture, for example, is there for all to see in Ludwig Mies van der Rohe's Farnsworth House in Plano, Illinois (1946–1951): the exterior walls are entirely of glass, and the interior, except for a small core in its middle, is entirely open (Fig. 21). Nothing could be simpler. Again, this did not recommend this house as one that afforded sufficient privacy, or that was particularly energy efficient—it would probably be too cold in the winter and too hot in the summer. But there was no question in anyone's mind that it had a single organizing principle. And that quality distinguished it from any other house ever built before and made it into a thing of beauty.

What was the single organizing principle that I was following in my scale design? Did I have such an organizing principle in mind, or was I trying to blend a crowded wish list into a single form?

Originally, the reader may recall, I set out to invent a travel scale. I read that to mean that the scale needed to be as small as possible and as light as possible, so that it would be as portable as possible. Now I was no longer so sure about my original agenda. How small could I make the plate without making it too small? Typical bathroom scales that were on the market at the time—like a scale called Thinner that came out then—were ten inches square and one-inch high. Some were bigger, eleven-by-eleven inches or more. A travel scale then advertised by Hammacher Schlemmer in New York was nine-by-eight inches, probably on the smaller side.

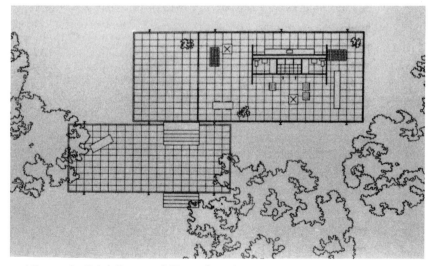

21 *Mies van der Rohe's Farnsworth House, floor plan*

Was the scale I had in mind a travel scale, or a regular bathroom scale that could also be used for traveling? I now opted for the latter. People who cared about their weight were interested in tracking changes in their weight, I reasoned, and that could only be ensured if they always weighed themselves on the same scale. A regular, yet truly portable, bathroom scale would also have a bigger market than a specialized travel scale. And if the scale were to be used regularly, it should not be too small. It would need to be at least ten-by-ten inches and possibly more, to be truly comfortable to stand on.

Given what I already knew about sandwich structures there was no question that the thicker the plate, the lighter and stiffer it would be. A one-half-inch sandwich plate, for example, would most probably weigh less that one pound. But I did not want it to be that thick. In fact, given that the scale had to have a minimum surface area to make it comfortable to stand on, the only dimension I could really reduce—so as to make the scale smaller—was its thickness. In the final analysis, if I had to choose between making the scale lighter or making it thinner, I would opt for the latter.

As far as I was concerned, the quarter-inch thickness requirement was a do-or-die requirement for the duration of the scale project, and its single organizing principle. It was the one requirement I truly adopted as my own. In my vision, the scale was a quarter-inch thick, and all the other requirements it had to meet would be subject to that one requirement. I stubbornly insisted on remaining true to this one single principle in the face of countless arguments by people along the way—engineers and marketing directors, among others—who tried to get rid of it so as to make their lives more comfortable.

The scale industry as a whole was clearly moving towards thinner scales, but for the industry thinner still meant breaking the one-inch barrier. I wanted to break the one-inch barrier and to run way ahead of the pack, all the way to the quarter-inch barrier, where I was willing to stop and wait for the others to catch up.

"The obsession with thinness," mused Dan Bucsescu, an architect friend, "was part and parcel of our relentless efforts to negate the materiality and solidity of objects. Making objects flat was tantamount to obliterating their third dimension and making them disappear. It was yet another aspect of our struggle to free ourselves from the oppressive force of gravity pulling us down, to become weightless, and to soar to the skies."

I couldn't agree more. When two dimensions were enough, the third one was superfluous. If there was any way of obliterating the third dimension with a new technology, why not go for it? Calculators had already lost their third dimension, and laptop computers followed. My scale would soon join them on the march to flatland.

The relative importance given to various design requirements for any form was, in the final analysis, very personal, and my insistence on a quarter-inch thickness as my single organizing principle was no exception. Specific design requirements were often associated with specific people, and when these people left or passed away, the requirements they insisted on often disappeared with them. In this sense, design was political, since issues regarding the relative importance of various requirements that shape the form in question were determined through the exercise and sharing of power in teams, boards, or committees that produced designs.

Yet the fact that the requirements that a form was designed to meet were decided politically by its producers did not mean that such decisions necessarily resulted in forms that could actually survive out there, among those who consume designed products. Consumers—fickle and ill-understood as they were—placed their own values on specific attributes or features of any given form. They determined, or at least helped determine, the chances of survival of particular products and services, whatever they may be.

It followed, then, that the relative importance of this and that requirement could not be decided upon arbitrarily by anyone in a position to decide—be he or she a politician with a new policy, an architect with a new building, a lyricist with a new song, a film director with a new movie, or an industrial designer with a new product.

Indeed, "because I want it" was rarely advanced as a serious rationale for moving ahead on any new design. New designs were advanced because their creators believed that they had a wide appeal—a specific niche appeal for a certain group of people, or a mass appeal for humanity at large. How did they come to believe that?

At one end of the spectrum were those who believed that, by going into the deepest recesses of their own consciousness, they could and would connect to an archetypal, shared humanity that was far greater than themselves. They looked for their commonality with the rest of humanity inside themselves. They made their discoveries and inventions alone, and having made them, they pronounced them or showed them to the world, calling on people to come and share their discoveries.

Whether they succeeded in attracting a following, acquiring a reputation, or accumulating a loyal clientele was another matter. What mattered to them was that they were not pursuing their own private agendas but an agenda that could be shared by all those who could see what they saw and feel what they felt. They had articulated a vision, and they wanted others to share it and to move together towards its realization.

At the other end of the spectrum were those who did not have any inner visions at all. Instead, they looked outside themselves seeking to discover the common features of what sells, and then to fashion themselves or the design of the products they wished to sell in a manner that embodied as many of these selling features as possible. They based their beliefs that their designs would have mass appeal on their knowledge of what lay out there in the marketplace, and they sought some level of proof—through polls, market surveys, or focus groups, for example—that the people would want to buy what they planned to offer them.

Needless to say, this method was far from scientific—it was not possible to point a finger at particular features of, say, a movie that made it successful, and rarely had a sequel been as successful as the original, no matter how many of the original features it incorporated. A sequel, like many other products based on what sells, is designed to reduce risk—both financial and political risk—at the expense of true innovation, which is, by its very nature, untested.

Opinion polls, market surveys, and focus groups were designed to gage the public's response to a new policy or a new product so as to reduce those risks, and they transferred some power in design decision making to those who conducted the surveys and could claim to know what the people really wanted. And, yes, that claim to know what the people really wanted, or to have identified a new and unmet need, certainly wielded power over design—whether it was grounded in a mystical inner certainty, a knack for guessing market trends, or a meticulous pursuit of statistical evidence.

I, for one, realized that bathroom scales, like many other artifacts, were destined to become thinner and thinner, and I knew that if I created a very thin scale, a certain group of people (people of good taste, to be sure) would welcome it as something they were after all along and be willing to pay a premium to get it. I also knew that a still larger group of people would gladly buy it if that premium were not exorbitant. How large were these groups, I had no idea.

Whether anyone else saw the value of investing time and money in developing a very thin scale I did not know. I also did not care because I was on my own, and I did not need to report to a superior or a partner who might not have shared my zeal or the depth of my commitment. In my aloneness, I saw the thin scale in my mind's eye, and I found that vision an attractive one that I wanted all to share. For now, since I was working with my own money, I did not have to listen to anyone or to convince anyone that my vision was worth pursuing. Eventually, I would need to find out what other people thought about it and whether it possessed enough commercial appeal. That would have to wait until I had a clearer idea of how to turn my vision into a finished product. For now, it was still quite blurred. Except for a vague idea about employing a sandwich plate design, I had nothing. But that was already a start.

8

The Rush to Patent

Where was the best place to be for someone with an invention to develop and patent? Thailand, I already knew, was surely not the place, and, sad to say, neither was any other developing country. Inventive action was concentrated in the rich industrialized countries—in the United States, in some of the larger countries in Western Europe, and in Japan. As for me, the States were surely more familiar, more accessible, and hence more attractive. This, then, was the place to look for a base of operations. Where in the States were inventors concentrated?

It seemed likely that inventive activity would be concentrated in and around the big cities rather than in small towns, and more likely to be found along the populated East and West Coasts rather than in the underpopulated middle. So I narrowed my choices down to three metropolitan areas—San Francisco, Los Angeles, and New York.

In retrospect, my informal geography was not too far off the mark. Figure 22 shows the distribution of patents granted to residents of the United States in 1999, for example. During that year, a total of some 89,000 such patents were

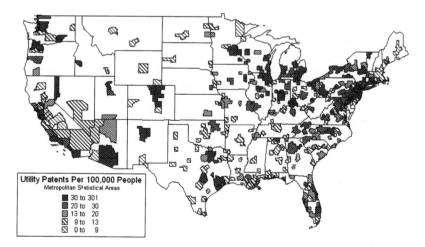

22 *The geographical distribution of patents granted in the United States in 1999*

issued by the United States Patent and Trademark Office. Of that total number, 18,000 were issued to inventors living in California; 13,000 to inventors living in the Tristate area (New York, New Jersey, and Connecticut); 6,000 to inventors living in Texas; 4,000 each to inventors living in Illinois, Michigan, Ohio, Massachusetts, and Pennsylvania; 3,000 to inventors living in Florida, and some 30,000 to inventors living in the remaining 43 states and territories.

Was there a sensible explanation for that particular geographic distribution of patents? Yes. All in all, patents were to be found in larger numbers where the money was (that is, in the rich, populated states); where there were substantial investments in R&D (research and development); and where there were good graduate schools of engineering.

There was no doubt, then, looking at the numbers, that California and the New York metropolitan area were—at least in terms of generating patented inventions—the most inventive and creative places in the country at the close of the twentieth century. Their primacy was even more pronounced when the numbers of copyrighted works were added to the numbers of patents. Both areas were indeed major producers of what has come to be called intellectual property.

Not surprisingly, this was clearly reflected in the large number of patent attorneys that practiced in both places. Of a total of some 20,000 patent attorneys registered with the United States Patent and Trademark Office in 2001, for example, 2,600 lived in greater New York, 1,500 in greater San Francisco, and 700 in greater Los Angeles. Surely, California could boast more inventions, but when it came to lawyers in general, and patent lawyers in particular, no place could surpass New York. I had to choose between ensconcing myself in or around San Francisco, Los Angeles, or New York, and that was not too difficult a choice.

* * *

I had a deep connection with the San Francisco Bay Area, and I am more than grateful to it for the large number of new experiences that it bestowed upon me. Surely, like other veterans, I now carried with me a bag of good war stories of my turbulent student days there in the '60s. In truth, like other veterans, I had a marginal role in the unfolding historical events. I had stumbled upon them, found them to my liking, and joined the fray that soon became more of a party than a fray.

But in 1988, other than still nurturing a modicum of nostalgia, I had utterly outgrown the place. In fact, it took me years to get my feet back on the ground after I left the dizzying atmospherics of Berkeley. Returning there felt like going back to an old place rather than moving forward to a new one. Berkeley was an earlier chapter and that chapter was now closed.

Los Angeles, now that was a more attractive possibility, but for the wrong reason. I assumed that the scale saga would be over, sooner or later, and I toyed with the possibility of enrolling in film school and edging myself into the movies as my next foray outside the confines of housing policy. It was an old and tantalizing dream that I had stored in the back rooms of my mind for as long as I could remember. But I had to admit that, for now, the thought of film school was a distraction, and, without the prospects of a career in film, Los Angeles seemed somewhat less appropriate.

New York, though the least familiar, remained, therefore, the weightiest contender among the three. My younger brother Joe lived there, and he was more than happy to ease me into the city. At that time, Joe—a graduate in baking engineering and management from Kansas State—operated a small bakery on Broadway, opposite the Federal Building in lower Manhattan.

At street level, he sold designer sandwiches to the office crowd at lunchtime. In the basement, he baked jumbo muffins that he himself never touched—they were loaded with fat and sugar and otherwise quite tasteless. But that was beside the point. Joe was not one to let his own taste buds dictate his business strategy. Muffins sold in the hundreds of dozens out there, distributed during the early morning hours by tough-talking jobbers that plowed the empty streets in their graffiti-covered vans. That was reason enough to bake them.

Joe was particularly adept at educating his workers—new immigrants all—in the art of baking engineering and management, and then delegating full responsibility to them. As a result, he never really had anything pressing to do, and whatever he did do he didn't do for very long. You had to give it to the man; he was not in the rat race. On the contrary, he made his money feeding the rats, and he was one of the very few inhabitants of Manhattan who was a master of his own time.

Joe was happy to lend me money for the scale venture as long as I could manage with little amounts of it at a time. He didn't mind kibitzing on the scale venture either. He had time on his hands in general, as I said, and he had time for me in particular, his long lost brother who disappeared into the far reaches of the East so many years ago. We had some good talks about possible business models for the scale venture; we looked for various materials and tools for the new prototypes on Canal Street in Chinatown; and we occasionally explored over lunch possible new venues for marketing muffins and bagels. As the days went by, I gradually became more comfortable in the city, but only gradually.

In terms of what it did to your mind, there was no city more different from Bangkok. In Bangkok, when I smiled at strangers, for example, their faces invariably lightened up with a smile of their own. In New York, when I attempted to simply make eye contact with strangers, never mind smiling at them, they countered with an angry gaze or turned their eyes away. In Bangkok, people went to great length to avoid contradicting me, even when they were in possession of an indisputable fact or an invaluable piece of information. In New York, I found contrariness to be second nature, confrontation a pastime, assertiveness a must, and smart people freely dispensing commentary or advice whether I asked for them or not.

Bangkok was patient with me—I had time to think before I spoke. New York expected a rapid-fire response—speak first, think later; we haven't got all day. In Bangkok, raw ambition (not to mention greed) was frowned upon, recognized, as it was, as the ultimate cause of suffering—the Second Noble Truth revealed by the Buddha. In New York, unbounded ambition— preferably accompanied by a killer instinct—was regarded with awe and admiration, and "aggressive" was an adjective that best described the venerated role models of the corporate world. Bangkok for me was about being, New York was more about becoming: it was vastly more purposeful than Bangkok.

New York was a magnet that attracted a self-selected group of particularly ambitious people, people who were driven by a desire to get somewhere; to

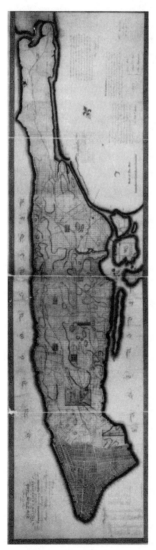

become somebody; to make it, so to speak; and preferably to make it big. In Bangkok, winning and losing were only a game. In New York, winning and losing were the only game in town.

For the scale venture, I figured, this would be an ideal base of operations. After all, there was nothing like a heavy dose of mental discomfort to keep your mind wakeful and alert. I was not at all sure that I could count on my killer instinct surfacing from my subconscious any time soon, but I certainly did harbor an ambition, a purpose, and an agenda. In that sense I surely fit the personality profile of the generations of immigrants that flocked to New York with a dream.

All these people with all these dreams made New York into a giant conglomeration of original talent, into a creative community that had been able to reinvent itself time and time again, miraculously managing to maintain its leading position on the cutting edge of cultural, technical, and commercial innovation for extended periods since its founding in 1625.

One of its most striking innovations, and, for me, one of the best examples of the visionary spirit of its people as a creative community, was its city plan of 1811. This plan still stands out for me, almost two centuries later, as the best example of effective urban planning, an example still to be emulated, especially by the rapidly growing cities of the developing countries of today.

In 1811, when New York City had only 100,000 people crowded into the southern tip of Manhattan, it adopted a plan to expand its street grid so as

23 *The New York City plan of 1811*

to prepare for a more than tenfold increase in population (Fig. 23). The three commissioners who presented the plan remarked: "To some it may be a matter of surprise that the whole island has not been laid out as a city. To others it may be a subject of merriment that the commissioners have provided space for greater population than is collected at any spot on this side of China."

I did end up deciding on New York as my base of operations. I had one more reason, over and above those already mentioned, for staying in the city. I shall explain that reason in the next chapter.

* * *

I did not yet have a *working* prototype of the thin scale, but—like other naïve inventors before me—I was in a rush to patent. I hated the idea of someone else getting there before me. That meant, among other things, that there was not much to patent yet. I did not yet have a thin and accurate load cell, for example, one that really worked and that could fit into a thin scale; so there was no use claiming an innovative load cell. I did not yet have any thin electronics, and there was no way of knowing whether once I had them they would embody anything new. I was essentially left with one single novel idea—the application of sandwich construction to scales so as to make them light and thin, essentially an old way of producing something new. I also had in mind all manner of design ideas that could make that thin scale into a beautiful object, but, as it turned out, not one of them was patentable.

In short, I knew nothing about patents, what they entailed, and what they promised, but I somehow managed to convince myself—having read too many self-help books, maybe—that I wanted one badly. And I wanted a patent for what I supposed were the usual reasons.

First, not being a secretive person, I loved speaking about my project and showing my prototypes to anyone who might possibly help, but I was reluctant to do so for fear that they would run with it and leave me behind. Second, I knew that I could not manufacture and market scales by myself, so I needed to sell my idea to someone who would. Other than going into business with a partner or an investor—an option I had hoped to avoid—the only way to do that was by patenting my idea and then granting a license to a corporation that could make it and sell it. Without a patent, I could never hope to get paid for my efforts— captains of industry were not in the business of paying unknown entities like me large sums of money for their good ideas.

And I did need to get paid, eventually. Inventing was an expensive pastime, I had already discovered, and I could not afford to keep at it for long unless I could sell some kind of product that embodied my inventive efforts. I clearly enjoyed the invention game, and I did not need a powerful financial incentive to stop whatever else I was doing in order to pursue it. But I certainly needed to at least break even to stay in the game. A little nest egg to keep me comfortable in my eventual retirement would be nice too, of course, but if that were too much to ask, I supposed I could do without it.

Finally, there was some glory to be had. Having a patent in your name, I thought, no matter for what object, bestowed upon you the credit you deserved for being the first person to have put something together, and confirmed you as an inventor. To be granted that elusive title, you have to have traveled to the frontier of human knowledge, into uncharted territories that only a select few can ever visit, and to have returned to claim it—to show proof that you deserved that title and that it was rightfully yours.

* * *

Filippo Brunelleschi (1377–1446)—the Renaissance architect-engineer who built the largest dome of his time, the *cupola* that graced the cathedral of Santa Maria del Fiore in Florence—once complained to a friend thus: "Many are ready, when listening to the inventor, to belittle and deny his achievements, so that he will no longer be heard in honorable places. But after some months or a year they use the inventor's words, in speech or writing or design. They boldly call themselves the inventors of the things they first condemned, and attribute the glory of another to themselves."

Brunneleschi was the first on record to be granted the right to exclude others from copying his invention. In 1421, using his not inconsiderable clout in government circles, he obtained official protection for "some machine or kind of ship, by means of which he thinks he can easily, at any time, bring in any merchandise or load on the river Arno and on any other river or water, for less money than usual." The Florentine authorities decreed that designs that copied his invention would be set aflame.

He was so confident of the commercial value of this invention that he actually built it using his own funds. It took him seven years to bring it to perfection, and in 1428 he was granted a contract to transport 100 tons of white marble along the heavily silted and fickle River Arno—from Pisa to Florence—for use in facing the arching ribs of the great dome.

The ship-cum-machine, mockingly known by his detractors as *il badalone* (the monster), sank with its entire cargo shortly after it weighed anchor, at great financial loss to Brunneleschi—an equivalent of ten years of his salary as the dome's architect and one-third of his fortune—and at a great loss to his prestige as an ingenious inventor. Thus began the recorded history of patent protection.

The Senate of the city of Venice is credited with the original introduction in 1474 of the first patent system, granting official protection to all inventors of useful devices, half a century after Brunneleschi's first patent:

> We have among us men of great genius, apt to invent and discover ingenious devices; and in view of the grandeur and virtue of our City, more such men come to us every day from diverse parts. Now, if provision were made for the works and devices discovered by such persons, so that others who may see them could not build them and take the inventor's honor away, more men would then apply their

genius, would discover, and would build devices of great utility and benefit to our commonwealth. Therefore:

Be it enacted that, by the authority of this Council, any person who shall build any new and ingenious device, not previously made in our Commonwealth, shall give notice of it to the office of our General Welfare Board when it has been reduced to perfection so that it can be used and operated. It being forbidden to any other person in our territories and towns to make any further device conforming with and similar to said one, without the consent and license of the author, for the term of 10 years.

The use of the word *patent* to describe the granting of a right is explained by the jurist Sir William Blackstone (1723–1780) in his *Commentaries on the Laws of England* in 1768:

The king's grants are also a matter of public record. . . . These grants, whether of lands, honours, liberties, franchises or ought besides are contained in charters, or letters patent that is, open letters, *litterae patentae*, so called because they are not sealed up, but exposed to open view, with the great seal pending at the bottom: and are usually directed by the king to all his subjects at large.

As with many other words in the English language—such as *convertible, epic, editorial,* or *short,* to take a few examples—the word *patent,* an adjective originally meaning *open,* has come to be used as a noun. In fact, most people now seem to believe that in the expression *letters patent*—still used occasionally in patent legalese—*patent* is the noun and *letters* is an adjective describing it, and not the other way around.

The Venetian formulation of the patent system was in itself an important invention that was broadly disseminated, and—with a few minor, yet important, modifications that will be discussed shortly—it has become the norm. With the exception of the Netherlands and Switzerland, which abolished their patent systems for short periods—the former between 1850 and 1912 and the latter between 1869 and 1888—national (and eventually international) patent systems have accompanied all industrial and technological development since the Renaissance.

Modern patent law, which by now has been largely standardized in global trade agreements, differs from the original Venetian law in several important respects. Patents have now come to protect inventors, rather than the importers of inventions from abroad. The requirement that inventors actually build their inventions and demonstrate that they work has been eliminated—patented inventions are no longer required to be operable. A search to verify novelty is now a prerequisite to the granting of a patent. The length of patent protection has been increased, and now stands at 20 years from the date of the initial application for a patent.

But, most important of all, while earlier inventors were not expected to formulate their patents in writings and drawings, today's patent applicants must provide a complete written description of their inventions. In the application it is the verbal claims to novelty that truly matter, rather than the drawings describing the invention. It is the claims that have to be upheld or voided in a court of law.

* * *

In early 1988, the only way I could hope to be remunerated for my untiring efforts was by getting a patent for my invention—a thin personal scale embodying the idea of a sandwich plate. I met Marc Gross—my trusted patent lawyer—through my brother Joe, shortly after my arrival in New York. Despite the intimidating Park Avenue skyscrapers visible through his office window, I found Marc's boyish, self-effacing demeanor rather comforting. He was a model of dispassionate rationality and cool objectivity. And like my father, if he had any strong opinion or any passionately held belief, he surely kept it well hidden from view. The only ill feeling he ever exhibited in my presence (or on the phone) was the occasional sense of mild frustration on Monday mornings when he had too many things to attend to at the same time.

Marc let it be known that what he enjoyed most about his work was meeting and getting to know interesting characters, and that he found me to be a worthwhile addition to his character collection. He also generously offered to connect me with everyone else he knew who might be distantly useful. Not the litigious type by a long shot, Marc urged clarity and full disclosure so as to avoid petty challenges down the line. He also advocated self-help, tutoring me into doing as much of the writing as possible so as to cut down on his fees. The self-help approach dovetailed nicely with the injunctions in David Pressman's *Patent It Yourself*, my favorite instruction manual at the time.

I explained my thin-scale design to Marc in great detail, and I found out to my chagrin that he was not at all interested in my design. From my perspective, I had in mind the best and most beautiful scale I could imagine, and I imagined it in great detail. It would be a flat and rectangular sandwich plate with slightly rounded corners, not more than a quarter-inch in thickness; with a top surface warm to the touch, four thin load cells embedded in the plate; an electronic readout with large numbers at the center of the plate, and so on. What I had in mind, in other words, was one single design embodying a set of essential qualities in one beautiful and functional form based on a single organizing principle.

From Marc's perspective, I could either apply for a *design patent* or a *utility patent*. Yet that singular design I had in mind was not really unique enough for a design patent. One could apply for a very restricted design patent if one had a clearly distinguishable shape that could be described in drawings—a Coca-Cola bottle, for example—and wanted to avoid imitators who tried to defraud buyers into thinking they were buying a Coke. Any singular shape could be the subject of a design patent. But a design patent was not appropriate for a very thin scale that could take on the shape of a square, a rectangle, a circle, a trapezoid, or an ellipse and still be very thin.

What remained, then, was a utility patent for a new and useful invention. A utility patent—unlike a design patent—did not apply to one singular shape but rather to a class of objects, as broad and as varied as possible, that embodied a novel and useful feature—a feature that could be plainly phrased in words (rather than described in drawings).

Making scales more portable was clearly a worthy objective and could therefore furnish the *usefulness* criterion. But it was the *novelty* criterion that was at the heart of a patent claim. To claim novelty one needed to distinguish the new invention from the *prior art*. The new form had to be distinctly different from anything already in the public domain and from anything already claimed by patents still in force. In addition, one had to prove to the patent examiner in Washington that the novel feature in question was not obvious to a person skilled in the art of making scales.

In other words, whether the plate was rectangular or elliptical did not matter, surfaces warm to the touch did not matter, and the fact that the scale was particularly thin did not matter either. Getting rid of the levers inside existing scales and using four load cells instead did matter, but that was already disclosed in the prior art. Others have already noticed that using several load cells is one way of making scales thin, and there were a lot of scales on the market—mostly commercial and industrial ones—that used several load cells.

It took me some time to leave my cherished design, and to broaden my perception so as to include an entire class of scales—including commercial and industrial ones that were of no interest to me—in my main patent claim. Basically, scales with a sandwich construction did not exist and had not been disclosed in any prior art. All that remained to claim it as a new and useful invention was to write it all down, again and again, in patent legalese, changing words from *consisting* to *comprising*, from *parallel* to *substantially parallel*, from *two* to *a plurality*, and from *four* to *three or more*, all the while keeping the claims as general and as broad as possible. I also had to describe a preferred embodiment of my invention—my actual design—and then provide enough detail so as to enable people to make it. Refusing to disclose an essential feature or ingredient—as those miserly souls giving away their cherished cake recipes have been known to do—could result in the patent's being disallowed. So I did describe my design in excruciating detail, but I described something that I later found out did not work at all.

I submitted the patent application to the Patent Office in early March of 1988. The patent examiner replied in mid-July, less than five months later, promptly rejecting all my claims because of "obviousness in combination." He uncovered two patents, he wrote, that I had not cited in my discussion of the prior art: one patent issued to a Mr. Tulloch for a scale with three layers, and one patent issued to a Mr. Holm for a load cell made from several bonded layers. "It would be obvious to one of ordinary skill in the art," he argued, "to use bonded layers in Tulloch and lower the profile of the scale as is suggested by Holm." Hmmm.

That was a cruel and not-at-all obvious rejection, and it took me a while to calm down. But once I got my bearings, I realized that the examiner did not understand that simply bonding layers together does not a sandwich make. Marc bolstered my spirits by assuring me that "obviousness in combination" was a good thing actually, for it implied that the examiner acknowledged the novelty of the invention.

In almost no time I ended up feeling that the examiner was in fact trying to be helpful by bringing forth these two patents, and that distinguishing my claim from theirs was not difficult and would actually strengthen it. It now boiled down to making it perfectly clear that—unlike all other scales—my scale had only one plate, comprising several layers that acted together as one rigid structure.

We sent the patent application back to the examiner with the amended claims some two weeks later. The word *comprising* was now everywhere. The main claim, for example, stated:

> A low-profile and light-weight portable electronic scale, *comprising* a thin and rigid load-bearing composite plate *comprising* a plurality of layers rigidly bonded together to act as a single structural plate . . . *comprising* a top layer of high elastic modulus having high compressive strength . . . a bottom layer of high elastic modulus having high tensile strength . . . and an intermediate light-weight layer . . . which acts primarily in shear.

Marc called me in mid-August to inform me that the patent was allowed in its entirety and in record time, less than six months after my initial application. I should have been suspicious about getting that patent in record time. As it turned out, the narrower the claim, the easier it is for the patent examiner to allow it, because he is not giving away a lot. Patents with broad claims are worth much more than patents with narrow claims, because they can restrict a lot more people from moving ahead without permission. Therefore, they also take a lot longer to approve and are much more likely to be rejected altogether. My patent was approved so quickly, I should have realized, because I was not claiming much that was new.

But that was August already, and by that time the scale saga involved a lot more than the pursuit of that first, rather minor, patent.

9

Arriving at the Square

February 1988–May 1988

William Goldman, who wrote the screenplays for *Butch Cassidy and the Sundance Kid, All the President's Men,* and *The Princess Bride,* among others, describes how it felt to hand in a screenplay he had just completed:

> And then comes the moment of mourning. Because the relay race must go on and my lap is ending: I must pass the baton to the other technicians. And when you give it away, the loss, of course, is the end of your imagination. The movie in my head is going to leave me. Other people's fantasies are going to take over. . . . At the time of his greatest usefulness, the screenwriter is cast aside. That's the way movies are made.

Goldman understood that he had to let go and was never involved in the transformation of his screenplays, his inventions if you will, into films. Was I only interested in inventing the thin scale, floating my scale patent into the world, and then leaving its realization to others? Or was I interested in actually making it happen, in making sure that the thin-scale design I had envisioned was transformed from a concept into a real object? There was never a doubt in my mind that I, for one, opted to strive for the actual realization of a new form of personal scale. It was the thin-scale design that was driving the invention in the first place, and there was a lot still to be discovered along the way.

My patent would never define an actual form for a personal scale anyway. I already knew that I could not patent the dimensions, the shape, the details, or the texture of the scale, for example. At any rate, having a patent for the sandwich-plate principle underlying the construction of thin and lightweight scales and moving on to bigger and better things was never a real option for me.

So, while it was not yet clear to me how to transform the scale I had in mind into an actual artifact that would grace the shelves of stores, I knew that there was a lot more work to do beyond getting that patent, a patent that solved only one of the three problems I had posed, anyway. I now had to move on several parallel tracks. One of those tracks involved the determination of the appearance of the thin scale in more complete detail.

This entailed shifting my focus from the scale's internal workings to its look and feel, at least in a preliminary sort of way. The final act of design—involving the elevated craft of bringing all the parts into a harmonious whole—would have to wait until all the parts had acquired their essential forms. Only then would I be able to join them seamlessly with one another.

For now, however, I posed myself a more general question: What would a beautiful personal scale look like? With this question in mind, I proceeded to explore my own aesthetic convictions, to build simple prototypes that veteran designers and ordinary people could fondle and comment on, and to develop a deeper awareness of the sheer beauty of the many designed objects that I saw as I began to explore the novelty shops, the museums, and the bookstores of New York City.

* * *

My reconnection with the issue of aesthetics in design—after so many years of wrestling with the nonvisual aspects of the housing problem—should be traced to those long lunch conversations with Lucinda at the Bridge Café, when we would easily polish off a bottle of Freemark Abbey Cabernet between us before she would courageously get up and I would walk her back to her office, a few blocks to the south.

The Bridge Café was a small and noisy restaurant-slash-bar in downtown Manhattan that, except for its creative American menu, had no visible intention of catching up with the times. It occupied the ground floor of a low wooden building at the end of Water Street, right where the Brooklyn Bridge starts crossing the East River. A modest and unassuming place built in 1794, it held the unbroken record of serving liquor since 1847 (occasionally—it must be admitted—in conjunction with raunchy brothels on its upper floors), making it the oldest drinking establishment in New York City. Its present décor was still 1920s, its walls were only suggestively vertical, and its old ceiling of embossed sheet-metal squares had been painted over so many times that one could barely distinguish its ornamental pattern. At lunchtime it was usually full of laid back regulars who gladly welcomed newly committed regulars—like the two of us—into their midst.

Who was Lucinda? At that point in my story, she was an architect working full-time on the design of office interiors—more specifically, trading floors—in a large office downtown. With her short black skirt, her flowing black hair, and her black everything else—except for her light skin and green eyes lined with a shade of blue mascara—she was beautiful, very beautiful, in fact. And she knew it too.

At the time, she was still married to a talented Israeli sculptor of South African origin, and they had two small children, had been living in New York for a dozen years or so. They inhabited a loft in SoHo that they had bought for a pittance a few years after arriving in the city, after their landlord raised their rent yet again. They remodeled that high-ceilinged loft—formerly occupied by an industrial workshop, possibly a printing establishment—in a minimal, uncluttered way, retaining its original open loftness, yet imbuing it with a noble, gentle, and serene elegance that it surely did not have before. It had Lucinda's signature writ large over it, an unabashed commitment to the "less is more" philosophy of modern design.

Her artist husband was among the few leading figures in the Israeli art establishment of the 1970s, and was modestly successful in New York too. He devoted himself entirely to his abstract sculptures and drawings, which he sold from time to time, edging closer and closer toward that elusive New York dream—the big break. Lucinda, on her part, worked away to make ends meet and then came home via the supermarket to cook dinner and take over from the nanny. It was her way of "supporting the arts," she used to say jokingly.

She loved visual art; she felt comfortable among artists; and she felt nourished, sometimes even elated, by the new art she feasted her eyes on in the many galleries that sprang up in her SoHo neighborhood. No matter how enigmatic or perplexing, what she saw was speaking to her. She listened, she understood, and she reacted—always in a passionate yet thoughtful way. A note she left me at the time in her squarish, back-slanted designer handwriting said: "Beauty means clarity and honesty. An object can be really beautiful only when it avoids the issue of aesthetics—when it tells you the truth about itself, when its purpose is clear. When its inner soul is revealed, you see it, you know how to use it. An object is really ugly when it lies, evades, or distorts the truth about its real nature."

My brother Joe saw them from time to time. In fact, Lucinda's husband had a pretty younger sister in Israel who was Joe's high-school sweetheart—a kindhearted dancer whom Joe did not marry but did not exactly let go of either. It was mutual. Now he was married and she was married and it was all too late anyway. But they kept in touch. And so it was that through Joe I met Lucinda, or rather, to be more precise, met her again.

* * *

The first time I met Lucinda was some 15 years earlier, before I left for Bangkok. I was a fresh Ph.D. from Berkeley, newly recruited to teach architecture and town planning at the Technion, the Israel Institute of Technology in Haifa. We stood side by side, almost touching, on the first day of classes, strangers to each other in a room crowded with students assembled to hear their professors market their courses. I made my pitch, promising to actually teach design in a fourth-year architectural design studio. Sensing a breath of fresh air, she and a dozen of her classmates signed on.

It was difficult to deliver on my promise. The students were more or less disaffected. No building ever built before was good enough for them. Nothing they saw in the glossy journals turned them on. Nothing their fellow students came to class with mattered to them in the least, because, as far as they were concerned, it was empty of novel content. No instructor had anything of consequence to say to them. They had taken upon themselves the task of creating new architecture from scratch, but, without any building blocks, that proved impossible.

I took it upon myself to get them to fall in love with small parts of conventional, nameless buildings—not whole buildings—that would be asking too much too soon—but maybe an occasional detail, a sunny clearing, a shaded seat, an inviting gateway. I took them on long walks along old residential streets on the slopes of Mount Carmel, pointing to places that seemed to be alive—a corner here, a verandah there, a window here, and a tended garden there that I found to be special and attractive.

I wanted them to see the beauty inherent in the simple manifestations of built form, and to develop personal connections with the places they found enchanting or, at the very least, sensible. I wanted them to start gathering personal collections of forms that appealed to them or moved them in some way because the forms worked, whatever that meant to them. From these building blocks, I believed, they could assemble a language, a pattern language if you will, that they could use in putting together their own building designs. To quote Robert Venturi:

> The architect should accept the methods and elements he already has. . . . Present-day architects, in their visionary compulsion to invent new techniques, have neglected their obligation to be experts in existing conventions. . . . The architect's main work is the organization of a unique whole through conventional parts and the judicious introduction of new parts when the old won't do. . . . Through unconventional organization of conventional parts he is able to create new meanings within the whole. . . . Familiar things seen in unfamiliar contexts become perceptually new as well as old.

When the students brought their first design sketches to class, I let it be known that I expected everyone to comment on everyone else's work, but I insisted on two separate rounds of comments—first, only the positive ones, and then, once the positive comments were exhausted, the negative ones. I then stopped anyone who tried to cheat with a comment such as "I liked the skylight in the corridor, but . . . ," and once it was clear that only purely positive comments were admissible, an oppressive silence descended on the room.

There was a frown on everyone's face. Who was I to trample on their freedom of speech? I looked into the void and started counting my breaths, letting it be known that I considered silence meditative. Slowly but surely, as the silence became unbearable, positive comments started flowing haltingly from mouths of people who seemed surprised to hear their own voices. Once it became clear that seeing something of value in someone else's work and acknowledging it did not diminish one's own standing in the community, positive comments came forth with more and more conviction. Not surprisingly, by the time the positive round of remarks was over, the negative aspects of the designs were there for all to see and did not really merit any additional commentary.

At the root of architecture, in other words, there was a love affair with special places one discovered, with alluring details one eyed in passing, with streets and enchanted squares one fell upon, and with cities one was purposefully lost in. It was sensual, to be sure, but Platonic all the same.

* * *

My love affair with Lucinda had to wait until a year later, when she was no longer a student and I no longer a teacher. One starry night in the summer of 1973, we drove down from Jerusalem through the Judean Desert, via Jericho, to the shores of the Dead Sea, and fell head over heels over each other. From that day on, we could not let go of one another. Come fall, we parted with a promise to live together, at least for a while, the next time we met, which was to be in Bangkok. I had just accepted a teaching job there. Lucinda planned to visit her father at her birthplace in Argentina and, from there, to come directly to Bangkok.

But that was not to be. The Yom Kippur War of October 1973 shredded our little blueprint into small pieces and cast them to the cold, desert wind. About a week after the beginning of the war, I was called out of the classroom and told that there was an urgent phone call for me. It was the secretary of the military attaché at the Israeli Embassy in Bangkok.

"I am afraid you will have to go back," she said. "We got a cable today that asked for all officers in the armored corps to go back. Apparently too many were lost during the first few days of the war and they need reinforcements." As a personal invitation to war, it was the best she could do.

As I left the class, Brito Mutanayagam, a student from Kerala in Southern India, gave me a small and shiny red seed tied to a thin cotton string. "This seed contains 100 miniature ivory elephants," he explained. "Wear it around your neck. It will protect you." I obliged.

The telephone service between Bangkok and Buenos Aires left much to be desired. There was no direct line. The connection involved several unhelpful operators who spoke Thai or Spanish, and long, frustrating waits that ended in unexplained silences. I had to leave Bangkok without getting through to Lucinda to tell her not to come, I could not get through to her while I was on my way, and I arrived in the Sinai desert without having spoken to her at all.

I found my little unit—the artillery command unit of a tank brigade—in the middle of the night. A few hours later, we crossed the Suez Canal into Egypt on our old M3 half-track—an open-top World War II–issue personnel carrier—to a loud welcome of unfriendly Egyptian artillery fire that rained shells all around us. From then on it was war, mostly a desert war fought at great distances between tank forces that could only see each other through binoculars.

I shall pass on the war stories. It suffices to say that I felt safe surrounded by the open, empty desert, much safer that I would have felt had I had to do battle in a densely populated city. Much to my surprise, I moved about as though I were protected by an invisible shield, and never for a moment did I experience real, gripping fear. In contrast, half the people on our half-track sat silently along its walls, hunkered down with fear. Miffed by the very idea that they could get themselves killed, they hid their sad faces under their helmets and waited for the whole sorry affair to finish; the sooner the better.

In a few days of intense fighting, our tank division completed the encirclement of the Egyptian Third Army that had crossed into the Sinai in the first days of the war. Then, rather abruptly, we were commanded to stop right there. Why stop, just when we were getting the upper hand?

Nixon and Kissinger—we were eventually told—in response to a vague Russian ultimatum, issued a strongly worded ultimatum of their own. They did not want the Egyptians humiliated, and they preferred an ambiguous outcome to the war, in which each side could claim victory. In their thinking, it would be a good basis for peace talks, and they were certainly proved right—a peace agreement between Israel and Egypt was signed three years later. And so, while the two sides started talking haltingly, we were encamped in the desert with nothing much to do, besieging the now deeply entrenched Third Army and rehearsing a deadly offensive we would mount against it—code-named Knights of the Heart— should negotiations break down. Weeks went by and then months.

Every two weeks or so, I went on a rest-and-recreation leave to Israel proper, where I found morale much lower than "back home" in the tent in the empty desert. The surprise Egyptian and Syrian attack on Yom Kippur shattered the country's confidence in the invincibility of its army and in the good judgment of its government. The people I knew were, on the whole, deeply depressed, and did not provide me with the nourishment and the support I needed to carry on with that interminable siege.

I kept calling Lucinda in Argentina and asking her to come to Israel to be with me. I told her I needed her close to me. She promised to come soon but she took her time. I felt more and more heartbroken, abandoned, so to speak, in my hour of need. I started to think that maybe she did not care for me enough, or that maybe she was just dishing out the proverbial Latin *mañana* without any real intention of coming. These thoughts were amplified into something resembling "betrayal" during the long nights in the flat, cold, starlit desert, when there was not much else to think about.

Lucinda finally came, but only after three long months. It was good to be with her again, even though we could only manage a couple of days here and a couple of days there. We wanted things between us to be as they were before, but they weren't. We could not talk it out either. We were both awed by the long silences that engulfed us; they were bigger than us, and our timid voices could not penetrate them.

My days in the desert became longer and longer, and there was no end in sight. One early morning, I was awakened by a telephone call from brigade headquarters. "Knights of the Heart," a voice said, "have your unit ready to move in 30 minutes." When I put the receiver of that field telephone back into its cradle, I discovered I could hardly breath. As far as I was concerned, this war was over and our little unit was lucky to escape it unscathed. In my agitated state, I was unsure that I could stand yet another battle. Now, for the first time in this campaign, I was scared, really scared.

But there was nothing to say. So we lumbered out, packed our half-track with rarely a word exchanged between us, and joined the assembling convoy, only to be told that it was just a drill and we could go back to sleep. The air escaped from my lungs as I dropped like a sack of potatoes on my disheveled bed. Not more than a day or two later, rummaging through the many zipped pockets of my khaki overall, I found that red seed that Brito Mutanayagam gave me. I opened it and spilled out the miniature ivory elephants. Out of the original hundred, there were only three left.

Eventually, after four months of active duty, I was discharged and told I could return to Bangkok. I asked Lucinda if she wanted to come with me. She said no, and we left it at that. That *no* was only explained in New York, many years later. A lame invitation that consisted only of asking her whether she wanted to come was not enough of an invitation, she felt, and rightly so—it neglected to mention whether I wanted her to come. Expressive we were not during those tense last days. I never told her how much I missed her, and she never explained what kept her away. And so, we parted our ways. She married a year or so later. I was there at her wedding, yet another invited guest, plainly disconnected from any real feeling I may have harbored. That was the last we saw of each other for some time. We lost touch and we lost each other.

Fifteen years went by, and then, while searching for the thin scale, I came upon the lost Lucinda. We were older now, more grounded, and definitely more articulate, and we now found time for each other, time to make up for all the lost time.

But we kept a respectful distance between us, moving around each other in wide invisible orbits, attracted to each other yet not knowing exactly whether it was safe to get closer. She, on her part, was estranged from her husband yet still married, and I, on my part, had vowed long ago to refrain from having affairs with married women. Plato would have been proud of us. And now—as for the choice of a base of operations for the scale venture—New York, with Lucinda there, made infinitely more sense than Los Angeles, for example, without her there. Cities, I discovered, have this quality—their fortunes rise and fall with the company you keep, especially the company of women.

* * *

Without a workshop and with no tools to my name except a pair of metal shears, I proceeded to build two show-and-tell prototypes. They were to be looked at, touched, and photographed, but not meant to carry any loads. The first prototype consisted of two ten-by-ten-inch aluminum sheets—rounded at the corners— with a quarter-inch panel of balsawood in between. I sprayed the aluminum sheets in matte black, and along the entire perimeter I stretched a quarter-inch diameter O-ring of black rubber.

The second prototype was simply a matte-black, quarter-inch plastic plate of the same size with the same rounded corners. On both prototypes, on the top side near one edge, I glued a rectangular piece of gray paper with slanted electronic numbers drawn on it to simulate the readout window, and on the bottom side, near each corner, I glued a one-inch-diameter thin plastic disk to simulate the feet supporting the scale from below.

Lucinda took the two prototypes to her interior design office downtown and showed them to seven designers, jotting down their comments. All in all, they were very enthusiastic: "This thin and this light! How wonderful!" "Fabulous," "Gorgeous," "Revolutionary," "A knockout," "belongs in the MOMA [the Museum of Modern Art]," "Will make a fortune" were some of their comments.

Most preferred the square design to a rectangular one, and the plastic prototype to the metal one with the rubber O-ring. They also favored the almost vertical, boxlike edge of the plastic prototype to the rounded edge of the O-ring model. Most preferred black to any other color. Some, but not all, opted for a matte finish.

"My husband travels, watches his weight, [and is] crazy about finding a scale he could take with him," said Kathleen. "Finish it with dots to avoid scratching," said Joe. "It should hang on the wall; I hate things on the floor," said Shelly. "If it has to have a rim, make the rim shiny and the rest matte," said Nancy. "No rim," said Lila. "It looks cheap. Let me know when it becomes available."

Those, I felt, were very encouraging comments indeed. Some time later I went with Lucinda to visit the third floor of the Museum of Modern Art. It housed a permanent exhibit of product design—from a small helicopter to a portable typewriter. I was thrilled to see everyday objects in a museum. They were imbued with intelligence and creativity, and a few seemed to have attained a measure of nobility as well.

"Design," wrote Peter Dormer, "has arrived as a serious cultural 'object' in its own right. . . . All manner of designerly objects . . . are collected, put on exhibition, curated, catalogued, classified, and eulogized. Design is not only commerce, not only about the here and now but, thanks to the museum culture, it is also culture, also timeless, also *classical*—the favorite word of praise."

It seemed natural and effortless for me to add one more objective—or rather one more imperative—to the scale project right there and then: getting it into the MOMA's permanent collection. Right.

* * *

Why, I must ask myself, was I committing myself to the modern agenda in 1988—having never signed on to it before—at a time when designers had already abandoned it in droves? This surely requires an explanation, one I could not offer then, but that has become quite clear to me since.

What was the modern agenda? It surely was not simply the principle *form follows function*. This principle was first articulated in 1852, I found out to my surprise, by a mediocre and long-forgotten American figurative sculptor, Horatio Greenough (1805–1852), who had little to do with modernism. But in his short critical essays lamenting the absence of an American architecture, Greenough uncannily formulated most of the modern agenda, half a century ahead of his time:

> If there be any principle of structure more plainly inculcated in the works of the Creator than all others, it is the principle of the unflinching adaptation of forms to functions. . . . If you will trace the ship through its various stages of improvement, from the dugout canoe and the old galley to the latest type of the sloop-of-war, you will remark that every advance in performance has been an advance in expression, in grace, in beauty, or grandeur, according to the functions of the craft.

While modern architects adopted form follows function as a slogan, they were not more concerned with function than the builders of old. The rediscovery of function did prove an essential element of the modern credo, however, because it called for a return to first principles, seeking a truthful expression of modern needs, and rejecting any further attempts at adaptation of old forms that no longer fit the demands of the times. Old Greenough understood that as well: "The laws of expression are such that the various combinations which have sought to lodge modern functions in buildings composed of ancient elements, developed and perfected for other objects, betray, in spite of all the skill that has been brought to bear upon them, their bastard origin."

It was the new building technology—more specifically, the use of steel column-and-beam (as well as truss) structures and reinforced concrete floors—that freed modern architecture at the turn of the century from its earlier reliance on heavy load-bearing walls and from constraints on the spans of ceilings and roofs, rendering irrelevant much of the building traditions of earlier periods. In this sense, it did make possible a pure break with the recent past, a break that coincided with the revolutionary fervor of the times, and that led to the call for the total and radical abandonment of old forms and anything reminiscent of them.

Not only was the old architecture no longer appropriate for meeting new needs, for modern eyes it was morally corrupt as well, employing excessive ornamentation and embellishment "to disguise its incompleteness." That was its biggest "crime," to use the language employed by Adolf Loos (1870–1933) in his book *Ornament and Crime* of 1908. In Greenough's words:

> The turning point was the first introduction of a fanciful, not demonstrable, embellishment, and for this simple reason, that, embellishment being arbitrary, there is no check upon it; you begin with acanthus leaves, but the appetite for sauces, or rather the need for them, increases as the palate gets jaded. . . . And by

degrees you find yourself in the midst of a barbaric pomp . . . whose enjoyment is
satiety, whose result is corruption.

The insistence on a return to function provided the moderns with a theoretical and rational base for a blanket rejection of any and all ornament, as well as all
other historical references and connotations that seemed unnecessary and
inessential. Shedding all obligations to the past and armed with the new technology, modern architects were now free to explore new forms. What old Greenough—being still locked into a figurative sculptural style—could not see yet
was the introduction of the abstract into modern art at the turn of the century.
And it was the introduction of the abstract that eventually provided the impetus
for a new aesthetic in modern architecture and design, a truly revolutionary aesthetic that clearly distinguished it from anything done before.

An abstract form was created through a highly disciplined rejection of the
particular and the unessential in order to bring out the
true essence of a form. A typical example would be the
1924 *Bird in Space* (Fig. 24), an abstract sculpture by Con-
stantin Brancusi (1876–1957) that tried to capture the
essence of birdness, if you will, without describing a specific bird.

Through the systematic rejection of any function that
was not deemed absolutely necessary, modern architecture
became free to employ the simplest, purest, and most powerful of geometric forms, forms that embodied its abstract
spirit, captured most poignantly by the dictum *less is more.*
The ultimate accomplishment of this aesthetic was the 1958
Seagram Building on New York's Park Avenue, a pure black
box designed by the architect who coined this aphorism,
Ludwig Mies van der Rohe (1886–1969), together with
Philip Johnson.

In truth, it was the design logic behind the minimalist
black-box aesthetic that I found attractive. It provided me
with a clear insight for approaching design: a small number of simple functions resulted, and should have resulted,
in a simple form. As the number of functions increased
and as functions became more complex, so did the resulting form. In other words, a form could and should remain
simple, unless there were good reasons to make it more
complex.

The simplest form—simple in the sense of requiring
the least information to describe it—was the one that
embodied the most symmetry. The simplest three-
dimensional form was a sphere, and "thus the lowest

24 *Brancusi's* Bird in
Space, *1924*

forms of animals, small creatures suspended in water, are more or less spherical." As for man-made objects—a straight-edge being a simpler tool than a compass—the simplest three-dimensional form would be a cube.

In parallel, for modern architecture and sculpture, black (and, more generally, the monochromatic) was the absence of color, and its use signified the rejection of color as unnecessary and inconsistent with the purely physical nature of a three dimensional form. In the words of the minimalist sculptor Robert Morris: "The qualities of scale, proportion, shape, mass, are physical. Each of these qualities is made visible by the adjustment of an obdurate, literal mass. Color does not have this characteristic. It is additive. Obviously things exist as colored. The objection is raised against the use of color that emphasizes the optical and in so doing subverts the physical."

It is a small leap to arrive from the cube to the thin square scale, in which the vertical dimension of the cube—because there is no longer a functional need for it—would be rendered almost unnecessary and collapsed to a minimum. In any event, thinking from first principles, it stands to reason that the shape of the scale would be symmetrical in at least one direction because of the reflective symmetry of the two feet standing on it.

The contour of a man in an upright position with his arms outstretched was found by the Renaissance scholars of the late fifteenth century to be embedded in a square, a finding immortalized by Leonardo da Vinci's famous *Homo ad Circulum* drawing of 1487. Similarly, the contour of two feet of an average person—with the toes slightly apart to maintain a good balance—does indeed touch the edges of a square in which it is embedded.

Insofar as the square is a sufficient, adequate, and economical platform to stand on, there is no reason to seek a more complex form—be it a rectangle or a more curvilinear form that follows the contour of the feet more closely. And there is no reason to make it in any particular color, or colors. Black, to the extent that it is the absence of color, would do. This, in short, was the reasoning behind the radical minimalist aesthetic of the moderns, the design logic that I professed to share.

* * *

Not surprisingly, this reasoning proved to be the Achilles heel of modernism too. It was accused of throwing the baby out with the bathwater. Paul Rudolph (1918–1997), for example, remarked: "Indeed it is characteristic of the twentieth century that architects are highly selective in determining which problems they want to solve. Mies, for instance, makes wonderful buildings only because he ignores many aspects of a building. If he solved more problems, his buildings would be far less potent."

Writing in the same spirit, Robert Venturi finally broke the chokehold that the modernists had on architecture for the better part of the twentieth century. In his wonderful little book entitled *Complexity and Contradiction in Architecture*, published in 1966, he wrote: "Architects can no longer afford to be intimidated by the puritanically moral language of orthodox architecture. . . . The doctrine 'less is more' bemoans complexity and justifies exclusion for expressive purposes. . . . Where simplicity cannot work, simpleness results. Blatant simplification means bland architecture. Less is a bore."

Yet the rejection of modern thinking and the modern aesthetic was never total and complete. What came after it—postmodernism in its various manifestations—was, surely enough, highly critical of the black box. Still, it incorporated a variety of modernist influences, while insisting on going beyond the black box in search of meaningful variety and a new, and more appropriate, visual aesthetic.

As I see it, the various important critiques of modernism have led to the development of four more-or-less different visual aesthetics, or styles, if you will:

1. The *neotraditional* style, based on the revival and conservation of the old and established forms rejected by modernism;
2. The *expressive* style, based on the premise that, unlike black boxes, forms should communicate their use and function, as well as their internal workings;
3. The *embellished modern* style, based on the creation of requisite variety by giving black boxes individual identities through the application of superficial ornaments; and
4. The *sculptural* style, based on a total rejection of any connection between form and utilitarian function, freeing the designer to create pure *objets d'art*.

Each one of these four visual aesthetics evolved from a different critique of modernism, and each critique has different implications for the form and appearance of the scale. The question I had to ask myself was whether any one of these critiques merited abandoning or modifying the modern thin-black-square design I had in mind.

* * *

A scale in the neotraditional style: I, for one, having been educated in architecture in the '60s, was never comfortable with the abstract geometrical forms of modernism. My first design exercises in architecture school were indeed boring compositions of small boxes, looking as tired and repetitive as all my other classmates' boring compositions of small boxes. My later years with Christopher Alexander at Berkeley entailed a total rejection of the black box aesthetic—a rejection with which I felt entirely at ease—and it should come as no surprise, therefore, that among the many hundreds of illustrations of good architectural practice in *A Pattern Language*, there is not one single example of a modern building.

The rationale for such a rejectionist attitude was, first and foremost, the realization that the puritanical modern agenda suppressed an entire spectrum of human needs. Instead of searching for the minimal functional essence of a building, our work moved in the opposite direction—toward identifying and exploring the effects on built form of as many functional needs as possible, including a variety of psychological, social, and cultural ones.

Still, we were searching for order, a more complex and less geometrical one, to be sure, but still an order. While broadening the form-follows-function agenda, we were looking for invariant arrangements of the built environment that had stood the trials of time and acquired the patina of timelessness. We wanted to codify the underlying principles of spatial organization that could regenerate the beautiful *unity in diversity* of the towns and villages of old.

To confess, we ended up rejecting modern forms not to create a new formal order, but rather to reopen the door for the earlier built forms—forbidden by the modern aesthetic—and allow them to reemerge as legitimate and viable answers to present-day design problems. In this sense, *A Pattern Language* was a manifesto for a conservative, conservationist, and what I would call neo-traditional movement, reconnecting with the past and reaching back to the familiar forms, the folk traditions, and the symbolic languages of long-gone days.

In 1985, for example, Alexander and a new group of collaborators designed the Eishin School in Japan (Fig. 25), a clear expression of this neotraditional style. As a style, I found it appealing, I must say. It was warmer, richer, and more attentive to real human needs than modernism. I could even see it as an appropriate

25 *The Eishin School in Japan, Alexander and Associates, 1985*

style for furniture, pottery, and various containers, but certainly not for instruments and electronic appliances.

The *Pattern Language* critique of modernism—the critique that rejected its reductionist and minimalist approach to functional essence in favor of a broader list of what should pass as function—should also apply to artifacts that have a specific single function, such as the personal scale. Like the pocket calculator, for example, the personal scale had one single use—to tell the weight of a person standing on it, day in and day out, in any and all places.

Were there additional, more subtle, functions that the scale or the calculator should incorporate into its design in order to fulfill its basic single function? None that I was aware of (except for the need to be more expressive of function, discussed below), and if that was true, then the thin square shape of the scale could remain a simple shape. The scale, therefore, disregarding this first critique, could still be a black box.

To the extent that this critique degenerated into a simple preference for a revivalist neotraditional style, however, it would call for the rejection of the black box scale design in favor of a more traditional and more familiar design. The upright doctor's scale—with its eye-level horizontal bar and the small poise moving across it to balance it—was one such design, still actively and successfully marketed with minimal improvements on its original form. As for my own preferences and my own scale agenda, I had no difficulty in ignoring this particular aesthetic in favor of the simple square.

* * *

A scale in the expressive style: a second critique of modernism—still in the form-follows-function tradition—was the objection to the black box itself because of its failure to communicate adequately, to tell us about its function and use, or about its internal workings. Black boxes, it was argued, no matter how beautifully poised, hid much more that they revealed, leaving us guessing, confused, and ill at ease, because they no longer talked to us in a familiar language we could all understand. In short, they were mute and inexpressive. Contemporary espresso-making machines designed for home use, for example, were

beautifully streamlined, but they were much less expressive of the process of preparing a cup of espresso than the older La Pavoni machine (Fig. 26).

Some artifacts, argued Peter Dormer, were by their nature more expressive than others: "An old-fashioned set of kitchen scales expresses the act of weighing a quantity whose weight is unknown

26 *The La Pavoni espresso-making machine*

against a set of standard weights. It is as expressive as trying to weigh two things relative to one another using just one's hands. With the old machine one knew what weighing *felt* like." A platform scale, he suggested, was much more vague about its function. It did not tell us a story about itself, about what it did, or about how it was operated. This may be true, I admit, but only in relative historical terms. Initially, of course, even the most open-minded public would be "unready to accept the unfamiliar." But as users of new artifacts gradually became more familiar with them over time, they became more willing to accept them into their midst.

Surely, the balancing of the horizontal bar on the upright doctor's scale by moving a small poise across it is still suggestive of the ancient steelyard Roman scale. The steelyard scales found in Pompeii, for example, with their small sculptured poises in the shape of heads, were still very expressive of the way they measured weight (Fig. 27).

27 *A steelyard scale found in Pompeii, first century* A.D.

But by now, I would argue, a thin square box standing on the floor—probably in the bathroom or in the bedroom—with slightly rounded corners (to prevent stubbing one's toe); with a nonskid, floorlike top surface (to stand on); and with a display window in its middle (to glance at one's weight) was recognized almost everywhere (in the industrialized part of the world) as a personal scale. This fact was demonstrated, conclusively in my opinion, by the appearance of simple line drawings of bathroom scales in a large number of cartoons (Fig. 28). The extreme thinness of my design should not have rendered it unrecognizable as a personal scale. Whether it answered the important questions "How do I use it? Can the product walk you through its use?" was another, more complicated, matter, to be discussed in a later chapter. It was certainly a central question for those committed to the expressive style. "Posted signs," says Donald Norman, "are an indicator of bad design."

It had also been argued that black boxes failed to inform us about their internal workings. "That building will generally be noblest," remarked John Ruskin in 1849, "which to an intelligent eye discovers the great secrets of its structure, as an animal form does, although from a careless observer they may be concealed." But noble as this precept may have been in the past, so many contemporary artifacts

28 *"Rose is Rose," comic strip by Pat Brady, 1986 (reprinted by permission of United Feature Syndicate Inc.)*

now incorporated miniature electronic components into which their functions were embedded, that they left nothing of their internal structure for their designers to bring out. The shift from mechanical technology to electronic technology at the end of the twentieth century had vastly reduced the possibilities for functional expressiveness, the kind of expressiveness that would have revealed how things work.

It is true that there were still mechanical elements in personal scales—the load cells, for example, in our case—that sensed one's weight (by bending imperceptibly) before transforming it into an electronic signal. And it is true that the thin square platform could have been made of transparent Lexan plastic, through which one could see the load cells, the wiring, the printed circuit board with the miniature electronic components mounted on it, and the batteries powering it. That would have been a cute novelty maybe, but it would not have explained anything. Rather it would have retained much of the mystery of the black box. If so, why abandon the black box?

* * *

A scale in the embellished modern style: a third critique of modernism (and specifically of modern architecture) faulted it for its embrace of industrial mass production of *machines for living*, to use a favorite expression of Le Corbusier. These machines for living were designed with average people in mind, ignoring the peculiar needs—not to mention the tastes and preferences—of the boundless variety of ordinary individuals, groups, and organizations, and preventing them from expressing their unique identities in their habitations, places of work, or gadgets.

This critique was particularly vocal in the case of the unadorned and nearly indistinguishable apartment blocks that made up the ubiquitous housing projects, nearly all of them built in the international style favored by the moderns. The Unité d'Habitation housing project, for example—designed by Le Corbusier and built in Marseille shortly after the end of World War II—was the archetype and precursor of this new housing form, although it was far from being mass produced. Public housing projects everywhere emulated it for several decades, but most of them were poor imitations that lacked the panache and the sense of proportion of the master.

In retrospect, the mass production of apartment blocks on a grand scale, using industrial prefabrication methods, was taken seriously only in the centrally planned economies of the communist countries—where it generally proved to be an expensive failure—and never took hold in democratic countries. Fortunately, the failure to introduce mass production into housing went hand-in-hand with the creation of a splendid variety of housing solutions, enabling families to choose a home to their liking, and then to modify it so that it responded to their own needs and preferences. In so doing, they exercised the power to establish, declare, and celebrate their identity.

The postmodern concern for giving buildings identities—be they individual identities in the case of private homes, or corporate identities in the case of organizations and firms—required distinguishing them from one another. Given that the modern boxes were, after all, the most efficient and cost-effective way to build, especially in denser cities, the simplest way of distinguishing one building from another would be through the embellishment of their façades. The embellished modern style thus called for the reintroduction of ornament and color—so despised by the moderns—into architecture.

Following this logic to its ultimate conclusion, we should expect to see entire façades of office buildings made up of video walls displaying advertisements that can keep changing forever; a rather frightening, yet predictable, prospect given the subjugation of corporate architecture to corporate marketing. For office buildings to still have windows, however, this futuristic scenario would require the invention of a see-through video wall, but—given the windfall profits in sight—that would not prove impossible.

Surely enough, catering to individual preferences for objects imbued with a personal identity eventually penetrated the design philosophy of mass-produced smaller objects as well. In the early days of mass production, Henry Ford could roll out identical Model T cars from his factories and still boast "you can paint it any color, so long as it's black" (Fig. 29). In his time, the universal need for an affordable car overshadowed any personal preferences consumers may have had regarding its design.

But once basic needs were satisfied, more refined and more differentiated preferences came into light. Moreover, once users and consumers became more powerful and found their voice, and once they became more discriminating, their concerns had to be incorporated into product design.

This could be accomplished in one of several ways: by involving users and consumers directly in the design of products or built environments; by pretesting new products with selected users and consumers before bringing them to market; or by offering consumers a large variety of products from which they could choose the one that suited them best. There was no doubt, however, that

29 *The 1926 Model T Ford*

no matter which venue was chosen, once consumer preferences were seriously taken into account, product design would move away from production for the mass market into niche markets, and eventually into highly personalized custom-made designs.

In doing so, it also moved away from the essential and common functional needs and into the more nonfunctional and ephemeral considerations. "Thinking of life as a whole, what is the purpose of a watch?" asks John Christopher Jones, the author of *Design Methods*. "Not only to let you know the time . . . but also to enjoy buying the object, wearing it, matching it to whatever else you choose to wear today, *to be the figure that you like to think you are.*" This, no doubt, is the underlying philosophy behind the Swatch—the watch as a fashion accessory—and it is spreading.

For example, the highly successful Classic model of the Nokia mobile phone, introduced in 1998, incorporated a great variety of removable faceplates, allowing people not only to personalize their phones by choosing a faceplate to their liking, but to change the looks of their phones depending on their mood, their clothes, or the occasion. Its designer, Frank Nuovo, is convinced that "within a few years having just one phone will seem as odd to most people as owning a single pair of shoes."

This much-hailed development in design thinking does have serious implications for the form of the thin scale, implications that I am not so sure I want to contemplate. It rejects the black box design aesthetic altogether, reintroducing color and ornament as the central elements of a personalize-and-customize approach to design. It implies, in the case of the thin scale, that the preferred design would be a sandwich plate with a flat top, on which a large variety of non-skid rubber decals, in hundreds of colorful designs, would be glued. They could be removable too, with new designs made available regularly.

The scale could surely retain the shape of a thin square with rounded corners, but embellished modern would call for generating lines of fashionable decals in glowing colors, year in and year out. This kind of fashion design, I confess, is entirely out of my ambit—I was diagnosed as color-blind when I was 18, and my understanding of color combinations had never advanced beyond the elementary.

* * *

A scale in the sculptural style: Finally, while the Swatch, the mobile phone, and the thin scale still retained an important aspect of the modernist "less is more" agenda by their highly efficient use of materials, there was a further development in postmodern design thinking that sought to abandon that remaining minimalism altogether. This further development—exemplified by Frank Gehry's Guggenheim Museum in Bilbao, Spain—moved design into the realm of sculpture in the spirit of "Why Not?" Often with a "money-is-no-object" license, talented designers sought to turn utilitarian objects into exquisite one-of-a-kind objets d'art meant, first and foremost, to create a moving aesthetic experience. Fulfilling their function was almost an afterthought.

With a money-is-no-object agenda, the only limit to sculptural scales was one's imagination. Any abstract form that one could stand on, sit on, recline in, lie in, or hang from could serve as a scale. In fact, anything that could be mounted in any manner that ensured that all of one's weight was bearing on it could be turned into a scale. All it involved was incorporating some load cells in strategic locations and then transferring the weight readings (with or without wires) to a remote display or directly to one's computer.

If one preferred scales made out of found objects or replicas rather than abstract sculptures, I would suggest Cinderella's glass slippers; a hemp hammock from the South Seas; an antique merry-go-round horse bouncing up and down on a pole; an old barber's chair; a tire swing hanging from the ceiling; or (if you can find it) the podium from which Einstein delivered his physics lectures at Princeton. One could also turn any number of useful objects into scales—a toilet seat, a tile on the bathroom floor, a treadmill, a bar stool, or the driver's seat in one's car.

But all of those elaborate fantasies were really of no interest to me. I was interested in going in the opposite direction, finding the minimal form that would function as a scale. The "anything goes" sculptural approach to design left me cold.

* * *

It was easy—it always was—for Lucinda and me to see eye to eye when it came to questions of design. We easily arrived at the square. And having arrived at the square, I already felt uncomfortable and mildly anxious about the prospect of having to confront manufacturers who embraced a different design aesthetic, and who had strong ideas about what their customers wanted or what corporate image they wanted to convey in their products. But I was running ahead of myself again. After all, I did not yet have any manufacturer interested in my invention, let alone in my design, did I?

10

It's Beautiful, Now Make It Accurate

King David of Scotland (1084–1153) decreed the Scottish inch to be the average width of the thumbs of three men, "a mekill [big] man, and a man of messurabel [moderate] statur, and of a lytell man. The thoums [thumbs] are to be messuret at the rut [root] of the nayll [nail]." We can assume that before his decree, the Scottish inch was measured as the width of any thoum at rut of the nayll. If that were so, then the benign king made the national inch more precise and subject to a much narrower variation than just any Scottish thumb.

That degree of precision may have been enough for what his subjects wanted to measure at the time, say, for example, the length of their quilts. How one went about finding three such men and getting them to put their thumbs next to each other every time one wanted to measure an inch (without getting mekilled by a short-tempered mekill one, for example) is altogether a different matter. The king wisely left that for his loyal highlanders to sort out by themselves.

Maybe he was not the most practical of kings, that King David, and his decree—like many "weights-and-measures" decrees elsewhere—was in all likelihood largely ignored. But his heart was in the right place: he decreed more rather than less precision, and in this important sense he was a true champion of progress.

———

By early 1988, I already had a patent application pending and a novel design for a personal scale, and I was resolved to make New York City into my home base for the scale venture. I soon found a small studio apartment in a rather rundown apartment hotel on Fifteenth Street in Chelsea known as the Chelsmore.

The modest little studio on the second floor at the Chelsmore suited me fine. It was quiet and well lit. A couple of windows looked out at other windows across an inner courtyard some 20 feet away, but the sun sometimes managed to find its way in. There was an alcove big enough for a large bed and ample room for a sitting area and a small desk—an entirely adequate live-work environment. I had the place repainted. I replaced the furniture with less objectionable stuff I found in disorganized piles in the basement. I made curtains from yellow cotton fabric that filled the room with warm light. I bought plants in the open market not far away, and soon enough the place was livable.

No, it was not nearly as luxurious as the two-story stucco house and the lush garden I had in Bangkok, with the sorely missed live-in maid who cleaned, cooked, gardened, ran errands, paid bills, and occasionally arranged parties as well. I was on my own here, back to having to remember to make my own bed and tend to my own laundry.

But now I had a New York address and that was something. The immediate neighborhood was rather squalid, yes. The buildings were almost uniformly ugly, yes. There was rarely a tree to be seen, yes. Nearby Fourteenth Street was very much a Third World street, lined with discount stores that sold cheap goods to new immigrant families, with men sitting on small ladders in front of each one, watching the store, keeping an eye on shoplifters.

All in all, however, the old buildings in Lower Manhattan felt more familiar and more inviting than the newer, high-rise apartment blocks on the Upper East Side, where my brother Joe resided. I myself was not yet ready for living so far up in the air. The neighborhood got nicer too as one went further south, below Fourteenth Street, toward Greenwich Village, and still further south towards SoHo and Little Italy. This could get comfortable, I said to myself.

* * *

Comfortable maybe, but I was still entirely on my own, with no one, except for me, even remotely interested in my inventions and designs. For that matter, no person of consequence even knew about my idea. Sooner or later, I knew, I had to bring it out into the open and find the people who could help me mass-produce and mass-market it on a large—and possibly global—scale. I could maybe assemble the resources to develop it into a marketable product (and even that was doubtful). Beyond that, I needed to involve others.

Basically, there were only three different ways to bring a new product like the thin scale into the market. One was to continue to work on my own and to license (i.e., sell the rights to) my patents and know-how to a large, established corporation in the scale business that would then produce and market it. The second one was to create a company or a partnership, with the technical know-how, the financial resources, and the marketing expertise to manufacture the scale (or to have it manufactured by others) and to market it directly to consumers. And the third one was to be offered a job in the research and development department of a corporation already in the scale business, to develop the thin scale as an insider, and then to have the corporation produce and market it. That last option was not available to me: no personnel officer looking at my curriculum vitae would be able to recognize that I was the right man for such a job, not even if that officer was trained to read between the lines.

There was really no rational and principled way for me to decide between the first two options, especially since I was not confronted with real choices at the time. For now, I resolved to avoid becoming personally involved in manufacturing— that much I knew—and I did not want a nine-to-five workplace of any kind to tie me down. Now that I was free to pursue the scale wherever it took me, being a master of my time and being footloose felt like a necessity. I also had a sense that the way of the freelancer—the solitary knight on his lone quest—carried the right level of risk, a risk I wanted to carry on my own until it was safe to involve others.

In the absence of any contacts in the scale business in New York (or anywhere else, for that matter), the only way for me to find a corporation that would be interested in licensing my invention was to resort to my own "old-boy" network—the people I had come to know in my professional work in housing. A former colleague and a close friend of mine at the Asian Institute of Technology in Bangkok—a tall, blond Dutchman by the name of Koos de Goede—was now back in the Netherlands working for Hasköning, a large international consulting firm. Maybe he could help.

Koos (pronounced *Koss*, like boss) spent several years in Bangkok with his wife after a sojourn in the Karachi slums in Pakistan. They adopted a couple of beautiful Thai children there, and occupied a nice bungalow in an enclosed compound, right next to a bustling slum on one of the meandering lanes off Sukhumvit Road.

Shortly after their arrival in Bangkok, I remember, their new maid almost left them because—the egalitarian and liberated Dutch souls that they were—they expected her to sit down to dinner with them, share their food, and participate in their intelligent conversations. She, on her part, thought that this was beyond her call of duty, and she somehow managed to communicate to them, before it was too late, that—much as she liked and respected them—she preferred to eat her own food on her own.

Koos was a first-rate field investigator and not much of an armchair academic, but he did have a wall-to-wall bookcase at his institute office. One morning, while pulling a book from one of its lower shelves, the entire bookcase collapsed on top of him in a thunderous rumble. I ran over, opened the door to his office, and looked in, wondering what had happened. He was sitting upright on the floor, half buried in books, and sporting a broad smile. "I think this is trying to tell me something," he said.

I contacted Koos and asked him if he could somehow link me up with Philips, the Dutch corporate giant. I found out that, among its long list of products—from consumer electronics and light bulbs to domestic appliances—Philips also manufactured scales for the European market. It also owned Norelco, one of the largest personal scale manufacturers in the United States.

Koos was happy to oblige. He soon made some inquiries and found out that a member of his board of directors at Hasköning, a Mr. Piet van Tilburg, was a former employee at Philips and now sat on its board of directors. Koos—always the activist—set up a meeting with him in Eindhoven, Philips's hometown, at the end of March and promised to come along. I now had a real deadline and I was devoting my entire time to the scale venture.

* * *

My plan of action called for moving everything ahead. There were the patent application to complete and file and the black square mock-ups to build and test, both already described in the two previous chapters. The most critical part of the plan, on which everything else rested, would be the assembly of a working prototype of a thin and lightweight scale that actually measured weight.

But that was not all. I also wanted to learn about the ins and outs of licensing contracts and what mattered about them. In addition, I wanted to prepare a brochure with text, tables, drawings, and photographs describing what I already had and what I proposed to do. And finally—now that I was readying myself to engage in a business transaction—I wanted to create and register a company for myself (complete with a name, a logo, a New York address, a letterhead, and a calling card) so that I would no longer be just poor me—yet another man off the street with a cockamamie idea—but rather the managing director of a corporation in the scale development business.

Assembling a working prototype of a scale should have been straightforward. I had metal parts for new circular load cells that I had designed myself and had made at a plastic factory in Bangkok. These load cells were audacious shots in the dark, of course. What I knew about load cell design was mostly tidbits I had picked up during my days with Harry, who, as it turned out, knew very little about load cell design himself. I found someone in Brooklyn who was willing to bond a couple of strain gages to each load cell, I hoped in the right places.

For a sandwich structure, I had a couple of quarter-inch Lexan top plates prepared, also in Brooklyn—with a beehive pattern of shallow circular holes drilled underneath them to make them lighter. These plates could be used, in conjunction with aluminum bottom plates, to make stiff sandwich plates.

All I needed to complete the assembly were the electronics that Harry Jones was working on. Harry had a simple task: finish the electronic design, populate a printed circuit (PC) board with components, make sure the board worked, and deliver it to me before the end of the year. Well, he managed to complete the design to his satisfaction, he told me, but getting someone to print the board proved to be a challenge. Harry, it turned out, was not a great motivator of people and was rather helpless when it came to getting his agenda on anyone's priority list. So, while printed circuit boards were being made across America by the thousands day in and day out, often at a 24-hour notice, our little board was not quite managing to get printed.

Weeks went by. Harry made great efforts to keep me from coming over to Massachusetts, assuring me again and again that he was promised the PC boards "in a matter of days." There was little left for me to do except phone him regularly and egg him on. That was one kind of price one had to pay for having to rely on contractors rather than on one's own employees, I told myself. And, yes, there was also a price to pay for being a bad judge of character, as well as an additional price on top of that for not learning from one's own mistakes. He had already let me down once, hadn't he, so why give him yet another chance to let me down?

Eventually, when Harry did get the PC board printed, it was already the middle of February, and the board was of the wrong thickness. There was another long wait for the much thinner board I had originally ordered. Harry then pulled apart the electronic components from his experimental board and populated the new board, and in the process he burned the only amplifier he had. Then he had to wait on new parts. He eventually did put it all together, but now it was noisy again because he had replaced a couple of components (the high-profile polypropylene capacitors with low-profile tantalum ones, he said) so that the PC board would fit into the thin scale.

So, sad to say, even though I had all the other components ready, I never managed to assemble a working scale in time for the Eindhoven meeting on 29 March. I did file the patent application; I did manage to build black square mock-ups and to photograph them (Fig. 30); I did put together a simple brochure; I did learn about licensing; and I did register a company (calling it Libra, an appropriate name, I thought, for a company involved with scales). Going to meet the Philips people without a working scale was just short of embarrassing, but I decided against postponing the meeting and got on the plane. Progress had been made, I figured, and eventually it would all work out.

I stayed overnight with Koos and his family in their small stone house in Nijmegen, and the next morning we drove together, Koos and I, to meet the enigmatic van Tilburg at his office in Eindhoven. I gave a short presentation. He did not seem particularly interested in my invention. But he did want to make sure that I understood that getting into Philips required connections that he could provide if it were of interest to him. I suspected that this was some kind of an allusion to money changing hands further down the road, but it was too early to tell and it was fine with me anyway.

Van Tilburg invited a Philips engineer to the meeting, a stocky man with a receding hairline and thick eyeglasses by the name of Rijk (pronounced *Rick*)

Nienhuis, who seemed to be his good friend and later turned out to be the former lover of his wife's younger sister. Now Nienhuis, in contrast to the rather remote van Tilburg, was in an enthusiastic mood, fully intent on making himself useful. He liked the whole idea, it seemed, and was happy to

30 *The thin-scale mock-up*

bring it to the attention of the right people at Domestic Appliances, but not before I could produce a reliable working prototype.

The helpful Koos, to gauge Nienhuis's level of enthusiasm, offered, "Maybe Philips will not be interested because it already has a product in this line," to which Nienhuis replied, "No, on the contrary. It is better for us to compete with our own products." Both Koos and I agreed that a valuable contact had been made. I left Nienhuis with the black square mockup, the documentation, and the photos, and promised to get on with completing the prototype. A week later I received a short fax from him that lifted my spirits. It was handwritten in large block letters in telegraphic style: "Have discussion with Director of Domestic Appliances on 25th of April. Could not make it earlier because he was on holiday. Consulted with van Tilburg and we decided not to enter lower down in the organization. I will fax you any questions he might have. Case is clear to me. All our secretaries (6) love your scale! Regards. Nienhuis."

* * *

That fax reached me in Israel, where I thought I could find fresh leads to a no-nonsense electronics engineer and to some knowledgeable scale people through my extended-family network. A couple of days after my arrival from the Netherlands, I was directed to Dan Atlas, a short man with a gray goatee beard, a shaven upper lip, a thin mocking grin, and intelligent, penetrating eyes. The day I came to meet him at his laboratory, he was meticulously putting together a set of apnea monitors, devices that woke people up with a start before they could choke on their soft pallets in their sleep.

The Atlas Research Lab—considerably more serious looking and better equipped than Harry's kid's bedroom—occupied a second-floor apartment in a cheaply plastered squat building in Hod Ha' Sharon. That sleepy town used to be a thriving market on the main road between Jerusalem and Haifa, surrounded by orange orchards that gave off an intoxicating smell when the flowers were in bloom and that dazzled passersby with their golden colors when the thick-skinned Jaffa oranges were in season. Now intercity traffic moved along a freeway that avoided the town, while its aging orange groves were gradually being bulldozed into the outlying suburbs of metropolitan Tel Aviv.

Atlas assured me that he could build and test a low-profile electronic circuit for the scale and then assemble the scale and test it, all in a matter of six weeks. He agreed to substantial penalties for any delays in delivery, provided I agreed to equally substantial awards for finishing before the deadline. The man exuded confidence that, I confess, was pleasantly refreshing, especially for someone so nauseous from the gyrations of the Harry Jones merry-go-round.

He had a contract typed up even before I managed to explain what I wanted. In fact, he was already explaining what I wanted to his assistant, in a technical language I was not exactly familiar with, and the assistant was already on the phone ordering parts while I was affixing my signature to every page of the ten-page contract. I informed Nienhuis that I would be ready to confront the people at Domestic Appliances with a working prototype by mid-May.

Atlas and his assistant assembled an electronic circuit in no time, using the thin PC board that Harry sent me as a base, and rewiring it with hundreds of thin colored wires. It was soon complete and functioning. Next, they wired and tested the circular load cells I brought from Bangkok, and got reasonable results. For a top plate, we used the quarter-inch Lexan plate I brought from New York. At the center of the beehive pattern of shallow circular cavities drilled on its bottom, it had one large rectangular cavity for the electronics. For a bottom plate we used an aluminum plate, bolting the two plates together with a long row of short screws—half an inch apart—along their entire perimeters.

The two bonded plates formed a sandwich plate of sorts that was rigid enough to stand on without sagging too visibly. There was still a bit of noise in the circuitry, but they got rid of it by electronic trickery: once someone mounted the scale, a motion sensor in the electronics froze the display at the acquired weight. Thereafter, no matter how much one swayed on the scale, one's weight remained the same.

The Atlas prototype was by no means a precision instrument, but it did display one's weight to within a few pounds and, for the time being, that would have to do. At that point, some four weeks into our productive collaboration, Atlas declared the project finished and informed me that I owed him extra monies for finishing earlier than expected. There were still things to do, but—I had to admit—they were over and above whatever was stated in our contract. I had no choice but to comply, and I agreed to pay him more for extra work.

All of our experiments until now—both at Harry's and at Altas's—were conducted with large batteries or with an external power supply. A week before my departure for the Netherlands, we finally installed a set of thin lithium batteries into cavities in the prototype; the kind of batteries used in common calculators. The batteries—according to their written specifications—had enough current to last us for some 40 hours, but much to our astonishment they dried up very quickly. It turned out that these batteries—as well as all the other common batteries used in calculators and watches—had an upper limit on how much current they could discharge for continuous use. We had far exceeded that limit.

The diary entry for 9 May 1988 had this to say: "For a while there last week my heart dropped to my pants. . . . The power supply disappeared, maybe forever. Maybe there are no batteries on the market that could do the job. Eventually I found some (zinc air batteries for use in hearing aids), but they are still not the right ones for a commercial product. This needs more work."

I boarded the KLM flight to Amsterdam on 11 May with a working prototype of the thin scale. After the plane took off, I pulled out the prototype from my briefcase and held it in front of me, looking at it closely for a long time. It now looked so simple, almost too simple. I felt a kind of a letdown. Once something worked, I carped, everyone immediately took it for granted. We have developed such confidence in technology, I carried on, that every technical accomplishment now seems trivial. Still, it felt good. I was quite tired from lack of sleep, too excited, and slightly anxious. There was a lot at stake—this was not just another presentation of yet another paper on housing at yet another conference.

* * *

Koos and I took the train from Amsterdam and headed north along the flat Dutch plains, passing through small picturesque towns separated by green fields that exuded a strong stench of pig manure. Groningen, our final destination, was a 1,000-year-old city on the shores of the North Sea and for hundreds of years of its long history a thriving and independent city-state. It was now an enterprising city of some 200,000 people and home to the headquarters of Philips's Domestic Appliances and Personal Care Division (DAP). We arrived at the Groningen railway station in the early afternoon to find Nienhuis waiting there in a state of high alert, ready to do battle.

The large rectangular table in the DAP conference room was surrounded by half a dozen directors, heads of development, and product managers in suits and ties, sizing me up and waiting patiently to hear what I had to say. I pulled out a yellow manila envelope and placed it on the table before me. I then made my brief presentation and, when I finished it, gently pulled the thin scale out of the manila envelope and showed it to them. I swear I could hear their gasps as their jaws dropped. For a brief moment they were transformed into kids watching a magician pulling a white rabbit out of a top hat. They then took turns weighing themselves and nodding their heads in acknowledgment as if to say to each other: "Yes, this is what I usually weigh." It worked.

In the discussion that ensued, three issues took center stage: the protection afforded by the patent, the desired accuracy, and the cost target. First, they questioned the validity of my patent and wanted to know if and when it would issue. I tried to elaborate. It took them a while to convince themselves that it was novel, and they eventually said they needed to study it some more.

Second, they were interested to know if I could ensure a high level of accuracy. They had agreed to meet me in the first place, they intimated, only because in my brochure I promised a 200-gram (less than a half pound) accuracy. Yes, I did remember promising that, I thought to myself, but more in the spirit of a lofty goal than as anything I knew how to achieve in practice. Now they wanted to know if I could attain a 100-gram (less than a quarter-pound) accuracy. Their competition—Soehnle, the leading German scale manufacturer—already had a personal scale with a 100-gram accuracy, and they now needed to match it. They thought they could sell some 20,000 such scales a month, they said. Would I accept the challenge? "Sure, why not?" I said.

Third, they wanted to know whether the scale could be manufactured for $15 and, more particularly, whether the load cells could be had for $1.50 each. I guardedly replied that my preliminary calculations suggested that both cost targets were indeed attainable, but that I had no firm quotations from anyone willing to deliver either complete scales or complete load cells at those prices. That would have to be looked into in the coming months.

At some point in the discussion, Koos noted later, there was a nod from the director to another man, signaling that he wanted this project to go ahead. He then got up, instructed his colleagues to agree on a timeline for advancing the project, and, before leaving, asked me bluntly what I wanted for licensing the patent rights to Philips. I said I needed to consult others on the matter. "When he asked you he already knew the answer, he just was curious whether you knew it too," Nienhuis later remarked. He volunteered to write the minutes of the meeting, and promised to play an active role in moving the project ahead. "He turns out to be a wonderful man," I wrote in my diary, "an inside man on our side."

The meeting ended in an upbeat mood, with an agreement to meet again for two whole days in late August—only three-and-a-half months away—by which time I was expected to have a valid patent, a prototype scale that met the specifications they would send me, and assurances that we could indeed meet the cost targets. Assuming that these three challenges were satisfactorily met, we would jointly build and test some additional prototypes, and then come to a "go-or-no-go" decision by the end of October.

I could not ask for more. I now had a sounding board, a reality check, and some worthy fellow travelers on my quest. And I was now offered a real opportunity, for the first time, to realize my vision.

So, by the end of that first Groningen meeting, my quest took yet another turn—away from lightweight panels, patent applications, and modernist industrial design and into the unfamiliar territory of transforming personal scales into precision weighing instruments.

I had just enlisted myself in a campaign aimed at making precision weighing instruments affordable to ordinary consumers. This was not, I admit, what I had in mind when I started thinking about the thin scale. At the outset I was mainly thinking about design, about changing the look and feel of the personal scale. Now, all of a sudden, it made perfect sense to me that a new generation of personal scales would not only look and feel different, but would also be different—they would measure weight accurately.

People involved in fitness training—like Laurence Moorhouse, for example, the author of *Total Fitness in 30 Minutes per Week*—are forever frustrated by the inaccuracy of personal scales:

> A bathroom scale is not a precision instrument. The pointer doesn't return to zero each time after you've weighed, or to the same reading when you step back on again. The kind of engineering that degree of accuracy requires would make scales too expensive for home uses. Even when your dial registers zero, your weight won't necessarily be measured in the same way it was the day before. Just by shifting your weight around, or standing in a different position, you can cause the dial to

move as much as five pounds in one direction or the other. By accepting your bathroom scale as your master, you indenture yourself to a vacillating tyrant.

For a moment there in Groningen, the scale quest was transformed into a struggle for the liberation of the suffering masses from the vacillating tyranny of scales that did not care enough about their users to tell them the honest truth—even if it were the simple fact of their correct weight, or the correct change in their weight since they last weighed themselves. Precision, after all, was the hand-maiden of truth.

So, in the service of truth, I willingly added high precision to my growing list of goals for the scale—it now had to be a quarter-inch in thickness, weigh one pound, sit on the shelf on the third floor of the Museum of Modern Art, and attain 100-gram precision. It also had to be affordable. Right. Now I had better get to work. There was not really much time before I had to present myself in Groningen again.

11

Beginner's Luck

What I needed now were leads, new leads to people who could actually supply accurate, low-cost load cells, or who could show me how to produce such load cells and then put them together into a scale with the target accuracy. I was past the stage where a general understanding of the parameters of the problem would suffice, and I now needed the services of specialists—people who knew how to design and manufacture load cells. I immediately thought of Gary and Randy Baker, the father and son team from Transducer Techniques in Rancho, California. Back in May 1987, they promised to make load cells for me and I didn't follow up on it. This time, I would. I resolved to pay them another visit as soon as possible.

I also had a new lead—through my extended family in Israel—to Tedea, the leading load cell company in the country, and I flew back to Israel to talk to the Tedea people right after the meeting with Philips. I met with the three directors at Tedea a number of times. They were not sure that a $1.50 load cell was an attainable goal, but they did find the idea of producing a million load cells a year for Philips enticing enough. They were willing to take on the development of such a load cell—subject to the required specifications and within the required time schedule—at their expense. That sounded very promising.

The problem was that we could not come up with a satisfactory business arrangement, which is a nice way of saying that the deal fumbled on the absence of trust. The load cell community, it appeared, was shrouded in secrecy. Load cells were, after all, just pieces of metal with some strain gages bonded to them. Most of their value, it seemed, was bound up in privileged information and specialized know-how that their producers were not eager to share.

To keep me interested, the Tedea directors informed me that they already had a promising idea for a load cell that would meet my specifications, but that they were not willing to show me anything or tell me anything about it—especially since their idea would probably not be patentable—for fear that I would then find a cheaper producer. Why would I want to do that?

With the help of a common acquaintance who was on their board of directors, I drafted an agreement that precluded me from doing any such thing, but they would not sign it. They concluded that—provided Philips itself consented in advance to a financial arrangement with them—they would send prototypes directly to Philips by the end of August. I, on my part, offered to inform Philips of this distant possibility if and when they had prototypes ready.

This absurd deal never materialized, of course, and I never found out what they had in mind. But one of them—Matti Raz, the most friendly of the three—did give me two useful leads. He told me that Philips itself owned a load cell company in Hamburg, Germany, a fact the people at DAP never mentioned. He also suggested that I contact a John Hall, the president of a company that manufactured strain gages in California.

Through Nienhuis, I tried to arrange a meeting with the Hamburg people to seek their advice. They proved to be even more suspicious of me than the Tedea ones. "I think they know fully well," I wrote in my diary on 27 June 1988, "that they are producing and selling something that could be had for much less." After some polite exchanges, they refused to even meet me. "We are not sufficiently well equipped for this type of product and market segment," they wrote Nienhuis. And that was that.

* * *

I returned to California, one year after my first visit, to again try my luck with Gary and Randy Baker at Transducer Techniques. They still remembered me, even though we had lost touch for a year. We zeroed in on the design of a one-piece aluminum load cell in the shape of a thin diaphragm with a protruding boss at its center, surrounded by a thick and broad ring (Fig. 31). Surely, this diaphragm design would have to be machined, and I already suspected that it would not meet the target cost. But I had already learned my lesson: I was not going to give up on the Bakers again. I placed an order for eight load cells, half of them with strain gages mounted on them, to be shipped to New York as soon as possible.

My friend Tom Heinsheimer, the mayor of Rolling Hills, was more forthcoming this time around. Instead of deflating my bubbling enthusiasm as he had during my earlier visit, he actually gave me a lead. He arranged a meeting for me with a friend of his, Harry Norton, at the Jet Propulsion Laboratory in Pasadena. Norton had written a handbook on sensors, transducers, and load cells. He was kind enough to sell me his book, to instruct me in the basics of testing sensor performance, and to send me on my way with two other leads that ended up canceling each other. One lead was to Nova Sensor in Fremont, a city on the San Francisco Bay, not

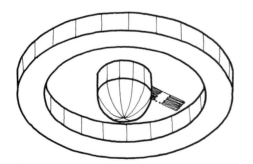

31 *The thin-diaphragm load cell proposed by the Bakers*

far from Silicon Valley; and the other to a Professor Alexander Khazan at the Lowell campus of the University of Massachusetts, who was also writing a book on sensors. A few days later I visited Nova Sensor, a futuristic-looking and spotless plant that made miniature strain gages with a new technology that—in Silicon Valley spirit—sought to replace thin-foil gages with silicon chips. The chief operating officer was quite confident that Nova Sensor could supply silicon strain gages for $0.25 apiece and load cells for $1.50 apiece, delivering prototypes in 20 weeks and beginning production in 30 weeks.

The stumbling block there—apart from their not being able to meet our tight schedule—was the $65,000 in Non-recurring Expenditures (NRE) that was required right away for them to get started. I also suspected that Nova Sensor was in the silicon chip business, but not really in load cell design and development. I may have been wrong, but they surely did not speak the same language that the Transducer Techniques and the Tedea people spoke. Accuracy, for example, was not discussed at all, never mind 100-gram accuracy.

A couple of weeks later, I met Professor Khazan—Norton's second lead. I told him about the possibility of using semiconductor strain gages. He was adamantly against it. "Drop it," he proclaimed imperiously in a strong Russian accent. "Too many problems. Stay with regular strain gages." I surmised he was referring to accuracy. I dropped it and I let go of Nova Sensor. It was one of these forks one encountered on invention road, and to remain focused one had to make a choice. This time I went down the safer road—staying with thin-foil strain gages—and I shall never know where that other road might have taken me.

Khazan was both encouraging and discouraging in an anxious and short-tempered kind of way. He believed it was possible to build a load cell with the desired accuracy and stay within the budget. But he also knew that developing such a load cell would take at least a year and cost a lot of money—some $50,000, he estimated—and he was too busy to help. Imparting a few basic suggestions regarding the design of diaphragm-type load cells, he dismissed me and went back to work, presumably on more serious things.

All in all, the most important contact I made in California that summer was with John Hall, the president of Micro Measurements II. Micro Measurements II—located in Upland, California, yet another faceless suburban community at the foot of the San Gabriel Mountains, some 45 miles east of Los Angeles—manufactured traditional thin-foil strain gages in a great variety of patterns for a great variety of load cells. The plant was fully automated, or rather almost fully. In the main hall there were still dozens of women in white frocks bent over magnifying glasses through which they peeked at strain gage patterns, connecting each gage to a voltmeter and gently wiping it down with a powdered Q-Tip until it attained the desired resistance.

Hall was a big, handsome all-American man in his early sixties, with glasses and a short, narrow nose. In both demeanor and philosophical outlook, he was the exact opposite of anyone else I had encountered until then in the load cell business. He was generous with his time, innately helpful, and, to my surprise, the exact opposite of secretive. In fact, he made it his business to disseminate the practical knowledge he had acquired over the years far and wide. Instead of keeping his expertise to himself, he helped set up strain gage production plants in Brazil, Taiwan, and mainland China using his technology, and was happy to help anyone else who was interested.

I explained my predicament and asked for his advice. He was friendly. He listened patiently. I felt as if he had taken me under his wing. He said that for a personal scale I needed a load cell design that would be insensitive to shifting one's weight from one place to another on the scale platform. The simplest load cell that had that property was one that measured the "difference of moments," he said, and that type of load cell usually required a two-gage pattern that should cost not more than 40 cents in large quantities.

"When you get back to New York," he said, "you should contact Charlie Kientzler. Charlie would know what to do." Before we parted, he also gave me the fax numbers of his strain gage people in São Paulo, Taipei, and Beijing—"once you decide on a gage pattern, ask them for a quote," he said. "American gages would probably be too expensive for your project."

* * *

I cannot fully account for the two months that went by following my meeting with Philips in mid-May, but by the time I drove out to meet Charlie Kientzler in Wayne, New Jersey—about an hour away from my Chelsea apartment by way of the beautiful George Washington Bridge—it was already the middle of July and time was getting short.

Charlie lived with his wife—the children having left already—in a summer home he winterized on the shores of Pompton Lakes, among the lush hills of the Ramapo Valley. There was a tall bird feeder hanging outside the kitchen window with a couple of birds balanced on it. I also saw some noisy wild geese on the grass by the lake. The place was calm and inviting.

Charlie was tall and trim, and no doubt in very good physical shape. I could not tell his age from his smooth face or from his thick and wavy white hair, and I never bothered to ask. He was a mechanical engineer, he told me, and he was now retired, working occasionally on the assembly, gaging, and testing of load cells for a small number of clients. Dentronics, the wire gage company that had employed him, had gone out of business some years ago; its gages could not compete with the newer thin-foil strain gages.

When Dentronics went out of business, Charlie got hold of many of its instruments and much of its assorted inventory and moved them into his basement, turning a corner of the basement into a small load cell laboratory. The rest of the basement was still a typical American basement with a large freezer, several bicycles and lawn mowers, boxes of jars and cans bought wholesale, lots of tools, some discarded furniture, piles of firewood, yellowing magazines, the usual.

By the time I got to Charlie, I had the Philips specifications with me, and most of them were about accuracy. "Very stringent and most probably impossible to meet," I wrote in my diary. But now, for the first time, I was with a patient and level-headed load cell engineer who understood what they meant and could explain them to me. As for me, by that time I was really eager to learn too, if only to make myself somewhat less anxious and a bit more comfortable with my project.

By now I had accumulated tidbits of knowledge here and there, but they did not amount to a coherent picture—I did not yet have a mental map of the territory into which I had stumbled. In the following paragraphs I summarize what I learned from Charlie about how to measure accuracy, that most important property of scales. Most of the measures of accuracy, it turned out, applied not just to scales and load cells, but to other types of sensors as well.

* * *

Basically, all you need to test an electronic scale for accuracy is a set of weights and a voltmeter. Charlie, for example, had a set of 10-pound, 25-pound, and 50-pound stackable weights, shaped like flat cylinders that fit on top of each other, and he would lift them from the floor and stack them up as though they were made from balsawood. The man, as I said, was in good shape. My job as his self-appointed apprentice would be to look at the voltmeter connected to the scale (or to a single load cell) and write down the red numbers I saw flickering there every time he added or removed a load.

Testing for accuracy involved a series of standard tests that were by now in common use in the commercial scale industry. The Philips specifications now required no less than eight such tests, and the permitted error or variation in each test had to remain within narrow specified limits. The stringent requirements and the rather humorless mechanical language used to specify them introduced a note of seriousness into the scale project that, I had to admit to myself, was never there before. Testing the scale—as opposed to inventing it, designing it, or building prototypes—suppressed my inspiration, imagination, and intuition and brought out my painstaking (and rather boring) yen for dogged exactitude.

I remember sitting in a lobby of a luxury hotel on the banks of the Chao Phraya River in Bangkok, in the company of a half-dozen seasoned gem dealers of Iranian and Afghani extraction. They were discussing some large blue sapphires they had seen earlier in the day and intended to buy. There were no stones in front of them, but they referred to each stone as though it had its own name and its own personality.

The operative word they used was *illusion*. "The stone I saw at so-and-so today had illusion," one would volunteer. Each in turn would then agree or not agree with the observation; in the majority of cases, they agreed. They all trusted their innate ability to identify illusion, and sapphires that had no illusion were worthless to them.

When it came to capturing the beauty hidden in precious stones one could still hope to perceive some now-you-see-it-now-you-don't illusion. But not when it came to accuracy. A scale was accurate to within 100 grams if, and only if, it passed some down-to-earth tests, objective and rather mechanical tests that could be repeated by others. When it came to objective testing, art and science parted ways. Expressions commonly applied when looking at art or architecture in the making—like the seemingly objective "it works," or the more subjective "it works for me"—failed to carry any weight when it came the rather uncompromising pursuit of accurate measurement.

What does accuracy in measurement mean, exactly? I found it to mean at least three separate, yet complementary, things: (a) that the measurements themselves must be accurate; (b) that the measurements must remain accurate despite changes in environmental conditions; and (c) that the measurements must remain accurate after the measuring instrument is subjected to abuse.

What does it mean for the measurements to be accurate? If a scale were perfectly accurate, it would be linear—the voltage reading for each load would be exactly proportional to the load, and if you graphed one against the other all the readings would fall on a straight line. The first important accuracy dimension of any sensor is its nonlinearity, which is the maximum deviation of any reading from the perfectly linear. Perfect linearity means "if you double the load, the reading exactly doubles; if you triple it, the reading triples." An example of nonlinearity confronts you when buying papayas from a street vendor in Chinatown: "One papaya, two dollars; three papayas, five dollars; five papayas, seven dollars."

A second important property of an accurate scale is its insensitivity to whether a load being measured has been arrived at by adding weights or by removing weights from the scale. In other words, it is the degree to which the scale manages to forget how the load being measured got there. The maximum difference between any pair of ascending and descending readings is referred to in sensor jargon as *hysteresis*.

A third important property of an accurate scale is the absence of creep—its ability to retain the same reading for a given load over time. In other words, it is the degree to which the scale is free from fatigue. The first scale prototype I built—the one with the water-filled tube between the two plywood rectangles described in chapter 2—exhibited creep, although I could not call it by its proper name at the time. The water level in the vertical part of the tube went down a couple of feet overnight, probably because the soft plastic tube expanded, much like abdominal muscles that gradually give way to a bulging beer belly.

A fourth important property of an accurate scale is its insensitivity to eccentric loading, and testing for it is referred to in the scale jargon as *cornering*. This property measures the ability of a personal scale, for example, to frustrate anyone who tries to change the reading by swaying in different directions, shifting weight from one foot to another, or standing on the ball of one foot on the corner of the platform. Most people try to find a position where their weight is at a minimum. The opposite is true, however, for rookie defensive linemen in the National Football League, for example. They are typically force-fed to a 300-pound industry standard, and when they sway on the scale, they probably try to find the position where their weight is at a maximum, not at a minimum.

To test for both nonlinearity and hysteresis, one would have to load the scale in 25-pound or 50-pound increments up to its full load (in our case 300 pounds) and then unload in increments all the way back to zero load, while recording the voltage output for each load. This loading and unloading cycle would have to be repeated several times to ensure the repeatability of the results.

To test for creep in line with the Philips specifications, we would have to leave a load on the scale for eight hours and then come back and see if there was any difference in voltage output from the initial reading. Cornering tests amounted to placing a load—usually a third or a half of the full load—on a small square piece of wood at nine different locations on the scale platform and measuring the maximum difference between any pair of measurements.

Philips specified the requirements for nonlinearity, hysteresis, creep, and eccentric loading, as well as the requirement for the overall repeatability of measurements during consecutive trials. For the scale to qualify as a scale with a 100-gram accuracy, all had to be within a narrow range with permitted deviations of 50 grams (0.1 pound) for some tests and not more than 150 grams (0.3 pounds) for others. But that was not all.

The scale had to retain its accuracy when environmental conditions changed—the temperature in the room, the presence of water and humidity, and even the inclination of the floor from the horizontal. In other words, to fulfill its function the scale had to be very sensitive to the loads placed on it and very insensitive to everything else. This insensitivity to the external environment, says Herbert Simon,

> is an important property of most good design, whether biological or artifactual. In one way or another, the designer insulates the inner system from the environment, so that an invariant relation is maintained between inner system and goal, independent of variations over a wide range in most parameters that characterize the outer environment. The ship's chronometer reacts to the pitching of the ship only in the negative sense of maintaining an invariant relation of the hands of its dial to the real time, independently of the ship's motions.

To retain its accuracy, the scale had to be indifferent to variations in room temperature between 50° and 100° Fahrenheit. Over and above that, the scale had to be waterproof. It also had to be resistant to the humidity levels commonly found in bathrooms, especially after long meditative showers or extensive bubble-bath sessions. It also had to remain indifferent to uneven and not-exactly-

horizontal floors. Its reading for any load when the scale was inclined—say at 2°
inclination from the horizontal—had to remain within a narrow margin of the
reading for that load on a perfectly horizontal floor.

Finally, the scale had to retain its accuracy after being subject to two common
kinds of abuse: mechanical shock and overload. In the Philips specifications, for
example, a 30-pound weight was to be dropped on the scale five times from a
height of 4 inches to simulate a mechanical shock. Philips also required each sensor to withstand a load of 450 pounds—one-and-a-half times the 300-pound
design load for the scale—without being damaged. That specification did not
strike me as entirely reasonable. It would require that 300-pound, force-fed
rookie football player mentioned earlier to stand on the ball of his foot at one
corner of the scale while balancing his girlfriend in his arms; but, then again,
why not?

* * *

The scale I demonstrated in Groningen in May was nowhere close to meeting
these specifications. I had to simply put it aside and start afresh. By the end of
July, Charlie and I had a design for a diaphragm-type load cell that, among its
many promising features, should have been able to resist overload (but not 450
pounds—Charlie did not have 450 pounds of weights in his basement; he barely
had 300). I was having the metal pieces for that load cell prototype machined
when the diaphragm load cells from Gary and Randy Baker arrived. I immediately set out to Charlie's to test them. Thus began my long apprenticeship under
Charlie's tutelage.

Before testing the Baker load cells in a scale, Charlie—suspecting something,
I guess—set out to test one of them on its own. He placed it on a horizontal steel
beam supported at both ends, with the boss at the center of the diaphragm protruding upwards and the wires from its strain gages connected to a voltmeter. He
then put a 70-pound point load on the boss.

One could see that the steel beam on top of which the diaphragm was placed
also deflected under that 70-pound load, and Charlie suspected that the ring surrounding the diaphragm deflected with it too. If that were the case, the deflection in the ring would distort the diaphragm in unpredictable ways and affect
our measurements. In a second test, Charlie placed a stronger beam under the
diaphragm. Both beam and ring now deflected less, and this resulted in a completely different reading for the same 70-pound load. He was right.

It turned out that the aluminum ring surrounding the diaphragm, which in
theory should have been "infinitely rigid," was not rigid enough. Given that the
thin-scale plate—the sandwich plate I had in mind—was going to deflect under
load in unpredictable ways (depending on where a person stood, for example),
that presented a serious problem. I could not make the aluminum ring more
rigid by making it thicker than 0.2 of an inch, because it had to fit into a quarter-
inch plate. I could make the ring wider, or I could make it out of steel, or both.

At any rate, I needed a new set of diaphragm load cells, and Charlie was doubtful whether any 0.2-inch-high ring would be rigid enough, no matter what. Where did that leave us?

I had just learned an important lesson: the accuracy of the load cells in the thin scale could be affected by the deflections of the plate. Surely the load cells and the plate were separate parts that could be designed and developed independently; but not completely independently, because as we had just found out, the behavior of one affected the performance of the other.

That meant that to increase accuracy we should try to minimize these deflections and to make the plate as rigid as possible. It also meant that the connection between the plate and the load cells was not a trivial one. The joint between them had to be carefully designed, so that—among other things—the forces acting on the plate did not create stresses and strains on the load cell that distorted its accuracy.

This was fast proving to be a more complex design problem than just creating separate parts and throwing them together. Although I had already accepted that the scale had three distinct parts—the plate, the load cells, and the electronics—it was slowly becoming clear to me that the interfaces between these parts had to be cleverly designed too. To quote the architectural theorist Vittorio Gregotti, in his book *Inside Architecture*: "The methods for joining different parts of the construction system thus become the elements requiring the most effort, and are often the points at which the application of specific inventions becomes most critical."

It follows that solving the three thin-scale problems separately without attending to the interfaces between them would simply not do, because there were no sharp boundaries between them, only fuzzy ones. In an important way, therefore, my design would have to attend to the boundaries of the three parts, so that when they were joined together they formed an articulated and orderly whole. The Greek root of the word *harmony*, by the way, is *harmos*, which means joint or to join.

"I hate to think of it," I wrote in my diary on 31 July 1988, "but I might have to drop the diaphragms altogether." There was not really much time left to ponder that question, was there?

*   *   *

The diaphragm load cells were laid to rest, and it was back to basics again. This was an opportune time for Charlie to explain to me some elementary notions about load cell design, and to introduce me to the hook load cell, which he thought would be a more productive venue to follow.

Imagine a beam projecting horizontally from a wall—a *cantilever*, in engineering parlance—with a second beam mounted on its free end (a second cantilever) projecting back towards the wall, just past the middle of the first beam. If a load is now applied to the top of the second beam exactly above the middle of the first beam, the first beam distorts into a shallow S-shape or wave shape (Fig. 32).

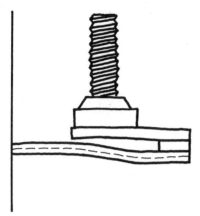

32 *A double-cantilever bending into an S-shape under load*

Under load, the part of the beam attached to the wall bends downwards, the part away from the wall bends upwards, and the midpoint of the beam does not bend at all. In engineering terms, the load produces a clockwise *moment* (or torque) on the beam that is at a maximum near the wall and zero in the middle of the beam, and an anti-clockwise moment that is at a maximum at the free end of the beam and zero in the middle of the beam too.

If we bond two identical strain gages on top of the longer beam, at equal distances from its midpoint, each gage will produce an equal change in resistance under load, but the one near the wall will be in tension (increased resistance) and the one near the free end will be in compression (reduced resistance). The difference between the resistances in the two gages will essentially be proportional to the load—when we double the load that difference will double too.

One can now see the brilliance of the hook design. When the load is shifted away from the exact center of the beam, say toward the wall, the resistance of one gage is increased by the same amount that the resistance in the other one is decreased, with the result that the difference between the two resistances remains the same. In other words, the hook arrangement is insensitive to a shifting load. It will produce the same reading of a person's weight, no matter where she stood on the scale or how much she swayed. That was the "difference of moments" arrangement that John Hall had talked about in passing, as I recalled.

Over the next two weeks, Charlie and I designed an elementary hook-shaped load cell and had it machined to our specifications. It was essentially made from two strips of one-eighth-inch steel with a thin steel spacer between them. The middle section of the longer strip was narrower. This increased the stresses in the middle section, making it possible to bond the strain gages away from the edge of the beam and still have them read high stresses; the higher the stresses, the more accurate the gage readings.

The stresses were, of course, at a maximum at the edges of the beam, but there were a lot of other forces there that could affect the strain gages. It was always better, Charlie said, to keep them away from the edges. He bonded a pair of gages on top of the longer metal strip, and the three parts were then connected with flathead screws. We added a semispherical foot under the shorter metal strip. The hook load cell was now complete (Fig. 33). We then screwed four such load cells tightly (through flat off-the-shelf washers) to thin cavities at the four corners of a square quarter-inch-thick aluminum plate and wired them all together.

The aluminum plate was very rigid and sagged very little under a full 300-pound load. But it weighed three pounds, a far cry from my one-pound goal. The hook load cells with their semispherical feet jutted down some half an inch from the aluminum plate, and were far from being embedded in the plate, as my design called for. This prototype was not light and not really thin enough either, but at least for now it would have to do. I needed to get the desired accuracy now and then trace my steps back to the thin-light scale.

Assembling this prototype took time, Charlie being a most meticulous and thorough man. He proceeded at his own pace, one step at a time, and could not really be prodded along in any way. He also needed regular time off for long treks in the surrounding mountains with members of his hiking club. He was an outdoorsman, Charlie, not content to live out his life in a dark and stuffy basement.

While Charlie was taking his time, I tried to put together the information I had gathered on the target cost of the scale and to prepare the report for the coming meeting. A couple of reliable electronic engineers in New York assur-

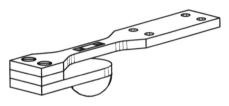

33 *The hook load cell*

ed me that the electronics could be had for $6, and provided me with a breakdown of parts. A more reliable quote, they said, would involve considerable investment up-front on developing and testing the circuitry. I also had some quotes for low-cost strain gages from the leads that John Hall gave me. He said that I could eventually get gages for 40¢ a pair, but the quotes from China and Brazil were still for twice that. There was not much more I could do now. Firmer quotes would have to wait.

Eventually, with one week left before the meeting in Groningen, things started to move at a fast clip, and it seemed that nothing could stand in our way. We were on a roll, Charlie and I. We tested the scale prototype over three whole days down in his basement, surviving essentially on grilled cheese sandwiches and cans of five-bean salad—these people did not believe in elaborate meals; they ate to survive. Much to my amazement, the results we got on all the tests were all within the required specifications—the scale, in fact, overperformed. This Charlie certainly knew how to build and test scales; there was no doubt about that. Why did it take me so long to find him?

Then, to top it all, just as I was ready to leave for the Netherlands, the United States Patent and Trademark Office formally approved the patent for the sandwich-plate scale. Good timing! I crossed the Atlantic at the end of August with a scale prototype that for the first time measured weight accurately and with a patent to my name.

"We are almost at the level of accuracy of commercial scales," I wrote in my diary on 28 August 1988. "This really feels good. My head is now clear and empty of this particular anxiety. Yes, we can improve. Yes, we may lose some accuracy when we use our own electronics and a less rigid plate. But we are definitely in the ballpark. From now on, as Nienhuis says, 'it's only engineering.'" Little did I know.

12

Price *Is* the Object!

The past few decades have seen the rise, here in America, of a new and unique phenomenon in human history, the mass consumption society. It is unique by virtue of three major features:

Affluence. Not a few individuals, nor a thin upper class, but the majority of families now have discretionary purchasing power and constantly change and replace their stock of consumer goods.

Consumer power. Cyclical fluctuations, inflation or deflation, and the rate of growth of the economy—all now depend to a large extent on the consumer.

Importance of consumer psychology. In our economy, consumer demand is no longer a function of money alone. Discretionary demand, which has assumed a decisive economic role, is influenced and sometimes determined by consumers' willingness to buy. In turn, this willingness to buy is a reflection of consumer motives, attitudes, and expectations.

All three of these characteristics emerged only in recent decades. All three now prevail in the United States, and increasingly in Western Europe as well.

George Katona, *The Mass Consumption Society*

————

AUGUST 1988–OCTOBER 1988

I arrived in the Netherlands a couple of days before the crucial meeting with the Philips engineers. On my first evening there I set out with Koos and his wife to a village fair near their home town, Nijmegen. His secretary had a small table there selling paper flowers she made. Her husband shared her table. He sold hand-bound notebooks, clad with a wave-patterned paper that he printed himself. I bought a red-and-purple one for the second volume of the scale diary, and a yellow-and-blue one for the third volume. The first volume, comprising 188 pages, had just ended, and the gray notebook I bought at Pearl Paint in New York to take its place felt uncomfortable. It was not inviting enough. Diaries should be inviting.

I met Rijk Nienhuis in Amsterdam the next day and we drove up to Gronin-gen together. We checked into the Golden Tulip (not a very original name for a Dutch hotel) and then went out to dinner in a dark cellar off the town square, squaring off two bottles of Côtes du Rhône-Villages. Rijk, an amateur chef by his own admission, was more than happy to offer a running commentary on the excellent food that was put before us.

He was outgoing and most encouraging about the prospects of tomorrow's meeting. He assured me that the DAP people were more than interested in working with me, and in forming an exclusive relationship if at all possible. "You proved by your performance during the past four months," he offered, "that your continued participation would be worthwhile. You did the work of ten of our engineers. . . . I didn't know people like you still existed."

He promised to get me in touch with the Philips plastics engineers as well as with the people at the Corporate Center for Industrial Design in Eindhoven. He wanted to talk about the next invention down the line. He could envision a thin kitchen scale, one that doubled as a cutting board; a scale you could wash with the dishes when you are finished. "Once you break the price barrier with a new commercial product," he ruminated, "there are many new possibilities for new products. . . . You have to talk to my wife about a scale which corrects your posture, she works in rehabilitation." "What a nice, positive man," I wrote in my diary on 30 August 1988, "I am going into the meeting with a good, relaxed feeling. Some kind of mature confidence. I do feel blessed, for sure."

* * *

I went into the first of two days of technical meetings with the Philips engineers with Rijk Nienhuis by my side. I distributed my report and presented my results. The scale was placed on a universal testing machine and various accuracy tests were performed in succession. It passed them all effortlessly. "They appeared quite stunned and did not know how to react," I later wrote, "but they did not appear very happy." Well, they were doing their job, I suppose, trying to find where the design was vulnerable and attacking it there. And the scale, with my help, was resisting their attacks.

The military analogy here is not too far fetched. There is indeed a direct parallel between good design and good military strategy. In his classic book *Strategy,* Sir Basil Liddell Hart quotes Helmuth von Moltke, the Prussian general who expounded on the art of war: "A clever military leader will succeed in many cases in choosing defensive positions of such an offensive nature from the strategic point of view that the enemy is compelled to attack us in them."

Good design also involves choosing defensive positions of an offensive nature. A novel design is necessarily offensive because it challenges existing designs and accepted modes of thinking, and it is a good design only if proves to be defensible—if it can provide satisfactory responses, first to all sensible criticisms and later to all possible complaints. I parried most of the blows with patient explanations that made better-than-average sense, and promised answers by tomorrow for the questions I could not answer.

The basic challenge, of course, was still the Gary Baker challenge—to produce that elusive $1.50 load cell—and this was a challenge that could not be fended off so easily. Much as I had tried, I did not have the solid answers they needed to convince themselves that this was indeed a real possibility. After all, the cheapest commercial load cells with the contemplated level of accuracy cost at least 50 times that much.

Surely, I had already gone a considerable distance towards the target price. I had some engineering estimates and some initial prices from strain gage makers, but they were still engulfed in a mist of uncertainty that made everyone uncomfortable about moving ahead at full steam. It was the kind of uncertainty that could only be overcome with real quotes from reliable manufacturers, and I was not there yet, that much was clear. But that was not all.

It was Engineer Beets, the product manager in charge of the scale, who then marshaled the attack on what he referred to as the *ultralight* scale design. Blond and blue eyed, tall, agile, confident, yet mildly anxious, and absent any trace of a sense of humor, he was willing to concede that the scale I demonstrated was accurate enough. His primary concern had always been with accuracy, he confessed, and the four-load-cell design I presented seemed to have attained it to his satisfaction.

But he thought that the ultralight design was not viable. "We cannot use a thin plate with four shallow feet, because the scale has to retain its accuracy on thick carpets," he insisted. "We also need enough room for a commonly available battery, say an AA penlight battery." And to hammer that final nail in the ultralight coffin, he declared: "Fat people are afraid to step on thin scales." In short, Beets was of the opinion that it would be better to use a conventional two-plate arrangement, in which the bottom plate rested on the floor or on the carpet and the load cells, the batteries, and the electronics were all stowed between the two plates.

I had no ready carpet defense. Personally, I doubted that many bathrooms had thick carpets, and I wondered whether the market for the scale would shrink at all if the thin scale could not be used on thick carpets. Of course, it could not maintain its accuracy if the plate touched the carpet—the entire load needed to pass through the load cells to the feet that were pushing against the floor; that much was clear. If need be, I figured we could supply attachments that would elevate the plate above any carpet.

An AA battery was no less than 14.5 millimeters or 0.6 inches in diameter, more than twice the overall thickness of my present design. With AA batteries inside a two-plate scale, I thought to myself, its minimum thickness could be as much as 20 millimeters or 0.8 inches, not much thinner than some of the scales already on the market.

But AA batteries were available everywhere. The batteries I had in mind were found in camera stores and electronic shops but not in supermarkets and drug stores. Since, like watch batteries, they would only need to be changed every few years, a trip to an electronic shop should not have presented a problem. For all I cared, neither carpets nor batteries nor the fears of stepping on the scale were serious issues, but I harbored no illusion about their attack value. They could certainly kill the thin-scale project, at least at Philips.

Much of that first day of meetings was spent on technicalities that do not merit further comment here. When I got back to my room at the Golden Tulip that evening I called Charlie in New Jersey and John Hall in California, seeking precise answers to some of the more technical concerns expressed in the meetings. I got all the answers I needed, and that felt both reassuring and refreshing. Still, I went to bed that evening exhausted, with an unruly bunch of worries elbowing their way past each other into my jet-lagged mind; not a conducive combination for a good night sleep.

* * *

My list of answers the next morning put a stop to the technical critiques. We moved on to talk about my new patent. Beets then offered, with a subtle yet recognizable sense of self-satisfaction, that if the scale was 20 millimeters thick and was made of two separate plates, then the protection that my patent afforded would not be needed. No patent, no royalties, I mused in lonely silence. Rijk Nienhuis tried vainly to suggest that the patent would still hold, but I had to concede that it would not. I had to admit to myself that the exchange was becoming rather unpleasant. Things were not going according to plan.

The afternoon meeting with the director was devoted to summarizing our findings and charting a plan for moving ahead. The main conclusion was that the scale I presented was indeed accurate, but that no one was convinced that it could really be manufactured for $15 or that the load cells could be had for $1.50. When it came time for me to offer my summary, I had to concede that both the scale and the load cells required more work.

I then zeroed in on the design issue: "Apparently Philips wants the accuracy and the low cost but prefers to remain with traditional forms, while I am personally interested in a third-generation scale." (Rijk Nienhuis liked that expression, "a third-generation scale"; he said later that it was a very powerful point to drive home to these gentlemen.)

It was then that Engineer van der Riet, who was rather quiet throughout the proceedings, took the lead. "We will not take a new technology and put it in an old box; we have made this mistake too many times before. Sure, accuracy and cost-price are the key issues, but the new design is attractive."

Getting practical, he turned to me and added, "I want you to leave the prototype here so that we can show it to the Norelco people when they come in September." He wanted to focus on a business plan for moving ahead, he said. I thought I saw a distant light shining again at the end of the tunnel, and I pressed on. I said that Beets worried that people would be afraid to get on the scale. Van der Riet brushed it aside with "We can overcome that with advertisements and guarantees." Beets became very quiet.

Then the director spoke. He did not offer his views about the choice of a design for the scale. Instead, he inquired about my own plans for the coming weeks. I replied that I had to agree with the emerging consensus: we needed a breakthrough on the load cell; we needed a load cell that could be had for $1.50; and that was what I planned to attend to as my first order of business.

He then asked me a question that caught me off guard: Would I be willing to take on the entire project and deliver finished scales at $15 apiece to Philips's door? I did not expect that. I said that I was not interested but that I was willing to look for manufacturers who would be.

The meeting ended with an agreement to meet again in early October. It was clear that Philips had yet to decide whether or not it wanted to develop a new scale at all; and, if so, what kind of scale it wanted. The promised "go-no-go" decision by the end of October retreated for now. I left Groningen with a mild case of cynicism: "As usual," I wrote in my diary, "things remain in the air, and the final decisions are left to the whims of individuals and to internal political struggles." A year had now passed since I started to work on the scale project on a full-time basis, and I was still chasing shadows.

* * *

On the road back from Groningen, passing through misty green fields with cows in black and white strolling quietly along, I began to come to terms with the fact that the focus of the scale project had shifted yet again; this time from the accuracy issue to the issue of whether it could be realized at all. The key obstacle to its realization was—to use the Nienhuis formulation—the price barrier. So my efforts now had to shift from "it's beautiful, now make it accurate" to "it's accurate, now make it affordable."

My primary objective now was to provide Philips with information that would make it easier for them to come to a decision to produce a new scale using my technology and, better yet, my design. The only way to do that now was to reduce the cost of production in any way possible. Both the scale and the load cell I showed them were still too expensive.

Again, cost reduction was not a goal I had in mind when I started out on the scale quest. It was not something I now looked forward to doing either—too prosaic, I thought; not fascinating enough. But it was something that simply needed to be done if the scale was to be realized. It was, as far as the scale was concerned, a matter of survival, survival in the global mass market as one of an untold number of products vying for the consumer dollar (or mark, or peso, or yen).

The scale was now at a point where it needed to leap across the price barrier into the consumer market. Failing to execute this leap, it would remain on paper as one of many nice ideas (including many patented ones) that never saw the light of day. This was something I could not let happen. So I enlisted myself in the cause of making the scale affordable to ordinary consumers.

* * *

It had finally dawned on me that I was dealing with a product of mass consumption, and that once one entered the mass consumption market, the consumer—through her willingness (or unwillingness) to buy—imposed a harsh discipline on the cost of production. My thin scale would see the light of day only if it promosed to sell in large numbers, and it would sell in large numbers only if it were affordable by masses of people.

Affordable personal scales for home use only became consumer products with the slow rise of mass consumption in the 1930s and 1940s. They initially competed with and eventually displaced the ubiquitous coin-operated scales that had been mass-produced (but not mass marketed) since the late nineteenth century.

The first coin-operated scale was brought to the United States from Germany in 1885. A few years later, in 1889, the National Scale Company manufactured the first coin-operated scale in the United States. During the 1920s and 1930s there was a coin-operated scale on almost every corner, most of them belonging to the Peerless Scale Company. For a penny, people could afford to weigh themselves even in the middle of the Depression.

The popularity of these scales reached its pinnacle in the mid-1930s, when there were over 750,000 scales all across the country. The advent of inexpensive bathroom scales was probably the major cause of their demise; vandalism and the increased cost of repair were contributing factors too. Interest in these scales waned rapidly in the 1940s, and by the 1950s they were considered junk. By the 1970s they had become collectors' items (Fig. 34).

The weighing of persons for medical purposes had a longer history. It originated with Santorio Santorio (1561–1636), a professor of theoretical medicine at

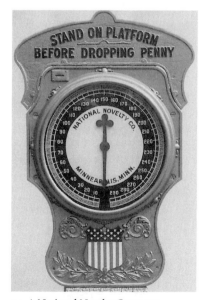

the University of Padua in Italy, who is credited with introducing quantitative measurement—counting, in other words—into the study and practice of medicine: "His most famous experiments involved the study of bodily weight. He placed himself on a platform suspended from an arm of an enormous balance, and weighed his solid and liquid intake and excretion. He found that by far the greatest part of the food he took in was lost from the body through *perspiratio insensibilis*, or 'insensible perspiration.'"

According to some accounts, Santorio measured minute changes in his weight for 30 years. He eventually published his findings in 1614 in a little book, *De Medicina Statica Aphorismi* (Aphorisms Concerning Static Medicine), the first

34 *A National Novelty Company coin-operated scale*

systematic study of metabolism. Santorio was also the first to measure body temperature: "The patient grasps the bulb" of the thermometer, he wrote, "or breathes upon it into a hood, or takes the bulb into his mouth, so that we can tell if the patient be better or worse." A drawing showing Santorio in his "weighing chair" having just finished his dinner appears in his book (Fig. 35) with the following explanation: "The Chair is set as it is represented in the aforesaid Figure wherein the Beam is fastened to the Rafters, at a secret place, in a room above that where you take refection [have a meal], because it would be somewhat unsightly in the same room; as also by reason of the unlearned, to whom all things that are unusual seem ridiculous."

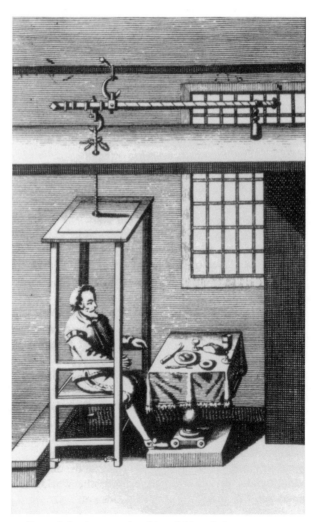

35 *Santorio having a meal on his weighing chair*

Note that for his measurements to be precise, he would have had to lift his feet off the carpeted platform. Otherwise some of the load would pass through his feet into the ground. This is another example of the carpet problem raised by Engineer Beets. To obtain an accurate measurement of a load, the entire load must pass through the load-measuring device. It cannot be allowed to pass through strands of wool in the carpet or through Santorio's buckled shoes.

Santorio, a pioneer in self-experimentation, did not see it as at all unusual or ridiculous to have his meals while sitting on his weighing chair as long as the scale he used remained out of sight. To weigh himself, he used the ancient principle of the Roman steelyard scale, invented as early as 200 B.C., which consisted of a beam with a sliding poise to counterbalance the load.

The steelyard was a cheap, compact, and relatively accurate instrument, and it remained in use for 2,000 years. The disadvantage of the steelyard scale was that the objects being weighed—like the heavy cannon in Fig. 36—had to be lifted off

36 *Weighing a cannon with a steelyard scale*

the ground. That limitation was only overcome in the eighteenth century with the invention of the platform scale.

Both coin-operated scales and their bathroom scale descendents made use of a platform supported by a compound-lever arrangement (as shown in Fig. 7 earlier). The first such platform was built by John Wyatt of Birmingham (1700–1766) in the last years of his life. A patent for a platform scale with a compound-lever system was issued to an Alsatian—Alois Quintenz—some 40 years earlier, in 1722.

This novel compound-lever arrangement eliminated the need for lifting heavy loads—even carts, vehicles, or locomotives—off the ground in order to weigh them. It transferred the loads at the four corners of the platform to a single point, where a cable pulling down on a steelyard beam with a sliding poise, for example, could be used to measure the loads on the platform. This is in fact the combination still in use today in common doctors' scales.

The first generation of bathroom scales used the compound-lever system to pull on a spring and turn a dial that displayed one's weight to within a few pounds. The second generation of these scales used the compound-lever system to transfer the load to a single load cell of some kind, and that made it possible to display weight electronically with a modest increase in accuracy. My earlier allusion to a "third generation" of personal scales referred to scales that eliminated the compound-lever arrangement altogether and replaced it with four load cells—one in each corner—thus making it possible to increase the scales' accuracy and to reduce their profile.

Surely, there were many very accurate commercial scales that already used the four-load-cell arrangement. In fact, commercial scales had to meet strict accuracy standards and had to be officially certified because they were used for trade. But they were expensive, heavy, and bulky; clearly not suited for home use; and surely not affordable by the average consumer. The issue I now confronted was the transformation of the four-load-cell commercial scale into an affordable and attractive consumer product without the loss of accuracy.

* * *

To get a grip on what affordable meant, I needed to know how much consumers were willing to spend on their bathroom scales. More specifically, I needed to understand whether the $15 cost target set by Philips should be taken seriously. To find answers to these questions, I compiled a list of 31 scales from catalogs and from those cool design stores I visited and revisited with Lucinda in New York— places like The Sharper Image, Brookstone, and Hammacher Schlemmer—that were packed with well-designed novel objects (my thin scale still glaringly absent). I passed over the cheap dial scales in the department stores and the drug stores, and collected data mainly on electronic scales, "designer" dial scales, and scales with special features—like the talking scale (Fig. 37), the remote readout scale, or the memory scale.

37 *"Frank and Ernest," comic strip by Bob Thaves, 1992 (reprinted by permission of the Newspaper Enterprise Association, Inc.)*

It appeared to me, in the absence of more reliable statistics, that the scale market was stratified, much like many other markets since the onset of mass production in the nineteenth century. It was split into at least three distinct submarkets: (a) the lowbrow market, with prices between $10 and $30 and an average price of $20; (b) the middlebrow market, with prices between $30 and $90 and an average of $60; and (c) the highbrow market, with prices between $90 and $120 and an average of $100. There was yet another market, the market for the more accurate doctors' scales that had a raised beam with a steelyard arrangement (or a raised beam with an electronic display) and sold for an average of $240.

A 1983 *Consumer Reports* evaluation of 37 bathroom scales showed them to vary in price between $13 and $119, with an average price of $64, not far from my own estimates. A 1986 "Market Profile on Scales" estimated that the number of bathroom scales sold during that year in the United States amounted to 7.3 million, but there was no breakdown into submarkets.

It was clear, however, that the lowbrow market accounted for a very large share of the market, the middlebrow for a smaller share, and the highbrow for a very small share. There were also indications that the market shares of the middlebrow and the highbrow markets in Europe were much higher than those in the United States, but that their respective shares in the United States scale market were now on the increase. In other words, the Americans were still cheap, but they were gradually acquiring a taste for taste.

In one of our meetings at DAP, Engineer Beets showed some pie charts that displayed electronic scale sales in Europe in 1987. One million such scales were sold, and 55 percent sold for less than $50. He interpreted that to mean that we should price our scale just below $50, aiming to capture 15 to 20 percent of the electronic scale market. He said that Norelco—Philips's United States subsidiary—was now conducting a market survey. It was estimated that 1.5 million electronic scales were sold annually in the United States, and that the market there was even more concentrated at the bottom end.

Beets projected that we could sell 300,000 to 400,000 scales per year when we reached full production if we offered 100-gram accuracy and kept the cost under

$50. To do that, he said, we had to produce scales at a cost not exceeding $17, including return on investment ($1 per scale) and development costs ($1 per scale). This, he said, was how he came up with the $15 figure. It included the cost of four load cells ($6), the cost of the electronics ($6), and the cost of the plate, assembly, pretesting, and packaging ($3).

So there it was for me to see. There were three forbidding price barriers to cross, one after the other. Rijk said that once Philips went into production, costs usually fell by an estimated 10 percent per year. In any event, one thing was made perfectly clear to me right there and then: carrying the load cell across that $1.50 barrier was critical to the realization of the Philips scale program.

* * *

Where did the 3 to 1 markup between the $17 production cost and the $50 retail price come from? As far as I could tell, this was just a rule of thumb, a working assumption that the Philips engineers used for assessing the commercial feasibility of new products. It implied that other costs, mostly those associated with advertising, financing, warehousing, transportation, and—most importantly— retail sales were twice as high as the cost of production.

Markups varied considerably between different industries and sometimes between similar industries in different countries. When it came time to publish A Pattern Language, for example, an editor from Oxford University Press visited us at the Center for Environmental Structure in Berkeley—a solid two-story wooden house on a quiet, tree-lined street.

During a creatively prepared lunch in the kitchen there (everything we did back then was creative), we explained to her that we wanted the book to be as cheap as possible so that ordinary people, not just architects, could afford to buy it. She explained that because it was a 1,200-page book with many pictures and drawings it would cost $3.50 to produce. It would then have to sell for $35, she said.

We were aghast. How could that be? Our self-image as servants of the people was instantly shattered. We suspected profiteering. Why such a huge markup? "Simple," she explained. "10 percent for producing the book, 10 percent for royalties to the author, 40 percent to the publisher for advertising, financing, and warehousing, and 40 percent for the bookseller." That was that. Books have a 10 to 1 markup.

Some of the lowest markups I encountered were for new homes. Typical developer profits, real estate agents' fees, mortgage closing costs, and transfer taxes added less than one-third to the total cost of land, land preparation, and house construction, implying a total markup of not more than 1.33 to 1.

The highest markups, as far as I knew, were in the heroin trade. In 2002, for example, the farm gate price for a kilo (2.2 pounds) of opium in the Golden Triangle—Laos, Northern Thailand, and Myanmar (formerly known as Burma)—was $135. Ten kilos of opium were then processed in jungle laboratories into one kilo of high-grade China White heroin that sold locally for $2,500.

By the time that kilo arrived in New York City it fetched $200,000 in whole-sale prices; an additional 80 to 1 markup. The big money was clearly in smug-gling and transit. The heroin was then cut (read: diluted) with other powdery substances at the ratio of, say, 3 to 1, and a 50-milligram "dime bag" was then sold on the streets for $10, another 4 to 1 markup. The total markup for heroin, from lab prices to street prices, amounted to 320 to 1—240 times the markup for new homes.

There was clearly no universal rule of thumb for estimating the markup for different products. I had no choice but to take Engineer Beets at his word.

* * *

A propos the Golden Triangle: during a five-day trek through the opium poppy fields and the hilltribe villages in a remote corner of the Golden Triangle—somewhere along the Thai-Burmese border—we stopped for an overnight stay at the home of a headman of a poor Karen tribe village. It was a house made of woven bamboo mats, built on wooden stilts, and covered with a thatched roof. The only building materials that were paid for in cash were the few nails that were used to put it together.

We were five, six including our guide, and it was left to me to negotiate with the headman. I agreed with his suggested price for lodging, and I then asked him what we could have for dinner. He said there was rice and vegetables, and some chicken too. "How much for the chicken?" I inquired. "Well," he said, "there is a 20-baht chicken (80¢) and a 25-baht chicken." "We'll have the 20-baht chicken," I said.

The next morning, as we left, I went to pay the man. "How much for every-thing?" I asked. "So much for the place and so much for the food and 25 baht for the chicken," he replied. "But I asked for the 20-baht chicken," I protested. "I know" he replied apologetically, "We couldn't catch it." Free range is free range.

* * *

Shortly after I returned to New York I received a fax from Rijk Nienhuis that cast the story in new terms. The conservatives at Philips appeared to have gained the upper hand. They wanted a 16- to 20-millimeter-thick scale (0.6 to 0.8 inches) with a bottom plate to avoid carpet problems and enough room for an AA pen-light battery, a design that had no need for my patent protection. They didn't need any help on the electronics—my cost estimates proved correct and they could develop the electronics themselves. The same went for the two-plate platform—they could develop that platform themselves too.

The load cells remained the main issue for which they still sought my help. "DAP feels that price and performance of load cells need confirmation through firm offers from a supplier and prototypes from different production batches," he wrote. "This is a field they would like to delegate to you completely." In other words, the Philips manager was not interested in my thin scale. They were still interested in me, because they believed (or wanted to believe) that I could deliver cheap and accurate load cells.

Where did that leave the thin-scale project? I, on my part, was not interested in their two-plate design at all. Never was, never will be. It was neither thin enough nor light enough for my taste. My gut reaction was to move on and focus on my thin-scale agenda. If they were not interested in it, so be it. This was not the end of the world. Would I abandon the thin scale and pursue the goal of finding that mysterious $1.50 load cell for Philips? No.

As I cooled down, though, I had to admit to myself that the thin scale needed the cheap load cells too. And if that was the case, then I should be willing to enlist myself in the pursuit of the affordable load cell. Yes, but only if it advanced my thin-scale project. Fine. Not all was lost, then. I did not have to give up on Philips just yet. In my more optimistic moments I also entertained hope that we could somehow arrive at a compromise two-scale solution—to produce both their scale design and my scale design, using the same load cells and the same electronics.

* * *

After two more days of meetings in Groningen in early October, I was finally confronted with the grim realities of the marketplace for mass consumption. I shall skip over the technical details and come right down to business.

At our closing meeting in the presence of the director, Engineer Beets reported that in all likelihood the thin scale could not be produced for $15, and that a two-plate design could possibly be had for that price. Engineer van der Riet echoed Beets, declaring that an accurate $15 scale was indeed essential as the mainstay of the new scale program. He envisioned a program that would market 200,000 to 250,000 scales a year in three price ranges: $50 for the economy model; $63 for the midrange model; and $75 to $80 for the luxury model. The luxury model, he said, would sell not more than 40,000 to 50,000 scales per year. The feasibility of the whole program, they both agreed, revolved around the availability of the $1.50 load cell.

The director then offered me a $50,000 contract to develop a final design and to produce 100 prototype load cells by mid-December. "We will work in parallel," he said. "You will work on the load cells and we will work on the electronics and on the plates. If the project proves to be feasible, Philips will buy 0.5 million to 1.5 million units from you per year, and we will pay you 3 percent on every load cell we buy."

I protested feebly that my development expenses to date had already exceeded $50,000. He replied tersely that my development expenses included technologies they were not interested in (anything having to do with the thin scale, that is), and reminded me that we had initially agreed to cooperate with no strings attached, anyway. "What I am offering you are the usual terms we give our vendors," he said.

Funny being called a vendor, I reflected: that did not feel right. The image of the street vendors and their carts and tables lined densely along Pratunam Road in Bangkok sprang to my mind. These vendors—I recalled—were regularly evicted by the police every two or three years, because they blocked pedestrian traffic. They always cooperated with the police, and on the appointed day they all promptly disappeared. A photograph of Pratunam Road, spotlessly clean and cleared of vendors, would then be published on the front page of the *Bangkok Post*, and the new chief of police would be complimented profusely on his unflinching commitment to civic order. The issue would then be quickly dropped, and within a couple of weeks all the vendors would be back en masse. Everyone concerned was happy with the outcome. Everyone understood who was in charge. No one was hurt and no one lost face.

Never before, I confess, had I ever thought of myself as a vendor. But now that my vendor status at Philips had been firmly established, it was also made clear to me, rather obliquely, that if I myself could have the load cells produced for less than $1.50, then I could, of course, pocket the change. "That is up to you," the director said with a knowing smile.

That sounded rather absurd to me: the budget was already way too tight. But I reluctantly agreed. I could not just walk away from it all and start from scratch again. Not yet, anyway. The $50,000 payment was puny, no doubt, but it would keep the work on the load cell going for a while. How far? Difficult to tell. It was all quite vague, I admit, and I was out of my element. But for the first time I was offered money for my scale work, and that felt good.

Vendor or no vendor, I insisted that I wanted some commitment on their part to have the thin scale as one of the products in their scale program, as a midrange or a luxury model if need be. A long discussion in Dutch between Engineer van der Riet and the director ensued. They eventually told me that the commitment was there, but not yet in writing. A written one had to wait until I could demonstrate the commercial feasibility of the thin scale.

The scale could then fit into a higher price category, depending on its cost of production; but the higher the price, of course, the lower the sales. If it could be produced for $20, for example, it would still be feasible, they said. I could relax, they advised amicably in closing, so I should stop worrying about the thin scale for now and get to work on the load cells. They'd fax me the development contract in a matter of days.

13

The License to Fail

Here, then, is the central idea: the form of made things is always subject to change in response to their real or perceived shortcomings, their failures to function properly. This principle governs all invention, innovation, and ingenuity; it is what drives all inventors, innovators, and engineers.

Henry Petroski, *The Evolution of Useful Things*

This library is full of stories of supposed triumphs, which makes me very suspicious of it. It's misleading for people to read about great successes, since even for middle-class and upper-class people, in my experience, failure is the norm. It is unfair to youngsters particularly to leave them wholly unprepared for monster screw-ups and starring roles in Keystone Kops comedies and much, much worse.

Kurt Vonnegut, *Hocus Pocus*

———

There was no doubt in my mind that completing the development of the load cell was now the first and highest priority; that the survival of the scale project hinged on the invention of an accurate and affordable load cell; and that all other aspects of the thin-scale project would have to wait on back burners until the load cell performed to everyone's satisfaction and its development was largely complete. I now had to become an active participant in the engineering design process, and I welcomed that prospect: engaging in design was the most fun part of the scale project.

The hook design for the load cell that I presented in Groningen in late August was already quite thin and quite light. It was not yet thin enough to fit into a quarter-inch scale, but it embodied the idea of thinness more readily than other known load cell designs. And it certainly produced the desired accuracy.

Three critical functional requirements—thinness, lightness, and accuracy— were more or less satisfied, and that was not something to be scoffed at. The most logical next step was to look into the requirements that the hook design did not yet meet and to modify it in such a way as would satisfy them too. The $1.50 cost ceiling was the most important requirement it now had to satisfy. But it also had to be able to resist excessive loads and sudden impacts. It had to be protected against water, humidity, and dirt. And, while satisfying all these demands, it still had to retain its 100-gram accuracy.

But that was not all. I soon discovered another functional requirement that the hook design did not meet, one that Charlie had neglected to mention earlier. The person to point out a crucial deficiency of the hook design was one of the three directors at Tedea: Amir Rahav, who was also its chief load cell designer. I flew to Israel for a few days of rest after the August meeting with the Philips people. On one hot and humid afternoon I drove north from Tel Aviv to the Tedea offices to tell Matti Raz—one of the other directors—how grateful I was for the John Hall connection. The air-conditioned Tedea offices were located in the midst of a high-tech industrial park in Herzliya-by-the-Sea, right next to a high-end beach community. I did not really expect anything of consequence to happen there. It was just a courtesy call.

Amir saw me in the hall and, to my utter amazement, called me into his office immediately for a serious discussion. He had been trying to reach me in New York for the past few days, he said, because he wanted to know if an 8-millimeter-thick load cell (0.3 inches) would be acceptable. If it was indeed acceptable, then he had a design in mind that might work. He had been thinking about it on and off, he offered haltingly. That simple admission was enough to let me know that he loved design too, more than anything else that came his way. He was probably addicted to it and couldn't help it. Up close, his childish excitement showed through the hairline cracks that lined his sculptured, almost lifeless face.

He showed me his sketches and I showed him my drawings and my test results; no more secrecy and no more paranoia—we were sharing our toys. Our eyes were now leveled too. "I was no longer someone coming to ask how to make a load cell," I wrote in my diary on 6 September, "but someone who has already made and tested one while theirs was still on the drawing board."

Amir then explained to me that our designs were not too different, but that when the scale was loaded, the hook arrangement would act as a lever: one side

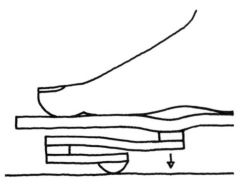

38 *The hook load cell pulling down on the plate under load*

of the hook would be pushed up from below by the floor, causing the other side to pull down on the scale plate. This could be a problem if the connection to the plate was not strong enough, or if the plate itself was not strong enough, in which case it might deform (Fig. 38). This, I had to admit, was indeed a cause for worry, especially if the plate was to be a thin and lightweight sandwich plate. It was yet another interface issue—the load cell design I needed had to accommodate thin, lightweight plates comfortably without bending them out of shape.

Amir described his design, which was a low-profile variation on the well-known Z-clip load cell; well known, that is, to those skilled in the art, but not yet to me. The Z-clip, I learned, is essentially made from three parallel beams, or two hooks, one on top of the other. The middle beam still deforms into a shallow S-shape under load, exactly as in the hook design. But when a force pushes the bottom beam from below—roughly below the center of the middle beam—the top beam pushes the scale plate upwards in simple and even compression, without creating a lever effect on the plate above it (Fig. 39).

While the hook design required four layers altogether—two parallel beams and two spacers—the traditional Z-clip design had five layers—three parallel beams and two spacers separating them. Amir proposed a novel design that would shrink the vertical dimension of the traditional Z-clip into four—rather than five—layers. This, he suggested, could be done by making the top beam in the shape of a horseshoe, allowing the middle beam to deflect into the empty space in the center of the horseshoe (Fig. 40). The horseshoe would be attached to the scale plate from below, exerting a compressive force over a wide area but no bending forces that could deform the plate.

Amir also proposed that the bottom beam would be shaped like a disc that—with a spherical rubber foot below it—would absorb a sudden impact. All in all, I had to agree, the horseshoe design was clearly an improvement over the earlier hook design. When I showed it to Charlie upon my return to New York in mid-September, he concurred. I then drew it up. A new prototype was in the making.

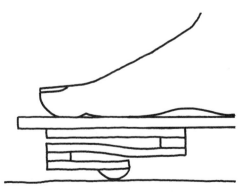

39 *The Z-clip load cell under load does not pull down on the plate*

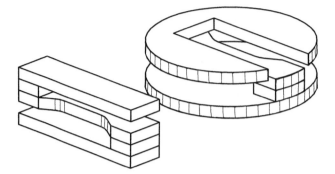

40 *From a five-layer Z-clip to a four-layer horseshoe design*

I had just added a new functional requirement that the load cell design had to satisfy, a requirement that basically ruled out the hook design because the hook arrangement exerted some pull on the scale plate. This requirement was an expression of my desire to come up with a load cell that would be a natural for a thin, lightweight plate. Was that a sensible desire? Would it not have been simpler to keep the hook design and strengthen the plate somehow, so that it could handle the bending forces exerted by the load cell?

In truth, there was no logical answer to this question. To some extent it was probably a matter of personal preference: the hook design was a nice and simple idea, but maybe it was too simple; and, in any event, it was not my idea, nor was it new (two strikes against it, to be honest). More generally, like all decisions having to do with making up a list of design requirements, the new requirement was to some extent arbitrary. David Pye, for example, in his book *The Nature and Aesthetic of Design*, makes it perfectly clear that

> all designs for use are arbitrary. The designer or his client has to choose in what degree and where there shall be failure. Thus the shape of all things is the product of arbitrary choice. If you vary the terms of your compromise—say, more speed, more heat, less safety, more discomfort, lower first cost—then you vary the shape of the thing designed. It is quite impossible for any design to be the logical outcome of the requirements simply because, the requirements being in conflict, their logical outcome is an impossibility.

For me, a preliminary list of functional requirements was always to be taken seriously. In my limited attempts at architecture, for example, I usually tried to avoid accepting new requirements uncritically, or abandoning old ones simply because they were difficult to meet in practice. Still, I already knew that the final list of requirements for a design is never given in its entirety in advance. Louis

Bucciarelli, in his book *Designing Engineers*—an anthropological study of the engineering design process—found that the final list of requirements was indeed an outcome of the engineering design process itself: "Nothing is sacred, not even performance specifications, for these, too, are negotiated, changed, or even thrown out altogether, while those that matter are embellished and made rigid with time as design proceeds. They themselves are artifacts of design."

* * *

One did not have to be an expert to observe that, in their present form, both the hook and the horseshoe designs did not yet meet the basic requirements for mass production, for example.

They required too many manufacturing operations: Each one was made of several separate steel parts. Each part had to be machined to a high degree of precision, be drilled, and then have its holes either tapered or threaded to receive machine screws while avoiding the use of bolts. The steel parts—that would initially be soft so that they could be machined—would then have to be hardened in a controlled heat-treating process. Then they would have to be assembled into load cells: to have gage patterns bonded to them and wires soldered to the gages. Finally, each load cell would need to be tested and sorted into groups of similar sensitivity (more on that later). In short, it was clear that there was no way that the cost of the load cell could be brought down to $1.50 without incorporating key manufacturing requirements into the design, and the sooner the better.

One of the more absurd courses in architecture school, I remember, dealt with construction details—looking into how windows were put together, for example. In my time, you could get by simply by copying drawings of window sections made by students of earlier years, line for line, without having the least idea how these windows were constructed or why. The entire grade for the course was based only on the quality of the drafting, anyway.

In architecture offices, I soon learned, construction drawings were typically left to the lowliest employees—usually to students working part-time or young interns on their first professional assignment—who had no clue how buildings were made. Construction drawings were an uncomfortable and anxiety-ridden chore to escape from as soon as practicable into the loftier pursuits of overarching aesthetic concepts.

"For most architects," writes Duo Dickinson in his book *Expressive Details,* "working on the details of a building is akin to spending time as a slave on a Roman galley, blindly pulling on an oar in a battle that you never see, gripped by the fear of the unknown, and attempting to survive great emotional and physical strength by flailing effort."

It is indeed lamentable that architects—originally employed as *architektons* or master builders—have become white-collar office workers, alienated from the actual making of buildings and oblivious to the demands of good and efficient construction. More generally, to quote from Stuart Pugh's book, *Total Design*:

> Design and manufacture, particularly in the Western world, have unfortunately over the years become divided into almost separate functions, resulting in design and manufacturing occurring as serial activities. . . . The manufacturing or process engineers have not traditionally been involved in the design of the product until the 'designers' have done their thing.

This has frequently led to the neglect of two important aspects of good design—incorporating manufacturing requirements into the design at the outset; and designing the manufacturing process concurrently with the design of the object.

What would design for manufacture entail? For one thing, it would entail simplicity, but surely not the simplicity that is attained through the denial of the complexities of the problem at hand or through the neglect of critical functional requirements. To quote Gregotti again: "Eloquent simplicity can be reached at great effort, but it is never a good starting point, nor, above all, an objective at any cost. Architecture is not simple; it can only become simple." Surely, this insight applied to engineering design and to product design as well.

The attainment of simplicity in design for manufacture—be it the manufacture of buildings, machines, or consumer products—translates into minimizing the number of parts; minimizing the amount and complexity of operations on each part; minimizing material usage and waste; minimizing assembly time; minimizing the number of drawings and instructions required; and as a consequence minimizing cost, while increasing product reliability and quality. If I wanted a load cell that was to be part of a product of mass consumption, I had to attend to designing it for manufacture.

* * *

Some months after my arrival in New York, Lucinda introduced me to an Israeli-born mechanical engineer she knew who occasionally helped her artist acquaintances with their projects and installations, usually free of charge. Amos Shamir was a few years older than I. He was taller and broader, his hair was graying, and the top of one of his middle fingers was missing, a permanent reminder of what machinery can do. He had a good sense of humor, and a good ear for classical music. When I met him, he had already been living in the States for some two decades but still read two Israeli newspapers regularly as if he were still abroad.

Amos was now a partner—or shall I say the working partner, or more precisely the only partner working—at Paramount Tool and Die Products, a dark and run-down factory shed somewhere between Red Hook and Park Slope in Brooklyn, not far from where the F-train from Manhattan comes out from the bowels of the earth and climbs onto an ugly overhead bridge.

Most of the machines at Paramount were old power presses noisily stamping out identical metal parts. One or two newer (and smarter) custom-made machines, designed by Amos to operate on timed bursts of compressed air, assembled several components coming from different directions into finished parts. Each machine at the plant had its own rhythm, and all these rhythms together were music to the two partners' ears—they knew that when the machines were pulsating they were making money, and the more polyrhythmic the cacophony the merrier.

A diary entry from 22 October 1988 describes my evolving relationship with Paramount Tool and Die in general, and with Amos Shamir in particular:

> Most of the workers stand near machines that produce the same thing every day of the year. There are a couple of Polish machinists there who are supposed to fix the machines when they break down, and are otherwise free to work on "development projects" such as mine. Amos has a partner called Bob whose father owned the shop before. Bob wants the factory to make money and cannot see the value of all these development projects. Amos, on the other hand, is bored with the factory and has to do something that requires his head. I can come out there but I cannot stay for long because Bob thinks that when I am out there Amos is not making money. When one of the machines is not working, Henry and Andrzej (pronounced *Anjay*) cannot work on my prototypes. If they do, Bob cannot know about it, and I have to stay in Amos's office while Amos goes out to see what they are doing. Such are the conditions and we do with what we have.

In short, the parts for the new prototypes were now made at Paramount, and Amos had been unofficially recruited as the production engineer and senior manufacturing advisor on my emerging design team. We worked out an informal arrangement—nothing on paper, mind you—whereby he offered me free engineering advice for now, sometimes almost on a daily basis, with a wide-open future for collaboration later on. In truth, it was more like the beginning of a friendship.

Amos, like Charlie, was a real find. He was perceptive and inventive. He grasped problems quickly, and his improvising mind veered naturally toward simple and elegant solutions that were often refreshing. He had a natural affinity for metals and the way they behaved, much like people with green thumbs have a natural affinity for flowers and shrubs. He also possessed a boundless repertoire of tricks and shortcuts.

He was a fountain of knowledge, this Amos, being largely wasted on a relatively mindless enterprise, stuck with a lazy partner who spent his days exchanging the latest tasteless jokes with salesmen who happened to drop by. To be fair, tasteless or not, some of the jokes were rather good. The short bursts of laughter they elicited were flickers of light that for a moment lifted that somber factory out of its overwhelming gloom, only to sink it into heavier darkness a moment later.

I gave Amos the drawing for the four-layer horseshoe design in mid-September, after discussing it with him at length. For the next two weeks I pestered him to get the parts made but to no avail. He then told me that he had thought of a better idea: the horseshoe design could be manufactured from one strip of steel, punched into the desired form in one operation, and then bent into an S-shape in a consecutive operation (Fig. 41). This design, he ventured, would eliminate all machining and fastening. He had a host of other suggestions for minor improvements as well. I went along, rather uncritically, with blind trust in his overwhelming engineering talent. Thus was born the bent-horseshoe load cell. In retrospect, it could never have performed as a load cell; it was too crude for that. But it did turn out to be an important conceptual step along the way.

Charlie bonded gages to the center beam of the bent-horseshoe prototype, and we tested it together during the two hectic days before my departure for Groningen in early October to meet the Philips engineers. It did not perform at all well. Where did we go wrong?

The hook design worked, that much we knew. But to arrive at the new bent-horseshoe prototype, it turned out that we changed at least six parameters at once. First of all, we changed the load cell from a hook to a Z-clip, to reduce the bending forces on the scale platform. Second, we changed the material from carbon steel to stainless steel, so that it would not rust. Third, we halved the thickness of the metal, so that we could stamp it. Fourth and fifth, we shortened and widened the center beam carrying the gages—the thinner the beam, the shorter and the wider it had to be to retain the same strength it had before. And sixth, we bent the metal instead of using spacers and fasteners, so as to reduce the number of parts and operations. Some of these changes were commendable improvements, no doubt. But any one of these six changes could now be responsible for the loss of accuracy, either alone or in combination with others.

There was no practicable way to test these changes one at a time in a dogged trial-and-error procedure. That would have required building and testing 64

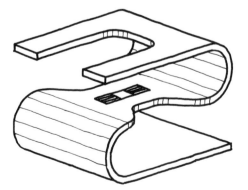

41 *The bent-horseshoe load cell*

prototypes ($2^6 = 64$), and I hated to think what kind of snide remark Bob at Paramount would choose to offer at the mention of such a prospect. I concede in retrospect that maybe we made too many changes at once. But I must also insist that, at least in theory, some of these changes should not have made any difference while others should have made a difference for the better.

After all, the hook design was still there, embedded in the bent horseshoe. The stainless steel we chose was in common use in the load cell industry. And we dimensioned the central beam so as to maintain the same levels of strain near the strain gages. Surely, the combination of new design parameters was a new trial and it produced new errors, but it was by no means a random trial. It was a trial specifically designed to move the project ahead. To quote Herbert Simon again,

> [Problem solving] ordinarily involves much trial and error. Various paths are tried; some are abandoned, others are pushed further. Before a solution is found, many paths of the maze may be explored. The more difficult the problem, the greater is likely to be the amount of trial and error required to find a solution. At the same time the trial and error is not completely random or blind; it is in fact rather highly selective. The new expressions that are obtained by transforming given ones are examined to see whether they represent progress toward the goal. Indications of progress spur further research in the same direction; lack of progress signals the abandonment of a line of search. Problem solving requires *selective* trial and error.

The underlying method for moving the design project ahead generally involved keeping the physical features (subassemblies, components, or patterns) that worked, and replacing those that failed to meet expectations with new physical features that should work. This allowed the design to evolve rapidly, much as a biological organism evolves—through the assembly of hierarchies of true and tried components in new arrangements, rather than by starting from scratch from elementary building blocks again and again in the hope of coming up with a better design.

The ability of designers to introduce new components or physical features that should work into the design is a function of their experience or their design repertoire. "We see this particularly clearly when the problem to be solved is similar to one that has been solved before," writes Herbert Simon. "Then simply by trying again the paths that led to the earlier solution, or their analogues, trial-and-error search is greatly reduced or altogether eliminated."

Budding designers may find themselves sketching a design, discovering something wrong with it, throwing it away, starting from scratch on a new design, discovering something else wrong with the new design, throwing it away, and starting again from scratch in seeming perpetuity, confronting a blank sheet day in and day out with not a sign of progress in the offing. They are like infatuated young lovers who fall out of love at the first sign of a problem, quickly become infatuated with someone else, fall out of love again, and become infatuated yet again in seeming perpetuity, as though destined to repeat the first chapter of their love story ad infinitum, without ever moving on to chapter two.

More experienced designers, once they have started working on a design problem, rarely start from scratch again. They may reject a failed design, but they keep certain physical features in some form in their next sketch, making it possible for their design to evolve. Only when they reach a dead end, having exhausted the possibilities inherent in the physical features they kept returning to, do they abandon them altogether and start afresh with a clean slate.

* * *

I had one measly specimen of the bent horseshoe with me as I crossed the Atlantic in early October. I showed it to the Philips people in one of our technical meetings in Groningen and told them rather meekly that I thought it had potential but did not yet work. They were not amused. It was too different an object from what they had come to expect. They hoped for a ready-for-manufacture version of the hook load cell I demonstrated in August. And they looked at my little gray piece of bent metal with some scorn, as though it lacked seriousness, and, by extension, as though I lacked seriousness too.

Their load cell engineer, van der Brug—a big, quiet man with a baby face topped by reddish curls—explained to me why it did not work. The center—or middle—beam was bent out of shape, and that destroyed accuracy.

Having killed the bent-horseshoe design earlier in the day, he took me out to dinner later that evening. During dinner, he told me how to fabricate the load cell without bending the center beam. That turned out to be a major unproductive detour and a dead end, but there was no way to tell that at the time.

The design van der Brug sketched on a napkin that evening was a Z-clip that consisted of three parts and still used stamping and bending instead of machining. The top and bottom beams were identical in this design for the time

42 *The double-grip load cell under load (in theory)*

being—they were flat metal strips with no cutouts, parallel to and slightly offset from the gaged beam. Each strip was bent backwards on one side to create a recess into which one edge of the middle beam slipped and was then held there snugly, with or without stiff glue. The top and bottom beams thus gripped the center beam from both sides in a double-grip arrangement. Under load, as I understood van der Brug that evening, this load cell would behave as an ordinary Z-clip, with the middle beam bending into an S-shape (Fig. 42).

*　*　*

I returned from Groningen to New York in mid-October, energized by the promise of a Philips development contract and its associated initial payment of $25,000, and I immediately set out to work on the design of a double-grip load cell prototype. Charlie, Amos, and I quickly agreed on the dimensions of the new design, and I drew it up. Amos promised to have the parts made in stainless steel in less than a week.

We now had a firm deadline to meet—mid-December 1988—by which time we needed 100 load cell prototypes and firm offers from manufacturers to deliver them in large quantities for $1.50 apiece. There was no time to waste.

While Amos prepared the metal parts for the new prototype, I made some inquiries about the cost of buying the steel in bulk and about hardening the stamped parts in a commercial heat-treatment process. In large quantities, I found, the material for the three steel parts together would cost 9¢ and hardening them would cost 3¢ more. That was good news. It was about half the original estimate I discussed with the Philips people.

I also talked to John Hall in California about the cost of strain gages, as well as about the cost of bonding them to the steel and soldering wires to them. Again, he was very cooperative. Two of the companies he recommended to me—one in Brazil and one in Taiwan—should be able to deliver the gages, bonded to the beams and wired, for 50¢ per load cell, he said. If necessary, he himself was willing to supply sheets of gages, uncut and untrimmed, for 15¢ apiece. The $1.50 price barrier was not looking as insurmountable as it did before, and that was encouraging.

We were on the move again and that felt good. Then, just as we were gathering steam, I received a short fax from the director of domestic appliances at Philips. In the fax, he informed me that they had "had internal discussions about the industrialization of the project, and there were still heavy doubts whether there exists any possibility to reach the cost price." They were now looking into it, he wrote, and to avoid unnecessary expenses on my part he asked me not to start any development work before the twentieth of November.

That was unfortunate, not the least because I had make some rash financial commitments earlier that week. I had promised my brother Joe, for example, that I would start repaying the loan he gave me, and I had even paid the patent lawyers money that I could have paid them later. Sometimes, sad to say, a verbal agreement is not worth the paper it is written on. It took me a few days to recover from that harsh disappointment before I faxed my reply: "We have now decided to continue this work despite the postponement of our contractual agreement, in order not to break the momentum and in order not to waste valuable time."

There was no way I was going to stop now. On the contrary, I was determined to finish the development of the load cell by the end of the year as originally planned, and that required moving at full steam. Eventually, though, running out of cash was going to slow me down.

At the very least, I now knew that I needed to earn some income to continue to pay for my scale habit. To that purpose, I had committed myself to teaching two courses at MIT in the coming spring term, starting in early February. That would require spending two days a week in Cambridge, Massachusetts, and it would inevitably slow me down for a few months the following year.

But there were still a few months left in that year, and I intended to put them to good use. My plan was to finish the design and testing of the load cell as soon as possible, and then to make steel parts for 100 prototypes, sending them for gaging and wiring—some to Brazil, some to Taiwan, and some to Charlie—before the end of the year. That was my plan, but, sad to say, I was ahead of myself.

* * *

The metal parts for the double-grip prototype were ready by mid-October. They were well made, and they fit into each other snugly even without glue. Charlie and I tested the prototype in late October, subjecting it to the standard tests for nonlinearity, hysteresis, and off-center loading. That load cell failed miserably too. Moreover, its behavior under load was surprising: instead of bending into an S-shape as expected (see Fig. 42), the top and bottom beams bent toward the

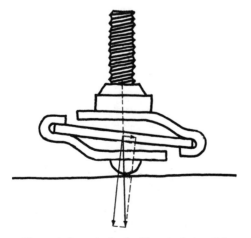

43 *The main beam in the double-grip design tilting under load*

middle beam, while the middle beam remained straight and simply tilted—the heavier the load, the more pronounced the tilt. In fact, it tilted almost six degrees from the horizontal with a 100-pound load (Fig. 43). We didn't expect that at all.

In the simple terms of engineering statics, that meant that the load was creating two force vectors on the tilted middle beam, one force vector perpendicular to the beam and one force vector along the beam. The gages on the beam only measured the force vector perpendicular to the beam, and that force became a smaller component of the total vertical load as the angle of tilt increased, accounting for most of the nonlinearity.

"I need patience with the load cells," I wrote in my diary on 13 November.

> They are still the key to moving ahead. Yes, I want to move ahead on other things as well, but nothing can move or really needs to move until the load cells work. . . . The time is short. Philips should answer by 20 November, a week from now. . . . My world has shrunk. I now focus on minute forces on small pieces of metal. There lies the solution or the opening needed to the wide-open road ahead. It is somehow confining. I have less and less to say to my friends about what I am doing: the story and the problems are becoming too specific. . . . I keep searching for the right balance between my optimistic problem-solving part—the part that can always see a way out of a difficulty—and my critical part—the part that looks for the hidden pitfalls and searches for self-deception. Both already know that they need each other, but they cannot avoid overwhelming each other from time to time.

The double-grip design failed, and it most probably failed because of the grip connections. They were not rigid enough, apparently, with or without stiff glue. "It was time to let go, move on to the next love affair," I wrote on 16 November. "We tested it, we improved it, and it still did not perform." In retrospect, it was just another blind alley along the way.

Not all was lost, however, because by then, a new design had presented itself. It came up in a discussion I had with Amos about going back to the single-horseshoe design, but this time, we decided to squash it flat, so that the three layers of the bent horseshoe lay one on top of the other. This would entail bending the three beams along deep crease lines in the metal. The top and bottom beams would be U-shaped and the middle beam would be I-shaped. Under load, the middle beam would still flex into an S-shape, as in the traditional hook design. This new load cell would be formed by folding one piece of stainless steel that looked like a wrench into three layers, so we called it the folded-wrench load cell (Fig. 44).

We would then spot-weld the parts together in several places along their common surfaces, clamping them together rigidly. Charlie concurred that this was a promising approach. He also suggested that the top and bottom beams could be dimensioned so that they would eventually touch each other, so as to protect the load cell from being overloaded. I liked that.

There was clearly something attractive and elegant in using U-shaped beams in a design that sought to reduce the vertical dimension of the load cell to a minimum, while at the same time not pulling down on the plate to which it was attached. Surely, the design as a whole did not yet meet the stringent accuracy specifications it faced, but the U-shaped top and bottom beams worked. They eliminated the need for the spacers separating the three beams in the traditional Z-clip load cell; and the top beam exerted only compressive forces on the plate above it. In that sense the U-shapes signaled progress.

That was why they were worth keeping. To quote Herbert Simon again: "Cues signaling progress play the same role in the problem-solving process that stable intermediate forms play in the biological evolutionary process. . . . In problem solving, a partial result that represents recognizable progress toward the goal plays the role of a stable subassembly."

But the idea of using a U-shaped beam to reduce the profile of the traditional Z-clip load cell was not simply a cue that signaled progress. It was—to borrow a term from Michael French's book, *Invention and Evolution*—a "pivotal" idea that seized me and now refused to let go:

> [The designer] thinks about the problem and the possible choices until some pivotal idea seizes his imagination, some particular way or ways of performing one or two of the more crucial functions which appear particularly satisfying or elegant, which have unlooked-for advantages or combine in a peculiarly helpful or apt or economical fashion. Then he tries to add all the other functions, to complete the outline of the whole solution; it may be he will come up against insuperable difficulties, and have to seek for another promising starting point, again, by the use of his aesthetic judgment. It is aesthetic in the sense that the emergence of the pivotal idea is accompanied by the same kind of intellectual pleasure as is excited by an inspired development in a great piece of music or a striking painting, and it may be recognized by that circumstance. It is a beautiful idea.

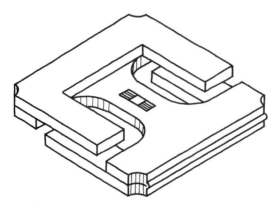

44 *The three-layer folded-wrench load cell*

I quickly drew up the new folded-wrench design. Amos had some parts made in stainless steel, I had them hardened in a heat treatment plant in New Jersey, and we were on our way again.

In early December—before I left for a trip to Thailand with Lucinda, her first—Charlie and I managed to test four stainless steel prototypes of the folded-wrench load cell. "They don't work," I wrote on 3 December.

> There is hysteresis . . . in all of them regardless of the way we test them. We thought it was the clamping on the edges and we welded them again and again. The clamps are now very strong, but the beam is weak apparently. . . . Sad and frustrating. It would have been nice to have a working prototype, no? But I don't. There are still some secrets to be uncovered. Is it the design? Is it the metal? Is it the hardening process? . . . Still, we have to proceed slowly and learn as we go. This is easy to say now, a couple of days after finding out that the load cells did not work. But as the numbers came up on the computer at Charlie's basement, I experienced that horrible feeling of "I don't want it to be that way, I want it to be my way, I want this long wait to end now, now!" I was just refusing to accept defeat, refusing to accept not getting what I wanted right there and then.

That was as far as we got in 1988, not very far. My plan—to finish the development of the load cell before the end of the year—simply refused to materialize. I journeyed to Thailand with Lucinda, leaving it all behind. We had some two weeks for ourselves, for the first time, and the house on Railei beach was the perfect place to spend them.

Philips, on its part, never came through either. The director of domestic appliances sent me a fax in late November, asking me to wait a few more days for "a green light" to start with my development work. Start? I was immersed in it already. I wrote back telling him politely that I would like to have my scale prototype back, and hinting that I had initiated contacts with other scale companies. (This was true. I now knew people who knew people at Krups and Siemens in Germany and at Black and Decker in the United States, and I was preparing to approach these companies if and when the Philips deal failed.)

He replied saying that the promised development fee of $50,000 was contingent upon exclusive deliveries of load cells to Philips and to no one else. If I agreed—he added the proverbial carrot—then the contract would be sent to me immediately. No more delays.

That was not part of the original understanding in our October meeting. At that meeting, it was made perfectly clear to me that Philips only wanted my load cells; and I, on my part, had made it perfectly clear that I needed them for my thin scale too, whether Philips was interested in it or not. It was understood then that I could not offer Philips exclusivity unless Philips agreed to manufacture the thin scale.

The rules of the game were now being rewritten yet again. I replied with a counter offer of limited exclusivity that left me free to use my load cell design for my thin scale in case Philips was not interested in manufacturing it, while giving Philips exclusive use of the load cells in ordinary bathroom scales. The director faxed me back, rejecting my offer and informing me that if I could not guarantee exclusivity then Philips was not interested in contributing funds for the development of the load cells.

"He still expressed some interest in buying load cells once we completed their development," I wrote in my diary. "This essentially means that I have to finish the development with my own funds, which is quite OK. It also means that they are not committed to anything. No timetable, no meeting, nothing. The ball is in my court. Once the load cells are ready, we can talk again. And the load cells are not ready."

* * *

The engineering design process, and more specifically the development process, was now clear to me, perhaps too clear: you have a design for a new object that you believe will perform its function adequately in the real world. If you can, you build a prototype and you test it under laboratory conditions that simulate the real world. You find out that it does not work, but you don't necessarily know why it does not work.

However, the specific failures in your tests are symptoms—signs or indications that something is amiss. These symptoms give you important information about the design that then allows you to weave a story about why it does not work. Once you have the beginning of a story, you look for more information to corroborate it. Then, once you have convinced yourself that you have a good story, you are ready to modify the design to remove the flaws you have discovered, you hope without reintroducing flaws that you discovered earlier; "earlier" meaning either in the current project or while working on other, similar projects in your past.

In short, when working on a new object you need your prototypes to fail in order to find out how to improve your design. To quote Henry Petroski, who has celebrated the importance of failure in engineering design in a number of his books, "It is the part that does not work that gets the attention in the model and the prototype. It is the function that does not get executed as well as can be imagined that becomes the focus of improvements."

Little wonder, then, that the only document I found that addressed load cell design—course notes Charlie consulted from time to time by one Albert Brendel—had little to say about how one goes about designing load cells, but had a lot to say about how one diagnoses failure. In fact, except for a cursory review of known load cell types and the forces acting on them, most of Brendel's notes, entitled "Basics of Successful Transducer Design," were elaborations on a diagnostic matrix.

The matrix, drawn on a single page, was a dense grid of small squares. It had

19 types of test failure listed on the horizontal axis and 26 potential sources of failure listed on the vertical one with the letters P (for primary) and S (for secondary) written by hand in any little square where a specific failure was associated with a possible source of failure.

The test failures listed were all failures to remain within acceptable tolerances in the familiar tests we were conducting ad nauseam in Charlie's basement. The listed sources of failure were physical features of the design, say, for example, "internal joint yield." There was no one-to-one correspondence between a particular test failure and a particular source of failure. One source of failure could lead to a number of test failures, and vice versa, one test failure could be attributed to a number of sources of failure.

The matrix, in other words, did not tell you how to improve your design, but where to improve your design and where to leave it be. It incorporated the maxim "if it ain't broke, don't fix it," and pointed you in the direction of what possibly needed fixing. That information, for someone desperate to know why his or her load cell design did not work—so that it could be made to work—was priceless.

Unfortunately, however, Brendel's "Basics" were written in jargon shorthand I could barely understand. Charlie had that matrix, or a similar one, hard-wired into his brain already. I did not, by any means. Our long postfailure talks, while we were sitting in his little kitchen and looking at the birds on the bird feeder or sitting on the verandah at the back of the house and looking at the geese by the lake, were design talks. We were searching for stories about our most recent failure that sat comfortably inside the matrix in Charlie's head, with the appropriate little squares checked off.

Depending on the story, many new variations on our latest design presented themselves to me, welling up from a rich compendium of geometric forms that were hard-wired into my brain over the years, my "design repertoire." "The mind of the designer should be like a rich, open soil, full of accessible resources, of which the chief is an ordered stock of ways and means, illustrated by many examples," writes Michael French. "The sum total of all such stocks might be called the 'design repertoire.'" I had an extensive repertoire when it came to making architecture, and I was now, slowly and hesitantly, bringing it to bear on load cells.

Charlie, on his part, rarely suggested a new form. He relied on me to come up with new three-dimensional objects, content to point out why they would or would not work, and confident that a new variation incorporating his latest critique was around the corner. The design process consisted of knocking our two heads together—one head with a design repertoire and one head with a diagnostic matrix—bringing up and discarding one geometric form after another in close succession, until we came up with a new form that merited a new prototype and a new battery of tests.

I came back from Thailand to New York in mid-January of 1989 to pick up the pieces of the failed folded-wrench load cell and try to make it work. Before I could get rid of my jetlag—there was a 12-hour time difference between Bangkok and New York, and it took almost 12 days to get over it—Philips came to life again.

Urgent faxes from Engineer Beets started coming my way. They never alluded to the now-defunct development contract, of course, but they informed me that Philips was now "anxious to know when we can expect samples of the load cells for testing." Beets informed me, in a fax sent on 2 February, that they were designing and testing the mechanical parts for a prototype; that they needed drawings of the load cells as soon as practicable, with 20 load cell prototypes to follow soon after; and that a manufacturer's price quote was to follow soon after that. I (hastily, much too hastily) promised to send him 20 prototypes by the beginning of March.

Those faxes from Beets were encouraging news. "There is interest on their part in continuing to work together," I wrote in my diary on 5 February. "They are investing time and money and they want to move ahead. Good. There is pressure, but this is 'real' pressure, not some undefined anxiety. . . . I don't mind that. I am moving ahead as fast as I can, and it feels fine."

Pressure or no pressure, the folded-wrench load cell prototypes still refused to perform, visibly oblivious to the rapidly approaching new deadline. It was not that the spot-welding connections between the parts were not rigid enough. The parts were slipping past each other no matter how rigidly they were clamped. Even when we substituted the spot-welding connections with four bolts on each side, we still got bad results. This was hopeless. Charlie was clueless and, needless to say, so was I. How could the parts be slipping past each other? Maybe the top and bottom flanges of the middle I-beam were now bending under load too, deforming the flatness of the beam? Maybe the material was too thin? Too weak?

It was then that the thought of paying a visit to Albert Brendel occurred to me. It was time for a pilgrimage to see the master and to ask for a teaching.

14

Embracing the Critic

Genius? Nothing! Sticking to it is the genius! Any other bright-minded fellow can accomplish just as much if he will stick like hell and remember nothing that's any good works by itself. You've got to make the damn thing work!

Thomas Alva Edison

For those men, it is an inestimable good fortune to find diaries by their forbears that expose the weaknesses they themselves are laboring under. The finished work has an oppressive supremacy. The man still caught in his own work, not knowing where it will lead, not knowing whether he can ever end it, can despair a thousand times. It will give him strength to see the doubts of those who succeeded in their work.

Elias Canetti, *The Conscience of Words*

———————

FEBRUARY 1989–NOVEMBER 1989

The repeated failures of the past six months exposed me to a number of existential and not-so-existential critiques of my project, critiques that I had thus far managed to evade. I now worried that, left unanswered, these subversive critiques would slowly drain me of the conviction—with its concomitant energy and enthusiasm—that I needed to sustain me in the face of persistent failures.

To persevere, I knew, I needed to remain aloft, buoyed by the rightness of my pursuit, however I chose to define it. Propelled by an unexplainable stubbornness, perseverance could only go so far. With a clear-headed understanding of what I was doing and why I was doing it, it could go a lot further.

* * *

What did I expect to learn from Albert Brendel, the master? The repeated (and not fully explained) failures of the last few months were gnawing at my confidence in the U-shaped designs. I could still remember fondly how wonderful the original hook design was and how well it performed at the time, and I was beginning to think that maybe I had accepted Amir Rahav's freely offered advice too hastily.

We had a working prototype load cell, the hook, six months ago. It was now mid-February, and I had an early March deadline weighing on me. I could delay the promised delivery of 20 prototypes to Philips for a while, maybe, but I did not want Philips to lose its patience. I felt I needed to deliver something, something that worked, and the sooner the better. Maybe it was time to give up on the U-shape designs and go back to the hook design? Could Brendel help me arrive at a sensible decision?

But even supposing I did go back to the hook design, I would still have to complete the development process, wouldn't I? It could not be left as it was before, because what we had before could not be manufactured for $1.50. True, it worked as a design. But it would still need to be miniaturized, so that it could be stamped. It would need to be made from stainless steel, so that it would not rust. It would need to be welded or riveted together, to eliminate the threading and counter-sinking operations that ordinary machine screws demand. These were, after all, the aspects of the design we were struggling with now anyway. So even with the hook design we were still a long way away from a set of drawings and specifications that could be sent to a manufacturer. Still, we would be closer than we were with the U-shapes, wouldn't we? Could it be that the whole love affair with the U-shapes was just a long and expensive detour?

* * *

I was toying with that unappetizing possibility while reading Tracy Kidder's *The Soul of a New Machine*, a gripping story about a group working on the design of a new computer, struggling to meet an impossible one-year deadline. For me, this story exposed a fundamental conflict between designers and managers, or, in my case, between the designer in me and the manager in me: "Often, they said, it was the most talented engineers who have the hardest time learning when to stop thriving for perfection. West [the team manager] was the voice from the cave supplying that information: 'OK. It's right. Ship it.'"

Was I striving for perfection? "No," I wrote in my diary, "I am not a perfectionist, I am ready to let go. I was always a 'low-A' student, trying to do the absolute minimum possible to get an A. Yes, not just a passing grade, an A, but a low A is fine. I need quality, not perfection. I need an elegant and intelligent load cell, not a major breakthrough in load cell design."

Still, I could definitely be suspected of leaning towards the designer in me. In truth, I loved the design process itself. The best part of the scale project so far was that it allowed me to spend a lot of time in the turbulent waters of the design process, time I had sorely missed during my years of teaching and working in the housing field. Now there was a part of me that engaged in design simply for the love of design.

Like every designer, of course, I had a vision of an end product in mind. It was a place I wanted to get to, a place of rest, but I was certainly in it for the journey itself. This must be a common experience among designers. Louis Bucciarelli in *Designing Engineers* captured it beautifully:

When designing is in process, that process is alive. The object is alive and laden with uncertainty and ambiguity. That is what makes designing the challenge that it is. When the design is complete, when the product gets shipped, when the documentation gets printed, and most significantly when the team disbands, then the process is over. The object as artifact is dead within the world of the firm; it no longer serves as the occasion for surprise. All is in order; all functions deterministically. No wonder most documentation, in its description of what once was alive as a design object, reads like an obituary.

Well, it was fine for me to acknowledge that I was in it for the ride: that was understandable. But, since I was wearing two hats—the designer hat and the project manager hat—I had to ask myself whether I was managing the scale project intelligently or whether, in my childlike fascination with design, I was neglecting my managerial responsibilities, moving along with no set plan and no visible end in sight.

There was no simple answer to this question, and, in the last analysis, it was probably not for me to judge. I had no previous experience in managing R&D projects that had a finished product as their outcome. But I knew for a fact that it was impossible to put a time limit on invention, or to estimate how much it would cost to complete the research cycle of a product that did not yet exist. All I could do was try to close in on my target, as effectively and as efficiently as I knew, one day at a time.

Surely, realistic budgets for both time and cost were easier to estimate when dealing with a mature technology and with a mature (read: reasonable) set of performance specifications. The inscrutable Professor Alex Khazan, I remembered, warned me that a new load cell normally takes a year to develop, assuming, I suppose, that one had a workable design in mind and a reasonable set of requirements it had to meet. He also said the development would cost $50,000. But these were ballpark figures anyway.

Lots of time and lots of money had been spent already, and, sad to say, we did not yet have a finished product that could be shipped. I was in a pickle, sure, but it did not surprise me. I concluded long ago that Parkinson's Law—"Work fills the time allotted for its completion"—simply did not apply in the realm of invention and design. Invention and design took their own time until the form in question came to rest. Project managers should push, and I was pushing as hard as I could. Yet, practically oblivious to my prodding, the design of the load cell was ambling ahead at its own unrushed pace, still far from a place of complete rest.

There was no question that I was going to miss the Philips deadline. I must have been overcome with optimism when I promised them a working load cell in early March. "Wishful thinking" would be a more appropriate description here, and I was not so pleased with myself for having succumbed to it. Instead of bargaining for more time, I promised a speedy delivery. "I have not been asked for promises," I wrote in my diary. "I volunteered them. All my deadlines have been self-imposed. I underestimate their patience, because of my own impatience that I attribute to them."

Was this taking too long? Difficult to say. I had expected this project to be over in a year. I had been at it for two and a half years already, and it was by no means over. In the sense of being longer than expected, yes, it had been too long. Could I think of a better way to have spent all this time and money? "There is no limit to thinking of better things to do," I wrote in my diary. "Whatever you choose to do, there is no limit to what you miss out. So what? You do what you do until it is done, and while you do it, you do it. Every once in a while you can remind yourself why, every once in a while. But you can't ask yourself why every day. That would be unkind."

Could somebody else get this far faster than I? Probably, but nobody was racing me along this path. It appeared that, at least so far, I was running entirely on my own; as fast as I could, but entirely on my own. Speed took on a different meaning as well. The formula fixing the relations between time, speed, and distance, I found, simply did not apply to mental space: since the correct path to the goal was unknown and the mental distance to the goal kept stretching, going faster did not ensure getting there earlier. I wanted to move, I needed to move, but motion by itself was of no help. "How can I go forward when I don't know which way I'm facing?" sings John Lennon. Most of all, I needed to find my way, my way forward, before rushing into yet another dead end. My energy and my resources were, after all, limited, and I had to use them wisely.

There is an ancient story about an old bull and a young bull that were standing on top of the hill. "Hey, look at all the cows down there," said the young bull excitedly. "Let's run down and mount one." "Let's walk down and mount them all," replied the old bull. This must have been the original formulation of the law of conservation of energy.

Was I managing project resources intelligently? As for my mental resources, maybe. As for my financial resources, probably not. I did not have a budget cap for the project, and had I had one, I would have had to stop in my tracks quite a while ago. For the last year and a half I had been working on it practically all the time, and I had lost track of how much money I spent. Maybe I didn't want to know? I made no distinction between the money I spent on myself and the money I invested in the scale. I had spent my savings, I spent the money I borrowed, and I spent the money I made with the occasional consultancy and now with the teaching appointment at MIT. I did not keep tabs on how much I spent in any given month and, what's more, I had no idea how much more money completing the project would entail. Having come this far, I was determined to go on until "money" ran out, and even that was not easy to figure out.

What money? I had some Angel Bakery shares that my father had passed on to me, for example. Was I willing to invest them in the scale project? Would I be willing to part with the house on the beach? Would I let the scale project drive me into the ground, or was there a point down the road when I would have to acknowledge that enough is enough? Would it not be wiser to give up some control over the project now and start looking seriously for OPM (Other People's Money)? Maybe working with my own money was a mistake to begin with? Spending my own money, I recalled, was what Tommy Heinsheimer, the disparaging mayor of Rolling Hills, warned me against.

With the fast-depleting resources at my disposal, I could not afford the scale splurge much longer. I had to economize simply because the threat of running out of cash was hanging over me. Harvey McKay, in his book *Beware the Naked Man Who Offers You His Shirt*, articulates this threat in simple, unambiguous terms:

> I attended a seminar on entrepreneurship taught by a Harvard Business School professor who told us the ten things he tries to teach students who want to be entrepreneurs. First thing on the list was 'Don't run out of cash.' The last thing on the list was 'Don't run out of cash.' And I'd have to say whatever the eight were in between, you really only have to remember the first and the last one.

I lived with that threat, aware and respectful of it, yet admittedly not bothering to think too far ahead. A familiar shudder of cash-flow anxiety would spiral through my spine from time to time with little or no lasting effect. To be honest, I was not respectful enough of the cash-flow menace, and the money kept running freely through my fingers.

* * *

I called Albert Brendel at Sensor Developments, his company, on 20 February. The next day, on the Northwest Airlines flight to Detroit, I wrote:

> I explained that we were in the process of debugging a load cell and that we had problems. He was willing to help but said the help was expensive—$1,000 a day. He asked me to send him drawings and test results by fax, offering to spend a day over a week and come up with some answers over the next two weeks. I told him I faced a crucial decision. I asked if I could fax the material immediately and come to see him today. He agreed.
>
> I am on my way. Unfortunately, the weather is not so good. The plane departed at 10:15 instead of 7:50. I won't get there for lunch, but that's OK. The flight cost $480. Ground transportation probably another $100. Three hours with Brendel—$375. $900. That feels OK. . . . If Brendel can tell us why our [stainless] steel does not work or why we have hysteresis, we will have saved a lot more than $900.
>
> What crucial decision am I facing? Well, I cannot really let go of the [folded-wrench] design. At most, I am willing to proceed in parallel, testing the two designs together. But I admit to being quite attached to it. It is elegant, and I have

a feeling it will work even if it is not supposed to work. I am willing to listen to Brendel. He may point out why it does not work, but then I shall have to get it to work.

I rented a car at the Detroit airport and drove slowly north on a freeway covered with fresh snow. The village of Lake Orion, population 3,000, was just slightly beyond the northern edge of the Detroit metropolitan area. Sensor Developments was housed in a modern, square, squat, and indistinct industrial building, a freestanding structure in the middle of . . . not much. The work at Sensor Developments centered, not surprisingly, on the development of new sensors for the Detroit automotive industry, but then branched out to more generic sensors for any and all industries. During the time of my visit, for example, they were testing, calibrating, and sorting load cells for measuring the weight of a bedridden patient. The hospital bed itself was to be transformed into a scale, by suspending the flat part of the bed at each of its four corners on load cells that were attached to the bedposts.

Albert Brendel was a big and overweight man in his sixties, with thin-rimmed glasses and a white goatee beard, and, as for attitude, I would say almost cuddly. He exuded a Midwestern niceness that was simpler, ingrained, and much more natural than the run-of-the-mill business civility of the coasts. Been in the load cell business since the late 1950s, he said. Our talk—not as planned, but as expected—focused entirely on the failures of the folded-wrench design, and I never once mentioned the possibility of abandoning it and going back to the hook design.

I showed Brendel our latest folded-wrench prototype and explained to him that we could not get rid of the unacceptably high levels of hysteresis it exhibited under load: the readings for a 100-pound load when we added weights on the scale were significantly lower than the readings for a 100-pound load when we removed weights, and we didn't know why. He looked at our data sheets—much like a doctor looks at the results of lab tests—and confirmed, in no uncertain terms, that the reasons for the hysteresis were the unaccounted-for friction forces at the top and bottom flanges of the center I-beam, where it began to touch the top and bottom beams. These forces reduced the load when the main beam was loaded, he explained, and increased the load when it was unloaded.

To this day I do not understand his patient explanation, despite the sketch he drew to illustrate it. Two things were clear to me, though. One, there was not a shadow of doubt in his mind that the friction forces he identified were the source of our problems with the latest designs. And two, these friction forces tormented us only because we had several layers of metal parts attached to each other and no matter what we did to fasten these layers together, they moved away from each other—however minutely—under load.

On my way back from Detroit and through the sleepless night that followed, I toyed with the idea of getting rid of those nasty friction forces altogether, by having the load cell made from one flat piece of steel. I envisioned all the beams on a single plane, in a sort of double-anchor arrangement. One anchor would be wider and the other one would be narrower, so that they would fit into each other. The middle beam would connect the centers of the two anchors together. In diagrammatic terms, what I was thinking of is illustrated in Fig. 45.

The double anchor would simply flex into an S-shape under load, as any other hook or Z-clip load cell. This is illustrated in the following figure. In this figure, the wide anchor is connected to the scale plate through a pair of thin washers. The narrow anchor is connected to a flat round plate, also through a pair of thin washers. There is a spherical rubber foot under the thin round plate. When the plate is under load, it presses down on the wide anchor, along the middle line of the load cell. The floor below responds with an equal and opposite force. That force is centered at the middle of the load cell, and it pushes the narrow anchor up. The middle beam now flexes into an S-shape, with one strain gage in tension and one in equal and opposite compression (Fig. 46).

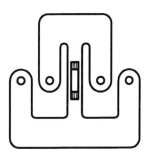

45 *A diagrammatic sketch of the double-anchor load cell*

By early morning, I had a sketch drawn up, and I faxed it to Brendel. He faxed back a drawing with a suggested slight modification a few hours later, a modification that did not challenge the basic idea at all. But other than that, he did not write me anything. The fact that he did not say it would not work was enough for me. I read his silence as an acknowledgment that I was on the right track. Deadline or no deadline, a new prototype was in the making.

* * *

Right around that time, as though to taunt me personally, a book by Jane Hirschmann and Carol Munter entitled *Overcoming Overeating* was published. That book advanced the simple thesis that people get fat not because of what they eat, but because they eat too much. It suggested, for example, that instead of going on an aggressive diet, simply giving up on second helpings at meals would be enough to keep one trim. It recommended that people forswear

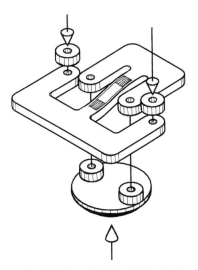

46 *The double-anchor load cell under load*

dieting (thus avoiding the binging that inevitably follows it) and instead learn to eat in moderation.

I found that line of argument and the research supporting it very appealing. Even though the only diet I ever tried was eating green apples and only green apples for five days in a row (and quickly losing a few pounds that I quickly gained back), I swore right then and there never to diet again.

Eating in moderation? Now that was much more difficult. By then, although still calling the Chelsmore my home, I was sharing my evening meals with Lucinda and her children at the SoHo loft. She cooked exquisite meals day in and day out, and I found it impossible not to help myself to second and third helpings. We were also gradually discovering the infinite variety of delicacies in New York's restaurants, and I could rarely resist ordering too many dishes. In short, I blame the beauty, the aroma, and the savor of the food put in front of me for my repeated failures to apply these lessons more effectively.

Lucinda herself had no visible trouble eating in moderation. It was easier when the food placed in front of her was tasteless or unattractive, she confessed. But even a sumptuous meal had a limited attraction for her, compared to the attraction of her size-eight wardrobe. Lucinda was never so entranced with the food placed in front of her to become oblivious to two relevant realities that were not present in the here and now—the inevitable bloating after a heavy meal, and the way she looked to herself in the mirror, with or without her clothes. With those two fierce images standing guard over her, she effortlessly resisted overeating. And on the rare occasion that she did eat too much—when her defenders were lax or when she allowed them a short leave—she ate less than usual on following days to make up for it.

My own difficulty with *Overcoming Overeating*—over and above not being able to follow its advice—was that it also recommended tossing away the bathroom scale as an act of rebellion against weight watching:

> Every day, millions of people allow their bathroom scales to determine their general outlook. Most of us who live in a fat-phobic culture are addicted to the scale. When our weight is high, we feel low; when it's low, we feel high. . . . If you are earnest about accepting yourself, the scale must go. Simply put, the scale is the most powerful symbol of nonacceptance in your life. It measures and it judges. . . . When you get rid of your scale once and for all, you are basically saying, "I won't allow the numbers on that scale to continue to torment me." . . . Once you get rid of the scale your vision will become more acute. . . . Without the scale you can see how things really fit. . . . You can feel for yourself if your clothing is too loose or too tight.

I read that as a critique of my project and one that required a response. "They suggest that 'the scale is the most powerful symbol of nonacceptance in your life,'" I wrote in my diary. "Quite an assertion. But getting rid of harmless inanimate objects is only symbolic, pitting one symbol against another. The scale is not a judge. It gives you feedback, and if it is accurate, it gives you honest feedback."

The scale, to be sure, dehumanized one's weight, as well it should have. It turned it into an abstract and objective quantity that was uncompromising, no longer raising any question whether it was a fair or an unfair assessment. "Traditional measures," writes Witold Kula in *Measures and Men*, "were 'human' in many respects. They were expressive of man and his work. They depended at times upon his will, which in turn depended upon his character and attitude toward fellow humans. Yet, at the same time, traditional measures offered endless opportunities for abuse and acts of injustice."

Surely, one could decide that there was no need for an accurate measurement of one's weight; that all one needed was a rough measure, say, of how tight one's pants were. But, just as traditional measures were subject to abuse in commercial transactions, informal measures of one's weight were subject to abuse through various forms of denial and compromise. Pants felt tight sometimes, and that feeling was subject to a great deal of autosuggestion: it would be very hard to gage accurately whether pants felt tighter today than yesterday or the day before. And a leather belt could remain fastened on the same hole for a long time—day in and day out—before one made the political decision to move to the next hole. The numbers on an accurate scale did not allow that kind of latitude.

There was probably still some primitive resistance to measuring oneself anyway, and in that sense *Overcoming Overeating* may have struck a hidden chord. In olden days, to count and measure was a sin. "Among the Czechs, at the end of the eighteenth century" writes Witold Kula, "a belief was prevalent that a child under six years of age would cease growing, become stunted, a 'measureling,' if the cloth intended for his shirt or outer garment was measured. Taking a man's measure, or the measure of some part of his body, invests him with symbolic and ambivalent significance." Maybe measuring oneself still made one somewhat ill at ease.

There was no question that one did not need to weigh oneself compulsively. That made sense to me. One should not do anything compulsively.

By extension [I wrote in my diary after reading *Overcoming Overeating*], having a portable scale that one can take along on vacation or business trips is catering to this compulsion. Leaving the scale at home would be an act of rebellion, running away from the restraint of day-to-day dieting to the vacation binge.

This suggests to me that somehow the attitude towards weight watching is wrong. Weight watching should tell you something about yourself, give you an objective measure of your body. That is all. It is not something to deride or to run away from. It can indeed promote awareness, without judging. It can tell you what makes you gain weight and what makes you lose weight. It need not be threatening. It can make you feel comfortable with some truth about yourself.

I'd hate to think that by putting the scale on the market, I am catering to yet another human compulsion. But let's face it. This is and always will be an unnecessary luxury, unless one day I get UNICEF to distribute these scales to health workers in developing countries. But let us not be naïve. This is not a "do-gooder" project. It has no social merit whatsoever. Just another novelty item among millions of others.

Have you no better problem to occupy your mind with? [I asked myself]. No. I don't, not now. I am quite happy to do something unimportant, something no one else needs and no one else told me to do. Why not? There is room for all of us here, and all our machinations. This little scale seems quite harmless, and may possibly even be conducive to some awareness of some body. So it is not on the list of the world's top priorities. For me it is. In fact, for me not having to worry about the world's priorities is a priority.

Still, even if it was not a global priority, the question of whether the thin scale was contributing to or detracting from human welfare did matter to me. I willingly accepted Victor Papanek's claim, in his book *Design for the Real World*, that "[the designer's] social and moral judgment must be brought into play long *before* he begins to design, an a priori judgment at that, as to whether the products he is asked to design or redesign merit his attention at all. In other words, will his design be on the side of the social good or not."

I would be the first to admit that the pursuit of the thin scale was frivolous, and at best a metaphoric quest in search of a deeper understanding of the design and invention process itself. The choice of the thin scale as an object that merited my attention was therefore a random choice, devoid of any deeper meaning. Any other object, as long as it passed the "do no harm" test, would have done as well.

As an object, the thin scale will never satisfy a basic human need, like food, clothing, shelter, or medicine. It was quite possible that my justification for pursuing it was primarily as a respite from the shelter problem. I could probably indulge in this respite for a while longer, I thought, but I doubted that I could spend a lifelong "career" designing frivolous objects, novelties, and other unnecessities.

I do have a soft spot for Papanek and his interminable admonitions, accusing industrial designers of being reckless and irresponsible when they submit designs that are criminally unsafe, wasteful, useless, harmful to the planet, and dishonest. "No longer does the artist, craftsman or in some cases the designer operate with the good of the consumer in mind," he laments; "rather, many creative statements have become highly individualistic, autotherapeutic little comments by the artist to himself."

The word *autotherapeutic* rang true to me: I did consider this work a form of personal healing in more than one way and maybe even a private comment to myself. As time went on, however, the thin scale became a more serious object, not as frivolous as it was at the outset. I became more enthralled by the idea of placing a beautiful precision instrument in the hands of common people. And although I did not think that this was a noble cause, I felt it was noble enough for me.

In short, the big picture remained clear enough through these difficult months, and the chains of inferences from the large to the small robust enough, for me to focus on the particular obstacles that I encountered along the way. I was stuck, and to move on I needed a cheap and accurate load cell. That much was clear.

* * *

Accuracy apart, the load cell I was searching for would meet its strict cost target only if it were manufactured intelligently at the minimum possible cost. In early 1989 I had already begun corresponding with two firms—Kratos Dinamometros in São Paulo and Scaling Instruments in Taipei—asking for quotes that I could send Philips. I explained in my faxes that I would supply them with metal parts for load cells in large quantities—up to one million units per year—and that I needed them to bond pairs of gages to the load cells, wire them, test them, and sort them. I specified the kind of gage pattern we needed, but I did not include drawings of the metal parts yet. They were not ready.

José Luis Azevedo of Kratos Dinamometros came to New York for two days in early March to discuss a price quotation and to work out a business arrangement between Libra, my company, Paramount, Amos's company, and Kratos, his company, for supplying load cells to Philips. We—Charlie, Amos, and I—met him in a plush conference room at Rockefeller Center in mid-Manhattan. That conference room was in a fancy suite of venture capital offices that an old classmate of mine occupied. It seemed like the right place for doing the kind of business we hoped to engage in. Charlie, for one, did not look at all comfortable in a jacket and tie and was clearly out of his element. His element was the great outdoors, and he much preferred checkered flannel shirts, crumpled if you please.

A good-looking Brazilian beau in his mid-forties—trim, impeccably dressed in a well-tailored suit, easygoing, well-traveled, and clearly comfortable in the company of others—José Luis arrived at the venture capital offices on a crisp March morning, full of enthusiasm and ready to do business.

We showed him the prototypes we had for the first time. He liked the concept and the designs, and he was excited about the possibilities for collaboration. Kratos was a family business, he explained. They started out 25 years ago making load-testing machines. They then moved into making their own load cells for the machines; then into the load cell business; then into making strain gages for their load cells; and finally into the strain gage business. They were now the biggest load cell manufacturer in Latin America, he said, with a factory outside São Paulo employing some 350 people. José Luis was the load cell and machine designer; his brother Mario was the electronics man.

After exploring the possible manufacturing sequences for the load cells, we zeroed in on a joint venture arrangement between Libra, Paramount, and Kratos. This led to a series of extended bargaining sessions that lasted for two days. We ended up agreeing to send Philips a firm quote of $1.79 per load cell. Late on the second day of our negotiations, Amos agreed to 33¢ for the metal parts, José Luis agreed to $1.30 for the gages, and I agreed to 17¢ as my share for putting together this venture. "There was a penny left and no one was willing to come down anymore," I wrote in my diary on 7 March. I finally relented, but I resolved to have someone bargain on my behalf next time we discussed prices. There was sure to be a next time.

Considering that commercial load cells cost more than 100 times that price, this quote was not to be scoffed at. At a dinner in Cambridge a few days later, my friend Bill Alonso commented on the fact that "today it is not surprising to hear of someone seeking a cost reduction of two orders of magnitude, for example from $150 to $1.50—they are trying it with chips, solar cells, probably many other sophisticated technologies." We were not yet at $1.50, but I thought $1.79 was close enough, being—to use Bill's term—of the same order of magnitude.

Philips did not think so. The diary entry from 28 March read:

Two faxes and a phone call from Beets. The $1.79 offer not acceptable. He saw a Soehnle scale with four load cells at the Cologne Fair in February. It sells for DM180 ($100). They took it apart. It has four aluminum load cells with strain gages on top of them, machined I suppose. The fax says: "We stopped the project of a bathroom scale with four prototypes pending receipt of your load cell samples. . . . We are looking for alternatives." I asked Beets about the alternatives— he meant basically following the Soehnle approach. Well, the others are catching up with me. Good. We have to move faster. The problem: will the present proto- types meet expectations? We are under pressure to deliver, but we are not yet ready. We might fail. Yes, we might. Such is life. Anyway, we know where we stand. $1.50 and no more. . . . There is already a consumer scale with four load cells on the market and for some reason it feels right. Others are moving in the same direc- tion. It seems all the more real.

In the hectic weeks that followed, we went through several design prototypes of the double-anchor load cell, while advancing the hook design halfheartedly at the same time. I developed the design I had sent Brendel into a more robust load cell and drafted it in early March. This design was still predicated on keeping the thickness of the metal part at one-sixteenth of an inch, so that it could be stamped in a common metal press. This required bending the anchors along their outer edges to make them stronger (Fig. 47). It took until the end of March to finalize this design.

By that time, Amos had let me in on another trade secret: wire cutting. There was a machine that could cut through several inches of steel with a high degree of precision, I learned, by discharging electrical sparks through a very thin verti- cal wire that moved along a prescribed path at the rate of several inches per hour. This process, Electrical Discharge Machining (EDM), was introduced in the early 1970s, and was used for—among other things—making tool and die sets for plastic molding. Amos suggested that I take a diskette with a CAD (Computer-Aided Design) drawing of the new load cell to his friend Ron Leone at Intricate Stampings in Paterson, New Jersey, with a stack of one-sixteenth-inch steel plates bolted together. Ron, he said, could cut right through the stack.

I drafted the double-anchor design on Amos's computer and I drove out to Paterson, New Jersey—the proud hometown of the hilarious slapstick comic Lou Costello of "Who's On First" fame—on the morning of 27 March. Ron and his brother had recently taken over their father's old business and modernized it. It did not look at all like Paramount Die and Metal. Old Bob at Paramount was either not interested or not capable of modernizing his father's business. In contrast to the tired old presses at Paramount, beautiful new machines colonized Intricate, all being fed computer drawings. "The precision is astounding," I wrote in my diary that evening. "He talks about 15 parts per million."

"Things are moving along, and I am in a clear and unclouded frame of mind," I continued.

> I need to keep the ball rolling, keep Philips informed of developments, keep the price negotiations going, and move ahead with the testing. The testing—that is the real confrontation with reality. When I have a new design it always "looks" so good that I fall in love with it, and pray it works. When it does not work, I fall out of love with it and start looking for a new design that would eliminate whatever is wrong with the old one. But, needless to say, I am drawn to the visual aesthetics of these little metal parts, the curves, the symmetries, the cleanliness of the design. I am searching for some natural beauty that works (sometimes introducing a symmetry when it need not really be there, I confess). . . . Anyway, for now we have a

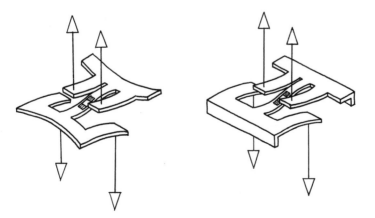

47 *The double-anchor under load without bending the edges of the anchors (on left) and with bending them (on right)*

new design for a one-piece load cell—the most beautiful one to date. It will be ready for testing in a few days, then we shall know whether its beauty is deep or superficial.

All the while during this difficult period, my mind wandered from the very intricate to the very broad, from the minute deflections of beams under load to the wide-ranging reflections on whether or not I had lost my bearings. Some of these reflections were articulated at the time in my correspondence with my friend Peter Swan, a tall, white-bearded Australian who came to Bangkok roughly at the time I did—back in 1973—to study Buddhism, and made the place his home. On 1 April I wrote Peter a letter, describing my state of mind at the time. I reproduce parts of it here:

> I have been wanting to write you for the past few days, after reading an essay by Umberto Eco called simply "Form as Social Commitment." Eco explains Hegel thus:
> "The moment man objectifies himself in the works he has created, and in the nature he has modified, he produces an inevitable tension. The two poles of such a tension are, on the one hand, his domination of the object, and, on the other hand, his total dissolution in the object, his total surrender to it. . . . Thus, alienation would seem to be an integral part of every relationship one establishes with others and with things. . . . We produce a machine and then the machine oppresses us with an inhuman reality that renders the relationship we have with it, and with the world through it, disagreeable. . . . To paraphrase Hegel, man cannot remain locked up in himself, in the temple of his own interiority: he must externalize himself in his work and, by doing so, alienate himself in it."
> I have become aware of some moments of intense suffering in my pursuit of the scale and the load cells—those little sensors that make it work. To realize it, I have had to become it, to breathe it, to dream it (my sleep is lighter and more disturbed than before). When the load cells fail to perform—I become insecure. Test results have been negative for months—failure after failure after failure.
> I look at myself: I am not as happy as I was before. The product manager from Philips says maybe they'll buy from someone else—I feel lonely and rejected. The parts I need are not ready. Why? The Polish workers at the stamping factory are quarrelling because the older one does not understand English, and he loses face every time there is a misunderstanding and a younger one stands by and translates. It has nothing to do with me but I feel I am being neglected.
> I can see it happening. Yes, I have committed myself to realizing the scale. Yes, I have committed myself to delivering the load cells. I shall do whatever needs to get done. I shall go wherever it takes me. I shall spend all the money I have to get it done. I am free to do it and I can sense that freedom. Yet it enslaves me, chains me to the object. I can leave, I know, but not now. I shall leave one day, I tell myself. I shall get tired of it all and leave, like I left the "Building Together" project, like I left

the Asian Institute of Technology. But not yet, no. For now I have to persist, to persevere. This is my present mental state. Moreover, I believe that it is a necessary
state. . . .

As you already know I have always pursued "projects." I am always involved in
some project or another, usually totally involved. "Project," even the word implies
projecting oneself into something else, losing oneself in a thing. . . . I pursued projects with a mixture of optimism and pessimism—seeking quality and success
while knowing that decay and destruction inevitably set in. Back to Eco: "The
availability to the world . . . is fundamental because it allows us to commit ourselves to the world and to act in it. But the fear that accompanies our every dealing
with the world, and the awareness that our adjustment could turn out to be a failure are also essential. . . ."

I keep getting hurt again and again. I hurt for a while (to see what hit me, at
least) and then I let go. It is tiring, but I endure with a smile, integrating more and
more of it into my worldview, and renewing my commitment to remain open.
Reject nothing, I say to myself, and hang on to nothing either. I let go of the
thoughts and the feelings as they pass by, but I continue to hang on to the task at
hand, doing whatever is necessary to accomplish it in the most wholesome and
beautiful way. . . .

My father called me from Jerusalem on 28 April and at some point in the conversation said to me: "Stay in your profession!" This was not said in anger, nor
was it a command, but maybe there was some frustration in his voice, as
though his own "project" would never be completed until all his children were
properly settled down. "He obviously thinks that tinkering in other people's
field is 'bad,' and that one should stay in one's own field," I wrote in my diary
the next day. "But then, to say the least, we have always had different percep-
tions of risk."

Hearing "stay in your profession" is not what I would call a supportive statement
these days, [I continued]. But I cannot complain—support is not lacking. . . . How
far have I strayed from my profession? . . . What is my profession? Planning? Management? Design? Teaching? Writing? Research? No wonder my father, who settled
in his office in downtown Jerusalem some 40 years ago and still looks at the world
from that perspective, finds it so difficult to sympathize.

What is it about my "moving" from one field to another? Is it restlessness? Not
really. Dissatisfaction? I don't think so. More like exhausting it, getting the point
and then moving onwards. There is no disenchantment, no rejection, just tiredness and a feeling that the insights have been exhausted. I stay there long enough
to get my work done at a "respectable" enough standard, and then I move on.

Do I plan to do the same with the scale story? Probably. Learn a bit about technology, business, production, marketing, electronics, and the people that inhabit

those fields and move on. Maybe eventually I'll get tired and then I'll stay in one place longer, get more deeply involved, seek more and more subtle refinements. Maybe, and maybe not.

Peter Swan wrote back from Nairobi on 7 May:

> Your letter brought me up to date with your pursuit of your present project—the scale—the "sensors"—and, more importantly, your pursuit of your 'self'. . . . I note that your pursuit of this project, which has become bogged down in defeat and uncertainty for the moment, has brought some pain, some unhappiness: "I look at myself. I am not as happy as I was before!"
>
> Your ability to pursue one project solely, to the subordination of all others, is an ability I do not share. I have found this kind of obsession in very few of my close friends and colleagues over the years. It has occurred to me so often in recent years that my achievements in film or whatever will never rise above the middling because I lack this ability. Perhaps it is only when I tie my efforts to someone else's efforts and vision and ambition . . . that I can participate in the predicament that you describe in your letter.
>
> But another dimension to this experience mentioned by Eco is "the awareness that our adjustment could turn out to be a failure." And it occurs to me that you rarely fail in the pursuit of whatever project because you dare not fail—something that holds your self-confidence together instinctively eschews failure. . . .
>
> You asked me to comment on the scale affair and how I see you in it. In certain respects it is your boldest venture to date, moving into a field that is highly technical from what was fundamentally an aesthetic impulse—as I recall a random observation about the ugliness of the bathroom scale at your house. In other respects it is an absurd departure from the main body of your endeavour to date. . . . It lacks the social or psychological (spiritual) significance of much of your earlier activity.
>
> At best it can bring you some kind of ego-gratification that you can succeed in whatever you turn your mind to plus a lot of money. Maybe there is more to be learned from the cycle of disenchantment that you are currently experiencing.

I replied to Peter's letter on 29 May 1989:

> By the time I received your letter my mood had of course changed. I have often found that the need to write is associated with the lower moods, another source of error when one tries to create truth. . . .
>
> My friend Mo from Berkeley, who read parts of the Scale Diary, said he did not see the scale as something "important" enough to pursue, echoing your comment on its lack of social and spiritual significance. Not as exciting as the diary of the scientists who discovered the double helix structure of the DNA, he said. I agree.
>
> In the past, in my pursuit of socially important projects—from organizing

parties to combat assignments, from working with the poor to campus politics—I was always attracted by the privileges these projects bestowed. People had to make way for me, for I was doing something useful. Fair enough, and a high cost to pay for whatever privileges were attached to these pursuits, mostly respect, prestige, freedom from authority, and minor material comforts.

I was, after all, brought up in the socialist youth movement in Israel in the early idealistic years of the young state. In that environment one sought the approval and respect of one's peers, and such approval was ideologically linked to community service of some sort. For me as an individual there was no choice. To pursue my personal objective of "privilege" in a very egalitarian environment, I had to get involved in "approved" pursuits. But, believe me, I never really liked this enslavement to other people's approval. . . .

Thailand was the first place I found where nobody really seemed to care, but by that time the approval function was well internalized.

Eventually one comes to ask oneself who is it that determines "significance"? Not only that, one comes to realize that by throwing oneself wholeheartedly into a pursuit, whatever it may be, one lends it significance. Significance is created, not predetermined, even the so-called social significance.

The scale project exists only because I approve of it, only because I make it significant. I am attracted to it precisely because it does not have social significance (yet), not because I am averse to "society," not at all, but because it frees me from the enslavement to the "given" social mores I do not necessarily share. There was a bumper sticker in Berkeley that said, "If you want to die for a cause, make sure it's your own cause." I don't know that the scale is a "good" cause, but I do know that it is "my" cause. It fits my criteria for a cause. In this sense this project is a rebellion against respectable established causes of the common variety that I pursued before, notably championing the cause of our poor brethren in the cities of the Third World. . . .

Is it my failure to be as effective as I had hoped to be in Third World housing that had led me to it? Is it my frustration at not being able to influence events there? No, not at all. I can't complain. I have had the honor to become one of the more respected scholars and experts in this field, and I have provided inspiration for many practitioners. I may still have a role to play there. But I am not interested.

Is it just tiredness? I must confess that as an academic field housing is very slow and uneventful: rarely does anything interesting get written, let alone done. There must be more interesting pursuits out there. . . . But that is not a reason to leave the field either: one can always move sideways instead of breaking away completely. But somehow every path I think of moving along feels tiresome somehow: uneventful.

To tell you the truth, my friend, I really don't know what happened. Something gave, something snapped. My energies evaporated and my heart was no longer there. . . .

And then the scale problem simply presented itself to me, winked at me a few times from the sidelines. But it winked at me alone. I did not expect anyone else to join me, to get excited about it. I decided to proceed alone. That too was "significant." For many years I needed others to join in—coauthors, partners, associates, assistants. This time I felt I could "go it alone" (in the meantime I of course met many people who chipped in and shared my work, my worries, and the potential for success).

I could elaborate further, but you may fill in the details yourself. This is a "significant" project because it is significant for me. But is it significant for anyone else? Will it be significant if I fail, or does it have to succeed to be significant? I don't know. Is it significant for you to hear or read about it? Are there important lessons for you in this story? Can I make it significant for you and for others? Do I have to? Can I remain silent and not bother? . . .

Why struggle at all, one may ask? Makes for a more interesting story I guess, knowing as well as you do that there is nowhere to get to, nothing to attain except liberation from the desire to attain. And this desire is not likely to be attenuated whether one struggles or whether one gives up the struggle, so one has no choice but to be oneself. Warriors fight and so I fight. And in the fight there is great peace, so I rarely walk away from it. And sometimes walking away is the courageous path and then one hopes to be able to walk away fighting.

* * *

The Scale Diary entry of 18 June 1989 read:

Last scene of *Indiana Jones and the Last Crusade*. Ninety minutes of noisy excitement have gone by. Now the earth is cracking and moving. Indiana Jones is hanging over a precipice within an inch of retrieving the Holy Grail, but if he stretches any longer he will fall to his certain death. His father (Sean Connery) is holding his one free hand and is losing his grip. He calls for Indi to give him the other hand. No reply. Suddenly there is dead silence and Connery says in a wonderful paternal, considerate, and inviting voice: "Indiana, let go." Indi gives him the other hand and saves his life. They ride into the sunset without the Holy Grail.

It touched me somehow. This kind of letting go is different from giving up, from turning one's back to one's enterprise, from surrender. This kind of letting go has a Buddhist character to it. Hubert Benoit's classic book on Zen Buddhism is called *Let Go*. What it means is that the obsessive attachment to an object distorts one's perception of reality, and makes one vulnerable to making serious mistakes. Only detachment allows consciousness all the room it needs to make the right choice, the wholesome choice, the beautiful choice.

The pursuit of this thin scale cannot but have this character. Obsessive attachment to making it happen quickly, wanting it badly until it hurts will simply not do. Running quickly does not really help if one does not know the way. The issue here is not "getting there first," for which one needs to run fast, but rather "getting there," for which one needs to conserve energy and go the distance. The danger is not being overtaken by others, but burning out before reaching the goal. Patience and perseverance are the required qualities, not short bursts of energy followed by tiredness and frustration. Letting go of the gripping pull of obsession allows consciousness in, and it is in that purer light of consciousness that the path is revealed.

The first version of the double-anchor load cell with the wide wings let us down too. Initially, when we tested a single load cell, it gave promising results in the now familiar tests of nonlinearity and hysteresis. But then we found it to be sensitive to the tightness of the screws that fastened it to the scale plate. When we tightened these screws, the load cell became less sensitive and produced a lower voltage output for the same load. That was a distressing discovery. It meant that we could not keep the four load cells on a scale to the same level of sensitivity, and that promised errors in cornering or eccentric loading tests.

If that was not bad enough, when we assembled four double-anchor load cells into a ten-by-ten-inch prototype scale, we had yet another letdown. We placed a load cell at each corner of a quarter-inch-thick aluminum plate—fastening the wide anchor to the plate with screws (over some thin off-the-shelf washers). Then we placed a plate of exactly the same dimensions (over some thin washers) on top of the four load cells and fastened the narrow anchor to that plate with screws.

It turned out that the whole assembly was too rigid. The top plate, deflecting under load, pulled the narrow anchor toward its center. The bottom plate remained flat, keeping the wide anchor in place and not allowing it to move towards the center. The pull on the load cells created nasty horizontal forces that affected the readings in strange ways. That was inadmissible, and it destroyed accuracy completely.

The lesson for the next design? Only one plate—either the top plate or the bottom plate—could be rigidly connected to the load cells; they should be allowed to slide freely (however minutely) toward the center of the scale plate when it deflected under load, coming to a rest at a place where no horizontal forces still pulled at them. How could I have known that in advance? Was that written anywhere?

In theory, at least, the double-anchor design should have worked. "In the mind of the theorist, this is a simple load cell," I wrote in my diary on 19 June.

[It's] trivial in fact. Getting it to work in practice just requires experimentation and persistence. It should work: therefore, any good engineer should be able to get it to work. How he [or she] does it is immaterial and uninteresting—there is no new theory involved. It follows that good practical people are interchangeable, somehow situated below the theorists. Berkeley had that message broadcast so loudly, it veered me violently into more and more theoretical pathways. My doctoral thesis is so theoretical, I simply cannot follow the mathematics anymore.

Over the years, my interest in getting theory to work has grown. I had to stop writing about housing policy and actually carry out a housing project. I found reality so much more surprising, so much richer, and so much more interesting than the theories about it. . . . Practical know-how is so vast compared to theory because it is so specific. There is already so much I know about this scale of mine, and so much that I still don't know.

This, then, is design [I wrote on 21 July]. We try to find a form "at rest," one that provides answers to all the problems that have manifested themselves. Then we slowly discover others that have not manifested themselves, and we keep making corrections. This is why "forms that work" have so many details we cannot understand. They are responses to practical problems that have arisen when the forms were initially put to use.

The theory is so simple. The basic principles are almost trivial. It is making the form "insensitive" to forces that are not part of the basic theory that is so difficult. The theory assumes that so many parameters remain constant. The form has to ensure that they do. Clamping should not make a difference, but it does. Dirt between plates does. Heat treatment of the metals does. Expansion of rivets does. Hole size does. Everything does, apparently. And this is why R&D takes so long.

Beginner's luck, that's what these initial load cells were last August. They simply worked. We did everything right without even knowing it. And I was foolish enough to think that I could make all kinds of changes without losing accuracy. How innocent.

The failure of the latest experiment with the double-anchor load cells brought me to despair, convincing me that—at least for now—we were still too far from getting it to work. I fell back on the hook load cell—now made of two thin strips of steel riveted together—just so we would have something to send Philips. We sent them a dozen hook prototypes in mid-July for them to test, but the load cell saga was by no means over. I could not yet let go.

I told you before that I did not feel very comfortable with the load cell I sent Philips [I wrote Lucinda in Israel on 24 August]. It was ugly, not very original, only marginally accurate, and too sensitive. Sent it anyway. . . . [Amos and I] had a heart-to-heart talk about the situation. He said things were getting too complicated. Too many operations: we punch the load cell. Send it out for heat treatment. Bring it back and grind it smooth. Send it out for plating. Bring it back for riveting. All for a few miserable cents. For the thin scale we need a spacer too. We have to punch it and then make counter-sink holes and then repeat all these operations. Depressing.

But, as the saying goes, every cloud has a silver lining. That heart-to-heart talk over dinner with Amos revealed to me that he never really insisted on one-sixteenth of an inch as the outer limit for the thickness of the metal. He preferred the metal to be as thin as possible, so that it could be easily punched from a metal strip. But it was simply a preference, rather than a do-or-die requirement. For all these months, I had assumed that I could not break that rule.

Releasing the stranglehold of that thickness constraint opened a door that I never before allowed myself to enter. A thicker load cell meant a thicker middle beam. A thicker middle beam could be longer, moving the gages further away from the screw holes and making the load cell less sensitive to the tightness of screws.

If the screw holes were far enough away from the middle beam, we would not have to worry about the friction forces that Brendel talked about. We could then use cheap off-the-shelf washers as spacers. In addition, a thicker load cell could be strong enough in the lateral direction too, so we would not have to bend its edges. In short, we could rid ourselves of all the troublesome bending that had been torturing us all these months. The load cell could simply be one flat piece of steel in the shape of a sturdy double anchor with no bending at all.

Months ago, I had accepted these two manufacturing requirements—the one-sixteenth-of-an-inch thickness requirement and the no-spacers requirement—pretty much on Amos's say-so, without ever really questioning them. It was not for me to question them because Amos embodied manufacturing for me. "Designing is a process of achieving consensus among participants with different 'interests' in the design," says Bucciarelli. "The process is necessarily social and requires the participants to negotiate their differences and construct meaning through direct, and preferably face-to-face, exchange." So it was that Amos's say-so chained me to these two requirements. It was his say-so that now released me from their grip as well. You could say that at that fateful dinner we simply rewrote the rules.

"I went back to the design I had when I came back from Brendel in Detroit," my letter to Lucinda continued:

> The one that looked like an I with its four corners bending in towards the center—the one-piece load cell. The one I had to leave because it was impractical. Too sensitive to off-center loads. With this new thickness, the main beam could be much longer and the strain gages far away from where the distortions were taking place.
>
> I faxed the design to Amos that same night and, as I already told you, he had a part ready that same Friday afternoon. I took it to Charlie. He tested it for nonlinearity and your favorite hysteresis and got excellent results. A day before yesterday he tested it for off-center loads. . . . It was quite insensitive. Now we are talking. This beauty does not need spacers at all. It can be punched from one single part. It does not need any riveting or grinding. (If we made it from stainless steel, it would need no plating either.) . . . It has a natural overload stop. It is thin enough to fit into the thin scale. . . . In short, I am in love again.

"Almost there," I wrote in my diary on 28 August.

> This "double-anchor" design is the culmination of all our efforts. It incorporates so much of what we have learned. . . . The double-anchor load cells have performed better than anything we had before. All of them, again and again. They are

good. They are very similar to each other, and they are very well behaved. Amos caught the excitement too. The prototypes are arriving faster and faster. One day, when Andrzej was sick, Amos worked with the milling machine the whole day to produce the bottom plate. Charlie kept saying linearity was "terrific," and using adjectives he had never used before. It was all going to work. It was all there. Simple. Symmetric. Easy to produce. We started talking about ordering a punch-and-die set from Ron Leone to make some real-world prototypes. But there was a part of me that held back from the celebration—wait for the test.

And indeed, the tests failed. "We should have known," said Amos yesterday. Yes, the whole assembly was too rigid. Anyway, my confidence has not been shaken. I already had fantasies of a transparent scale, one you could see the load cells through. I kept talking about "revolutionizing" the scale industry. Why not? If we had a simple load cell that could be mass-produced, the entire innards of scales could be taken out and replaced with four load cells. Any outer design would do. "Dream, dream, dream," sing the Everly Brothers.

We overcame the rigid connections problem in late September by using rubber grommets (sleeves) around one pair of screws, making it possible for the load cells to move slightly under load. That did it. The lateral forces pulling on the load cell disappeared. Charlie and I tested a scale prototype with four double-anchor load cells with rubber grommets. The error in nonlinearity was 1 to 2 parts in 10,000 and the error in hysteresis 2 to 3 parts in 10,000, best we had ever had. The maximum error in cornering—placing a 100-pound load at nine locations on the scale plate—was 65 grams, the lowest error we had ever had.

"That was it," I wrote on 26 September. "We are through. We have a load cell that works beautifully. I shook Charlie's hand and thanked him. . . . I called Amos and we laughed together. I called Lucinda and had tears in my eyes. I felt that all the air went out of my lungs in sighs. After so many errors and so many trials, it finally works. It is simple. Precise. Easy to make. I spent a few more minutes with Charlie discussing the final design of the next model. . . . I drew it up in the early hours of the evening."

In the new design, instead of the square perimeter of our earlier models, I now made the perimeter an octagon with rounded corners. We had learned earlier that it was best to place the load cells with their center beams along the diagonals of the scale plate, as far into the corners of the plate as possible. That would be easier with an octagonal shape than with a rectangular one. Thus was born the cat face load cell. It was thin enough to fit into a single-plate, quarter-inch scale, and it could also be used for the two-plate Philips scale. It was robust. And it got better and better as time went on, with minute adjustments that never required major modifications, because it was a *form at rest*.

During the previous 14 months, we had built and tested no less than a dozen prototypes, one after the other, at the average rate of one per month. Each one had to be conceptualized, designed, drawn up, machined, heat-treated, gaged (i.e., have strain gages bonded to it), wired, assembled into a scale, tested, and analyzed to determine why it failed and where.

That long sequence of frustrating failures gradually led me—by the nose, so to speak—to a novel and simple solution of the thin load cell problem. To those investigating the creative process, like Dean Keith Simonton, for example, it comes as no surprise: "Creativity is a consequence of sheer productivity. If a creator wants to increase the production of hits, he or she must do it by risking a parallel increase in the production of misses.... The most successful creators tend to be those with the most failures." Simonton makes failure a bit more palatable by speaking of a "parallel increase," thus refraining from pointing out that in typical creative ventures the ratio of the number of failures to the number of successes may be quite large. Is a 12 to 1 ratio of failures to successes typical?

The thin load cell problem was solved, that much was clear. The cat face was a simple and therefore cheap solution to that problem, one that could be easily copied unless I had some patent protection. Given that I had invested no less than 14 months of work and untold thousands of dollars in developing this design, I thought I deserved some protection.

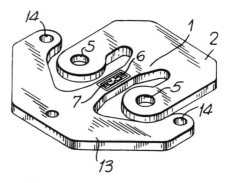

48 *The patent drawing for the cat face load cell*

With some pinpointed help from my patent lawyer—"I have just tinkered with the claim language to avoid possible rejections," Marc scribbled below his revisions to my draft—I composed a patent application for the cat face load cell (Fig. 48) in early November of 1989. It was entitled "A Mass-Produced Flat One-Piece Load Cell." The main claim read thus:

A low-profile load cell designed for mass production and comprising:
a. A one-piece configuration of flat mechanically deformable beams, comprising:
  1. A flat I-shaped flexure beam, possibly with a thinning midsection, on which electronic sensors are bonded;
  2. A flat U-shaped beam attached at its inner midsection to one side of the flexure beam with the two edges of the U-beam reaching beyond the midpoint of the middle beam; and
  3. A flat wider ... U-shaped beam attached at its inner midsection to one side of the I-shaped flexure beam ... [and so on].

My world had shrunk during these long months of incessant preoccupation with the minutiae of load cells. I could now escape that shrunken microcosm and survey the broader landscape. Communism, for one, was collapsing all around me and I had barely paid attention. For that matter, there were several other—admittedly less cataclysmic—developments on the scale front itself that had been vying for my attention for some time. The most troubling ones had to do with money.

15

In Pursuit of a Business Deal

People think of negotiating power as being determined by resources like wealth, political connections, physical strength, friends and military might. In fact, the relative negotiating power of two parties depends primarily upon how attractive to each is the option of not reaching agreement.

Roger Fisher and William Ury, *Getting to Yes*

If money makes you feel guilty because you don't feel like you deserve it, then it is difficult to increase your income, because if you did you would just feel more guilty. . . . Money is a topic that activates shame for everyone. People are ashamed they have so little or so much. When you are ashamed about money, no amount seems right.

Phil Laut, *Money Is My Friend*

_____

I had already started thinking seriously about the business angle of the scale endeavor back in early March of 1989, when José Luis was visiting New York from São Paulo to negotiate a price for supplying load cells to Philips. The reader may recall that at that time we ended up with an agreement on $1.79 per load cell, a price that Philips later rejected, insisting on the original $1.50 ceiling. While we were negotiating the price among ourselves, there was also some talk of forming a partnership between Paramount, Amos's company, and Kratos Dinamometros, José Luis's company, to supply Philips with load cells and to pay me royalties. Alternatively, Paramount would supply metal parts to Kratos, and Kratos would ship finished load cells to Philips and would pay me royalties. Both arrangements looked reasonable to me; I did not want to be directly involved in manufacturing anyway, and a royalty arrangement would suit me fine.

Amnon Shiboleth, my budding legal counsel on these and other business matters having to do with the scale, rejected these propositions out of hand. That surprised me, I must say. My brother Joe, who introduced me to him, assured me that, unlike other members of his much-maligned profession, Amnon was a deal maker rather than a deal breaker, and that he was very good at putting together business arrangements that worked. I expected him to simply formalize our arrangement by embedding it in a proper legal framework.

Amnon regularly played backgammon with Joe—usually at his own office—
and was a silent partner in Joe's newly established bagel production line in the
Broome Street bakery, the one near Caffè Roma in Little Italy. He was happy to
be of help to me, and he assured me that his help was free as long as Libra did
not have any income to speak of, which it certainly did not right then. It was
through his office that I registered Libra as a corporation, the first step I took in
convincing myself and prospective partners or investors that the scale was a real
business proposition and not just a toy.

Amnon, as a senior partner in a large law firm, occupied a plush corner office
on the sixtieth floor of the Empire State Building, overlooking the Hudson River
and the tall skyscrapers downtown. We met him there—Amos, José Luis, and I—
and explained the proposed business relationship vis-à-vis Philips. "Amnon simply disagreed," I wrote in my diary on 7 March. "He said: 'I am sorry but I will
have to strongly advise Solly against it.' He refused to have me out of the picture
and insisted on Philips' paying me for the load cells, and on my allocating the
money according to some agreed-upon instruction to the bank. José Luis
appeared very unhappy, making it clear that he expected to have a direct business relationship with Philips. Amnon insisted and I felt uncomfortable. Eventually José Luis relented and we left the office."

We never discussed this matter again, Amnon and I, but I understood without having to be told that I was too intent on pleasing everyone, even at my own
expense; that I needed protection; and that Amnon—who, no doubt, had the
demeanor as well as the vocabulary of a New York wise guy—could provide it
when necessary. Amnon was clearly one of those people that are good to have on
your side when you are putting together a deal. As President Lyndon Johnson
said of J. Edgar Hoover, the director of the FBI: "It's probably better to have him
inside the tent pissing out, than outside the tent pissing in."

* * *

A couple of weeks after the meeting at Amnon's office, my cousin Joe, passing
through New York, introduced me to his good friend Lorne Weil. Joe, like my
brother, was named after my grandfather on my mother's side, Joseph David
Farhi, a solid and respected businessman who thrived on the import of textiles
from Manchester to Beirut between the two world wars.

His ancestors, two Farhi brothers, were bankers who became ministers of
finance to the *pasha* (governor) of Damascus in the early 1820s, having enriched
themselves beyond measure by managing savings and loans for the *Hajj*—the
annual pilgrimage to the holy cities of Mecca and Medina. Their Moslem detractors accused them at the time of keeping official records in an obscure Hebrew-
based cipher, so as to make themselves indispensable to the governor, inscrutable
businessmen that they were. As far as I know, none of their business acumen
seems to have passed on to me, either by nature or by nurture.

My cousin Joe, in contrast, was clearly the direct descendent of one of the

Farhi brothers. He commuted between London, New York, and Los Angeles and was involved—in one way or another—in a wide range of exotic business ventures. He was very successful at doing business because, like the two Farhi brothers, he was very discreet. In fact, he was so discreet that I never found out the precise nature of any of his businesses. The diary entry of 18 March describes our early afternoon encounter with Lorne Weil:

Lorne Weil dresses casually and puts both his feet up on the round table of his rather disorderly office, a corner office on the eighteenth floor of a new skyscraper on Fifty-Seventh Street and Seventh Avenue surrounded by tall picture windows. You can see Central Park here and there.

Lorne Weil advises large corporations engaged in the electronics business. He has excellent connections in Hong Kong and Taiwan, and much experience in the scale business, having dealt with Hobart and Pencor before (who are they?). He uses rough language, coming across as straight and frank. My cousin Joe asks Lorne what he thinks about the thin scale. He and his associate, Bob, both think it is an excellent product. The question is how to launch it. We talk about the large companies in the scale business—there are only six, anyway. They know the people who make Borg scales. I mention Philips, and their U.S. subsidiary, Norelco. I tell them that the Norelco people visited Groningen, liked the scale, and said they were not interested because they were trying to get out of the scale business.

One way to launch it, they say, is to license it to a big manufacturer. Another is to start a company with sufficient capital to launch it. We talk of associated scales, a whole family of scales—for the kitchen (with a timer built in or with a scale built into a cutting board), for delis short of counter space, for letters, etc.

"One could buy the Norelco scale division," says Lorne. "Just what I was thinking," says my cousin Joe, and that strange New York feeling passes through my body. Here we are in the financial capital of the world, talking big. My brother, who drove me to the meeting, sells muffins and bagels to jobbers like Benny and Vinnie. "They pay cash every day," he says. "They don't talk big, they pay cash." Yes, true. But I came to New York in the first place to talk big. I liked the sound of it, getting hold of the Norelco scale division, letting go of the dead wood and the unprofitable practices and launching a new product line. Here I was in the midst of the "hostile takeover" world, where paper transactions decide the fate of workers and managers in unknown plants and offices somewhere. Where is Norelco, anyway?

"Well, they were nice to me," I wrote in my diary. "Lorne will think it over. He went skiing for a couple of weeks. We shall talk again."

We never did. I guess the hype level may have been a bit too high for me. I could see the attraction of this high-level matchmaking, though, bringing together idea people, money people, and production people to launch new ventures and make big things happen. Huge things. It surely was exciting, just possibly still a bit unreal for me. Much as I wanted to talk big, I was not there yet. I never did manage to make an offer, or to find someone crazy enough to make an offer on my behalf, to buy Norelco's scale division, and I have no idea what became of it.

It did cross my mind, though, that I did not rub shoulders with enough rich people, the kind of people who would be happy and willing to invest a few hundred thousands of dollars in a silent partnership with me in exchange for their participation in the scale saga, a saga that could certainly provide them with a ready-made topic to liven up their stodgy cocktail conversations, something more bizarre and more exotic, more *outré* if you will. Such a silent partnership—not so different from the one my brother Joe had with Amnon in the bagel venture—would certainly be most helpful to me, if only in providing the necessary flow of cash to finish the development of the thin scale; to establish the proper means to launch it, whatever these were; and to allow me to sleep more soundly at night, free of the haunting nightmare of running out of money.

But, come to think of it, even if willing silent partners materialized at my doorstep tomorrow, I was not yet prepared for them. The scale was, after all, a business proposition, not a charity. They would at least want to know what was in it for them, how much money they needed to put in, how much money they stood to make, and when they could expect to make it. That called for a business plan, the core of which was a cash-flow table showing how much money was needed when, how much money would flow in when, and how much of the money flowing in would be in profits. This much I understood. In fact, I was gradually assembling the numbers needed to construct such a table. Some really basic numbers were still missing, however, and it was still not clear whether there was any money to be made in this venture or not, let alone how much of it.

* * *

As more numbers started to come in over the following months, the original idea of a tripartite business arrangement between Kratos, Paramount, and Libra made less and less sense. First, there was an offer from Stephen Lee at Scaling Instruments in Taipei to do all the gaging, wiring, and testing of the load cell for $1—30¢ less than José Luis's last offer. Kratos was still in the game, but I could no longer see the point of a joint venture unless it could match Scaling's offer.

Second, there was an offer from W&H in Hauppage, Long Island, to supply finished metal parts for 25¢ a piece—8¢ less than Amos's last offer—using a much more accurate stamping process than the one employed at Paramount. It was actually Amos who went to a trade show and found out about this process, referred to as "fine blanking" in manufacturing jargon; "I talked myself out of a job," he said afterwards.

I called Stephen Lee one evening in early April of 1989 from my canopied bed at the Cambridge Bed and Breakfast—the place where I was staying overnight while teaching at MIT—to discuss his offer. He was surprised to get my call and hear to my story, he said; Philips had just asked him for a quotation on a four-load-cell scale with a 100-gram accuracy too. He had not yet replied because there were still too many unknowns for him to give Philips a real quotation. He told me in passing that Scaling Instruments now produced a million scales a year, mostly bathroom scales with 500-gram (1.1-pound) accuracy, for Counselor, Sunbeam, Sharp, Philips, and others. Most of their scales had the same innards, and his clients kept sending him different exterior designs every so often.

It was yet another instance of the separation between the working mechanism and the outward appearance of man-made objects that Victor Papanek deplores:

> [T]he vital working parts of a mechanism (the guts of a toaster, for instance) may remain unchanged for decades, while surface, finish, exterior embellishments, control mechanisms, skin color and texture undergo yearly mutations. This will be true even if the mechanism is faulty. . . . The 'skin' designers (Detroit's stylists) disdainfully avoid the 'guts' designers (engineers and research people); form and function are artificially split. But neither a creature nor a product can survive for long when its skin and guts are separate.

Stephen Lee understood that I was talking about new guts, not just a new skin, and was understandably worried about his ability to deliver load cells that were much more accurate than the ones he was used to making for his regular clients. As we got deeper into the intimate details of the processes involved, I got the sense that his $1 estimate might need to be revised upwards.

We met him, Amos and I, some eight months after that initial conversation, at his office in downtown Taipei. Taipei itself was not particularly charming or pleasant. The place was densely built, mostly with cheap construction methods and shoddy finishes. The streets, bustling with scooters and lined with vendors, were full of grave people going about their business. This was not Thailand, the land of smiles. Their faces were too somber, and their movements too rigid. What was even more disconcerting to me was that they all seemed to have lost their aesthetic sensibilities. Everything—the clothes, the trinkets, the furniture, and the buildings—appeared to be purposely gross and harsh, as if beauty and elegance no longer mattered in the least. "The treasures in the National Museum stand in great contrast," I wrote in my diary on 7 January 1990. "Such everlasting beauty."

By the time we got to Taipei, the cat face load cell was already fully operational. We had a candidate manufacturer for making the metal parts. We now needed Stephen Lee—or someone like him—to do the gaging, wiring, and testing if we wanted to meet the Philips $1.50 cost target. I say "we" because during that trip to Asia we were toying with the idea of creating a partnership, Amos and I.

Nothing ever came of it, though, because Amos's contract with Lazy Bob at Paramount forbade him from entering into any partnership agreement with anyone else. They had a symbiotic relationship, these two, that fed on their com-plementary insecurities—one needed a reliable worker to make his place useful, and the other needed a reliable place to make his work useful. And while Amos would complain about Bob on occasion, he never mustered the courage to leave and venture out on his own. Any business proposition that I had to offer him was surely not enough to entice him out of that dark and derelict factory in Brooklyn anyway.

"I was surprised to find him so young, 41 years," I wrote of Stephen Lee in my diary on 8 January. He was good-natured and laid back, yet clearly an ambitious man—he was already producing laptop computers as well as scales by that time. "We did not show him the load cell. . . . He did not seem impressed with our ver-bal descriptions of it, saying there were no secrets in this business, since this was a 'mature' technology."

Our main technical discussion revolved around the sorting problem. It was already clear that for the scale to maintain the 100-gram accuracy when people shifted their weights, the sensitivity of each of the four load cells in every scale had to be within 0.1 percent of the other three.

Amir Rahav of Tedea told me at the time that there was a way to do that elec-tronically—with an EEPROM (Electrically Erasable Programmable Read-Only Memory) chip that would store a sensitivity factor for each load cell. But that chip still cost several dollars, and that was out of our price range for now. Eventually, it could be had for pennies, no doubt, and the sorting problem would disappear.

For now, however, the cheaper and more labor-intensive alternative was to sort the load cells into groups of similar sensitivities (i.e., registering similar volt-age outputs for a given load). We expected the initial sensitivities of a large batch of load cells to vary by as much as 2 percent, because of differences in metal thickness and in the way the load cells were put together. We would then need to divide them into as many as 20 sensitivity groups, so that the variations within each group were kept to 0.1 percent. Then we could pick four load cells from the same sensitivity group when assembling a given scale.

Amos explained the sorting machine he had in mind to Stephen Lee. The machine will have a single station, where the load cell will be received, he said. Three spring-loaded probes will come down to make contact with the solder points near the strain gages. With them will come down a load of, say, 75 pounds, which will be pneumatically operated. The load cell being tested will sit on another precision load cell—the "mother" load cell. An electronic circuit will read both load cells and calculate the sensitivity factor of the load cell being tested (i.e., the ratio of its sensitivity and the sensitivity of the mother load cell). This factor will be marked on the load cell, either by hand or with a printer. The person sorting the load cells will put them in boxes depending on that factor.

Stephen listened carefully, asked a few questions, and after a while decided that the sorting posed no special problem. Eventually we got to discuss the price for gaging, wiring, testing, and sorting an individual load cell. "We narrowed the price range down to 90¢–95¢," I wrote in my diary, "and he did not seem particularly perturbed. He actually warmed up to us gradually, and eventually asked if he could use the load cells for his own scales. We said we would think about it. Got me worried about patent protection. . . . All in all, it was a good visit. We accomplished the two main objectives of getting him to relax about sorting and coming down in price."

I did not pay adequate attention at the time to his comment, made in passing, that there were no secrets in this business since this was a mature technology; I brushed it off as posturing, I guess. I left Taipei with the confidence that, sooner or later, the cat face load cells could be manufactured in large quantities for about $1.60, the number I had mentioned in my more recent correspondence with Philips over the past few months. I was beginning to believe that, given the price quotations we were getting from manufacturers, there was enough of a margin for good money to be made. With the protection I expected from the new load cell patent, I could ensure that at least some of that money came my way.

* * *

Philips, meanwhile, was taking its sweet time. It was months before I received word that the batch of hook load cells that I sent them in July of 1989, in a moment of despair, actually performed as expected. They were building and testing their own scale models using these load cells, they said, and it took time. Now, having received the new cat face prototypes in early December of 1989, they were building and testing yet more models. They expected to have a go-or-no-go decision by the end of February 1990, a year later than the original date for that decision. I had no clue what were the causes of the delays on their part, but I was glad that they were still in the running after so many postponements and so did not bother to ask.

A new, younger engineer was now in charge of the project: Albert Mey, a nice, sophisticated, and approachable man. I talked to him after we all returned from the Far East. He was still quite confident that our project would go ahead. "I told him that we had worked out the prices with Stephen Lee," I wrote on 11 January. "He asked whether our offer of $1.60 still stands and I said yes." I guess the new regime was no longer so religious about the $1.50 price ceiling.

There was a meeting scheduled for me on 14 January with the new director of domestic appliances, a Mr. Tolenaar, at the International Housewares Exposition in Chicago. He wanted to get to know me, Albert said. My diary entry of that day, written in the hotel room in Chicago, reads:

> Got up early and went to the exposition not knowing what to expect and losing my gray cashmere scarf on the way. Two enormous pavilions with thousands of booths, and a feeling of a place well organized. (The housekeeper just knocked with some bath gel, so I am going to have myself a hot bath before I continue.) It is 6:00 P.M. I am meeting Tolenaar at 7:30. Embarrassing: I had to look twice through

the list of hotels in the Chicago *Yellow Pages* before I could remember what hotel he is staying in.

I spent the afternoon in bed doing nothing much, watching the Denver Broncos win a place in the Super Bowl and mulling over the morning's events. In a span of a few hours I visited 20 booths that had bathroom scales and talked to top management people of the largest distributors of bathroom scales. . . .

I told them we were developing an accurate, thin, and lightweight scale. They were all interested. The man from Counselor indicated he wanted some exclusivity; the man from Krups said that if it is interesting he could send his man to New York in no time. The man from Hanson said that their travel scale, called Stow-a-Weigh, probably sold not more than 10,000 last year, even though it has been in Sharper Image's catalog. It is an eight-inch-by-eight-inch scale, one and a quarter-inch thick, weighing probably 3–4 lbs. I said our scale competed with it. He said he was more interested in a bathroom model, maybe a flat tile with a remote control display. I like the idea. I want to know how to make a remote-control readout, and maybe incorporate it into the prototypes. . . .

I also saw the Soehnle scale. Beautiful. It retails for $170.

The Counselor man said that to hit it big we have to make something that will sell for $39.95 and that its out-of-factory cost could be as high as $20—or maybe it was the Health-O-Meter man. . . . The Counselor man was the one who did not want to disclose his margins. . . . The Krups man was quite excited, the Measurement Specialties man quite suspicious. Black & Decker did not display any scales, and neither did Norelco. I also met a couple of aggressive Hungarians . . . who told me they had a factory in Budapest. They were very keen, perhaps too keen. . . .

It looks like the big market is still in the cheap end, although it is slowly moving up-market, slowly. . . . Nobody seemed especially excited about accuracy. Half-pound accuracy seems to be more than enough as long as there is repeatability. Spending so much time on increasing accuracy may have been barking up the wrong tree, but I have a sense that it will pay good dividends in the end.

I am getting dressed for dinner with Tolenaar and van der Riet—I don't expect much and there is really no agenda except getting to know each other.

I was wrong about that, completely wrong. But, in truth, there was no way for me to guess what was coming. No way at all.

* * *

The next diary entry was written at 6:00 A.M. on the following morning, aboard the plane back to New York:

Over a couple of dark Beck's beers and a sirloin steak at the basement restaurant of the Swiss Grand Hotel, Messrs. Tolenaar and van der Riet confronted me with a new reality: they handed me a copy of a Dutch patent issued to Philips in December of 1965 and now expired, which shows a drawing of a load cell almost identical to cat face [Fig. 49], and using the same loading arrangement to get a double cantilever arrangement. I could not read the text, but van der Riet promised to send a translation. Apparently, nobody has ever done anything with it, he said, and in their view it did not mean they were not interested in pursuing the project and buying load cells from Libra. It did mean, however, that I may not be able to register a patent, and that even if I did, I would have trouble protecting it.

It is clear that we are talking about the same basic shape. Maybe they did not think of stamping, but this is hardly a strong claim. For now, for better or for worse, I must assume that I can get no patent protection for the load cell; all the more reason for increased confidentiality. We agreed that all we have is an "edge."

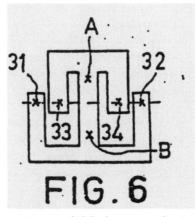

49 *Figure 6 of Philips's patent application of 1965*

Tolenaar wanted to understand "what makes Dr. Angel run," and my answers did not seem satisfactory. . . .

They kept talking about hiring me as a "consultant," helping them develop their scale line. They wanted to try to convince me that their designs were thin enough, and that I should let go of my insistence on the "ultrathin" version. I made an effort to convince Tolenaar directly that there was something unique about it. That it was light. He seemed interested and positive. We concluded that we should meet in Groningen during the second half of February, and I said I shall bring a thin, lightweight prototype with me.

No, I did not sleep much last night. For the first time I saw the end of the scale project: Angel signs a deal with Philips for the delivery of the load cells. Philips agrees to market the thin scale. Ten thousand are sold in the first year and the line is discontinued. It felt like the world was closing in on me. And so soon after it opened up in the morning, so full of new possibilities. No wonder they talk about "closing" deals. . . .

Interesting. I was not devastated by the Dutch patent. I was not sprung. My feet kept firmly on the ground. It felt like just another round of negotiations. After all, I needed a flat, low-cost load cell and I found one. No one else has one right now. If I can't protect it, I can't protect it. Patents are not foolproof protection either; they are grounds for litigation, that's all.

And who wants to spend time in litigation?

I must confess that the discovery of the Philips patent still hurts a bit [I wrote a few days later, on January 24]. Not too much. I was so proud of myself having a robust patent, a broad one. Now I find myself with either no patent at all or with some crumbs of a patent. Thin? How thin is thin? Stamped? Stamping a well-known form is hardly an innovation. Can I console myself that maybe the patent has not been registered in the U.S.? Hardly a consolation. It is quite plain. Some-body thought of it before me. Like Stephen Lee says: "this is a mature technology." True, my load cell works and can be done for little money. But the form, the dou-ble anchor, has been thought of before. Yes. It has.

So? Does it hurt? Where? Why? A blow to my pride, for one. But that is good, after all. Conceit is not a wholesome mental state. Less patent protection, for another. More need for secrecy, not a bad practice after all. I talk too much and too openly anyway; practicing discretion will be good for me. It may be easier for oth-ers to copy, yes. But we have an edge. They may not be able to copy it exactly either; some protection may be available after all. Lucky for me that the Philips patent is no longer valid. That would have been much worse. I would have had to pay them to use it for the thin scale, imagine.

Marc Gross, my patent lawyer, advised me to get the Dutch patent translated and to submit revised claims to the Patent Office as soon as possible. Patent law, he informed me, requires full disclosure of all the prior art that one has unearthed. Good counsel.

* * *

With the new cat face load cell prototypes, we were ready to assemble a thin scale in early February 1990, using a metal-and-foam sandwich for the scale plate (Fig. 50). I obtained some quarter-inch-thick rigid foam from General Plastics in Seattle that could actually be milled, like wood or metal. With two thin sheets of steel—each one of them one-fiftieth of an inch (0.5 millimeter) thick—we could

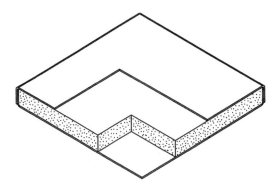

50 *The metal-and-foam sandwich plate*

form a sandwich plate, with shallow cavities machined in the foam for the cat face load cells.

The diary entry of 3 February, entitled "The Thin Scale Works the First Time," read:

> I spent Wednesday at Charlie's, talking about the assembly sequence, trying things out, preparing some jigs, placing pieces near each other in a leisurely manner, rehearsing the sequences out loud, and eventually making a nonreversible move by gluing the top plate to the foam with the load cells embedded in it. Charlie put it in the oven, clamped, and I went back to the city. He connected the electronics and glued the bottom plate, and by the time I arrived yesterday it was ready for testing. I set my computer up on the workbench as usual, and we proceeded to test for nonlinearity, hysteresis, and cornering, as if by rote, slowly and mindfully. The results came out quickly and unambiguously: It works. . . .
>
> We measured the scale itself. It weighs 500 grams, 46 grams over a pound, and it is 0.29 inches thick, 0.04 inches (or one millimeter) more than a quarter-inch. We are almost there. The most satisfactory test was that for the rigidity of the plate. We loaded it with 150 pounds over a three-by-three-inch block of wood at the center, and got a total deflection of 0.018 of an inch, less than half a millimeter. So the composite plate with the load cells embedded in it works! It works! . . .
>
> I have yet to digest it all, but this is very good news. We have a thin-scale proto- type that works. It is thin, lightweight, and accurate: all three together! True, we still don't have the electronics, but we have two out of the three: load cells and a plate. . . . We are no longer far from the goal. And that is good. Very good.

I made contact with people at Krups in Germany and at Counselor in Rockford, Illinois, right after the International Housewares Exposition in Chicago. By 24 January I had received a fax from Dr. Heinrich Komesker, the director of R&D at Krups in charge of the development of scales: "I will call you in a few days. I am very interested in the production of the scale and in a conversation with you." Bob Guinter, chief development engineer at Counselor, called some weeks later. He wanted to know about progress made with the prototype. "Looks like you are heading in the right direction," he said. "We are very interested in this project. Counselor is always looking for something new to put on the market."

After a number of postponements, the Philips negotiations were finally set for 27 and 28 March, and Amnon, my legal counsel, was going to join me in the Netherlands to negotiate on my behalf. I did not trust my ability to bargain with the Philips people effectively. I was reading *Getting to Yes: Negotiating Agreement Without Giving In* at the time, trying to hone my meager skills. The authors, Fisher and Ury, emphasized the need to develop one's Best Alternative To a Negotiated Agreement (BATNA) as a true bottom line. "*That* is the standard against which any proposed agreement should be measured," they wrote. "That is the only standard which can protect you from accepting terms which are too unfavorable and from rejecting terms it would be in your interest to accept." That made perfect sense to me.

It was comfortable to know that there would be life after Philips if the negotiations collapsed. I contemplated visiting both Krups and Counselor before the visit to Groningen in late March, to develop potential deals with them as BATNAs for the Philips negotiations, but I decided against it. There was no point in disclosing everything to them yet, and full disclosure was probably an essential precondition for getting them to even consider a serious deal.

This BATNA business was a bit of a chicken-and-egg problem, come to think of it, when secrecy was involved. I could not just present myself at Krups, for example, and say, "I have this wonderful invention. I can show you that it works, but I cannot show you how it works, OK? Now how much are you willing to pay me for it?" Instead, I planned to travel to Solingen in Germany to meet Dr. Komesker of Krups right after the Groningen meeting, in case the negotiations with Philips collapsed.

* * *

I was still not at all comfortable with the money angle of the scale project. I understood very well that I needed money to continue and that I deserved to get rewarded handily for my tireless efforts. Still, I was quite uncomfortable with the idea of bargaining with others for a bigger share of the pie, compelling or coercing them to accept less so that I could get more. I had to force myself to get more interested in money.

In fact, I added "making a million dollars" to the list of my objectives for the scale project in late 1989, as a challenge to succeed in the marketplace as well. Bringing the thin scale to market at a loss would be OK, I figured, but it would not be a very great achievement. Crossing the million-dollar barrier would lend it a measure of success that it would not have otherwise, I thought, while making my life in New York more comfortable at the same time. The diary entry of 12 February 1990, entitled "Flashback," reads:

> Just back home from *Flashback*, a movie with Dennis Hopper. At some point, Dennis and his captor come upon a small hippy commune in the mountains, with a loving, long-haired hippy abandoned there after all the flower children left to get on with their lives.
>
> I still long for a place in the mountains, a horse, a community of like-minded people, love, meditation, a simple life, growing things, having time on my hands, not carrying money all the time. Can I ever get there or is it all over? Are these values dead? Did they disappear with the 60s? (I resent the expression "the 60s," the commercialization of that period, the myth, and the abbreviated generalization that pretends to sum it all up. I can't stand it.)
>
> Yes, I was there, by some sheer coincidence, carrying picket signs in Sproul Plaza in '64, listening to Bob Scheer discover the Vietnam War in '65, planting trees

in People's Park in '69, sitting naked in the hot baths after long Gestalt Therapy sessions at Esalen that same year, I was there. It was there for me and I drank from it to my heart's content. . . .

But all that is now long gone for me—the commune ideal, even the daily meditation or the readings of the mystics of old. Only the beard (and the mind) remains.

I also ask myself, like that pathetic lawyer with the beard and the BMW in the movie: Have I sold out? Have I turned my back on what I believed in then? Did I compromise with the Establishment? Difficult questions to answer. We are all suspect, guilty until proven innocent.

Yes, some of my values are changing. I don't want to organize the poor in Asia. I have no need for ashrams. I want to start a family again. I want to be monogamous. I want to settle down. . . . But enforced poverty, hippy poverty, will no longer work for me. I am spoiled, I admit it, and doing the things I want to do costs more than before. Lucinda makes it clear enough, she does not enjoy poverty; she does not enjoy counting her pennies when she needs something, even though she is by no means a spendthrift.

Money did not seem to matter then. We somehow scraped by, and we had enough to do what we wanted. Money was something you came by, not something you focused on. Academia in Bangkok was like that too. I had enough for my needs, I was never in debt, and I never felt I was unable to afford something I really wanted. I feel poorer now, I am in debt, and I cannot afford to finish the development of the scale without depleting my savings. . . .

I am tired of spending so much money. New York is such a tyrant. It gives to you with one hand (or promises to give to you), and takes away more with the other. A bit like the casinos in Atlantic City: "You pay us for our promise to make you a winner." Inevitably, your mind turns to money and your objective becomes to make more of it, lots more.

This is what is happening to me. I confess: making a million dollars from the scale project was not one of the original Bangkok objectives; it was added here in New York. And on the rare occasion when I mentioned this objective to another New Yorker (my brother), all he had to say was, "Why only a million?"

Amnon and I arrived in Groningen at the end of March under something of a cloud. It was already clear by then that the Philips board of directors had not arrived at the expected go-or-no-go decision. The technical people who built new prototypes with the load cells we sent them could not repeat our results and could never attain the desired accuracy. The prototypes we sent performed as expected, they said, but the prototypes they built themselves did not. For reasons that remained unexplained, they did not apprise me of their difficulties, nor did they ask for my assistance, letting three whole months go by.

Now, Albert Mey told me, they had given the project to their development lab in Japan, of all places, and they expected answers by the end of June. June? Now that there were other companies interested in working with me, I had no patience left. I wanted to move on. Neither did I have much money left. I needed to replenish my coffers urgently if I wanted to complete the development of the scale. Most of all, I guess, I needed some commitment, some contractual arrangement that would put an end to all these long months of anxious uncertainty.

The negotiations were preceded by some unpleasant technical discussions led by Engineer Munnig-Schmidt. He was the one with the goatee beard and the small, piercing eyes, and he was in a particularly discouraging and disparaging state of mind. He had come to the sad conclusion that the load cells I sent them did not work.

Engineer van der Brug then showed us the prototype he had built. It was built purely for mechanical testing purposes, so why should its looks bother me? Well, they did bother me; what could I do? There was something about it that I found offensive. Anyway, the critical problem with it was at the interface between the load cells and the plates. For some reason, van der Brug had gotten rid of the rubber grommets we sent him and replaced them with rigid connections—screws. That, I already knew, would not work. Why didn't he ask? I thought that the two of us were on better terms.

At some point, after the technical exchanges calmed down somewhat, I showed them the new thin-scale prototype that Charlie and I had put together. We all strutted down to van der Brug's laboratory, where he had a universal testing machine. He loaded the thin plate with 100 kilograms (220 pounds), all concentrated on a two-inch-diameter disk at the center of the scale plate. There was barely a noticeable deflection. The voltmeter read 100.00. When he removed 10 kilograms, the voltmeter read 90.00; another 10 kilograms, 80.00; and so on down to zero, with an occasional 50-gram (0.1-pound) variation here and there. He then tried the cornering test, placing a 50-kilogram weight at different places on the scale; again, not more than a 50-gram error.

Munnig-Schmidt then tried to torture the poor prototype. He placed two steel wedges under two of the feet and then loaded the plate with 100 kilograms. The scale was at an incline and the load cells were really twisted out of shape, but they still performed: the total error was less than 250 grams. I sat by a desk, some distance away from the testing machine, and smiled from ear to ear while they slowly convinced themselves that it worked. Amnon was sitting next to me, watching their facial expressions. "We are whetting their appetite," he said.

We went back upstairs and the atmosphere changed. It was no longer dreary and heavy, as before. Munnig-Schmidt now became the most positive man in the room. "This concept clearly works," he said, "and it works because of the design of the load cells." He kept turning the prototype in his hands. "This is actually a load cell," he said, implying that this quarter-inch plate could probably be the guts for a new generation of scales with all kinds of new skins. They asked about the first patent, the one that protected the use of sandwich plates in thin scales, and were quite relieved to learn that it was now in force both in the United States and in Europe. It surely looked like they were now ready to move ahead.

Amnon, in a rather gruff way, made it quite clear that we planned to walk out of there with an agreement, a deal. No, we had not yet met any of the competition; and, no, we had not shown the competition anything. But, yes, we did have a meeting scheduled with a competitor before the end of the month, he said, which was quite true.

The end of June deadline was then dropped, and it became clear that Tolenaar, the director, could give the go decision in a matter of days, as soon as he returned from the States. It was agreed that we would finish the negotiations before noon the next day, so that Amnon could catch the earlier plane to New York; he could not get a seat on the later one. Everyone seemed to think it was possible.

The negotiation session the next morning was quite unpleasant. It was becoming evident that Munnig-Schmidt and Mey, the only Philips people in the room, had no negotiating authority anyway. They were there to listen and to comment on what we had to say, so that together we could present a common front to Director Tolenaar and the Philips board.

Amnon put forth the skeleton of the proposed agreement: first, I would be reimbursed for all my development costs at the time of signing the contract. Second, I would be appointed consultant on scale development for the next three years on a retainer contract; I would be available on call, with sufficient advance notice, for limited periods. Third, Libra would sell load cells to Philips at $2.00 per unit for 400,000 units per year, coming down in price to $1.60 per unit for 1,000,000 or more units per year. Fourth, Philips would commit itself in writing to produce the thin scale and to market it. Fifth, I was to be the designer of the thin scale, while Philips would have final approval of the design. And sixth, I would receive a 5 percent royalty on the sale of thin scales.

The Philips people occasionally protested or proposed minor changes, and they never wholeheartedly agreed with anything Amnon had to say. They had their own list of concerns that Amnon did not really bother to address. They still worried about technical issues, for example, and most particularly about quality control. They were not at all convinced that either the load cells or the entire scale could be produced to the required specifications at the targeted prices.

They told us that they had visited the Soehnle plant in Germany and were duly impressed. They were convinced that the Germans could maintain quality control, but they were not at all sure about Stephen Lee, whom they knew; or about José Luis, whom they did not know. They would do it in-house if they could, but they had no experience in either scale or load cell production. They needed someone to hold their hand while they set up a production plant, but I was not that person. "How can we guarantee quality?" they wanted to know.

But Amnon was not to be diverted. He essentially dismissed their concerns,

promising that I would submit a proposal on quality control by the following
week and then plowing on. Intent on employing intimidation as a tactic, he
repeated our contention that we planned to contact competitors in the near
future. "How much time do you need to arrive at a decision?" he asked pointedly.
"You tell us how much time you can give us," replied Munnig-Schmidt curtly.
"Two weeks," retorted Amnon, though the two of us had never discussed a time
frame before. "You'll have your answer in two weeks," said Munnig-Schmidt.
"The numbers look reasonable," he volunteered, more out of politeness than out
of conviction, I thought. We left it at that and parted, rather coolly but cordially.

We sat in the back of a new Mercedes taxi doing 90 miles per hour all the way
to Schiphol airport in Amsterdam. I felt rather heavy and uncomfortable, unsure
as I was of where the Philips people stood and trying to put myself in their
shoes. Amnon, in contrast, was of the opinion that the deal was in the bag.
"You'll make a million dollars out of this deal," he predicted. "As far as I am concerned, you can take the Concorde back to New York." Too early to celebrate, I
thought; I'll believe it when I see it.

Before we parted, Amnon advised me not to send too many friendly faxes in
the days that followed. He did not want them to know that I thought that we
were too tough with them. He must have seen it on my face. I thought that the
whole exchange was too adversarial and I was worried stiff. Anyway, I cancelled
the meeting with Krups and flew back to New York.

* * *

Albert Mey gave me Philips's answer by phone when I called him on 12 April,
and the official letter from Tolenaar arrived a few days later. The gist of it was
that Philips was not interested in a deal with me, nor was it about to make a
counter offer. They were now thinking of producing load cells by themselves,
based on their own design, and possibly on their own lapsed patent application
of 1965. Were I to have a functioning production line of load cells, Philips might
(or might not) buy load cells from me in the future.

They were not interested in my thin scale either, because they said, it was not
"serviceable"—its innards, being glued together into a stiff composite plate,
could not be opened for repairs, and that was unacceptable. Finally, they were
graciously offering to pay me a pittance—$12,500 in total—for the load cell pro-
totypes I had sent them, for the know-how I had provided them, and for my
travel expenses to the Netherlands. They were clearly not as concerned about
trying to put themselves in my shoes as I was about putting myself in theirs.

> Are you hurt? [I wrote on 12 April 1990] Are you covering up your pain? You went
> back and forth to and from Philips for two years. You visited them five times. You
> built four prototypes for them. You pursued their agenda—their need for 100-
> gram accuracy, which was not part of your own agenda. You studied manufactur-
> ing, heat treatment, fine blanking, plating, and gaging so that you could produce a

load cell for them. You went to visit manufacturers—Stephen Lee in Taipei, John
Hall in Los Angeles, the fine-blanking people in Connecticut and Long Island, and
the heat treatment people in New Jersey. You sent them samples of load cells at
three different times. You did a lot of work for them and they let you down.

Not completely true, [I continued]. There was no obligation on their part. You
chose to do it, and you learned many things along the way. You developed the load
cell for the thin scale at the same time; you made contacts with other manufacturers through them in Chicago; you learned and learned.

In retrospect, our so-called negotiations in Groningen were not really negotiations in the true sense of the word. No real agreement was ever reached at the
time; Amnon was essentially talking to himself and I was of no help at all. We did
not really address their concerns. We were both impatient and we were both in a
hurry—I did not want to be held back anymore and he had a flight to catch—
and both impatience and haste were anathemas to serious negotiation.

"Americans look at negotiations as a Ping-Pong game," writes Chester L. Karrass in *Give and Take*. "One side, then the other, serves. Then on to something
else. Not so the Japanese. A quick deal can get a Japanese executive fired. It is a
sign of bad judgment. The North Vietnamese leased a villa in Paris for two years
when talks began. Averell Harriman, our man, probably had a room at the Ritz
Hotel on a day-to-day basis."

Well, in some sense I was not in haste at all. I did not rent a villa on the outskirts of Groningen, but I kept "negotiating" with Domestic Appliances for two
long years and two generations of functionaries, tying my fortunes to theirs and
never getting anywhere. Amnon came in as the proverbial midwife who cut the
umbilical chord and set me free.

In yet another retrospect, taking on the responsibility for quality control of
load cell production in some faraway country by subcontractors that I could not
really control was ridiculous. What if a shipment of load cells was rejected? What
if a shipment was delayed or lost? What if the relationship soured and I needed a
new manufacturer on short notice? Because of Amnon's insistence that the funds
pass through my hands—to make sure that I was not cheated out of my share—I
would have been directly accountable for quality control. I am not sure that he
made that connection at the time, or that he understood the implications. A
great listener, probably an essential quality of a good negotiator, he was not.

Come to think of it, the whole idea of producing load cells for Philips was a
nonstarter, and I should have known it at the outset. I shouldered it in the spirit
of true chivalry, to get my foot in the door, I suppose, but my shoulders were
never broad enough to be able to carry it through. Maybe it was my association
with Amos that gave me the false confidence that I could do it.

I already said it before and I repeat it here: I was not cut out for manufacturing; that much was made clear to me a long time ago when, as a kid, I had a
chance to observe the intense goings-on at the Angel Bakery in Jerusalem. I had

no business making load cells. It was all wishful thinking. From now on, I vowed, I shall limit my activities in this venture to design and development, and my business relationships to consulting, on the one hand, and to licensing my inventions to others, on the other.

"The Philips people never fell in love with the thin scale," I continued on 12 April. "They rejected it way back in October of 1988, took another cursory look at it the last time we visited them, and rejected it again. . . . They never thought they had a hit there. . . . That is what I need now. Some company that will fall in love with the thin scale and be ready to back it, push it, make it happen, make it happen big."

On that same day, I wrote faxes to Dr. Heinrich Komesker, the director of R&D at Krups in Solingen, Germany; to Mr. Armin Soehnle, the president of Soehnle in Murrhardt, also in Germany; to Mme. Dominique Routhier, director of scale services at Tefal in Rumilly, France; and to Bob Guinter, chief development engineer at Counselor in Rockford, Illinois. I only had introductions to Heinrich Komesker and Bob Guinter, through their colleagues at the Chicago Exposition. I got Armin Soehnle's name and fax number from the Soehnle representative in New York; and Madame Routhier's name and fax number from a very distant friend of my mother's who did some administrative work at Tefal.

In a few days, I had appointments scheduled to see all these people before the end of the month. As it turned out, it was not at all difficult to set them up. I guess it was because I now had something to show them—something in their own field of expertise that they had not seen before—and they were curious. The Philips affair was now over, and towards the end of April—feeling much lighter—I was on the move again, this time in pursuit of a license agreement.

16

License It!

What you want to do—desperately—is to sell your idea to a manufacturer for a royalty deal. Anything else is second best. A fallback position. Collecting royalties is the cleanest, neatest, most profitable, simplest way for you to make a fortune in the inventing game.

Don Kracke with Roger Honkanen, *How to Turn Your Idea into a Million Dollars*

Grant of License—During the term of this agreement and subject to the conditions thereof, Licensor grants to Licensee personal, indivisible, nontransferable, exclusive, world-wide licenses, with the right to sublicense its Associated Companies, under the patents listed on Schedule A to make, have made for its own account, use, lease, export and sell Licensed Products.

Calvin D. MacCracken, *A Handbook for Inventors*

———

APRIL 1990–SEPTEMBER 1990

Dr. Heinrich Komesker, the director of R&D at Krups, was a man in his early forties—blue eyed, enthusiastic, broad shouldered, bubbly, and generous—who had just had his third child, a daughter, born on Easter Sunday. The Krups offices were closed because it was a Friday, and he came to work especially to see me. His young assistant, a thin and frail engineer with thick glasses and an unsure grip on the English language, drove me over to Solingen from Düsseldorf Airport.

Krups had two factories and about 1,100 people in Solingen, a green city of rolling hills and old houses with black slate shingles on their exterior walls. Like other relatively small German towns—this one with some 170,000 people—it seemed so convivial. It was compact rather than sprawling, surrounded by fields that were still cultivated. At the same time, it was a home to industries with a global reach—Solingen was known worldwide for its high-quality knives. These middle-sized towns dotting the German countryside were perfectly urbane and modern, yet still retained an intimate connection with their rural surroundings. I could sense something wholesome and fulfilling in this connection.

We talked in generalities a bit. Then I asked him to sign a nondisclosure form, agreeing not to make use of information that was not in his possession at the time of my disclosure. This he did quite willingly. I then took out the thin scale and the cat face load cell and explained how it all worked.

While I was explaining things, I pulled out some papers from my correspondence folder, and a fax with "Soehnle" written on it in large square letters fell on the floor. It was immediately spotted by Komesker who proceeded to comment on it. I felt the blood gushing into my cheeks but he was quite disarming. He readily acknowledged my right to talk to his competitors, and did not at all project any hurt or a sense of betrayal. In fact, we proceeded to court each other, me by proclaiming the great attributes of the thin scale, him by proclaiming the great attributes of Krups and its unique position in the market for a new, innovative scale.

At some point, quite early in the conversation, he got up to talk on the phone with the marketing lady who could not join us for the meeting. When he came back his main concern was how soon we could get it on the market.

A bit later in the conversation he asked about costs. I said that I estimated that for 200,000 units, $25 would be enough to pay for production and royalties, and he said there was no problem with that. Just before we got up for lunch he said, "I like it more and more." We talked about exclusivity—assigning a license to make use of my patents and know-how to Krups and to no one else. He was quite specific about each market and Krups's position in it: they were doing well on the continent, except for France; they were expanding into Eastern Europe and the former Soviet Union, but there was not much happening in England; they were doing well in the States but were just beginning to enter the Japanese market. Two years of an exclusive license would be enough, he thought, giving Krups a sufficient head start in the market. I did not feel that my hands were being tied like I had when I talked about exclusivity with Tolenaar of Philips.

By the end of lunch, I was convinced that Krups needed the thin scale. In four years or so, they would be 150 years old. They had started business as a scale company but had now lost the lead in the German market to Soehnle. They wanted to come out with an innovation, something that could be marketed in many shapes and colors, "like the Swatch," as Komesker acknowledged. He referred to the thin sandwich plate with the load cells inside it and the short wires coming out of it as a "sensor," thinking of it, no doubt, as the guts of a new generation of scales. All that needed to be done, he thought, was to connect it to Krups's scale electronics.

Did we get to talk actual dollars? No. I could not bring myself to talk about money. In retrospect, that was a big mistake, because I never found out from him what Krups would have considered to be reasonable licensing fees for me. I ended up saying that I would send him a detailed proposal once I got back to the States.

We talked engineering, we talked marketing, but I could not bring myself to tell him how much money I expected. He did not ask me directly either, and we let it hang there. I was given to understand that the scale should market for 150 German marks, $86, and that their markup was of the order of 3.0 to 3.5 times cost. The out-of-factory cost, including royalties and development expenditures, could be somewhere between $24 and $29, which, given what I already knew about production costs, was plenty enough. I left Solingen in high spirits, with a weekend to spare before my meeting at Soehnle.

It was late April and there were light rains. I thought that long walks in the German countryside would do me good, and I picked two small towns along the Mosel River—Eller and Cochem—as reasonable destinations, where I could have a cool glass of white wine in some small wine cellar waiting for me at the end of my walk—those light, fragrant wines of the Mosel region were particularly friendly to my palate. I wish I could say that my strolls in the Mosel valley were soothing and relaxing, that I ambled leisurely in that tranquil countryside with not a care in the world, but they were not. The scale had a vice grip on my mind during those days, and it just refused to let go; or to put it more precisely, my one-track mind had a vice grip on the scale and refused to let it go.

I thought of Dr. Komesker's comment about giving the scale a Krups design. They had very good designers, he said. When I told him that our next prototype would be only six millimeters thick, one millimeter less than the present prototype, he told me not to worry—it was already thin enough. As he said it, I sensed that familiar anxiety again—the design of the scale was getting out of my hands. They might still opt for thick batteries and carpet protection, my two enemies; who knows? They definitely wanted to change the size—to make the plate larger—and hence make the scale somewhat heavier too. Less of a threat, but still.

I began to worry that showing Krups an incomplete prototype—with an unsolved "thin-electronics" problem—had reduced the chances of realizing my thin-scale vision. And, I had to admit to myself, I was still not ready to give up on it, especially now that it was more realizable than ever before. I desperately wanted to be the designer of that scale, at least to the extent of determining that it would be 6 millimeters thick and not more, as well as weigh a pound and not more.

To that extent I wanted the "final cut," as they say in Hollywood. I did not want anyone to meddle with the design once I finished it. Anyone. But only the most powerful directors in Hollywood got final cut. So did top designers, I suppose, but not no-names like me. Who did I think I was? Anyway, I was not employed or retained as a designer in this scenario at all; I was simply negotiating the licensing of my patents and know-how to them, after which they could do with them all they wanted and I would be left out in the so-called wilderness.

That Saturday afternoon, strolling along a narrow path in the forest, I came upon a magical place where a small stream coming down from Eltz Castle joined the Mosel. I sat there on a wet rock to watch. The stream was fast, enthusiastic, quiet, and determined to disappear into the wide river below, to lose its identity in something larger than itself and to start its final journey to the great sea. How could it be so excited to lose its identity? That small stream kept disappearing into the Mosel. Nothing remained of it, nothing at all. A new stream was forming in its stead every moment.

Yes, the Greek philosopher Heraclitus already understood that "you cannot step into the same stream twice" as far back as the sixth century B.C. But was that ever really clear to me? Did I understand that I was that stream? That I too could make a contribution, a small contribution to the larger whole, and then disappear in the whole, leaving no permanent mark?

But it was not making a mark that was at stake, I tried to tell myself. I wanted my small contribution to be a design, a total design, not just a technical innovation. That technical innovation was made in the service of that design, and it was the design that was to be the true innovation. It was a demanding design, so demanding that it required a new technology to bring it to life. Others might not yet see its value, might not share my conviction that it had value, and might thus not want to make the necessary sacrifices to attain it.

Should I simply let go, make my technical contribution, and then allow it to blend into the greater whole; or should I insist on contributing a design? Licensing, after all, really amounted to letting go of the thin-scale vision. Was I ready and willing to let go?

There may be a middle way, I told myself in an effort to calm down. Maybe we could work together. Maybe I could somehow remain involved in the design and development process at Krups, even without that elusive final cut. The first scale may not be the quarter-inch, one-pound one I had in mind; but the second or third one may be.

* * *

On Monday, 23 April 1990, aboard the train from Stuttgart to Murrhardt, where Soehnle had its factory, I had an attack of cold feet. If I revealed to the Soehnle people as much as I had just revealed at Krups, would I not be revealing too much to too many? There was, I realized, an inevitable tension in the know-how business between trust on the one hand and greed on the other. In this business, revealing everything got you nothing. In fact, revealing anything—a precondition for establishing trust and credibility, I thought—had a price, because any know-how once revealed would never command any price.

Nondisclosure agreements did not really provide adequate protection against people "skilled in the art" working on a similar problem. Not least because the particular kernel of know-how that may have the most value for them would be difficult to predict in advance and put into words. It was the missing link in their thought process that they were after, and that missing link could be quite trivial. In my explorations, I may have walked further down the same path that these people thought was a dead end, and I found, or stumbled upon, a way out. All they needed to know was that this path was not a dead end. Then they could find their own way out. They would not need me to show them the way.

I knew myself enough to understand that, one way or the other, I would end up showing the Soehnle people everything I had. My academic publishing habits were partly to blame for that openness. In the academy, at least in the field I worked in—urban studies—the "publish or perish" imperative was predicated on putting new knowledge in the public domain, where it would be freely available to all. I liked that. I enjoyed sharing what I knew. My grandmother used to say: "Don't tell me anything that you don't want me to pass on; I can't keep a secret." I too disliked secretiveness, and if that was an essential quality of the good businessman, I sorely lacked it.

I would need to show the Soehnle people something to establish my credibility, no doubt. That was why they had agreed to see me in the first place. But in return I was hoping to visit their factory, the one that manufactured four-load-cell scales; the Philips engineers, I remembered, had described it to me in glowing terms. That factory surely held some secrets for me. And so, in the final analysis, we were going to exchange know-how; it would not be just a one-way street. Eventually, as the train neared Murrhardt, I calmed down, convincing myself that, one way or another, the cat face load cell would shortly be protected by a patent anyway.

* * *

I was ushered into a modern and impeccably clean conference room and left there waiting. Two walls of that room were entirely covered with personal scales; there were maybe 200 models on display. Some of the scales had 500-gram, 200-gram, or 100-gram labels on them, referring, of course, to their accuracy. The four-load-cell scale was there too: thin, elegant, and with 100-gram accuracy. The third wall displayed commercial scales, all looking distinguished and aristocratic, a bit out of place in a room full of inaccurate relatives. On the whole, there was something very serious and vigorous about the place. Soehnle had been in the scale business for no less than 125 years, and it did not look tired at all, nor did it rest on its laurels. It now produced six million scales a year and sold them in more than one hundred countries.

Armin Soehnle walked briskly into the room. In his early forties, thin and agile, he had already acquired the demeanor of the fourth-generation scale maker that he was—he was sharp eyed, relaxed, and on top of things. Definitely less enthusiastic than Komesker, he appeared more self-assured, more settled. Less friendly too, I thought. With him were two adjutants, Albrecht Stahl (Steel, in German)—the tall, sturdy director of R&D, who, like many of his countrymen, sported a blond moustache—and a withdrawn man from marketing. I showed them the thin-scale prototype and the test results. They readily acknowledged that both looked good. Then they talked in German, Soehnle doing most of the talking and Stahl replying.

They were not interested in light weight, Soehnle said after a while; "heavy sells better." "What about travel?" I inquired. "Travel scales are only half a percent of our market," he offered in reply. "When you don't have them people say they want them, and when you have them people don't buy them." Good to know, I thought.

We talked about their four-load-cell scale. It was selling for 140 German marks ($85), and it sold well. The load cells, they said, cost 4 marks ($2.50) to make. It sounded low to me. The discussion came back to the thin scale lying quietly on the conference table.

"It all boils down to the load cells," Soehnle finally said. "Can we see them?"

"I have a problem showing you the load cells," I said, "without a nondisclosure agreement."

"We have problems with such agreements," he said. "There are so many load cells we are working on now, we might already have your design."

"Yes, I know," I said.

"And in addition," he said, "there is no problem making a slight modification and circumventing your design."

"Yes, I know," I said, "but I would be more comfortable with a nondisclosure agreement. I also heard a lot about your factory," I added. "I would love to visit it." A long silence ensued.

"And do you have such an agreement with you?" he said finally.

"Yes, I happen to have one," I said, pulling it out.

They read it and discussed it, commented here and there, modified it a bit, and agreed to sign it. I pulled out the load cell. The rest of the discussion was in German. They were truly interested. They kept talking about moments and the rejection of side forces. I sat there quietly. I knew that the cat face could speak for itself. The atmosphere was pleasant and relaxed. They were cool and poker faced but I sensed their excitement. There was no intimidation in the air, no "know-it-all" superiority, and no "not-invented-here" resentment. Here was a cheaper, flatter, and apparently highly accurate load cell; and they had never seen one quite like it.

"I was a bit reluctant coming to you with something that may compete with your own product," I said sometime later.

"That is quite fine; we like to compete with our own products," Soehnle said proudly. "This load cell would definitely be cheaper than ours," he admitted. "It could in fact replace ours altogether."

"If this works out, we could sell 200,000 to 250,000 scales a year using this load cell," he said. ("Wow.") We talked a bit more about production prices, strain gage prices, and modes of production.

"You are probably showing it to everybody," he said after a while.

"I plan to show it to two European manufacturers and one American one," I said.

"That is everybody, isn't it," he said rather unhappily. "We would like worldwide rights." I had no problem with that, and the visit to Tefal in France looked more and more irrelevant.

Again we did not talk about money, just about principles—licensing, the recovery of investments, royalties, consulting, the commitment to bringing the thin scale into the market. They wanted me to leave the prototype and four load cells for a two-week testing period, but they said that negotiations could proceed in parallel. I agreed and forgot about going to Tefal right there and then.

Soehnle then took me to the factory in his little blue BMW and we spent over an hour there.

A beautiful factory it was: clean and quiet except for the rhythmic muffled sounds of machines; sparse in workers moving rather quietly about, supervising machines that did it all by themselves, moving parts around, making sure everything was in order, alert, clear headed, barely paying attention to us. Assembly was all streamlined and mostly automated.

There was even a robot working in a small dark room. Scales moved towards it on a conveyor belt. It lowered a weight on the scale in front of it, and then turned a small screw on the side of the scale until the correct weight appeared on the scale's display window. That could surely be done manually, I thought to myself. But not there. To keep manufacturing jobs in Germany—with its high labor costs and its extended social benefits—worker productivity needed to be continually on the rise. That meant more capital investment in machinery per worker. That little robot working in the dark was just a small step along the way.

The sorting machine for the load cells of their four-load-cell scale was, for me, the most attractive sight in that factory. There was a solidly built woman dressed in white there, placing eight load cells at a time in the sorting machine; soldering their wires to her testing equipment; and measuring their sensitivity, nonlinearity, and hysteresis with an assortment of cylindrical loads hanging below the machine. The results then appeared on her computer screen. Much better than ours, I thought. They went to the trouble of soldering the wires to the testing equipment and then unsoldering them. Even Charlie does not do that. But I suppose that is what German manufacturing is about. Meticulous. I liked it. In 1990, Germany still had 31.6 percent of its labor force employed in manufacturing. They still made things there and they made them well. In the United States manufacturing labor was down to 18 percent by that time.

I left Murrhardt having acquired a considerable respect for the people at Soehnle. They were ahead, they already had load cells and sorting machines, and I could talk to them in the same language that I talked to Charlie. They knew what there was to know about producing scales and about four-load-cell scales. I had less to teach them and more to learn from them. They were willing to talk about a thin travel scale with a larger plate, one that could probably also be used as a bathroom scale. They were also willing to talk about thin batteries. They were not concerned about carpets for now. They saw cost savings.

Soehnle said, much to my surprise, that their markup for retail was only 2.5 times cost because they distributed the scales themselves all over Europe. That meant that if the thin scale could be produced for $25, it could possibly sell for only $63—25 percent less than their present four-load-cell scale. They also saw the advantage of the thin design—"That is what everyone is working towards," Soehnle acknowledged at some point.

For Soehnle, I concluded, lightness was not important but thinness and accuracy were. Lightness would come in handy only in a bathroom scale that would also double up as a travel scale, and they were open to that possibility. For ordinary bathroom scale models, however, they wanted the scale plate to be bigger, not necessarily light, but still thin.

This was all quite acceptable. As things stood, if I had had to choose, I would have preferred to work with Soehnle. They were more advanced technically. Krups has better name recognition in the United States maybe, but that meant very little. The market for accurate scales was in Europe and possibly in Japan, but not yet in the United States. Soehnle felt safer than Krups, spelling less anxiety for me. These people were not taking what I said for granted but rather integrating it with their own experience. With Krups I would have to do more, and there would be more unknowns. That also meant that Krups would have more need for my know-how than Soehnle, and would therefore be more willing to work with me. Either of them would be more than good enough. I cancelled the Tefal visit and flew back to the States the next day.

* * *

I arrived at the United Airlines terminal at Chicago's O'Hare airport in the morning of 30 April 1990 on my way to Counselor. Walking through the tall barrel vaults of the terminal (Fig. 51) was in itself an aesthetic pleasure of a high order. They were all exquisitely detailed in contemporary steel and glass while, at the same time, reminiscent of the naves of Gothic churches of old. This building, completed in 1988, was not a postmodern hodgepodge of "one-liner" quotations from the past. It was a truly modern synthesis of past and present into a single,

51 *The United Airlines terminal in Chicago, Helmut Jahn, 1988*

unified, "total architecture," to paraphrase Helmut Jahn, the architect who designed it. "We see our work as an appropriate and innovative recomposition of classic and modern principles of the building arts," Jahn said.

But even beyond the comfortable familiarity that this recomposition generated, what appealed to me most about the place was that all its joints were "solved": its many parts all fit together gracefully, seamlessly, into a coherent whole, as if they were all made for each other. No connection seemed to be forced. On the contrary, every little interface in the design must have received plenty of undivided attention. I was humbled. The scale project was not there yet; there was still a long way to go before all of its joints were truly solved.

From the terminal, I boarded an empty bus to Rockford, Illinois, an hour and a half to the west through interminable cornfields. Rockford, a small town of 170,000, was situated in the middle of these fields, having gotten its name from the ford on the river Rock that was shallow enough for the covered wagons to cross on their way west. The Counselor Company been there for over 50 years, occupying what was now an old and rather ill-maintained brick building.

Bob Guinter, Counselor's 62-year-old development engineer, had been with the company for 29 years. He was overweight, bald, and jovial; and it was clear at the outset that his heart was no longer in scale R&D and had not been there for a while. His eyes lit up only once, when he told me (much later) that he was an aficionado of model trains. That's where his heart was, and he did his work at Counselor just to make ends meet and to feed his model train habit. Bob was one of the old timers there. He was recruited when Counselor was still a family business, long before it bought Borg and Detecto, and long before it was itself bought by Newell and eventually—some years after our encounter—sold to Sunbeam.

We sat in a rundown conference room and talked for a while, waiting for Wayne Dickson, the director of merchandising—the Counselor man I had met in January at the Chicago exhibition. While we waited, Bob told me how they turned their mechanical dial scales into digital scales. The old mechanical scales worked by pushing down on a spring that, as it went down, rotated a dial with numbers on it. They still used a spring, but now, instead of printing numbers on the top of the disk, they made radial notches at the bottom of the disc. An electronic eye could count those notches and display the number digitally. How about that?

Dickson eventually showed up, young, red haired, and gung ho. I showed him the test results. He did not understand anything about scales, he admitted, since he was a Newell marketing man. But he assured me that he could see the potential. If this scale did what I said it could do, he said, "we could market the bejesus out of it." "How many scales could you sell?" I tried to inquire, but to no avail.

Eventually he said, "Could we see it?" I had pulled out the prototype, still covered in plastic bubble wrap, when he said, "Surely you want to sign a confidentiality agreement?" "Yes," I replied and stopped unveiling the scale. "I have no problem with that," he said. I then brought out the standard nondisclosure form that I had copied from the book *Patent It Yourself!* and had the Krups and Soehnle people sign.

"We actually have our own form," offered Guinter as he got up to get one from his office. Dickson, meanwhile, read the form I gave him and looked quite satisfied. Guinter came in with the company's form. They then read both forms for a while, looking at one and then at the other in close succession several times, and then one said, "They are practically the same, aren't they?" while the other nodded hopefully in agreement.

The first page of the company's form was called "Statement of Policy Governing the Submission of Ideas." It made it plenty clear that "the Company declines to accept disclosures of any ideas in confidence"; that "no confidential relationship is to be established"; and that "the Company makes no commitment that the idea or material submitted in connection with it shall be kept a secret." The second page was a form that said something to the effect that I understood that my hand was being cut off; that I had no objection to my hand being cut off; and that whatever I signed would make the cutting off of my hand painless.

I politely pointed out to Dickson that this was precisely the opposite of the conventional nondisclosure form that I had put in front of him, and indeed it slowly dawned on him. "I wouldn't sign this if I were you," he said after a while. "Who would?" "No wonder we haven't been getting great new ideas lately," he added. "Other people all sign it," volunteered Guinter, albeit rather lamely. "I have a file full of them in my office."

At this point Dickson got up and started to make phone calls to legal counsel, but they were not there. He was now frustrated and he wanted action. Eventually, he understood that I was not going to sign their form, and he said, "I'll have to look into it, but I don't want to do anything against expressed company policy." Of course not. I felt pity for the man. I believed he really wanted to do business. I packed my bags and left with Guinter for the bus.

Talking with him on the way, I got the distinct impression that they were not interested in accuracy, the most basic measure of quality in the scale business. The people at Newell headquarters were interested in the bottom line, and at Counselor that meant a sharp focus on cost reduction, down to the fourth decimal point. This was all quite worrisome, I thought to myself. The air at Counselor was decadent and stale, and the place felt old and tired. Dickson was enthusiastic, surely, but he understood only sales, not scales. It seemed that they no longer loved their product. On the contrary, they were thinking of ways of making it for less, rather than of ways to give it quality. They were taking more and more away from it without giving it anything in return. Pity.

* * *

At the beginning of May 1990 I faxed proposed license agreements to both Krups and Soehnle. They were variations on template agreements available in the many how-to books on invention that I had collected by that time.

The agreement I sent to Krups, for example, described the kinds of know-how, patents, and patents pending in the possession of Libra, my company; it proposed providing Krups with exclusive worldwide licenses to the patents and know-how for an initial period of three years; and it offered my consulting services throughout the period of design and development.

In return, I expected to be reimbursed for my research and development expenditures incurred since August 1986—to the tune of $400,000—to be paid shortly after signing the agreement. In addition, I expected to receive royalties from the sale of scales incorporating the cat face load cell at the rate of 5 percent of the gross revenues. I also expected a minimum royalty payment of $200,000 per year, regardless of how many scales were sold.

Finally, I wanted to be paid for my consulting services at the rate of $6,000 a month plus expenses. The agreement I sent to Soehnle was identical. Again, as in the failed Philips deal, if either Krups or Soehnle agreed to my proposed terms, I stood to make at least a million dollars in licensing fees, no doubt a very respectable sum of money.

Where did I get these figures? They were basically the same figures that Amnon, my legal counsel, had presented to Philips not long ago. These figures were inflated versions of what I had told him I expected. Everyone I consulted at the time advised me to ask for a lot more money than I was willing to eventually accept. Such was the nature of bargaining, they said. The simple fact that Philips did not bother to reply with a counter offer did not bother me in the least. It should have.

My limited experience in negotiation involved bargaining with taxi drivers in Bangkok. Taxi meters did not exist in Bangkok at the time. You waived a taxi, it stopped, and you came forth to declare your destination and ask for a price. The driver would make the initial offer, you would make a counter offer, and after some give and take you agreed on a price you both thought was fair. Knowing what was fair, however, required knowing something about the prevailing prices for rides of different length. And sometimes, when the driver would offer what I considered to be an outrageously high price, I would simply walk away, offended at being taken for some ignorant tourist. The driver would then follow me slowly in his car, asking me what I was willing to pay. But I would simply ignore him, refusing to make a counter offer. Would Soehnle and Krups even consider getting back to me with a counter offer, or would they walk away? All I could do now was wait.

During the waiting period that ensued, assorted voices rang in my head every so often, competing for an audience: you asked for too much money, said one; you should not have shown it to their competitors, said another; they think they can circumvent your patent, said a third; they don't want to work with outsiders, said a fourth. Then, when all the disparaging voices exhausted themselves, there would follow a comfortable silence and a pleasant voice that said: "Let's just wait and see what happens, OK?"

* * *

There was no question that these license agreements hinged on getting a patent for the cat face load cell. Except for some marginal know-how—some practical do's and don'ts—I had acquired along the way, I had little to offer a potential licensee other than patent protection for the load cell and maybe for the sandwich plate for the thin scale.

After some phone inquiries and fax exchanges with the Netherlands, I found out that Philips did not really have a patent for the load cell design that was so similar to cat face. As I understood it, Philips filed a patent application in the Netherlands in August 1965. It lapsed in 1967 because patent maintenance fees were not paid. Still, the one-piece, double-anchor arrangement had been disclosed and was now in the public domain, the global public domain. Having come upon this patent application, I was now obliged by law to inform the patent office of it and—to use the customary legalese—to distinguish my proposed embodiment from the embodiment disclosed in the Dutch application.

The Dutch application did not refer to thinness at all. My load cell design was novel because it was thin, and—being so thin—it made possible the mass production of a new generation of very thin personal scales. Scales had to have minimal lengths and widths to be useful—a personal scale had to be broad enough to stand on comfortably. Making scales thinner was therefore the only way to reduce their volume and hence their weight, thus making them more transportable, more conservative in the use of materials, and less demanding of storage space and shipment volume. All these features had clear utility value.

Thinness as a distinguishing feature, however, was difficult to put into words. If it could not be expressed in the technical language of patent claims, it had no value at all as a distinguishing feature. How thin is thin, after all? I did contemplate using a phrase such as "less than one quarter of an inch thick" at some point, but I quickly realized that such language would be too limiting and too easy to circumvent with a slightly thicker load cell.

The United States Patent and Trademark Office approved my original patent application for the cat face load cell in late June 1990, without requiring any amendments. Just like that. That felt good, but it would not do. I now had to distinguish it from the Dutch application.

After a number of consultations with Amos, my chief mechanical engineering consultant, I resolved to incorporate the idea of stamping the load cell into my main claim. Making a load cell thin enough so that it could be stamped clearly had utility value because it made possible its mass production. Amos was of the opinion that the cost of making cat face–type load cells by any other method would be exorbitant, and would therefore not be suitable for mass production. Stamping clearly distinguished the cat face load cell from the Philips disclosure, and at the same time was a feature that could not be so easily circumvented. That would do.

By the way, the fact that the cat face load cell actually worked—in the sense that it produced highly accurate measurements—was not a distinguishing feature at all. The patent office was concerned simply with identifying new forms that promised to have some utility and giving them patent protection, without any regard at all to whether they actually worked in practice. Strange, but true: taking an idea that did not work and making it work did not merit patent protection. Patents were given for new ideas. And stamping load cells, until now considered delicate instruments that needed to be carefully machined, was indeed a new idea. After some more discussion with Marc, my patent lawyer, I filed an amendment to my application, revising the main claim in the patent application to read thus:

> A low-profile load cell designed for mass production and comprising:
> a. A one-piece, flat, mechanically deformable metal part, stamped from a single piece of thin stock material, comprising . . . [and so on].

The patent examiner in Washington was eventually satisfied that the cat face load cell was indeed novel and useful and awarded it the patent protection it deserved: United States Patent No. 4,993,506 was eventually issued in February of 1991. Patent applications for the cat face load cell were also pending in Canada, the European Union, and Japan, and were eventually approved everywhere.

At the time of my licensing negotiations with Krups, Soehnle, and Counselor I still needed to insist on nondisclosure agreements to protect the confidential know-how embodied in the new load cell. Eventually, once the patent application was approved, I would be able to let go of that cramping shroud of secrecy. The whole point of patents was that they were patent, literally meaning open, open for all to see. That would be a relief, I thought.

* * *

I am sad to report that the promising licensing agreements with Soehnle and Krups, and later with Counselor too, all came to naught. They dematerialized one after the other during a torturous sequence of exchanges that went on and on for months and left me exhausted and spent.

Soehnle sent me two communiqués, one towards the end of May 1990 and one in the middle of June. The first one was from sturdy Stahl, the R&D man. He informed me that they had completed their tests of the prototype scale and the cat face load cells; that they had gotten the same levels of accuracy that I had said they would get; and that they were satisfied with the performance of the load cells. They were discussing production methods and production costs, he wrote. The second one was a rather angry fax, I thought, from Armin Soehnle that said:

> The outcome of the comparison between your load cells and ours is however that we could not find advantages in using your load cells. I also have to tell you that we are very much disappointed about your proposal of the licensing agreement; its conditions are totally unacceptable. Under the given circumstances we have

decided to stop the project. Please tell us what we shall do with the materials received from you.

No advantages? We already agreed that it was cheaper than their own load cell and that it would allow Soehnle to design and manufacture thinner scales. Yet, he did not think that my proposal merited as much as a counter offer. That hurt. I felt ashamed, as though I was being punished for my excessive greed. I wrote back a lame letter offering them better terms, but it was too late. I never heard from them again. Actually, I did hear from them once again, but of that later.

The reaction of Heinrich Komesker from Krups to my proposal was quite similar, yet different in tone. "It seems to us extremely high and we are not willing to accept it," he wrote in late May. "Please send me a proposal stating your required licensing fee per piece. We are waiting for your comment." Not exactly a counter offer, by rather a "nice try, now try again" message.

I thought it over for a while, discussed it with my business advisors—Lucinda and my brother Joe in that case, as Amnon was away—and decided to offer them a more modest proposal. I offered a lower royalty rate; I agreed to be reimbursed for my development costs in two installments, rather than one, and now as an advance on my royalties, rather than as an up-front payment; I accepted lower minimum royalties and a two-year grace period before they were due; and I offered to provide them with free consultations for limited periods while the scale was being developed. Gone was the million-dollar dream. I was in a survival mode now, thinking more of recouping my investments, paying back my loans, and replenishing my depleted coffers.

There followed a long wait while nothing much happened on the scale front. Komesker and I exchanged a few more faxes over that long hot summer. I understood from him that they were studying my proposal and taking their time. The Counselor people were working at an acceptable nondisclosure agreement. There was really not much for me to do.

* * *

On 20 June 1990, I wrote the following lament in my diary, titling it "Stuck!":

> Nothing is happening. Nothing.
>   All hope has evaporated
>   And there is nothing, or next to it,
>   To look forward to.
>   I keep it all on simmer
>   And the energy is gone . . .
>   In the meantime,
>   While nothing is happening,
>   The noose is tightening.
>   I have virtually no money left.

I stopped all work on the prototypes
(Charlie is away on vacation anyway.)
And, most frightening of all,
I have no idea of what to do next.
The green energy is gone.
No money.
I am working for a living:
Joe asked me to help
In planning a new bakery.
$50 an hour.
I have been at it for a week
And it is moving along. Nicely.
I may have $5,000 a month from now . . .
In truth,
I am in dire financial straits.
I have debts,
Luckily with no great pressure to pay.
Yet.
I have more expenses coming,
And no money to pay them with . . .
It hurts.
I am stuck!
And the scale project?
What is happening to the scale project?
It has become a monster
That eats money
And gives nothing in return.
Nothing.
Yes, it is interesting, challenging, adventuresome.
Sure it is better than a nine-to-five job.
But I am starting to hate it.
I have a nice product.
It is beautiful.
It works.
It is accurate.
It can be produced at an affordable cost.
And still,
I got nothing.
Nothing.
I can't do it myself.
I can't even finish a production prototype—
The electronics cost $40,000 to make.
I can't manufacture it myself—

If each scale will cost $25,
I'll need a million dollars in working capital
To stay in business.
What could I do?
I could stop spending on it.
I could get a partner.
I could look for more licensees . . .
For the first time,
I feel that I need a break.
A rest from the scale.
There is really nothing I can do right now.
It is better for me to just work
At making money.
As much of it as possible.
Doing anything that needs doing.
Interesting or not, make it interesting.
Just put in hours . . .
What else is there for me to do?
I can't feed the monster anymore.
I have to stop that . . .
The scale is no longer my friend.
It demands too much
And gives nothing in return.
I will not be as generous with it
As I have been in the past.
I gave it anything it wanted . . .
No more.
Others have to pay too.
Philips got everything free, absolutely free.
I visited the others—free.
I sent prototypes—free.
Nothing in return.
And now I am angry.
Maybe not angry,
But not as generous as before.
Most of all,
I am confused.
I feel betrayed by the scale.
And I feel weird.
A mystical feeling is lurking there.
Its voice says it is all OK.
Wait patiently and something will happen.
Don't do anything, just wait.

And I resist this feeling.

I don't want to start believing in magic and Divine Grace.

I want to make things happen, *make* them happen.

And the voice says Do Nothing.

Just rest for a while.

There is no need to do anything now.

You are tired; rest.

Wait for the new energy to come up.

Wait for a clue, a message.

Krups bowed out of the scale project in early August 1990. Komesker explained to me that their calculations showed that the R&D expenditures required to bring the scale to market would be substantial; that the market for the scale would be limited; that the dollar was too strong to merit production of scales in Europe; and that management had recently decreed that scales were no longer an important product line for Krups. He wished me luck with the thin-scale venture and told me that they were sending back the prototypes.

The Counselor affair dragged on and on. Wayne Dickson sent me a real nondisclosure agreement at the beginning of July 1990, two months after my first visit. I came to Rockford again in mid-July—this time carrying a new prototype—and again, nothing seemed to move. At that point I realized that there was little hope that any licensing agreement with Counselor would ever materialize, and from then on I pursued it with little or no zeal, mostly for lack of a more engaging alternative.

I presented myself there yet again in mid-November at Dickson's invitation. This time the top management was all there: the president of the company, the vice-president for manufacturing, the vice-president for merchandising, and a few others. A nice group of Midwestern gentlemen who were interested in the scale for the duration of the meeting, stood on the prototype and nodded their heads, asked relevant questions, and looked thoughtful.

Yes, they wanted to pursue it further. They needed to ascertain the costs, of course, but the estimates I presented did not strike them as outrageous. They liked the simplicity of the design. The load cells were a bit strange for them, and—like Philips before them—they needed to source them somewhere else. They did not have the right kind of electronics people in-house, they intimated to me; and, more seriously, I sensed that they did not have anyone who could take this project on and bring it to fruition.

By mid-December someone at Counselor managed to test the prototype scale I had left there. As I surmised later, it was tested mainly for repeatability, the least demanding test of all. A 100-pound load was placed on the scale, a reading was taken, and the load was removed. This sequence was repeated numerous times. It turned out that the maximum difference between any two readings was a measly half-ounce. Bob Guinter told me over the phone that Dickson was all over the office waving his arms and shouting, "Half an ounce!, half an ounce!" like a man possessed.

Dickson indeed kept calling me on the phone that December. He really wanted the project to move ahead but, as I said, did not have anyone there—a "product champion," to use Chris Floyd's term in his *Managing Technology for Corporate Success*—who could be relied on to move it ahead.

He did pay for my ticket (for the first time) to come to Rockford for a fourth time—at the beginning of February 1991—to talk to a potential producer from Hong Kong. That producer must have sent Counselor some quotes, but it took Counselor a few more months to finalize its cost estimates.

I received a letter from Dickson on 16 April 1991—15 months to the day after our initial meeting at the Chicago Housewares Exhibition and one year after my first visit to Rockford—informing me that their cost estimates came out to be too high—$3.80 per load cell (excluding the metal part) and $31 for an assembled scale. Those numbers were indeed way outside the range of Counselor's main market segment. "I am disappointed that we could not bring this product to fruition," wrote Dickson, "but its niche in the marketplace is one in which we are not able to focus our efforts at this time." And that was that.

But by that time I had long given up on Counselor. To be precise, I had actually given up on Counselor by the end of the summer of 1990, when the Krups deal fell through. By the end of that summer I had effectively despaired of the licensing option, and having despaired of that option, I had no clear idea of how to pursue the scale project further. I was also embarrassingly short of money, even for my basic personal needs, not to mention the boundless needs of the scale.

* * *

In mid-September of 1990 I started a new venture with Steve Mayo at the World Bank, a venture that would require at least half of my time for at least a year as well as a serious intellectual and emotional commitment. The days of working full-time on the scale were now over.

Following in the footsteps of Lord Kelvin—who was quoted earlier saying that "when you measure what you are speaking about and express it in numbers, you know something about it"—Steve and I were going to introduce measurement into the global housing policy debate, so that one could tell whether housing conditions in one place were better than in another; or whether housing conditions in one place were improving or getting worse over time.

We proposed an ambitious research agenda that involved creating a comprehensive system of housing indicators and then collecting comparative data on these indicators in some 50 countries around the globe. We were fortunately able to obtain a considerable amount of research funds for this purpose, both from the United Nations Centre for Human Settlements in Nairobi and from the World Bank.

In theoretical terms, we needed to articulate a broad and systematic understanding of what in the housing sector needed to be measured and why. In practical terms, we had to create a comprehensive set of housing indicators, simple quantitative measures each of which would provide a summary status report on a particular aspect of the housing sector; measures that could be standardized, so that housing conditions in different cities and countries could be compared. Taken together, these indicators were to inform policymakers of all the key dimensions of the housing sector, highlighting particular aspects of the sector that required special attention and comparing housing sector performance at different times and in different places.

Our survey of the prior art yielded all the housing indicators that had already been defined in one context or another. We eventually had to invent new indicators for important aspects of the housing sector that needed to be measured but for which we could not find an indicator in the existing literature. In a sense, inventing new indicators was no different than inventing new products and services to meet identifiable needs.

My initial motivation for signing on to the housing indicators venture was no doubt economic—I had to find a sustainable source of income to keep me going while I continued to attend to the scale. I did not seek full-time employment—that would have entailed dropping the scale project altogether. Instead, I opted for the indicator work as a part-time job. It involved commuting to Washington once a week for two days, and usually spending the night with Steve's family at their suburban ranch-style home in Great Falls, Virginia, with Steve usually cooking a sumptuous meal and me performing the more mundane duties of a sous chef.

And the scale? I was now pursuing the scale project with much less zeal and with the more modest and much less pleasant objective of recovering my investment. I still sorely wanted a lightweight, thin, and accurate scale to see the light of day. But I was not as confident as before that I was pursuing the right objectives.

Accuracy, especially in the United States, did not appear to be a major concern, nor did the scale have a very large mass market. The lightness and thinness of my design—I was beginning to realize—were two-edged swords. They looked good and felt good, but they also made the scale look too fragile and too dangerous to stand on, especially if it was slightly raised from the floor (to ensure that the plate did not touch it). Lightness as an objective, introduced with the idea of travel in mind, did not really have a mass market either, if Soenhle's word was to be taken seriously. Maybe, I wondered, it could be discarded as an objective altogether without any great loss.

To the extent that my energy and my enthusiasm in the pursuit of the scale were directly proportional to my commitment to my objectives, I could feel my enthusiasm subside. My objectives no longer felt pure and clear, especially while the costs of pursuing them further kept escalating. "Is it all worthwhile?" kept requiring new answers. Now it was my sense of responsibility—recovering my investment, or at least paying back my debts—that gave me energy and kept me working on the scale project. But it was a part of me I didn't particularly like. I would have rather pursued the scale work because it was fun.

Now, slowly but steadily, it was the housing indicators work that was providing the fun. In October of that year I took a two-week trip to Eastern Europe and Southeast Asia, setting up pilot projects for testing the housing indicators in Hungary, Thailand, and the Philippines. The work was almost effortless. In two or three days in each place I managed to meet senior government officials, negotiate for funds, talk with our research teams, set up advisory groups, and generate enthusiasm for our project. I felt like a fish in water.

My self-esteem batteries, largely depleted by my failed licensing efforts of the past year, were recharged during that trip too. In Manila, for example, I met the gentle and silver-haired Theodoro Katigbak, the de facto minister of housing in Corazon Aquino's cabinet. I thought I was just paying him a courtesy call, to introduce myself and to tell him about the Housing Indicators Program. But, much to my surprise, he kept me in his office for two and a half hours, enjoying my company and picking my brains. At some point he told me a story: "I was once very depressed by a problem I had and our mutual friend Bill Keyes brought me that article of yours on upgrading slum infrastructure. That article lifted my spirits and made it clear what it was really all about. From then on, I give it to anyone that comes to me with a problem he thinks he cannot solve." That was nice to hear. I needed that.

* * *

To confess, after coming back from that trip I thought of ditching the scale and forgetting all about it. I imagined yet another possible ending to the scale saga: Angel gets involved with housing indicators; falls back in love with housing, his old flame; and drops the thin-scale project as if it never happened.

It was then that Ziggy Zee called me. Ziggy was an enterprising electronics engineer whom I had consulted a couple of times before on cost estimates for the electronics of the thin scale. He told me over the phone that some people he knew (no names were mentioned) were interested in producing the scale and marketing it globally. We needed to talk, he said. The scale saga was not yet over.

17

The Mismanagement
of Product Development

I have been told the saying "May you live in interesting times" is considered by the Chinese to be a curse. Being in product development, you probably already knew that.

Erwin Frand, *The Art of Product Development*

The conditions of labour and life, the sense of joy, anger or frustration that lie behind the production of commodities, the states of mind of the producers, are all hidden to us as we exchange one object (money) for another (the commodity). We can take our daily breakfast without a thought for the myriad people who engaged in its production.

David Harvey, *The Condition of Postmodernity*

———

When I met Ziggy Zee to discuss the new venture he proposed, I had already despaired of licensing the scale patents to Soehnle, Krups, or Counselor. The prospect of a new venture offered me some consolation after that sequence of disappointments. There was still hope for my thin scale. Ziggy proposed that the two of us develop and design the scale together, getting it ready for manufacture in one year. I liked that. We would have all the financial backing we needed, he said. I liked that too.

I welcomed the idea of working with Ziggy, both because he knew his electronics and because he was experienced in product development. He struck me as a solid businessman and a brilliant engineer; an inventor with a firm grounding in the practical aspects of bringing a host of new electronic products to market; a bit secretive maybe—like all inventors that have been burned by talking too much—but that was to be expected. He was about 50 years old, of medium build, with straight black hair brushed back, a trimmed black goatee, wire-frame glasses, and street-smart eyes.

Ziggy was the president and CEO of a small company that manufactured and sold sophisticated electronic circuitry for use in industrial control systems. The company, Think Systems, was located in Lower Manhattan, not more than a ten-minute walk from Lucinda's loft. We met after working hours in mid-December of 1990 at his deserted offices.

He showed me a couple of faxes he had received from "Victor" (no last name), the president of Home Products of Detroit, Michigan. Victor said he could sell 100,000 scales in the first year, Ziggy explained. There were three other investors interested in coming in on the deal, he added; and, in partnership with Home Products, they were ready to finance the development of the scale into a marketable product—getting it ready for manufacturing, that is. Home Products would then manufacture and distribute it. Ziggy wanted to be in on it too, he said, and he would take care of the electronics.

"I have no doubt that he can do the electronics," I wrote in my diary on 14 December 1990, "I have doubts that I can make any money out of this deal. Too many fingers in the stew, as they say. . . . I asked about the deal. It was 10:30 by then; Ziggy was too tired to talk about it. I thought we already agreed on it, he said." I didn't quite get it. Maybe it was too early to talk about money. I did experience some discomfort just then—something didn't feel quite right about the whole affair—but I let it pass.

* * *

The deal started to take shape when we all met at the Chicago Housewares Exhibition in early January 1991, some three weeks after the meeting with Ziggy in Lower Manhattan.

> Other than meeting Victor of Home Products (and Nora, his product develop-
> ment lady) [I wrote in my diary on 13 January], there was nothing to learn there.
> The scales were again old tricks in new clothing, exteriors dominating interiors,
> glitter dominating essence, and maximalism dominating minimalism. The *New
> York Times* reported last Thursday, "At a Housewares Show in Chicago, the Old
> Reliables Shine." The picture accompanying the article shows the Big Foot scale
> ($80), which can accommodate size 15 feet, and that is an electronic version of a
> model introduced 70 years ago [Fig. 52]. "Moreover, the digital display produces
> two-inch-high numbers—the largest readout in the industry, according to Health-
> O-Meter officials." How tiresome.

Victor was somewhere in his fifties, tall, lanky, and restless. He had a prominent nose and deep blue eyes that kept shooting forays of registered glances around the room. He must have a lot on his mind, I gathered: putting out an array of "home products"—hundreds of articles with no common technology to bind them—trying to keep abreast of the shifting tastes of unreliable consumers; worrying about his company's cash flow; and remaining always on the lookout for the next novelty, the coming attraction. For the moment, he was focused on scales, but only for the moment. He could now envision a new Home Products scale in his mind's eye, a scale that would not only be thin, light, and highly accurate, but would also have a memory feature (he suggested storing the last 14 weights of three or four persons), as well as a clock, date, and temperature display. It would also have a feature for weighing babies.

I had thrown in that last suggestion myself after seeing a recent newspaper clipping from the *Bangkok Post* that a friend had sent me: "UNICEF is about to produce 150,000 solar-powered weighing scales.... When a mother or health worker stands on them, they see their weight, then zero it by covering the display and solar cell. Next they are handed the infant whose weight is displayed."

The clipping said that the scale was patented in Australia. What was patented, I could never imagine; surely not the well-known tare feature. Every counter scale in every delicatessen had one: first you put an empty container on the scale; then you press a

52 *The electronic Big Foot scale*

tare button that zeroes the reading; then, when you place the full container on the scale, the scale displays the net weight of its contents. Still, using the tare function for weighing babies—even though not patentable—was an attractive feature that I had not thought about before, and I was now happy to appropriate.

The baby-weighing idea was accepted without further ado, and a preliminary list of features was hastily agreed upon in Chicago in a matter of a couple of hours while we had Victor's attention. Buoyed by the excitement in the room and the sense of camaraderie and anticipation that came with planning a thrilling journey together, I signed on to this list too, without giving it much thought. But in retrospect, as a product development strategy, it made little, if any, sense.

The thin scale had guts that were different from the personal scales that were on the market at the time, scales that utilized the compound-lever system first introduced by John Wyatt in the 1760s (Fig. 7). Getting rid of the lever system was thus a departure from the *dominant design* of personal scales.

"A dominant design," explains V. K. Narayanan in *Managing Technology and Innovation for Competitive Advantage*, "is defined as the product that wins the allegiance of the marketplace, the one that competitors and innovators must adhere to if they hope to command a significant market following." If we were to introduce the first product of a new generation of personal scales that challenged that dominant design, it would have made more sense to focus on a core product with no features beyond those deemed absolutely necessary to launch it.

Robert Burgelman and his colleagues, in their *Strategic Management of Technology and Innovation*, explain the distinction between the core product in a new line and other products in that line:

A *core* product is the engineering platform, providing the basis for further enhancements. The core product is the initial, standard product introduced. It changes little from year to year and is often the benchmark against which consumers compare the rest of the product line. *Enhanced* products are developed from the core design; distinctive features are added for various, more discriminating markets. . . . The *cost-reduced* model starts with essentially the same technology and design of the core product but is a stripped version, often with less expensive materials and lower factory costs, aimed at a price-sensitive market.

These distinctions were not at all clear during our meeting in Chicago. In fact, to use the terminology of Burgelman and his colleagues, we were discussing an enhanced version of the core product that would be sold at the price of a cost-reduced model. We wanted everything: the design, accuracy, and special features of the best of the luxury models at the cost of the standard electronic scales in the market that Home Products catered to, that is, $50 or less. Surely, if it could be made to happen, this kind of product required no market research because it was a no-brainer: consumers would be getting something for nothing—more features and an innovative design at no extra cost. No wonder that the Home Products people thought they could sell 100,000 of those in the first year.

The correct approach to developing the thin scale, as a new core product, would have focused on getting the scale plate and the load cell ready for manufacturing, and on introducing the minimally necessary electronics for making it work as a scale. This scale was conceived, after all, with a minimalist agenda. But now—while still retaining its minimalist look—it was all bells and whistles when it came to features.

For some unobvious reason, we have all come to believe that electronic features—particularly those involving software—can be added on at virtually no cost, ad infinitum. And so, we piled them on: memory of the past weights of several persons, baby weighing, a pound-to-kilograms switch, an electronic clock, a calendar, a thermometer, a low-battery indicator, and so on. Why not? Too bad all of these features were invisible. Had they been visible to the naked eye, the scale would have looked like a Jeepney, the much-venerated Filipino taxi so full of bells and whistles that sometimes you could barely recognize that it was, after all, a car (Fig. 53).

The Chicago meeting ended with an agreement to meet again in New York in late January, by which time Ziggy and I would have prepared draft contracts for all to sign, as well as a development plan with a detailed budget. The goal we were all aiming at was to have production prototypes on display in the next Chicago Housewares Exhibition a year hence. That target date looked entirely feasible.

For the first time, there were real people ready to invest real money both in bringing the thin scale to market and in using my design. That certainly meant a lot to me. Finally, after all these years, there was Other People's Money, just as I was running out of steam and out of cash. I had been waiting too long for that to happen, for other people to acknowledge that I had something there and to be willing to back their trust in my invention and in my design with their money.

But now that it was finally happening, I wanted it so badly that my judgment became quite clouded: "Whirled by the three passions," writes Ungo, a Seventeenth-century Zen Buddhist poet, "one's eyes go blind." The meditative and detached state of mind with which I started the scale project was all but gone now, replaced by what amounted to craving, one of the three passions. All I knew was that I had to realize that thin-scale design, to somehow make it happen, to bring it out so that I could let go of it and get on with the rest of my life. I wanted to see my cherished scale finally grace the shelves of stores. Never mind a million dollars, as long as I could eventually recover my investment and as long as I had final cut on the design.

It was then—as I started to work with Ziggy—that the scale, first imperceptibly and then unabashedly, began to require ever more painful sacrifices. These sacrifices were not simply monetary ones—I was already accustomed to those— they were sacrifices that, slowly but surely, drained all the fun out of the scale project, and a lot of my residual enthusiasm along with it. I became so enchanted with the promise that the Home Products deal offered, that I was willing to compromise the two most important things in my life—love and work.

There were two contracts to be drafted—a license agreement and a development agreement. The license agreement was a contract between the investors and me alone, whereby I allowed them to use my two patents—the sandwich

53 *A Filipino Jeepney*

plate patent and the cat face load cell patent—in exchange for royalties on the sales of scales. In my desperation, I agreed to receive no up-front payment for the use of my patents and to forego minimum annual royalty payments as well. I also agreed to reduce my royalty rates. Even if Home Products sold 100,000 scales a year, at $30 apiece, both here and abroad, I stood to make no more than $100,000 a year for a few years under the best of circumstances. Gone, as I said, was the million-dollar dream.

Gone was another dream, too: a sabbatical year in Nagoya. Lucinda and I planned to take her two children with us in the fall to Nagoya, where I would be teaching urban planning at Nagoya University while we all started living together as a family. We were all ready to take that step, and starting it there was an exciting proposition. The deliberations about going to Japan together took a long time, as did finding the right school for the children. We talked for many an evening about daily life in Japan, about visiting Zen temples, about sleeping on *tatami* mats, about living among the Japanese, and about spending a lot of time together. The university was especially generous, agreeing to cover all our expenses handsomely—our travels, the children's schooling, our lodging, and our living expenditures. But that was not to be.

Once the scale contracts were signed, I had to write Nagoya and back out of the sabbatical, so that I could attend to my duties in the development of the scale. Our future hosts in Nagoya were very understanding: "There are always unpredictables around us," they wrote back. Lucinda understood too. We both let go of Nagoya to start a new chapter in our deepening relationship: living together as a family in the SoHo loft. But it hurt us all the same: it cut into our love and our togetherness, and the pain of that cut stayed with us. "The thin scale is an altar on which the trip to Japan was sacrificed. What else will it want?" I wrote in my diary.

The development agreement was a contract between Ziggy and me as the "developers," and Home Products and the three partners as the "investors." Ziggy and I promised our best effort to bring the thin scale with all the agreed-upon features into production in one year. The investors promised to invest $150,000 in our efforts, to be disbursed according to an agreed-upon schedule of payments.

From Home Products' perspective, this project involved the external acquisition of technology because the technical and managerial resources for inventing and developing new personal scales in-house were not available. The acquisition— rather than the in-house invention and development—of new technology, by the way, has by now become ubiquitous the world over: it was estimated that by the end of the 1990s, 30 percent of European companies, 40 percent of United States companies, and 60 percent of Japanese companies relied heavily on external sources of technology. This required the development of new management structures. It also placed new demands on leadership in the development of new products, especially in cases where the external resources were not under the direct control of management, as was the case with our scale project.

Companies, writes Vittorio Chiesa in *R&D Strategy and Organization*, may acquire new technology by acquiring other companies; by recruiting experts; by mergers; by purchasing licenses; by joint ventures and alliances; by funding R&D contracts; or by outsourcing technological activities, as Home Products did in our case:

> Outsourcing implies a very low impact on the firm's resources: only financial resources are allocated by the company and no external resources (technology, know-how or people) used for the collaboration, are integrated within the company.... The level of control over activities is low.... Control over results is high.... As a consequence, outsourcing implies a very low level of risk, given that activities remain external to the company.... Outsourcing typically has a brief time horizon.... The level of reversibility is very high.

This description proved to be very precise in our case: Home Products could not control our activities, but it could control results through the flow of funds and it could opt out at any time. The Home Products management could still provide leadership by sustaining a climate of innovation and risk taking, by keeping open lines of communication, by ensuring the smooth flow of funds, and by insisting on quality and on-time performance.

The development agreement put Ziggy and me in charge of getting the scale ready for mass production, as comanagers of the contract in some form of a loose partnership, without specifying the distribution of authority between us any further. We were in it together, so to speak, and we were both responsible for making it happen. It was assumed, I suppose, that any and all management decisions would have to be made by consensus, arrived at through mutual agreement.

In practice, it meant that I would have to run everything by Ziggy and that he could veto any and all proposals I had about how to move forward and especially about how to spend money. When it came to providing leadership, I was seriously handicapped because I knew next to nothing about product development. I had to rely on Ziggy both to guide the development process and to lead the progress along the electronics track. I also consented to Ziggy's holding the purse strings and depositing the money we would receive from the investors in his bank account. As far as product development went, I was his apprentice. Given the circumstances, there was nothing inherently wrong with this arrangement, or so I thought.

* * *

The beginning of my collaboration with Ziggy was quite promising. He had a very clear idea of how product development was initiated: it was initiated with the creation of a product development plan. The core of this plan was a flow chart that had a built-in time schedule and a budget for all the project's activities, all the intermediary products, and all the decision points along the way. Our work on the Home Products project started by sitting together in front of his computer at his deserted office at night, for hours on end, creating our plan. The plan looked like an array of boxes—each with a name, a dollar budget, and a time budget—connected together with arrows in such a way that it was possible to tell which activities, decision points, and intermediary products were on the critical path. Those that were on the critical path needed special attention because failure to complete them on time would delay the entire project.

A schematic diagram of our initial $150,000 product development plan is shown in Fig. 54. The plan proceeded along four parallel tracks: a marketing track that moved towards the final determination of features, specifications, package design, costs, and prices; an electronic track that moved through software and hardware development towards final prototypes ready for production; the scale-plate track that moved towards the final design of the top and bottom plates and the preparation of steel molds and dies for producing them; and the load-cell track that involved finalizing the design of the load cell and its associated parts (e.g., the rubber foot below it) and the preparation of steel dies for their mass production.

The electronic track was found to be on the critical path (shown in hatched boxes) throughout the development process. The development of the load cell and the scale plate was already more advanced, and was not likely to delay the project as a whole.

The long hours required to produce our initial flow chart and its many revisions over time were generally well spent. They allowed both of us to articulate what we already knew and to learn from each other what we did not know— Ziggy learned about plates and load cells, while I learned more about the electronics. I also needed to learn about the steps (and costs) involved in getting a new product ready for mass production.

The flow chart made possible the breaking of the project down into a set of discrete activities. Its value was in limiting the necessary coordination between these activities to a minimum, and thus allowing one to focus attention and resources on a single activity, solving one small problem at a time instead of being overwhelmed by all the problems at once. There was no question that, at

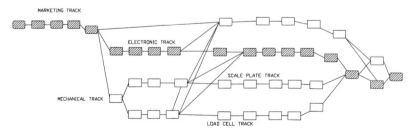

54 *A schematic diagram of our product development plan*

least in theory, this was a useful approach to product development. It paralleled the breaking down of a complex design problem into a hierarchy of manageable design problems that could then be solved one at a time (Fig. 10).

Our plan charted the path to the completion of the development phase of the thin scale in one year from the day the contracts were signed and the first installment of funds was made available. By the end of that year—we promised—all the necessary tools would be in place to start mass production. The drafts of both contracts, as well as the draft development plan, were ready for the meeting with Victor and the three partners in New York in late January, but Victor never showed up.

* * *

The prospects for having the production prototypes ready for the next housewares show in Chicago, as originally agreed, became dimmer and dimmer as weeks went by. The crucial meeting to launch the development plan only took place one late afternoon in early April in the office-cum-warehouse of one of the investors, Ruben Stamm, who was apparently in the import-export business. It was a shabby place full of unseemly piles of shapeless cardboard boxes, somewhere on Lexington Avenue and Thirtieth Street or thereabouts. We sat in a windowless room, in a clearing that for now was made into a conference area. It had a vomit-green carpet that screamed for a vacuum cleaner with a few uncomfortable chairs strewn around it.

I felt as though I was in a shadow play, where every participant had a scripted role. We were five. I was the inventor and the designer. Ziggy was the product development specialist. Horace Boneh—another one of the investors—was the interlocutor, the in-between man orchestrating the deal. Ruben was playing host, trying to read the situation and somehow make himself useful. At some point, when there was a lull in the conversation, he asked Victor what his plans were for later that night. The New York Knicks were playing the legendary Chicago Bulls, and he had two good tickets. He offered Victor to join him. That, by and large, was his sole contribution to the entire project. Later on, he appeared here and there from time to time, but he never managed to invest his share.

Victor was playing the man to be humored and enjoying himself immensely. He was animated yet relaxed. "We need the memory feature," he said, "all 14 last weighings. It's got to be a computer, not just a scale." He liked the baby-scale feature too. The three investors looked at our $150,000 development plan and were satisfied. The target place and date were now shifted to the San Francisco Housewares Show in late April the following year, roughly a year hence.

"This has not really sunk in yet," I wrote in my diary on 5 April 1991. "There is money to finish the development and there is a real deadline. Ziggy will supervise the development of the electronics, and Home Products will provide a plastics engineer to work with us, free of charge. . . . Charlie will help. I will get paid for every day of work I put in, and will not have to pay for consultants, materials, or prototypes anymore. This is all a bit unreal, but it is definitely on. It is on. . . . We are shooting for a $17 cost target. . . . This seems quite difficult, especially in small quantities. . . . I worry that we won't make it, but at least the ball is in my hands right now: it is up to me if we make it or not." In short, I was all geared up and ready to move. But as I was soon to realize, the ball was not in my hands, and it was not up to me whether we made it or not.

At the conclusion of that meeting, Ziggy and I were given a green light to start the project. But it quickly became clear that the green light meant very little because our car, to pursue the analogy further, had no petrol. Our draft development contract specified that we needed $20,000 upon signature and $20,000 every month thereafter. That contract went back and forth for months, with a change made here and there, and was only signed in late July, almost four months into our carefully crafted flowchart.

Even then, the funds due upon signature were not made available. The first payment of $10,000 was only received in mid-August of 1991, and three more small payments like that one trickled our way every two months, on average— one in October, one in January, and one in February. In other words, the cash never flowed as it should have. The expected delivery date for production prototypes, however, remained April, and the investors did not feel that this merited any further discussion.

Ziggy and I started to move immediately after the April meeting. We finalized our plan. Ziggy recruited an engineer to design the electronics package, and I started to work with Charlie on the design of a new mechanical prototype. But without any cash to fuel our work, everyone's progress was intermittent and lethargic. The project could never accumulate sufficient energy and enthusiasm to really take off.

In the words of Smith and Reinersten, the authors of *Developing Products in Half the Time*, we were simply victims of the "fuzzy front end" syndrome. They observed that in typical development projects, as much as half the total development time (and sometimes as much as 90 percent of it) is consumed before a full development team starts working on it. We were no exception to that rule.

* * *

Ziggy and I were off to a slow and rather shaky start, and the ritual launch of the project—with a full team in tow—never took place even when the money did start to drip our way. In early April, Ziggy brought Ken Kloome on board to design the electronics for the scale. He assured me that Ken, who had worked with him on a number of projects before, was the right man for the job. Ken was a big, broad shouldered, bald man with a highly developed sense of self-importance and a short temper; and, as it turned out, not the right man for the job at all, especially since his work was on the so-called critical path.

To begin with, he did not know much of anything about scale electronics and was learning on the job at our expense. Scale electronics was not something that you could read about in a book and master in a few hours. Like all technical know-how, it had to be accumulated through years of experience in making special electronics circuits for scales. To quote V. K. Narayanan again: "A characteristic feature of technical know-how is that it is not easily transmitted. . . . Pure scientific knowledge, the output of basic research, is equally available to all the actors in the technological field. . . . However, technical know-how, the output of applied and developmental research, is largely product- and process-specific."

That is why, for example, there are no good books on the design of specific types of objects—be it the design of hospitals, airplanes, cars, shoes, domestic policy, or scale electronics. The knowledge is out there, surely, but it is in the heads of specialists. We needed one of those specialists for this job, not a generalist like Ken. This does not mean that the man was not intelligent. He was, in fact, both intelligent and experienced but he was still not the right man for the job.

Actually, the theory underlying scale electronics is quite straightforward, and Ken understood it very well. It is based on a simple electrical circuit for the precise measurement of small resistance changes called a *Wheatstone bridge*. The circuit is named after Sir Charles Wheatstone (1802–1875), a shy English inventor who never even claimed to have invented it. He came upon a description of the circuit in 1843 and put it to good use—measuring the value of an unknown resistance. The mistaken attribution of that circuit to Sir Charles is yet another example of Stigler's law of eponymy, which states: "No scientific discovery is named after its original discoverer." Stigler himself, by the way, does not claim to have been the original discoverer of his law, and therefore feels perfectly justified in putting his name to it.

Wheatstone bridges are very common in electronics, and I am quite sure that Ken Kloome crossed many a Wheatstone bridge in his time; but the ones in scales were distinctive, especially when it came to connecting all the four load cells of the thin scale—with their eight strain gages—into one or more bridges. The complications started apparently when the four load cells were not exactly equal in sensitivity, as ours were.

The reliable Charlie Kientzler—himself a mechanical engineer who did specialize in scales—had to spend many hours patiently composing long letters to Ken—and annotating them with complicated formulas that must have taken him forever to type using only his two index fingers—explaining why Ken's ideas about Wheatstone bridges were plainly wrong in our case.

Ken started out by quickly producing a 12-page paper entitled "Specifications for an Intelligent Scale." It was ready by late May of 1991, even before our contracts were signed. I was impressed. It described in detail what button on the scale needed to be pushed for each weighing procedure—general weighing, general weighing with save, weighing baby, and so on—and what part of the display would light up or blink with each operation.

Sometime later on, Ken was the one to suggest, for example, that remembering the last 10 or 14 weights for three people was an exercise in overkill, proposing instead that each user simply register his or her baseline weight when starting a diet. The scale would then show each user how many pounds had been lost (or gained) since the onset of his or her diet, by simply pressing a button. That was a good suggestion, I thought.

According to Ken, a typical weighing sequence would proceed as follows: you press the lower part of the scale plate and the scale turns on; you mount the scale; your weight appears on the display, assay 128.6; you dismount and press your personal switch: I, II, or III. Then several displays appear in close succession: the word *last* appears; then the difference from your last weight, say -1.2, appears; then the word *base* appears; then your baseline weight, say 158.0, appears; then *diff* appears; then the difference from your baseline weight, say -22.4, appears.

"The scale thus gives your present weight, your progress, and your long-term trend," I wrote in my diary. "In short, all you need to know. Much better than your last ten weights. You can then change your baseline weight; say, when you reach your target weight of 125.0. It will then tell you the fluctuations from your target weight. This feels good, really good."

Then, once Ken completed the electronic specifications to his satisfaction, he stopped working, preferring to get paid before moving on. He got paid a few months later, when we had some funds thrown our way in August. Then he did some detective work, trying to identify the best microprocessor for the job. This work, originally scheduled for completion in a week, was only completed by the end of January 1992, some five months later. He stopped working again after that when one of his invoices went unanswered. And so it went. His erratic behavior, I must say, did not exactly endear him to me: I assumed he was a part of my team and he didn't act like one. We had a common deadline to meet, after all, and he couldn't care less about it. But he had mouths to feed, and I could not really blame him, after all.

In addition to his erratic engagement with us, the man did not have a lot of respect for our time and budget allocations for each of the activities on the electronics track, so accurately estimated in our carefully crafted flow chart. Because we changed his assignment from time to time, as we learned more about the electronics, he felt that he was given license to spend as many hours as he fancied he needed, entirely oblivious both to cost overruns and to the havoc it created on our critical path. According to my conservative calculations and his invoices, he did five hundred hours of stop-and-go work over a period of 18 months to complete four (out of ten) activities on the electronics track, for which our initial flowchart allocated 100 hours over a period of 2 months.

Ziggy, meanwhile, remained ever so cool and detached, too busy with his personal and professional lives to monitor Ken and guide him, let alone to discipline him. So much for leadership. He kept revising his flowchart from time to time, trying to convince me (and himself) that some of Ken's work could be accounted for under some other activity, and sinking deeper into denial. My occasional comment on the matter was ignored. I found myself staring at a blank and impervious face. He kept me at arm's length, letting me understand that "things" were under control, but never managing to be entirely convincing because they weren't.

"Why is it that so many development projects fail to deliver fully on their planned goals and anticipated benefits?" Because, say Robert Burgelman and his colleagues, "[i]n too many instances, management at all levels fails to provide the leadership required for success." This is a sensible conclusion, and it makes even more sense when one considers that "leadership" resources for new product development are frequently in very short supply.

"We don't need more ideas," says Gillette's Thomas Singer, "we need more champions." Since champions are hard to find, it would be irrational to allocate the limited supply of champions to marginal projects. And without champions, marginal projects were more than likely to fail. Unfortunately, the scale project was indeed marginal for all the participants except for me, and, not surprisingly, the leadership resources allocated to it were minimal indeed.

Ziggy, I found out to my chagrin, was practically never available. Beyond putting together the original project flow chart, revising it every two to three months, and showing up for a meeting here and there, he did next to nothing. More worrisome was my gradual realization that he did not behave like a business partner either.

It turned out that the three investor-partners were his friends. They were the ones who had the direct link to Victor, and they did some business with Victor occasionally. Officially, Ziggy and I were partners who—in my book—owed our primary loyalty to our partnership. Within our partnership, we were supposedly insiders who could share our confidences. Unofficially, Ziggy and the three investors were friends and neighbors who owed a longstanding loyalty to each other. In the unofficial realm, they shared their confidences and I was the outsider.

Some time later on, when I once casually asked Ziggy what he expected to gain from the project—beyond the measly fees we were both being paid for our time spent in development—he intimated to me, rather shamelessly I thought, that his investor friends promised him a cut of their profits, as a side payment for his help in developing the product; so much for avoiding conflicts of interest.

In fact, having Ziggy on board just added an extra layer of bureaucracy to the project. The three investors wanted to protect their investment, and they quickly figured that to remain informed they should remain in the loop, so to speak. Since their major contribution to the project was bringing Victor, Ziggy, and me together, they perceived themselves as the natural candidates for liaising between us.

So it came to pass that informal communication channels were established, channels that slowly and steadily became the official channels as well. I soon found myself at least twice removed from Victor (Solly-Ziggy-Horace-Victor), assuming that Horace could get past Nora and talk to Victor directly every time.

Given that all the people on this chain were difficult to reach, this arrangement ensured that I was permanently marginalized, and that my contacts with top management were nonexistent.

That state of affairs was made painfully clear to me on one occasion when I realized that I needed to go to Detroit at short notice to champion the scale project. I simply had to talk to the Home Products people directly, to explain to them where we were and why, and to get their feedback and their support. Yet both Ziggy and Horace refused to approve the funds for my traveling there. I could barely contain myself; I felt like a depraved prisoner trying to break out of his leg irons, his shackles tearing into his bleeding ankles. No wonder: I had just lost the power to champion my work.

That was bad enough. But to make matters worse, the scale itself—while attracting their attention for a short while at the onset of the project—was quickly marginalized too. Home Products, as a housewares company, at least had some cheap scales on the market, probably produced to their own skin design specifications by Stephen Lee in Taiwan or by his alter ego in Hong Kong. The three investor-partners has no business with scales whatsoever. Two of them—Horace and Virgil—owned a mail order company that sold office products through a fancy catalog. The third partner, as I mentioned earlier, was in some kind of import-export business.

Whether the development of the thin scale was successful or not—especially in the medium or long term—was of marginal interest to them (and to Ziggy, for that matter, too). The futures of their companies did not depend on it; they did not need this product to improve their overall competitive position in the marketplace; they were not interested in using the new technology to change their way of doing business; they did not have a long-term strategy for acquiring a market share with a line of new scale products; and they kept the development of the scale at arm's length from their own core businesses to minimize their risk. They were risking their money, but the scale project was not a central component in their overall business strategies, and therefore it did not deserve their loyalty, their long-term commitment, their undivided attention, or their loving care.

In Soehnle's case, of course, it would have been quite different. The introduction of my patented load cell would have improved their leadership position in the global scale market, as it would have allowed them to break the one-inch thickness barrier with a new generation of thin scales. The cat face load cell could have formed a key element of their overall product development strategy, a strategy that already included four-load-cell scales; and it would have been developed in-house, by their own development people, possibly with some marginal help from me. A pity.

Not surprisingly, I did not understand the relationship between individual inventions and the overall product development strategy of large corporations at the time. I understand it better now: corporations have specific needs for new technology, technology that could consolidate their leadership in the marketplace, modernize their way of doing business, ensure their continued competitiveness, and improve their profitability. If inventions address these needs directly, they become valuable as central elements in the corporate product development strategy. If they address these needs only marginally, they are likely to be marginalized.

* * *

Ken was paid a total of almost $20,000 for writing that wonderful paper about the features of the proposed scale; for drawing some preliminary schematic diagrams; and for carefully choosing a microprocessor and an analog-to-digital converter that in his view could do the job, but that—unbeknownst to him, apparently—would cost twice as much as our budget allowed.

But he never got as far as designing an actual electronic circuit, ordering any electronic components for a prototype, or writing any software instructions. The battery problem—that he thought could be handled by using a pulsating current instead of a continuous one, to save on power—remained unsolved. Like I said, he was not the right man for the job. He may have been one of those bright, creative thinkers, an idea-generator rather than a doer or finisher. Consequently, 70 percent of the money designated for the electronic track was spent on Ken while 13 percent of the work got done. By mid-March of 1992, for example, just before a crucial meeting with the Home Products people, he had very little to show.

While Ken was slowly ambling along the electronic track, I was trying to register some progress along the mechanical track. First, I had to complete the design of the plate, but I was no longer as confident as before that I was pursuing the right design objectives for the plate. Lightness and thinness—I already realized—were two-edged swords. The thin scale as a design object certainly looked good, but it could appear to be too fragile and too dangerous to step on, especially if it was slightly raised from the floor (to ensure that the plate would not touch the floor under load). The 18-pound Big Foot scale that I had seen in Chicago, for example, was really sturdy, the exact opposite of fragile. No person, no matter how heavy, would be reluctant to step on it.

Lightness as an objective, introduced with the idea of travel in mind, did not really have a mass market, if Armin Soenhle's word was to be taken seriously. He said, I recalled, that travel scales formed less than 1 percent of his overall market. A Sharper Image catalog that came out in early 1991 had a new travel scale that doubled as an alarm clock. It was 4.5 inches in diameter and weighed only 12 ounces, or three-quarters of a pound. To weigh oneself, one had to stand on the ball of one's foot (see Fig. 55), and lightly touch a nearby wall to maintain one's balance. This must be the

55 *The travel mini-scale*

ultimate in portability, I thought, but it would never become anything more than a novelty, and it could never double as a scale that would be regularly used at home.

I now wanted my scale to function mainly as a home scale that could be used for occasional travel as well. My interest in the scale as a pure travel accessory was a thing of the past. I was now interested in a minimalist design for an accurate personal scale for home use. Maybe, I speculated, the one-pound weight limit could be discarded as an objective altogether without any great loss. One-and a half pounds, even a bit more, would be OK too. But the thinness still mattered to me. When, in a moment of weakness, I proposed making the scale slightly thicker than a quarter of an inch, Ziggy would hear none of it. A quarter of an inch, he said, was a feature that we wanted to use in marketing the scale; and to do that, the scale had to be a quarter of an inch and not more. I did not need to be convinced.

The quarter-inch objective made the design problem of the scale a very demanding problem, requiring a high degree of discipline of all the participants. It restricted the available options and the free play of possibilities, forcing everyone to follow a strict set of self-imposed rules without diminishing their creativity. In essence, it transformed the design problem into a game. Bernard Suits, in *The Grasshopper: Games, Life and Utopia,* provides the following definition: "To play a game is to attempt to achieve a specific state of affairs . . . using only means permitted by the rules . . . where the rules prohibit use of more efficient in favour of less efficient means, . . . and where the rules are accepted just because they make possible such activity. . . . Playing a game is the voluntary attempt to overcome unnecessary obstacles."

The thin-scale design problem certainly fit this definition. The quarter-inch rule affected every design decision. To function effectively as a member of the design team, you needed to willingly abide by this rule as part of your design self-discipline. For those lacking in such self-discipline, there had to be an enforcer of that rule, someone like me who insisted on it despite a host of arguments brought forth by design engineers who had wonderful solutions that did not comply with it.

In the process of design and development, to make life easy for oneself, one naturally sought to question constraints, especially the artificial ones, the ones that made the design problem into a game. Why a quarter-inch? Why a one-pound weight? Why a 100-gram accuracy? There you have it. Get rid of the rules and the design problem becomes trivial and uninteresting. As for myself, I was gradually getting good at this particular game—the thin-scale design game—and the better I got at it, the more I wanted to play by the rules and the more I insisted that others play by the rules. But, since I was the one who came up with the quarter-inch rule, I had to convince others that this was indeed a good and workable rule that made for an interesting game; otherwise, I would end up playing by myself. For now, the others liked the rule and were willing to play the game, allowing me to assume the role of designer, which included the role of the referee who enforced the rule.

Conceptually, the thin-scale problem was now already solved, meaning that it did not appear to require any new research to realize it. It was now a matter of solving the practical problems associated with its development into a manufacturable product. There were still at least six technical questions along the mechanical track that needed to be resolved. Do we use a Lexan-and-steel sandwich or a steel-and-foam one? How do we ensure that the PC board does not weaken the sandwich plate? How do we attach the different layers to each other in manufacturing? How do we attach the load cells to the plate without affecting their sensitivity? How do we seal the scale without affecting its accuracy? How do we incorporate the memory switches into the plate?

We opted for the Lexan-and-steel combination, shown in Fig. 56. The square grid of ribs created small square cavities that would then accommodate the electronic components. The PC board on which the components would be mounted would be designed as a small urban neighborhood, so to speak, where the components occupied small city blocks, leaving the streets between them free for the plastic ribs to sit on.

A rigid connection of the Lexan plate to the steel plate was a must if the two were to act as a single sandwich plate. After exploring numerous alternatives, we settled on gluing the steel to the bottom of the Lexan plate with epoxy, although everyone involved in manufacturing made it clear to us that they hated gluing. For now, we could not come up with a better alternative that created a strong enough bond between the layers to ensure that they would act as one plate and not slide past each other under load. But it would mean that, once glued, the electronics and the load cells could never really be repaired; a distressing compromise.

It is important to note here again that many if not most of the technical problems we encountered during the development phase were interface problems

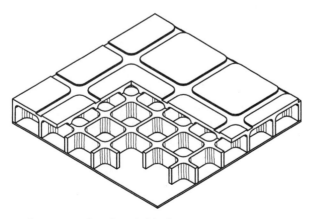

56 *The Lexan-and-steel sandwich plate*

that required the detailed design of the joints between the different parts of the scale; and that, in the design of these joints, each of the parts involved had to be modified to accommodate the other.

The plastic plate, for example, had to be designed so that its cavities would house the electronic components, while the arrangement of the components on the PC board had to allow for streets in critical places, so as not to weaken the plate. The Lexan plate, on its part, had to have special cavities for the load cell to sit in, so that it allowed the load cell to deflect under load without touching the Lexan, while at the same time providing an overload stop to protect it from damage under too-heavy loads.

Slowly, over a number of months, I put together a set of production drawings for the mechanical prototype. They were ready some three months behind schedule, but not as far behind schedule as the electronics on the critical path. Earlier experiments had shown that the mechanical prototype passed the structural tests: it could handle a 300-pound load without any visible deflection; and it passed the accuracy tests, too, using external electronics. But as of mid-March 1992, the actual parts for a production prototype were still to be made; it was not yet clear whether the scale could be produced within the required budget; and a producer that could manufacture it had not yet been identified.

The enterprising Nora Maher—Home Products' overworked chief of product development and Victor's right-hand person—came to see us in New York in mid-March of 1992, six weeks before our designated final deadline for the project. Ziggy was out of town. Ken and I met her at her midtown hotel. We reported on progress and I showed her the drawings for the mechanical prototype. Fine. She wasn't really listening anyway. All she wanted to know was "Can we have a production prototype ready for the housewares show in San Francisco on May 2?" Otherwise, she said, we lose the Christmas season.

Ken ruled it out immediately. The electronics would definitely not be ready, he said. Even if all the mechanical parts for a prototype could be produced in time, he added, the most we would have in San Francisco was a fake scale that looked like and felt like the final product, had a built-in display, and a few switches, but did not tell weight. She was not amused. In fact, she became quite agitated. This project, she decided, was in serious trouble. She was right.

* * *

Maybe I was not giving the scale the attention it needed during those months, and neither was anybody else involved. "This project will never get off the ground," a friend observed over dinner after I related the Nora story. "There is no burning passion in it. Nobody is pursuing it as if his or her life depended on it. You must leave everything and put everything you have into it."

I humbly suggested that this was impossible. Ken and Ziggy were ever so slow, and I depended on them to complete the development. We didn't have the electronics yet. We didn't have switches, batteries, or battery compartments. We didn't have rubber parts for the feet under the load cells yet. We didn't have prices, producers, a production line, or a testing machine for sorting the load cells. We still had a lot of work to do, way too much work to be able to meet the deadline for the show in San Francisco, no matter how much passion I put into it.

Yet I also had to admit to those sitting around the dinner table that even my own commitment to the scale project had been transformed. This was no longer my sole work, and it could no longer command my undivided attention or order me around like it had before, exacting more and more sacrifices. I could no longer afford to put all my eggs in one basket anyway, and I now had other work, paid work, that demanded commitment and creative energy as well—my housing work at the World Bank with Steve Mayo.

That work now involved both directing the Housing Indicators Program in some 50 countries, and drafting the bank's housing policy paper. The paper came out later as a small book, a kind of manifesto entitled *Housing: Enabling Markets to Work*. It was translated into several languages and widely distributed, and it certainly made a difference. In 2000, a British housing expert quite critical of our work commented: "The World Bank's 1993 Housing Sector paper is the base document around which most thinking about housing now takes place."

In fact, my two work commitments—to the scale and to the housing problem —were now empowering me, rather than rending me apart. Even if I had been entirely available, the scale project no longer would have required my full-time commitment. It mostly required the work of others, and there was only so much coordination involved, certainly not enough to fill a day's work. The same went for my housing work at the time—it did not demand a full-time commitment either.

Surely, they both required that I be fully engaged and fully present while attending to each one of them. That, I found, was something I could do. And being fully present was quite different from—in fact, it was the exact opposite of—being obsessed. Being obsessed means that you can never let go of something; that it is always on your mind; and being always on your mind, it prevents you from being fully present in attending to anything else except the object of your obsession. Now, I found, I could engage with one project totally, coming at it with an empty mind; entirely available to become involved and engrossed in it, having entirely let go of the other. Later, I could let go of it too and engage, just as fully, with the other project.

I found working on both projects—dividing my time roughly equally between them—both more meditative and more productive than before. It felt like a more mature attitude toward work too. The call for dropping everything and enlisting in the service of a totalitarian cause did not reverberate with me as loudly as it had before, and yet I did not feel at a loss for it at all. I still put in two or three working days every week on the scale project—certainly more than the development budget allowed for—trying as hard as I could to move the work

along the mechanical track. But there was little I could do to move the electronics or to take the entire project on my shoulders and carry it to completion.

* * *

In fact, I kept working on completing the mechanical prototype even after—
shortly after Nora's visit to New York—the investors froze the funds, alarmed at
our lack of progress and worried about cost overruns. The one thing that kept
me forging ahead during those months was working on the prototype, this time
a more advanced one than ever before. "If it weren't for prototypes . . ." I wrote in
my diary.

This one took the longest to make. It required many technical discussions
with Charlie; with the GE Plastics people (the plastic person promised by Home
Products never materialized, by the way); with Amos; and occasionally with
Ziggy and Ken too. It also required a large number of detailed drawings on my
part—plans, sections, and elevations for each mechanical part, with every single
dimension thought out to the nearest thousandth of an inch. But I liked that
work and it kept me going for weeks on end—there was something very relaxing
and fulfilling about drafting for long hours, I found out to my surprise.

In many ways, I preferred working than managing the work of others. At
heart, I had always been a worker. I loved work, especially the work involved in
the making of things, and most especially the work of turning ideas into things.
Why would I want to leave it to others? Even drafting, which I had once thought
was beneath my dignity, was now an attractive proposition. And so I drafted and
drafted. Then, once the drawings were ready, I started to get all the mechanical
components made. That part, I regret to say, I could not do by myself.

Getting all the parts together to start assembling the mechanical prototype
was a frustrating affair involving numerous delays as well. Everyone seemed to
take his time. Even Charlie went hiking in search of the new spring flowers.
Packages with parts were shipped to the wrong addresses twice in a row. Other
parts were waiting for Ziggy to send a check. Only in early June 1992, some ten
weeks after my unpleasant hotel-room meeting with Ken and Nora Maher of
Home Products, did Charlie and I begin to assemble the mechanical prototype.

> There I was [I wrote in my diary] back in the safety of Charlie's basement again,
> putting together yet another prototype. I love being in that crowded basement.
> Charlie is so even keeled, so slow and so practical, there is hardly any tension, any
> frustration. We both know it never works the first time, and we are both not in a
> hurry to get it working. In fact, there is always a long discussion upstairs—in front
> of the picture window with the bird feeder—about the sequence of operations,
> before even starting to work. The sequence of operations involves mostly "setup."
> Setup is in fact the key operational concept. One never attacks a hole directly, never.
> One sets up a jig within a jig to ensure that once the hole is in fact drilled it is

exactly in the right place and of the right diameter. There is always measurement, calibration. The caliper is out all the time, measuring thicknesses and depths.

We tested the prototype for three days and it eventually worked to our satisfaction, attaining the desired 100-gram accuracy on all the usual tests. There were still numerous changes to be made before we could ship it, so to speak. In mid-June of 1992 Ziggy and I sent photographs of the prototype to the four investors, together with the test results, an updated development chart, and a cash flow chart.

The development chart showed that we were behind schedule, and an appended letter explained why. The cash flow chart showed that since we had signed the contract 11 months ago, we had only received $40,000; that the last payment was received in February; that we had cost overruns of some $16,000; and that we needed $40,000 urgently to complete a "looks-like works-like" prototype by October 1992. But, by that time, it was too late. It fell on deaf ears.

* * *

There was plenty of blame to go around, and much of it was to be expected. But now people were upset.

> Ziggy and I had a conference call scheduled with Victor, the president of Home Products, on Friday, 10 July [I wrote in my diary on 19 July 1992]. We called. Ziggy introduced himself. "What can I do for you?" replied Victor in a cold and distant voice. Ziggy asked him whether he had received the photos of the mechanical prototype and explained that we need another $40,000 to continue our work, at which point the president of Home Products launched into a tirade: "All I get from you are nice little drawings and photographs, but that's just bullshit. All you guys want is cushy jobs, sitting on your behinds and asking for more money. Not with this company. All you've done is waste a lot of my time. We have already had three trade shows and put out a hundred new products. For all I know, you'll never produce anything." Ziggy mumbled something about needing the money to continue, and I mumbled something about the contract. "Don't talk to me about contracts," boomed Victor, "and you'll see no money from us until I see a working prototype." (This is a pretty good approximation of the exchange, except for a half a dozen missing curse words.)

Victor's invective—which I found unexpectedly offensive, I must say—set the stage for what was to come. We were now at an impasse, a double bind, so to speak, tugging us in opposite directions. On one side we had Ken and other subcontractors, who refused to complete the work unless they got paid, and on the other side we had Victor, who refused to pay unless the work was completed. No one would budge. Horace and the others—the investor go-betweens—tried to chime in from time to time with suggestions for compromise that got nowhere. There was no room for compromise. It was now an all-or-nothing proposition, especially as it became clear that no intermediate progress would be recognized as progress: as far as Victor was concerned, anything less than a complete prototype was worthless.

Further conversations with Victor led nowhere. "I don't believe in it anymore," he said to Ruben on 21 July 1992. "It's only in their heads. . . . Let them go to the bank and get the money. I'll pay later. I don't want to throw good money after bad." In a conversation two months later, he told Horace that he thought that Ziggy and I were two crooks out to get his money with false promises. "I want to see a finished working prototype with drawings for tooling," he repeated. "Then I'll pay everything." He had lost confidence in us, he said, and he had lost any hope that the project would ever be finished. He called us a bunch of morons "fucking up with my money," and said he considered the whole project a joke. But he did not want out.

What was I to do? I had no desire whatsoever to complete the prototype for them using my own funds or borrowing money from the bank. I too had lost trust in Home Products, as well as any hope that they would somehow produce and market the scale if and when its development was complete. But I was now in a real pickle. "Another doomsday scenario," I wrote in my diary on 19 September 1992. "The production of the scale is blocked pending a court decision. Home Products won't let go, and no one else will touch it until it does. I lose interest when it becomes nasty and entangled and I finally let go."

How was I going to get out of this mess? At the very least, I thought, I would need a written release from my contract with Home Products so that I could pursue other manufacturers. In early October of 1992, I called Marc Gross, my patent lawyer, to discuss the release option. "I think you're in a box with this guy. He'll not sign off unless he gets his money back," he said. Marc told me that I needed a contract lawyer, which he was not, and estimated that going to court might take two years.

My other advisor friends, upon hearing of my predicament, made one point clear to me: I needed a clean break not only with Home Products, but with the other investors, with Ziggy—who was their partner too—and with Ken, who was not performing. My brother Joe, for example, told me that I was still trying to behave decently with people who were not behaving decently themselves. "Forget about them," he said. "They have already demonstrated to you that they don't pay, they don't care for contracts, they don't trust you, and they don't support you. These are not the kind of partners you need. You can't work with these people anymore. You have lost control of the development process. You have to get back in control." I couldn't agree more.

Then I went to see Amnon, the same Amnon who had negotiated the Philips deal; my wrecking crew, as it turned out. I explained the situation to him in great detail. He asked a question here and there, looked at the contracts, and told me not to worry. My licensing contract, he pointed out, had a section called "Commencement of Production: Remedies for Breach." It said that if production did not start by 1 October 1992, I could cancel that agreement by sending the investors a notice of termination, "whereupon this Agreement shall terminate in one month from the date of such notice of Termination and Angel may grant additional licenses to others." We were already past that date. Amnon also advised against making any side deals with the other investors. "It would complicate your legal position down the line," he said.

"Am I afraid of their anger and resentment?" I asked myself. "Less and less. More fears are surfacing and as they surface, they expose themselves; and as they expose themselves, they lose their edge; and as they lose their edge, they are vanquished. Gone is the fear of letting go of this entire group, the whole lot of them, every one of them, the good, the bad, and the ugly."

Amnon wrote a rather conciliatory letter to the investors suggesting that the project was still salvageable, but only if they remitted adequate funds immediately. It concluded with: "In the event that the full amount of $55,000 is not received by our client within 10 days from the date of this letter, please consider this letter our client's termination notice, terminating the Agreements effective 10 days as of today due to your breach thereof." The funds were not received, not within ten days, not ever.

Instead, Amnon received a short reply from Victor on 25 November 1992. It said: "In reviewing progress, we found that no work in fact was evident despite having received $40,000. This company has suffered a significant financial loss of time and money as a result of false representation of your clients. We therefore request an immediate refund of funds paid to your clients. In the event this refund is not received within 10 days, we intend to file a claim against your clients for fraudulent representation, breach of contract, and damages incurred." And it was left at that. Neither Victor nor the other investors ever sued.

It was Ken, the electronic engineer, who sued Ziggy and me for non-payment of his out-of-control fees. The summons I received read thus: "From approximately April 8, 1991, through September, 1992, plaintiff rendered 500 hours of consulting services to defendants at defendants' request which, using an agreed hourly rate of $60 per hour, results in a total bill of $30,000, of which $19,260 has been paid, leaving an unpaid balance of $10,740, no part of which has been paid although duly demanded." We had to pay him out of our own pockets and, in due course, we did. And that was basically how the Home Products saga ended.

18

A Scale Approved for Trade

That all, both in the cities and in the monasteries, may have equal and correct measures and just and equal weights, whether they be used for giving or for receiving, as expressed in the Law of the Lord and again in Solomon, where the Lord says: "having two weights and two measures, both alike are abominations to the Lord."

Charlemagne, *Admonitio Generalis*

The manufacture and use of weights and scales have been supervised by government since remote antiquity.... After money, weights and scales are the most important instruments of national and international commerce, and in most countries only carefully selected and certified persons are permitted by law to make them.

Bruno Kisch, *Scales and Weights*

———

NOVEMBER 1992–SEPTEMBER 1993

Right around the time that the Home Products deal collapsed, I received a phone call from one Oved Sadeh, the export manager of Shekel, the leading electronic scale company in Israel. Shekel, now that was a name with a pedigree. The Shekel was the ancient unit of weight in the Land of Canaan. Abraham, for example, bought the property rights for the Tomb of the Patriarchs in Hebron sometime around 1800 B.C. for "four hundred shekels of silver." Not surprisingly, the Shekel was now the official currency of modern Israel. Currencies often had their origins in weights: the pound in Britain, the mark in Germany, the drachma in Greece, and the lira (libra) in Italy are examples.

The Shekel Company produced electronic scales and load cells for industrial plants, warehouses, shops and stores, hospitals, vehicles, and agricultural works, but did not make any personal scales for home use. It was owned and operated by a kibbutz on the eastern slopes of Mount Tabor in the Lower Galilee. Oved Sadeh was one of the kibbutz elders, now no longer a proud manual worker drying the swamps, tilling the land, or milking the cows, but rather—like his merchant ancestors in the Diaspora—peddling the kibbutz's industrial products in foreign lands.

He sounded like a very decent old man, entirely out of his element but completely at ease with the noble "we do what we have to do" of the country's founders. Shekel had gotten word of my cat face load cell, he told me, and he wanted to know if it could be used for the scales incorporated into baby incubators. I said I didn't know but was interested in finding out.

Real business with Shekel was ever so slow to materialize, however—yet another manifestation of the fuzzy-front-end syndrome. There was the occasional telephone and the occasional fax, but not much more. All in all, the first months after the Home Products debacle were painful in their emptiness:

> A new condition has arisen [I wrote in my diary on 29 December 1992]. There is no tempo, no excitement, no momentum. My suppliers have all practically forgotten about me.... Neglect. Neglect everywhere.... What to do? Can I pick up the momentum again? How much momentum does one have in one lifetime anyway?... "How's the scale?" my friends ask me. Sounds like "How's your back?" somehow. Laugh if you want.... Problems do not seem soluble anymore. With momentum, new problems just give in, buckle, drop out of sight, melt. Without momentum the slightest problem looms above you like an unsurmountable obstacle.... Without momentum one comes to a full stop, to a dead end. It is as if the angle of my body is no longer tilted forward as I move on, but backward, ready to collapse with the slightest contact.... This neglect business is not for me. I need motion, familiarity, warmth, contact. I have to ... move ahead. Breath normally.... Can I do it or what?

Gradually, as some healthy distance developed between me and my abandoned collaborators—Ziggy *et al.*—I started to entertain the notion of completing the development of a looks-like works-like prototype of the thin scale by myself somehow—electronics and all—before pursuing yet another company that could manufacture and distribute it. I felt that I could not leave the Home Products prototype unfinished. But more than that, I was addicted to design work on the scale by that time; the thin-scale problem had acquired permanent residence in my mind and would not be dislodged. I simply could not tolerate the absence of some scale design problem that I could grapple with: something, anything, except gazing at nothingness while waiting for something to happen. I wanted to keep playing the "game" and I wanted someone to play with. I could manage to complete the development of the scale, I figured, but not without depleting my remaining savings and sinking deeper into debt.

Like a true addict, I went for it. Why would anyone in his right mind invest good money to complete the development of a prototype—one already known to work—in the absence of a client or a prospective customer? I am afraid that I cannot supply a rational answer to this question. All I can say is that there was a big gaping hole that needed to be plugged, but that's what they all say, isn't it? In retrospect, not surprisingly, this proved to be a silly move, just money down the drain. Be wary of impatience in the guise of passion, of addiction posing as commitment.

Sam Cohen was definitely the right kind of playmate. I met him on 14 January 1993 in a well-lit public library in Pleasantville, New York, his hometown, not quite an hour north of Downtown Manhattan. Sam was in his sixties, maybe even late sixties, light haired, with a pleasant face and a rather squeaky voice that he most certainly loved to hear. He had mastered his electronics many years ago and kept up with its rapid progress. He worked in his well-organized basement laboratory, both as a consultant and as a prototype developer.

Sometimes he worked alone, and sometimes he recruited one of the whiz kids of the younger generation to help with software programming and such things. He loved electronics above all else, and he wanted other people to fall in love with it too. To that effect, he dedicated himself tirelessly to explaining it in excruciating detail, especially to a captive audience like me, and probably to his wife over breakfast too.

After agreeing on a plan for completing the development of the electronics all the way to a looks-like works-like prototype—as well as on a schedule of payments that I could maybe live with—Sam set out to work. He was as meticulous as anyone I had ever met before. He divided his work into some 50 different steps and set himself some 16 milestones. At the attainment of each milestone, he sent me a fax and spoke to me for two hours on the phone explaining what the fax said. I drove out to Pleasantville every week or two to visit him in his laboratory, yet another crowded basement in an old wooden house surrounded by tall trees, just outside of town. He was not moving along quite as fast as he had hoped, but there was motion all the same, and I needed that motion to sustain me.

The work with Sam added more bells and whistles to the prototype too. Instead of a simple on-off switch, for example, we now used a photocell, appropriating it from the UNICEF scale I mentioned earlier—the one that incorporated the baby-weighing feature. The photocell was located under a small hole in the plate, just below the display. When you covered and uncovered it, the scale switched on. Also, now only two dieters could use the scale to monitor their diets, and two load cells—the one on the bottom left and the one on the bottom right of the plate—were used as switches. Without switches, the scale now had no moving parts at all. Sam also suggested stopping the weighing operation and displaying *tilt* when one was not properly balanced on the scale. No more cheating.

Eventually, as the months went by, Sam did manage to complete the electronics for the thin scale, to prepare several PC boards and stuff them with components, and to program a microprocessor with all the bells and whistles incorporated into it. The PC boards were designed so that the components mounted on them fit into the cavities in the Lexan plate. It all eventually worked, and it certainly provided me with the satisfaction of seeing it all come to rest, not to mention the side benefits of the occupational therapy along the way.

At the end of the day, however, the estimated costs per unit for the electronics were still much too high—more than double my $6 goal—and the PC board was still too big (some three-by-five inches) and had too many components mounted on it. In due time, there was no doubt in my mind that the electronics for the thin scale—like the electronics for everything else—would become much more compact and much cheaper. In retrospect, other than allowing me the opportunity to think up new bells and whistles for personal scales, the third problem I had posed to myself at the outset of the scale quest—the thin-scale electronics problem—proved to be a nonproblem.

In March of 1993 Charlie and I turned our attention to modifying the cat face load cell so that it could be used in an incubator scale for Shekel. Shekel had already tested some of the load cells we sent them and found their performance satisfactory in the 300-pound range. They were now eager to move ahead, and they wanted a scale in the 10-pound range.

To generate the same levels of strain, the load cells for such a scale would have to be some 30 times weaker than those used in a 300-pound scale. The only ways to weaken them would be to use aluminum instead of steel, to make them thinner, and to make their beams longer and narrower. We ended up with an aluminum load cell prototype that performed reasonably well in some basic tests—the now-familiar tests for nonlinearity and hysteresis, for example—but failed miserably when subject to eccentric loads.

When we looked at a load cell up close and subjected it to an off-center load, we could see that the center beam simply twisted—the off-center load created a torque on the beam that bent it out of shape and destroyed its accuracy. We had never seen that torque effect before, when we tested thicker and sturdier loads cells, but it had always been there, apparently. As it stood, Charlie and I had to conclude, the cat face design was not suitable for measuring small loads.

"This really means that we have to stop the development of the load cells for the incubator scale," I wrote Oved Sadeh on 19 March 1993. "To continue will mean an open-ended R&D project for which we have no funds, and for which I do not want to ask you to contribute funds. I simply do not know what it will require." The Shekel people were disappointed to learn about our failure, but they still wanted to continue our collaboration. More specifically, they now wanted to use the cat face load cells for commercial scales in the 500- to 3,000-pound range.

The Shekel people and I were caught in same double bind that I had faced with Home Products: they, on their part, were reluctant to invest in the making of new prototypes unless they could be assured that scales incorporating cat face load cells would eventually pass the strict standards of the United States National Institute of Standards and Technology (NIST), so that they could be used for trade. I, on my part, could not provide Shekel with any assurances of a NIST approval without building and testing new prototypes, and I was reluctant to spend my own funds on the remote chance of a contract with Shekel at the end of the road. I had already been down that road with Philips, for example, and I was not about to embark on that journey yet again.

Getting a government seal of approval for the scale so that it could be used for trade was, for me, an entirely new requirement that I had not entertained before. Personal scales did not need government approval, I knew, unless they were used to verify commercial claims, such as "If you buy our diet products and follow our regimen, we guarantee that you will lose 20 pounds in six weeks." But commercial scales certainly did, because reliable measures of the weight of goods to be traded were, to quote Bruno Kisch, "the foundation of a just and ethical commerce."

Kisch, in his book *Scales and Weights: A Historical Outline*, notes that "governments early became aware of their duty to protect the citizens against being cheated in everyday commerce, and they turned their attention to supervising weights, scales, and money. . . . Wherever weight and scale making became a free enterprise, the instruments were checked from time to time by a government-appointed adjuster (*Aichemeister, ajusteur,* sealer) and were certified for use by a specific puncheon impressed on the object." A Babylonian lion weight found in Syria, for example, is inscribed in Aramaic: "Tested in the presence of the officers of the mint" (Fig. 57). NIST continues this ancient tradition to this very day, and requires that every scale used for trade be regularly tested and issued with a seal of approval.

I was not about to invest my own money in getting NIST approval, no matter what. So we went around in circles for a while, each of us trying to get the other one to make the first move, and both of us getting nowhere. They kept saying: "Why should we invest if we cannot be sure it will work?" And I kept saying: "How could you ever be sure it will work if you didn't invest?" By May of that year, it came time for a face-to-face meeting. Oved would be traveling in Europe then. I was planning to spend a week in Moscow on a crowded World Bank mission, giving a hand in the design of a $500 million loan project aimed at reform-

57 *A Babylonian lion weight, inscribed with "Tested in the presence of the officers of the mint"*

ing the Russian housing sector. I could meet him somewhere in Europe on my way back from my housing mission.

* * *

That week in Moscow was a humbling experience for someone like me, with unbounded confidence in the power of design. Finding a quick yet sensible way to disburse $500 million on housing sector reform in Russia in 1993—less than two years after the Communist debacle—proved to be simply impossible. I had brought my entire design repertoire to bear on this problem—all the possible solutions to all the possible housing problems, large and small—and none of it was of any practical use to the "client," neither to the Russian government nor to the World Bank.

Rampant inflation and shoddy banks ruled out the rapid development of a mortgage system, for example, normally an easy way to move money quickly. Without mortgages, there was no way to support a construction program either, because almost no one could pay for a house in cash.

Building more public rental housing did not make any sense either. Rents were still heavily controlled, miniscule compared to real market rents. The heavy subsidies that public housing still required were no longer sustainable. These and other subsidies were what had brought the Russian economy to its knees in the first place. What was needed now was more market-oriented solutions to the housing problem, and public rental housing was not one of them.

The minister of construction—a broad-necked, stocky fellow and a well-preserved specimen of the old order—wanted to use the loan to modernize his cement plants, also a nonstarter. Building materials factories were still making prefabricated components for apartment blocks with a technology that had not changed for some 40 years. Typical wall components were no less than 24 inches in thickness, three times the thickness of typical concrete walls in the West. There was no point in supplying such factories with more cement, not until they were modernized, or better yet, rebuilt altogether. The building industry had to be started from scratch, and that would take time.

The underlings in the Ministry of Construction had no better suggestions. On one sunny afternoon, for example, one of them took me out to a beautiful knoll overlooking Moscow—not far from Stalin's old *Dacha* (villa), he said—and asked me rather directly whether the World Bank would be willing to finance a new upscale residential community there for him and his fellow senior bureaucrats at the ministry. I politely replied that I thought it would be difficult to get such a project approved at the bank, and, to his credit, he did not insist.

I had one good suggestion, I thought: to sell off the prime real estate in some of the large housing projects from the Khrushchev era, and to use the proceeds from the sale to rehabilitate them. These projects consisted of hundreds of run-down walk-up apartment blocks, and they often bordered on the main avenues.

It should have been possible to tear down the first row of apartment blocks nearest the avenue, to sell the property along the avenue in the open market, and to use the proceeds to upgrade the entire community. This could have been done at no expense to the government, using World Bank funds only as operating capital. It would take time, of course, but it was the kind of project I thought could be done on a substantial scale, eventually biting heartily into that $500 million.

Unfortunately, it was also a project whose time had not come yet. The political coalitions, managerial skills, and intellectual capacities needed to implement it were not yet in place. More to the point, it had no champion in the Ministry of Construction—our Russian counterpart—and without a champion it, too, was a nonstarter.

On the last day of our stay there, the members of the mission met at the rooftop coffee shop of our hotel—overlooking the colorful onion-shaped domes of the Cathedral of Saint Basil in Red Square—to arrive at some conclusions. We had several serious ideas that would advance housing policy reform in Russia, but it was not serious ideas that the Russians wanted to hear about.

They wanted the money now, and the top management at the World Bank wanted us to find some way of giving it to them that would pass the so-called red face test, that is, be short of embarrassing. There was no way to do that. If it had been up to me, and it wasn't, I would have given these people very little money very slowly. Some problems, such as the one posed to the mission, did not succumb to design. Design, too, had its limitations.

I had just come out of the Home Products experience, in which the slow flow of too little money into the project proved to be its demise. Now I found myself in an exactly opposite predicament, in which the flow of too much money into the project too quickly posed no less of a problem. This mission, while quite instructive, was disappointing. I had no business being there, and—much as I had tried—I was really of no help. To console myself, I bought a few old Caucasian rugs at the Ismaelova weekend market. In retrospect, they clearly made that trip worthwhile, to me at least.

* * *

On 22 May 1993, on my way back from Moscow, I met Oved Sadeh and his colleague David Elbaz—the managing director of Shekel—for an after-dinner drink at the bar of the Sheraton Hotel outside Frankfurt airport. I could not help noticing that the old bartender looked familiar, and that felt eerie because I knew no one in Frankfurt, never having set foot there before. He was very small, and he had an aged baby face with ears jutting out, altogether reminiscent of the dolls used by ventriloquists. "You look familiar; do I know you from somewhere?" I said as I approached him for some beers.

"Jerusalem?" he asked with a faint, courteous smile. "Probably," I replied. "I am Moishé from My Bar," he said. Surely, he was none other than Moishé, one of the more permanent fixtures in Jerusalem nightlife for decades; a veritable institution considering that Jerusalem never really had any nightlife to speak of. "What are you doing here, Moishé?" I inquired, imagining him on some sort of a bartending sabbatical, I suppose. "I moved back to Germany," he said. "I feel more comfortable here. It's more civilized." I chose not to question him any further. I picked up the beers and went back to our table. The times they are a-changin', I thought to myself.

Oved and David—a much younger man with sharp facial features and an Afro—wanted one simple thing: to license the cat face load cell and to pay me royalties, at 5 percent of their wholesale prices, every time they made a sale. They were planning to invest some $100,000 in a new production line for the load cells, they said, and for that reason they did not think it appropriate to pay me anything up front for the promised license. Yes, they were willing to exclude scales "for weighing persons in erect positions" from the license, so that I could still use the load cells for making the thin scale if and when I found anyone who was interested.

I could not imagine ever making any serious money from this deal, but I consented all the same. By then I must have despaired of ever finding anyone who would be interested in taking my invention to market. These people were quite enthusiastic about it, I said to myself. Why not just give it to them? Maybe they could put it to good use. At least it would not be abandoned. Oved drafted a general Memorandum of Understanding sometime before midnight and, tired and exhausted, I agreed to sign it. What I did not understand that evening, while nursing my beer at Moishé's adopted bar in Frankfurt, was that this was only the beginning of our negotiations.

The haggling continued—mostly by phone and fax—for two more months. We finally signed the license agreement in Beit Keshet—their kibbutz in the Lower Galilee—when I came for a short visit at the end of July 1993. The only immediate advantage of this agreement for me was that Shekel took over the payments for the maintenance of the patent and its continued registration in the remaining countries on my list. These not-insubstantial payments amounted to thousands of dollars every year, and I was all too happy to rid myself of that obligation. This required some stubbornness on my part too: the Shekel people wanted to start paying the patent fees only after the NIST approval, possibly a year or more away; I threatened to withdraw and they eventually backed down.

In all other respects, the agreement was not a good agreement for me. The royalties would not amount to much of anything. There would not be any upfront payment. Shekel would obtain an exclusive worldwide license, but would not have to pay me any minimum royalty every year, as is generally expected in such exclusive licenses. Yes, at the beginning I did insist on minimum royalties, but eventually Oved tired me out. On 18 June, for example, he wrote:

> Let's face the facts: you invested a great deal in this product, but the only way to materialize this investment is to work with a serious partner (like Shekel). Your

patented prototype needs added investment by Shekel to develop it into a saleable product. . . . This secondary investment is very costly and it has its risks. Shekel will take on this challenge in the most efficient and aggressive way, using all our experience and expertise. I am sure we will not disappoint you at the end of the day, but, in all fairness, we cannot add a 'minimum quantity' to this risk.

I succumbed, partly out of having run out of options, and partly out of despair of ever finding yet another option. This arrangement essentially meant that Shekel could eventually sell only a few hundred load cells a year, and yet I could not offer the license to any other manufacturer because it was an exclusive one. In fact, our agreement stated that as long as Shekel continued to produce load cells "in production quantities" (whatever that meant) beginning not later than ten months after the load cells were approved by the National Institute of Standards and Technology, I could not back out of that agreement.

After our summer meeting in the kibbutz, Shekel slowly started to test the cat face load cell and to develop it in preparation for production. I kept sending long faxes, rich in know-how, in response to a bombardment of technical inquiries. I also occasionally sent Shekel steel parts for prototypes, for which they duly paid. I did not do anything beyond the absolutely necessary to help them along, though, and I made sure that I reduced my expenditures in connection with the development of the load cell for a scale approved for trade to next to nothing. The Shekel affair now retreated to one of the back rooms of my mind, and I gave it very little thought.

* * *

But the original problem that Shekel presented to me then—coming up with a cat face load cell for an the incubator scale—did not just disappear. It merely entered my mind, found a comfortable place, and went into hibernation—an incubation period, as it is often called—before it surfaced again.

19

The Effortlessness of Informed Design

There is a curiously sharp sense of joy—or perhaps better expressed, a sense of mild ecstasy—that comes when you find the particular form required by your creation. . . . What is the source of this curious pleasure? I propose that it is the experience of this-is-the-way-things-are-meant-to-be. If only for that moment, we participate in the myth of creation. Order comes out of disorder, form out of chaos, as it did in the creation of the universe. The sense of joy comes from our participation, no matter how slight, in being as such.

Rollo May, *The Courage to Create*

In the fall of 1993, the incubator scale problem that Shekel had posed months earlier completed its incubation period, presented itself to me, and demanded attention. It caught me at an opportune moment. The Shekel affair was over by then. Sam Cohen was putting his so-called finishing touches on the production prototype, and I occasionally drove out to Pleasantville to chat with him and urge him along. Other than that, there was not much else for me to do on the scale front.

Simply stated, the incubator scale problem was this: how could I modify the cat face load cell so that it did not twist out of shape when subjected to eccentric loads? The solution to this problem promised to be the solution to a more general problem: what would be the form of a load cell for very thin scales intended for measuring lighter loads? Or even more generally: what form of a new load cell for very low-profile scales (in all possible weight ranges) would provide superior performance under eccentric loads?

I shall attempt to describe the route to the solution of this problem in some detail, because it sheds some light on what has come to be known as the creative process; and because, in comparison with the torturous expedition to the cat face load cell, it was beautifully effortless. Instead of 14 months of trial and error and a dozen prototypes, this journey took less than 14 days and involved no trial and error at all—the first prototype worked the first time.

This time around I had a clear plan of attack. I was not approaching the general problem stated above as a fresh problem that involved giving my imagination free rein and boundless regions to explore. Rather I was approaching the twist problem of the cat face load cell itself, as a problem that required a disciplined imagination looking for a breakthrough within known bounds and well-established rules. That breakthrough did not need to start from scratch either. It could be based on the cat face load cell itself, seeking to modify it somehow to meet the new requirement—thou shalt not twist.

It did help, of course, that by then I was no longer a novice in the matter of thin load cells. On the contrary, I was already a decorated veteran of many a load cell campaign. My immersion in the matter was, no doubt, an essential precondition for inventing a new form that would be a satisfactory solution to the twist problem. Edmund Sinnott, in *The Creativeness of Life*, made that abundantly clear:

> Inspirations, it is well recognized, rarely come unless an individual has immersed himself in a subject. He must have a rich background of knowledge and experience in it. In science, he must be laboring to find the answer to a problem or to bring a mass of unrelated facts in his mind into a unity. . . . He is wrestling to bring into actuality these cloudy, half-formed products of his imagination. . . . Then, in a time of relaxation or when something else is actively occupying his mind, the answer which he seeks, or at least the creative nub of it, will come sauntering into his mind as if spontaneously.

In these pages, I have tried to describe the process I went through as the taking of five discrete design steps, one following another in strict sequence. This description required a modicum of simplification, of course. In reality, there was more movement back and forth between these steps and a larger number of intermediate steps as well.

As is often the case, my formulation of the problem had already brought me halfway towards its solution. How do you prevent something from twisting? As a car antitheft measure, for example, the steering wheel can be prevented from turning by locking it with a metal bar that attaches it to the break pedal. When there are two parallel columns attached both to the steering wheel and to the car floor, the wheel can no longer turn. In more abstract terms, a single column sub-

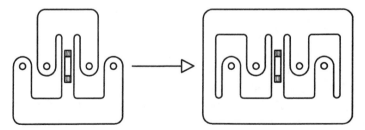

58 *Step 1: Adding two parallel beams to prevent the center beam from twisting*

ject to a torque will twist. But two columns attached to one another at their tops
and bottoms will prevent each other from twisting.

This insight points to a design solution to the twist problem. Indeed, the first
attempt at solving the twist problem involved adding two parallel beams to the
cat face load cell, one on each side, as shown in Fig. 58.

This modification certainly solved the problem. The center beam could now
no longer twist when the load cell was subjected to an off-center load. There was
no question about that. But this was a rather heavy-handed solution. It added
two elements to the five vertical elements already there—one flexure beam at the
center, a load-receiving tongue on either side of it, and two clamping tongues
further out—bringing the total to an unwieldy seven.

Together with the two elongated transverse elements on the top and bottom
of the load cell, the load cell now had nine distinct parts; too many. The two new
beams were single-function elements that did nothing else except guard against
twist. And the multiplicity of vertical elements, one next to the other, now
widened the overall shape of the load cell—making it almost twice as wide as the
flexure beam itself. This, in short, was not an elegant solution at all, and the
absence of elegance strongly suggested there was something wrong with it.

The mathematician Henri Poincaré highlighted the primary role of elegance
in guiding the discovery of new forms or new combinations:

> What are the mathematic entities to which we attribute this character of beauty
> and elegance, and which are capable of developing in us a sort of esthetic emo-
> tion? They are those whose elements are harmoniously disposed so that the mind
> without effort can embrace their totality while realizing the details. This harmony
> is at once a satisfaction of our esthetic needs and an aid to the mind, sustaining
> and guiding. . . . The useful combinations are precisely the most beautiful, I mean
> those best able to charm this special sensibility that all mathematicians know, but
> of which the profane are so ignorant as often to be tempted to smile at it.

The absence of elegance in this new form prevented my mind from coming
to a complete rest, leaving it agitated. What bothered me most about it was the
preponderance of single-function elements in that form. Come to think of it,
some elements performed only half a function. Except for the flexure beam at
the center, there were two vertical elements needed for every single function: two
for receiving the load, two for clamping, and two for resisting twist. This design
remained a combination of too many disparate entities, rather than an integrated form where each element played a dual role—that of fulfilling its own
function while lending support to the other elements in fulfilling theirs—or
where each element fulfilled a multiplicity of roles by itself.

Geoffrey Hyman—the brilliant esoteric mathematician who helped me with
the mathmatics of my doctoral dissertation—once explained his chess strategy
to me thus: "I never make a move unless I have two good reasons for it." The first

design move I made—adding the two beams to resist twist—did not have this quality at all. There was only one reason they were there, and that made the resulting form suspect. It was still immature. "The superior design," write Carroll and Bellinger, "is one which encompasses the necessary and protective functions with the absolute minimum number of components and connections." I was not there yet.

Discovering the next improvement in the design involved breaking a rule, a rule I was no longer conscious of, which had, in the meantime, actually become inoperative. I was still operating in the old mode—designing a thin load cell that would cost no more than $1.50. This required using the absolute minimum number of strain gages—two per load cell, and no more. The gages themselves, and the labor involved in mounting them to the metal and wiring them, were a significant share of the overall cost of the load cell, and so I never even contemplated using more than a pair of them on any given load cell. I had internalized this frugality, turned it into an absolute rule, and never given it another thought. But it was the breaking of this rule—allowing myself the luxury of using more gages—that was needed to take the next step.

Arthur Koestler, in *The Act of Creation*, speaks of the creative act as an act of liberation, of defeating the rules:

> The term 'matrix' was introduced to refer to any skill or ability, to any pattern of activity governed by a set of rules—its 'code'. . . . Matrices vary from fully automated skills to those with a high degree of plasticity; but even the latter are controlled by rules of the game which function below the level of awareness. These silent codes can be regarded as condensations of learning into habit. . . . The creative act . . . is an act of liberation—the defeat of habit by originality.

What is an example of breaking a rule that operates "below the level of awareness" in the process of solving a problem? Alan Watts—the author of many books on Zen Buddhism—told of a visit to Japan, when he went—accompanied by his little daughter—to see a Zen master. At some point in the conversation, they spoke of *koans*—the unanswerable riddles given to Zen adepts to tie their thinking minds into knots and to force them into no-thinking.

"Why don't we present a koan to your lovely daughter?" suggested the master. The girl was thrilled. "You carefully place a young shoot of a bonsai tree in some soil at the bottom of a glass bottle," started the master. "Then you take good care of the tree, watering it and feeding it, until, many years later, the tree completely fills the bottle. Now, how do you take the tree out of the bottle without harming the tree and without breaking the bottle?" The girl replied without hesitation: "You break the bottle." "You see," said the master with a smile, "children get it every time."

Rules are essential, no doubt, but sometimes they are there to be broken. Once the unwritten rule that stated "only two strain gages may be used" was broken, in

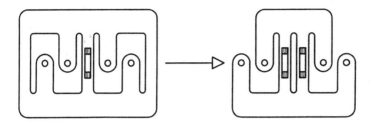

59 *Step 2: Using two center beams, instead of one, to overcome twist*

a fit of frustration with the large quantity of elements in the previous design, a new solution to the twist problem presented itself. It involved putting a pair of strain gages on two center beams, rather than only one, as shown in Fig. 59.

The two center beams were now no longer single-function elements. They functioned as flexure beams and they prevented the load cell from twisting. That was an improvement, but I was not there yet. There were now six vertical elements instead of seven, still too many. The number of strain gages was doubled, of course, but that was actually an advantage because it would increase the accuracy of the load cell. The added cost would not be a problem, because we were now dealing with products that were not consumer goods. Still, I had to admit to myself that this was not a very elegant design, and not yet a form at rest.

True, but in retrospect it was very helpful as an intermediate design. Looking at it intently, going away, and coming back to look at it again, I ultimately (and rather suddenly) discovered that the center of the load cell was now free. Before—in the original cat face design—it was occupied by the flexure beam, and now that there were two flexure beams, it was empty. Seeing it took time because the empty center was not an object, it was the absence of one, and as long as I focused too hard on the objects themselves—the horizontal and vertical elements of the load cell—I could not see it at all. Discovering the empty center involved a sudden shift from seeing emptiness as *ground* to seeing it as *figure*.

Now that I could see it as a figure, I could see it as a place. And if that place was made wide enough, it could house one of the load-receiving tongues. We could then have one load-receiving tongue instead of two. This insight then led to the next design, shown in Fig. 60. This was already a novel design for a useful object, not necessarily obvious to persons skilled in the art, and therefore possibly worthy of a new patent.

It was surely an improvement over the earlier configuration. It now reduced the number of vertical elements to five, the same number as in the cat face load cell. It had only one tongue to receive the load, and now, because that tongue was in the center, the load could be transferred to it directly. That eliminated the need for the additional plate bridging under the flexure beam. That plate, the reader may recall, was required in the cat face load cell to center the load on the

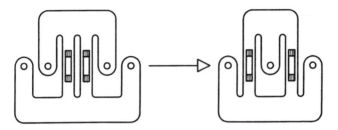

60 *Step 3: From a pair of load-receiving tongues to a single one*

load cell, so that it would act as a point load exactly at its center (see Fig. 61, left). Eliminating the bridging plate now meant that the new load cell would make possible even thinner scales than before (see Fig. 61, right).

As a design, however, this new configuration was still not elegant. It was still not a form at rest. Surely, the patent examiner in Washington would not care whether the proposed configuration was elegant or not, as long as it described a novel and useful device. But I did. For me, the shape of the new configuration still looked like a combination of single elements, rather than like an integrated whole. It took me a while to see the next step, but eventually I saw it: when I exchanged the places of the two flexure beams with the two clamping tongues, the outside perimeter of the load cell became a square, as shown in Fig. 62.

The square outline unified the design and made it into one whole. The new configuration now satisfied one of the cardinal requirements of elegant forms:

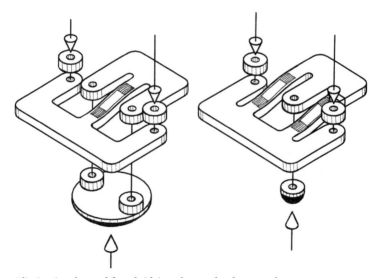

61 *Eliminating the need for a bridging plate under the center beam*

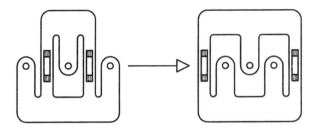

62 *Step 4: Making the outer perimeter into a square*

there were easily recognizable forms at every level with smaller forms nested in the larger ones. It was no longer an amalgamation of disparate elements that did not add up to anything, but rather a whole divided into parts by making progressive distinctions.

A beautiful example of a form that has that property, to an astonishing degree, is the Caucasian rug shown in Fig. 63, a Star Kazak rug from the early nineteenth century. The rug as a whole can be divided further and further into its component parts by making progressive distinctions. For example, the rug can be imagined as a rectangle divided into two—a thin border and an interior. The interior is further divided into two main medallions and three interlocking stars, or parts of stars. Each medallion is further divided into one central rhomboid, two arrow shapes, and four S-shaped figures, one in each corner. Each of the S-shapes is further divided into two squares. Each square has a border and a

63 *A Caucasian Star Kazak rug, 1829*

core, and so on. The rug as a whole can be disaggregated into a hierarchy of nested forms by making progressive distinctions. And each form—including the rug as a whole—is a recognizable whole it itself.

Getting to elegance required one more critical step, shifting attention again from the elements themselves to the empty spaces between them. Inside this new square outline there were still leftover spaces with random shapes. Good design required transforming them into positive spaces, into forms that had definite shapes and served useful functions. In *A Pattern Language,* for example, we discussed the shape of outdoor spaces in built environments in these terms:

> There are two fundamentally different kinds of outdoor space: negative space and positive space. Outdoor space is negative when it is shapeless, the residue left behind when buildings—which are generally viewed as positive—are placed on the land. An outdoor space is positive when it has a distinct and definite shape, as definite as the shape of a room, and when its shape is as important as the shapes of the buildings which surround it. . . . If you look at the plan of an environment where outdoor spaces are positive, you may see the buildings as figure, and the outdoor space as ground—*and,* you may *also* see the outdoor spaces as figure against the ground of the buildings. The plans have a figure-ground reversal.

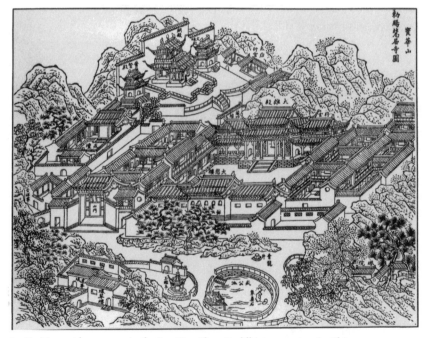

64 *Positive outdoor spaces in the Pao Hua Shan Buddhist monastery in China*

Some of the most beautiful examples of the transformation of outdoor spaces into positive spaces by the arrangements of buildings and garden walls are to be found in the old Buddhist monasteries in China. A woodcut of the Pao Hua Shan monastery in Kiangsu, from a seventeenth-century chronicle, is shown here as an example (Fig. 64). It can be easily seen that every outdoor space had been conceived as a place with a positive shape. There are no spaces that are leftovers or residues of buildings.

It was not difficult to transform the leftover spaces in the square design into positive shapes. In fact, the only functional requirement of these shapes was that they be of a minimum width (of some eighth of an inch) and have no sharp corners, so that they could be punched out with a tool-and-die set without breaking the tool too often. Narrowing the leftover spaces and keeping them to a minimum width now completed the design of the load cell, as shown in Fig. 65. The load-bearing tongue and the two clamping tongues now dissolved into the transverse horizontal shapes, further reducing the overall number of parts to four, and allowing each part to fulfill more than one function. The entire load cell was now of one piece. It had attained elegance and was now a form at rest.

In contrast to the painful old days, when ignorance was surely not experienced as bliss, working on this new load cell was sheer unadulterated pleasure. It felt effortless and it filled me with joy. There was a meditative and a curative quality to that design episode that had not been there before. Would I describe it as a mystical experience? Difficult to say, but it certainly involved "the sense of mild ecstasy" that Rollo May wrote of in *The Courage to Create*.

John Briggs, in *Fire in the Crucible*, writes: "Like the alchemists, who believed that the physical distillation of the *prima materia* [primal matter] was identical with the spiritual distillation of the soul, creators believe that transcendental experience can be manifested in a physical form—in an artwork or scientific discovery." I cannot vouch for the spiritual distillation of my soul, but I do believe that I had stumbled upon some kind of transcendental experience. I certainly had a strange sense of at-oneness with things-as-they-are at the time that my invention unfolded itself. The form of that load cell and my mind became one; and as that form came to a complete rest, so did my mind.

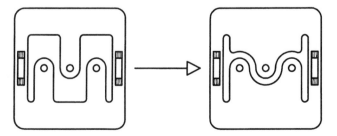

65 *Step 5: Making the leftover spaces into definite shapes*

Soon thereafter, I started to prepare another patent application, this time for a "Mass-Produced Flat Multiple-Beam Load Cell and Scales Incorporating It." I knew that this new load cell would merit a patent, and I felt I owed it to myself to pursue it. To confess, I still felt a trace of disappointment with the 1965 Dutch application beating me to the cat face load cell configuration. That left me with some unfinished business with patenting. I needed to prove to myself that I had, in fact, gone all the way to the knowledge frontier. A strong patent for the new and useful load cell would be my testimony that I had been there.

I was working away at that patent application when, out of the blue, Oshima called.

20

The Company Motto Is "Light and Thin"

There are some complex human activities, and management is one of them, in which it is the aesthetic fit (i.e., the form and harmony among things) that matters most. Division and subdivision of tasks and intellectualizing and verbalizing will never accomplish the learning that experiencing, watching, feeling, sensing, and imitating will. In Japanese organizations, the *sempai-kohai* (mentor-disciple) relationship helps achieve this kind of learning. The Japanese unabashedly acknowledge that the *sempai-kohai* relationship is made up of emotional as well as functional ties and they harness both.... Attempting to mask or deny emotional relations as an inescapable part of hierarchical relations is like trying to remove wetness from water.

Richard Pascale and Anthony Athos, *The Art of Japanese Management*

————

SEPTEMBER 1993–DECEMBER 1994

Toshihiko Oshima was the vice president and general manager of the Tanita Corporation of America, one of a number of subsidiaries of the Tanita Corporation of Japan. Tanita, founded in 1923, now had a 50 percent share of the Japanese scale market. By 1990, it had produced over 20 million bathroom scales and 10 million kitchen scales. It had recently opened a new assembly plant in China, and was now in the process of transforming itself into a global corporation—opening offices in Hong Kong, Germany, the United States, and the United Kingdom.

On the phone Oshima sounded abrupt, speaking in terse and confident staccato sentences, devoid of any color or ornamentation, a true minimalist. He informed me that his colleagues in Tokyo had recently come across my Japanese patent for a new flat load cell, the cat face, surely. (Marc, my congenial patent lawyer, must have been doing his job.) Oshima inquired whether I would be interested in licensing the patent to them for use in making low-profile wheelchair scales for hospitals, and possibly other scales as well.

In the exchange of faxes that ensued, he informed me that the scales they were interested in were in the 300- to 500-pound range with a 0.1-pound (50-gram) or 0.2-pound (100-gram) accuracy, and that they would all eventually require a government Certificate of Conformance. He also indicated that the company was rather unsure if it was really interested in the patent, and that it was a rather small project for them. "Due to a negative economic situation at the moment," he wrote, "we are a little bit hesitant to buy a patent. However, we would also like to know your opinion on this matter."

To that effect, he told me, he would like to invite me to meet his Japanese colleagues when they visited his office in Skokie, Illinois, in mid-October. They could all come to New York too, he said, but if I were willing to come to Skokie— a suburban village north of Chicago—he would be happy to send me a ticket and pick me up at O'Hare airport upon my arrival.

This, I must confess, was a rather refreshing and most pleasant beginning for a business relationship. I tried to sound calm and collected throughout our exchanges, just barely managing to suppress my excitement. I promised Oshima I would show up in Skokie with a working prototype of the thin scale, hoping against hope to have the almost-complete prototype—the one Sam Cohen was tinkering with—ready for the meeting and performing to perfection, with all the bells and whistles to boot.

Why I still kept making promises that I was not asked to make, I don't know. I was under no pressure at all. I could have waited patiently for the meeting, but no, I had to transform the date of the meeting into a deadline. I wanted to push myself as hard as possible until it came time to go. In truth, I had waited for that Sam Cohen prototype long enough, and now that a real deadline presented itself, I was longing for closure more than ever. That deadline, I hoped, would help generate the adrenalin I needed to finally attain that elusive closure.

Except that my adrenalin by itself was not nearly enough to finish that prototype. Charlie, I found out to my chagrin, was away hiking. I spent the weekend before the Skokie meeting at Sam's basement laboratory. It quickly became obvious that Sam's collection of electronic bells and whistles and his thin PC board were not yet operational. Without the dependable Charlie to help us, we barely managed to put together a Lexan quarter-inch scale that would show one's weight on an external voltmeter wired to the scale. That would have to do for now. I breathed a sigh of relief. There was, finally, some minimal sort of closure. Real closure—with a capital C—remained as elusive as before. The thin scale was still a work-in-progress.

The Tanita people I met in Skokie on 18 October 1993 had no trouble recognizing that the thin scale was still a work-in-progress, and they said so. They weighed themselves one after the other, and they satisfied themselves that it was indeed a scale. They were interested in it, they said, but any commercial interest on their part would have to wait until development was more advanced. Once I had a looks-like works-like prototype, they would like to be the first to see it, they said. For now, however, they were only interested in the cat face load cell. They could use it for low-profile personal scales, they said, and its use for a low-profile wheelchair scale would be particularly attractive.

There were six or seven Japanese men present. They were all in dark suits and ties, and they spoke at length among themselves, in Japanese, of course. From time to time Oshima would translate a question addressed to me. I would answer, he would translate my answer, and another long discussion in Japanese would ensue while I sat there patiently. It felt like friendly and familiar territory. Having lived in Asia for many years, having worked with Japanese engineering professors, and having been to Japan before all helped. I was at ease. They were all completely at ease with each other, of course, and much as I had tried to discern who was in charge, I couldn't. Except for a couple of younger men who clearly deferred to the others, the pecking order was not at all obvious.

It became obvious over lunch, when the conversation got more personal. One of the men was Daisuke Tanida, the president of the Tanita Corporation of Japan. He was of medium build and of medium height, in his early fifties. He was agile, supple, and comfortably erect. His sculptured face was luminous in its innocence, its humility, and its relaxed vulnerability. What a pleasant man to be with, I thought to myself. Daisuke Tanida was the exact opposite of an American CEO—no names need be mentioned—typically a master intimidator with a killer instinct, full of himself, and as distant as can be from mortals who worked for him.

The president's brother Kenzo was also present. He was taller, his hair was completely white, and there was no way of telling whether he was an older or a younger brother. He was handsome too, but not nearly as open faced as his brother. Kenzo Tanida was the export manager and spoke perfect English, while his brother Daisuke clearly understood English very well, but spoke it only slowly and reluctantly, preferring to speak to me through an interpreter. Kato, the director of the R&D department—an older, balder, and slightly nervous man—was there too, as was the company's legal counsel.

They returned from lunch ready to do business. By that time it was all decided already. They wanted to license the load cell for making personal scales, as well as wheelchair scales. If possible, they wanted world-wide, exclusive rights to the patent. They wanted to know whether this was possible and what I wanted in return.

It was right there and then that the not-so-distant memory of the Shekel deal came to haunt me. Exclusivity was unfortunately out of the question, I said. In fact, Shekel had exclusive rights to the load cell patent for any scale used in industrial, commercial, and medical applications. The only patent rights I had left were for scales used to weigh persons "in upright positions" in home, commercial, medical, and other applications, with a maximum capacity of 440 pounds (200 kilograms). I could grant Tanita these rights, even exclusively, I said, as long as they agreed to exclude the patent rights for the very thin personal scale I was developing myself.

To this they agreed, much to my surprise, and now they wanted to know what I wanted in return. After some bargaining, we agreed on a lump-sum $50,000 payment up front to cover some of my development expenses, and on 1 percent of the wholesale price of every scale sold as a running royalty. I started to regret it as soon as we agreed, and for no particular reason. Maybe I was so convinced I was never any good at bargaining, that any deal—no matter how attractive—would be disappointing. It was the best scale deal I had struck yet, wasn't it? So why carp and whine about it?

Is a person sitting in a wheelchair in an upright position? I said I did not know, but promised to find out. Oshima was then given instructions to follow up on the deal, our meeting ended, and I flew back to New York on that same afternoon. I called my patent lawyer, Marc, the next day and asked him whether he thought a person sitting in a wheelchair is in an upright position. He said yes, he thought so, but I was not convinced. Oshima called a couple of days later and said that this "upright position" clause was too restrictive. Would I be willing to contact Shekel and inquire whether they would be willing to share their rights for industrial, commercial, and medical scales with Tanita? I promised I would, but that it would not be easy or cheap.

* * *

How was I to transform Shekel's license from an exclusive to a nonexclusive one? What could I offer them in return? What if they refused me altogether? There was no longer any question that Shekel could kill the deal.

I called David Elbaz—the managing director of Shekel—in early November 1993. I explained that I was in the middle of negotiations with a Japanese company on using the cat face load cell for personal scales and that I needed his help. The exclusive license I had granted to Shekel was creating a problem for me, I said, because the Japanese wanted the rights for commercial and industrial scales as part and parcel of the deal.

"I am happy with our collaboration so far," I told him, "but at the same time I realize now that I made a mistake in granting Shekel an exclusive license, especially since there were no up-front payments or minimum royalties to compensate me for it. Since I made a mistake I am willing to pay for it, and I want you to tell me what you consider a fair and adequate payment for my mistake."

David's response was as quick and emphatic as it was unexpected. "I want to promise you one thing," he said. "We will definitely not take any money from you and we will not stand in your way. Let me think about it more thoroughly and I will call you back." That was a nice response, I thought. I felt as though a heavy stone had rolled off my chest. But that pleasant lightness in my chest did not last very long.

By mid-November, David informed me that Shekel's load cell development program was moving rapidly; that several R&D people—their best people, in fact—were working on it; that dozens of new prototypes were being prepared for testing; and that a new electronic circuit was being put together that eliminated the need for sorting load cells into batches of equal sensitivity. In short, he wanted to let me know that they were investing both money and effort in bringing the development of the load cell to a satisfactory completion.

He also informed me that he wanted to collaborate with the Japanese, maybe open a load cell factory together, maybe divide up the global market, and maybe all kinds of other things too. He wanted to be "in" on the deal, he said. I cannot say that his proposition agreed with me. It didn't. I promised him that I would introduce him to the Japanese, but only after we agreed on the revision of our licensing agreement.

Some ten days later, his secretary informed me that he would be away from the factory for two months on military reserve duty, and could not be reached. I was at a total loss about my next move. It was not hard to imagine the Tanita deal fading away.

David called me the next day, on his way to his army base, and told me that he had had a difficult and prolonged discussion with the Shekel board of directors the day before. Board members were of the opinion that changing our agreement into a nonexclusive one would lead to a significant loss of Shekel's market share and revenue. Moreover, now that Shekel had invested in the development of the load cell, it would need to be compensated for its investment. I did not follow the logic of his argument, but I did realize that he was now amending his earlier "we will definitely not take any money from you" promise. I had no problem with that. I had made a mistake and I had to pay for it. At least they were not going to stand in my way. Now it was only a question of money.

After some further exchanges of faxes, the Shekel people and I agreed on a co-exclusivity arrangement. Only Shekel and Tanita would have the patent rights to commercial and industrial scales using the load cell patent, but Tanita would not be able to sell load cells as separate items on the market. Shekel would continue to pay the annual fees for maintaining the patent and the expenses involved in prosecuting it, deducting them from future royalties due to me as it had before. In exchange for its agreement to cooperate, Shekel would receive a $20,000 up-front payment, and a discount of $35,000 on future royalties due to me from their future sales.

Oshima was quite relieved to hear of the results of my negotiations and more than happy to add compensating Shekel to our agreement. He also told me that the people in Tokyo preferred a one-time lump-sum payment to running royalties on future sales. It was cleaner that way, he said, meaning there would be no long-term obligations involved. In other words, this was just a one-time arm's length exchange. I said I didn't mind. In January of 1994, after exchanging drafts for some two months with numerous individuals, Daisuke Tanida and I signed our first license agreement. At the end of the day, Tanita bought the patent rights for the cat face load cell for $165,000. After paying Shekel $20,000 as agreed, I was left with $145,000. For the first time, after too many years, I breathed a special kind of sigh of relief—the kind you didn't know was in you—and it felt ever so good. At least I had gotten back the money I invested (my father would say "gambled recklessly") in the scale venture, and that was not to be scoffed at, especially after having come very close to despair of ever recovering it.

* * *

The money I received from Tanita was used to pay off my debts and to replenish my coffers. I was now resolved to complete the Lexan-and-aluminum version of a looks-like work-like prototype as soon as practicable. Sam, having been paid, was now happily working away, complaining from time to time that the microprocessor we chose did not have enough memory for all the bells and whistles, but assuring me all the same that he was far from giving up on crowding them all in. Getting his electronics to work as envisioned was no longer just a job: it was a mission.

While Sam was working on the electronics, Charlie and I sought to introduce some mechanical refinements to the prototype as well. The mechanical design included a circular bridging plate underneath the load cell, attached (through two thin washers) to the holes in the inner anchor of the load cell (see Fig. 46). A rubber foot was attached to the bottom of this plate and pressed against it when the scale was under load.

We now added a thin rubber diaphragm between the circular plate and the rubber foot, with a few bellows-shaped corrugations on its perimeter (Fig. 66). The perimeter of this diaphragm was now connected to a wide hole in the bottom metal plate, and the diaphragm now sealed the load cell compartment against humidity and dirt. Because of its corrugations, it did not transfer any loads from the plate directly to the floor when the scale was under load. After some experiments with different designs and rubbers of different hardnesses and different thicknesses, the diaphragm arrangement seemed to work.

Oshima called at some point and said that he expected President Tanida to visit Skokie again in mid-April 1994. Would the prototype be ready by then? It should not be too difficult to guess my answer. Nor should it be difficult to guess that the prototype was not really ready by then; it was still a work-in-progress. The electronic bells and whistles all worked, and so did the rubber foot/ diaphragm/circular plate/load cell arrangement. But we did not manage to include a proper battery compartment, nor did we glue the parts together into a sandwich plate. That was too scary a move. We knew that once we glued it all together, there would be no way to get to the load cells and to the electronics, and we were not there yet. On the last day before my departure for Chicago, I worked with Charlie until midnight to give the prototype its final touches. As

66 *A schematic drawing of a diaphragm with corrugations*

they say, "if it were not for the last day, nothing would ever get done."

I met Daisuke Tanida in Skokie on 12 April 1994, and this time there were fewer people in attendance. I apologized for not completing the prototype to my satisfaction, and explained what still needed to be done. Tanida suggested that no further development was necessary at this stage, as long as it was understood that I planned to complete the development in the near future. I showed him the results of our accuracy tests and explained them before bringing out the prototype. He then leisurely weighed himself a few times. Then he tested the *last*, *diet*, and *baby* modes—using the photocell and the load cells as switches—and was satisfied that they worked. I insisted on explaining a few rather esoteric technical issues, but there was really no point to that because there were no technical people around. Still, Tanida listened patiently and intently, looking straight into my eyes the whole time.

We broke off for a lunch heavy on gravy at the nearby Howard Johnson Hotel, and when we reassembled at the small conference room in Oshima's office, Tanida informed me that he wanted to obtain an exclusive license to my thin-scale sandwich patent, to the load cell patent for thin scales that I still reserved to myself, and to my know-how about the construction of thin scales.

He was now committed to making a new generation of very thin and lightweight scales, he said, and he wanted to enlist my help in educating the R&D staff at Tanita and helping them along. He believed that my approach to the thin-scale problem would be a good influence on R&D in Tanita. He also admitted to me that Tanita had never bought a patent outside Japan before, and that we had to tread carefully since this was all new ground for everyone. Then he leaned back in his chair and asked me what I wanted in return. The room became very quiet as I weighed my answer.

I started with the softer elements of the deal.

"Would Tanita be committed to making a quarter-inch scale?" I asked.

"Yes, if it proved to be feasible," said Tanida.

"Could I participate in the design of the scale?"

"We have a very good design department" was the answer, "but you could participate in the design, yes."

"If my design was eventually selected for the quarter-inch scale, could there be a label on the back that said *a Solly Angel Design*?" That question elicited a quizzical look on his face. (In Japanese companies, I understood only later, "rewards are based on group, not individual, performance.") "Only on scales sold in the U.S. and in Europe," I added, with the Museum of Modern Art still in the back of my mind.

"That would be possible," he said.

I then said that as for payment I wanted three things, the three things that all good exclusive agreements should have: an up-front lump-sum payment to cover my past expenses, a running royalty as a percentage of gross sales, and a minimum royalty every year, no matter how many scales were sold. That seemed fair to everyone present.

A bargaining session then ensued. By the end of the meeting, we agreed on a lump-sum payment of $250,000; a running royalty starting at 3 percent of gross sales and eventually coming down to 1.5 percent after a million scales were sold; and a minimum royalty based on the sale of at least 20,000 scales per year. When the bargaining session came to an end, we shook hands. I shook Tanida's hand to seal the deal, I thought. He shook my hand in return, probably in deference to the Western tradition of saying goodbye. From his perspective, the bargaining was not yet over: it had just begun.

It was left to Oshima, who drove me back to O'Hare airport, to complete the negotiations with me. By the end of April, our agreement was modified in three important ways. First, the up-front payment was reduced to $200,000, to be paid in three installments. Second, I had to return these installments to Tanita in full if it became clear, during development, that there were insurmountable technical difficulties or that it was impossible to produce the scale at a reasonable price. And third, a $50,000 nonreimbursable payment would be given to me for helping Tanita during the coming year in completing the development of the thin scale. It would be used to develop prototypes or to make parts in New York, as well as to travel to Japan a few times to work with the R&D people in Tokyo.

The reimbursement idea made me very uncomfortable, and it was eventually agreed that Tanita had only one year from the time of signing our contract to request reimbursement. That seemed more reasonable to me, and the thought of putting all the monies I received in some escrow account—so that I could return them if needed—never crossed my mind. I felt blessed and grateful. Existence was so kind and patient with me. It now gave me yet another chance to realize my thin-scale fantasy, under better conditions than ever before. There was no reason to fret about the deal collapsing yet again.

* * *

I made my first short trip to Tanit Tokyo in June of 1994. Oshima came too, to act as interpreter and to smooth all sharp corners. He had been living in the United States for five years by then and was the company's designated American relations expert. Being rather curt, laconic, and angular himself, he was not the perfect man for smoothing corners, but we understood each other perfectly and that was what counted after all.

Oshima arranged for me to stay in a small business hotel with tiny rooms, a short walking distance from a train station. It was only a few stops northwest of Ikebukuro—one of the main transportation hubs of the Tokyo metropolitan area. Tanita's headquarters were located in a nice residential neighborhood, a few stops further along that same train line. They were housed in a relatively new four-story building surrounded by a broad green lawn and encircled by tall trees. The president of the company lived a short distance away and walked to work.

The headquarters building itself was a rather nondescript contemporary structure, much like most of the other newer buildings in Tokyo. It was a clean and total break from the beautiful architecture of the past, the architecture that produced the exquisite Temple of the Golden Pavilion. Gone were the solid timber columns and beams, the exquisite details of the wooden joints, and the gently concave sloping roofs. They now succumbed to the International Style and to the sway of Western technology. Wood, tile, and paper were now replaced by steel, concrete, and glass.

The interior of the headquarters building was divided into offices and research laboratories. The office floors were all of the open-plan type with shallow partitions. To my surprise, there were no enclosed offices along the windows. Even Tanida himself sat in an open cubicle, amidst the rest of the work force. Except for the occasional conference room along the perimeter that blocked the view, everyone could see the trees outside from where they sat. There were also one or two designated smoking corners on every floor that were always full and bustling with conversation. *Nemawashi*—or informal discussion—was an essential ingredient of Japanese corporate life, and was encouraged rather than throttled.

There were some men in white shirts and ties, but at least half of the men—including the senior management—wore a blue work shirt over their white shirt that had a Tanita logo on the pocket. Upon my arrival, I was ushered into a conference room for a meeting attended by seven men. Except for Oshima, I had only met one of them before. Tanida walked in a few minutes after the meeting started, dressed in his blue shirt and gently fanning his face with a traditional bamboo-and-paper fan. I was wearing a jacket and a tie and sweating profusely.

The meeting, the first of many, was dedicated to contract negotiations. The discussion moved leisurely from one issue to another, and eventually centered on defining know-how. I was made aware—in a polite and circumspect way—that the engineers at R&D were offended by the know-how list that I had appended to the draft contract I sent them, because, they said, it included many things they already knew. Tanida said he liked one of my suggestions: to incorporate a keyhole on the bottom of the scale, so that people—especially those with little floor space—could hang it on the wall. The formal know-how list was dropped soon thereafter, but there was a lot that they wanted to know.

Here was a group of people who were truly interested in what I had found out about thin scales over the past few years. I had brought presents with me too: new parts and new load cells, a new prototype, and a complete set of new computer drawings on a diskette. They were anxious to see them. I quickly settled down to enjoying myself. They seemed to be enjoying themselves too.

That afternoon, there was a meeting with the engineers at the R&D laboratory. The two central figures working on the thin-scale project were Miyoshi and Yabé. Miyoshi was the head of the group, a larger man, and their electronics ace. Yabé was shorter, bespectacled, and dead serious; he was their mechanical engineer and load cell man. But there were a lot of other engineers around—some talking, some thinking, and some acting on the mechanism at hand. They were clearly a group working together. Oshima assured me that I could get as technical as I wanted with these people—they knew their job, he said. There was no question of that.

They had clearly done their homework before I came. They had new cat face load cells made with a new configuration, more rectangular and sharp cornered than mine. And they made them by punching them out of a flat piece of steel, as described in my patent claim. It worked! One less thing to worry about. They said that they now believed in the accuracy of the load cells, but that they did not believe that the load cells would retain their accuracy when mounted into the scale plate. That was what José Luis of Kratos Dinamometros in São Paulo—the engineer I had negotiated with for supplying load cells to Philips—kept telling me, I recalled.

They then showed me their one-inch-thick prototype scale: two thin, square metal plates with four of their load cells mounted between them—one in each corner. It had many parts—too many parts for my taste—but each part was immaculate, and all the parts were put together with great precision. They said that they suspected that when the plate deflected under load it pulled on the load cells toward the center of the plate and interfered with their accuracy. I already knew that. It was the same problem that Engineer van der Brug of Philips had encountered when he connected the load cells rigidly to a top and bottom plate.

But the Tanita engineers did not just leave it there. For the time being, they had solved the problem, they said, by placing rubber spacers between the load cells and the bottom plate. The rubber allowed the top plate to deflect and come to a rest, without pulling on the load cells. I showed them the single-plate prototype I had brought with me. The rubber feet under the load cells functioned in the same way, I said. Still, they remained worried. They felt that the rubber under the load cell would not be adequate if there was too much deflection, especially when it was compressed tightly under a full load. As it turned out, they were right about that.

When it came time to discuss the electronics, they simply brushed it aside. Miyoshi said that he would take care of it, and the way he said it sounded like he could design a new electronic circuit for a scale before breakfast. I believed him too. He showed me a PC board he had designed for a one-load-cell scale; it was only two square inches in size, less than one-sixth the size of Sam Cohen's PC board. Like I said before, investing my money and Sam's time on completing the development of the electronics was silly. There was no real need for it at the time, and anyhow, the first models of the thin scale would be core products without any bells and whistles. How was I going to break the news to Sam that his electronics were out the window? It would break his heart.

That evening, Tanida invited me to a traditional Japanese dinner—always in a restaurant, rarely if ever in a home. Only men were present. Oshima was there, as were three other Tanita *sararimen* (salarymen) out on yet another company evening. We sat on the floor on *tatami* (woven straw) mats, with Tanida facing me and Oshima sitting by my side, translating and often laughing to himself at what he heard before passing it on. There was no shoptalk and no business was transacted. We spoke of aging red wines in cellars and of fasting in Zen temples. The food was excellent and kept coming in small portions for a long time. We drank saké, the light Japanese rice wine. It was taken for granted that no one poured saké for himself: Tanida poured some saké into my cup whenever my cup was empty. I reciprocated. It was a way of remaining watchful of the moment and not getting carried away with idle conversation.

Tanida also made sure that my plate was full and kept replenishing it with food as soon as a new dish arrived at our table. This he did with grace and an assured hand. It was service that brought him to power in the first place, and once in power, his most important responsibility was to be of service to his group. Leadership, in the Japanese context, was often opposite in character to leadership in the West. "Whereas in the West work group leaders tend to emphasize task and often neglect group maintenance activities," note Pascale and Athos in *The Art of Japanese Management,* "in Japan maintenance of a satisfied work group goes hand in hand with the role." Richard Greenleaf, in *On Becoming a Servant-Leader,* goes one step further, calling for instilling that servant mentality among Western corporate leaders:

> It is more important to use one's power affirmatively to *serve,* in the sense that those being served, *while being served,* become healthier, wiser, freer, more autonomous, and more likely themselves to become servants. . . . The hierarchical organization postulates the leader as the *superior* of his followers. In the Catholic orders, the word *superior* is an actual title. We now need a principle of organization that postulates the leader as the *servant* of his followers.

In the days that followed, Tanida retreated, reducing his contact with me to a minimum and letting others take charge. Most of my time was spent with the R&D engineers—in their lab during the day, and in the karaoke bars at night.

The R&D engineers demonstrated to me that the scale prototype I had brought with me deflected too much under load, and that its excessive deflection affected its accuracy. They then subjected my prototype to two other tests: a carpet test and a concentrated load test. It failed them both. Its failure to retain its accuracy on a thick carpet was no surprise at all, neither to me nor to them, but they assured me that carpets were of little importance in Japan, where homes, not to mention bathrooms, rarely had thick carpets.

The "concentrated load" test was a test I had never encountered before. It involved comparing the difference between two readings for a 120-kilogram (260-pounds) weight: one in which the weight was placed on two three-inch-by-eight-inch blocks of wood, spaced two inches apart on the scale platform; and one in which the same weight was placed on two smaller six-inch-by-three-inch blocks of wood, spaced only one inch apart (Fig. 67).

When we began to test the Lexan-and-aluminum prototype for concentrated loads, the building started to sway and we heard a rumble. The inanimate objects in the room now came to life and were shaking, making different kinds of clicking sounds. It was an earthquake, a common occurrence in these parts. Everyone present was mesmerized. Our casual looks turned into fixed gazes and our faces froze in mid-smile. When we resumed the concentrated load test—as if the earthquake had never happened—the prototype failed to perform.

We were not getting any closer to closure. On the contrary, as our testing and our discussions progressed, there were more and more unresolved issues that needed attention. It was still too early to tell whether the R&D engineers were convinced that the thin-scale game was a game worth playing. These people were very serious about their work, about acting responsibly, and about making sure that nothing important went unnoticed. And they still reserved their judgment. It was too early to tell whether they thought that the problems at hand were soluble or insurmountable. Initially, I experienced their reserve as a slightly adversarial attitude towards me. At times it felt as though they were trying to prove me wrong. But as the days progressed, I slowly came to realize that it was not personal at all. They were just as eager to provide answers and solutions to the puzzles confronting us as I was.

It was quite easy to see that they felt comfortable with me when we sang "Summertime" and "When the Saints Go Marching In" together at their favorite karaoké bar in the evenings, accompanied by canned laser-disc music. The atmosphere shifted markedly from seriousness to silliness—the saké helped, of course—and the problems of the day faded away, giving way to light conversation, in-house jokes, and amicable character assassination. Differences in rank were of no matter, and everyone was made to feel at home. These were long and elaborate male bonding rituals that would never end. A pair of unmarried women colleagues would drop by occasionally, stay for an hour, and leave. On occasion, we stayed at the bar until midnight.

On the morning of the last day of my visit to Tokyo, over a Japanese breakfast

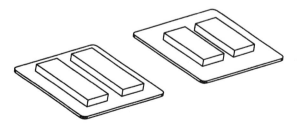

67 *Wooden blocks for comparing nonconcentrated (left) and concentrated (right) loads*

at my hotel—rice mixed with a raw egg and wrapped with thin strips of black seaweed—Oshima raised the specter of the cost of production. He said that if the present $30 cost estimates contemplated by R&D were correct, then the scale would have to sell for $150 in Japan. Too high, he said; we would probably need to bring the cost down to $20 to make the project feasible. I felt a familiar hardness in my abdomen. The cost question had come to haunt me yet again, and I felt powerless in its presence. I had pinned my hopes on the Tanita engineers. If anyone could think of ways of reducing costs in mass production, it would be them, certainly not me.

Why was there such a high markup in Japan anyway, five times the cost of production instead of the typical three times in the United States, for example? Americans often complain that the Japanese distribution system is antiquated and inefficient, preventing American products from gaining access to Japanese markets. A frequently cited statistic is, to quote Dennis Laurie's *Yankee Samurai*: "For every 1 worker in the U.S. distribution system between the manufacturer and the customer, there are about 2.3 in Japan." Laurie points out, however, that "What Americans call 'inefficient,' the Japanese might simply call 'exemplary service'. . . . There is a premium on customer service throughout the Japanese distribution system, with its 'greeters' at the door, gift wrappers, and myriad small mom-and-pop wholesale and retail operations that is often missing from much of the American scene."

In the long run, under the pressures of globalization, the American and Japanese distribution systems may or may not converge. As for myself, I had to contend with the high cost-multiple in Japan, about which there was nothing I could do. I left Tokyo with a queasy sense of anxiety—there was still a host of open questions ahead that needed urgent answers. Tanita might still decide to back out of the project after all, and the monies I would receive for granting them the license might eventually need to be reimbursed. Not a pleasant prospect.

For now, however, I was not strapped for money. And these somber thoughts on my future cash flow could not stop me from using the money I had already received from Tanita on renovating the SoHo loft I now shared with Lucinda and her two children—Adam and Daniella. That summer, Lucinda and I planned and executed a major home improvement project. It entailed building ourselves a new, bright bedroom with its own bathroom; building a big new bathroom for the children as well; and giving the whole place a much-needed facelift.

Working together on the design was a pleasant and nourishing experience. I thought of design largely as a problem-solving exercise, as in form follows function. Lucinda also subscribed to the form-follows-function imperative, but, for her, design was also the transformation of something ugly into something of taste. I willingly deferred to her sense of taste—it was more sophisticated and subtle than mine. But occasionally, in the spirit of an antimodernist rebellion, I could not help insisting on an ornamental feature here and there—I felt I needed to "decorate" the place somehow. Lucinda, an avowed modernist, pleasantly resisted most of my more ornate decorative impulses. I didn't insist, some ornamental traces remained, and all in all, the place ended up looking more beautiful than ever. It now also felt more like home.

* * *

Charlie went back to work as soon as I returned, focusing on two critical issues: the excessive deflections of our composite-plate prototype, and its failure in the concentrated load test. Over the summer—while I was away traveling—he had built two more prototypes and tested them using rectangular wooden blocks. He found that once the wooden blocks were put between the plate and the test weights, the behavior of the plate changed in strange ways.

First, the wooden blocks, acting like beams, strengthened the plate in one direction more than in the other, resulting in uneven deflections all around. Second, he found that—with our specific design—the sharp corners of the wooden blocks were pushing down exactly over the area where the load cells were attached to the plate and distorting his measurements. Once he cut the corners off the wooden blocks, they no longer interfered with the load cells, and the prototype performed adequately. Charlie tinkered some more with the hardness of the rubber feet, decided on softer rubber, tested the prototype some more, and then shipped it off to Tokyo.

* * *

I arrived in Tokyo in late September of 1994 for a second round of meetings at Tanita headquarters, bringing yet another prototype as well as new test results. I sensed a general discomfort when I arrived there. Word was out that the latest prototype that Charlie had sent had failed all the accuracy tests, every one of them. That was strange. Yabé, the engineer who had conducted the tests, was a very meticulous man, but so was Charlie. Once the customary meeting with the top management of the company was over, I walked over to the R&D laboratory, this time without Oshima.

Yabé presented his results in detail with a tight jaw, barely moving his mouth as he spoke. Miyoshi translated haltingly but very accurately. Everyone was nodding his head slowly while Yabé explained what he had done, and so was I. I then asked for a few clarifications, and I nodded my head some more when I heard Yabé's answers. I then politely suggested that we go and repeat the tests. Everyone nodded agreement. We all went together to the universal testing machine that stood in the middle of the laboratory. We repeated the tests, and sure enough, all the errors showed up again, just as Yabé had predicted. I courteously asked for this and that to be changed. The tests were repeated, and the major errors were still there.

This was impossible. I trusted Charlie completely, and if he said it worked, it worked. There must be something wrong with the testing equipment we were using, I thought. Suspecting that their electronics were faulty, I requested that an external voltmeter be brought in, to replace the one that was built into their universal testing machine. They were happy to comply. All the major errors now disappeared. Everyone breathed a sigh of relief. There was no loss of face. I could even detect a faint smile on Yabé's face. Another obstacle was removed and we could now move on.

I then demonstrated to them that the error on the concentrated load test disappeared as well when we used the wooden blocks with the cut corners that I had brought with me. Surprisingly, that did not go down very well. A few of them were shaking their heads. I tried to explain that the blocks with the cut corners resembled the shape of human feet, all to no avail. The square blocks were required by government regulations, they said. I proposed that Tanita formally request a change in the regulations. They were not so sure that this was a productive course, even though they agreed that it made sense.

Anyway, over dinner that same night, it turned out that the government required that the large square blocks be used in basic accuracy tests, but that the concentrated load test was an in-house test and could be conducted in the future with chamfered wooden blocks. I recommended hard foam instead of wood, and that appealed to them too. As the evening proceeded, they gradually warmed up to the idea of approaching the government with an improved block design. But they insisted that any such proposal would have to be very concrete, backed with serious testing. I concurred. After the dissonance in the morning meeting, it felt very comfortable sitting there on the *tatami* mats with them. "Things are on the up and up," I wrote in my notes the next morning. "The engineers seem to agree that the accuracy is there."

After some more testing over the next couple of days, we all agreed that the composite plate still deflected too much and that the deflections were interfering with accuracy. The engineers at R&D were also worried that the rubber foot arrangement under the load cell was still producing inaccuracies as well. They suspected that these inaccuracies occurred because (a) there was still too much friction between the rubber foot and the floor; and (b) the force exerted by the foot on the load cell above it was shifting from one place to another. If we could eliminate friction with the floor and ensure that the floor exerted a *point* load right underneath the center of each load cell, they predicted, these inaccuracies would disappear. This made good sense.

On a Hittite relief found in Karkemish—one of the oldest depictions of the act of weighing—an equal-arm balance is shown to be supported by a finger from below (Fig. 68). Such balances, despite their inexactness, were used for many centuries. Because they made cheating too easy—by moving the finger slightly to the left or to the right—their use for trade was later prohibited by several statutes.

Over centuries, equal-arm balances were improved in several ways to increase their accuracy. According to Chisholm's *On the Science of Weighing and Measuring* of 1877, for example, for a balance scale to be accurate, the two points of suspension of the pans must be exactly equidistant from the center of motion, and

68 *A Hittite relief showing a balance supported by a finger from below*

the friction at the center of motion must be at a minimum. In other words, the arm of the balance must exert a *point* load at its exact center, and there must be a minimum of friction at that point. A finger would simply not do.

The Tanita engineers pointed out, in fact, that these two basic requirements for accuracy—a point load and minimum friction—were still missing from the rubber foot arrangement under the load cell. To demonstrate that there was still plenty of friction present and that it was producing inaccuracy, Yabé and a young assistant placed small metal squares under each of the four rubber feet of the scale prototype, and then inserted three metal ball bearings under each square. The scale now floated on ball bearings. They then repeated the concentrated load test and got a tenfold improvement on our earlier results. I was duly impressed.

To get rid of friction and to center the load exactly under the load cell, they suggested that I introduce a steel ball-and-socket arrangement between the rubber foot and the circular bridging plate under the load cell (Fig. 69). I was more than happy to concur. They then explained to me what was involved and helped me with the dimensions. We were collaborating now in getting the thin scale to work. I no longer felt that they were simply trying to prove that my designs did not work for one reason or another.

Over breakfast at my hotel the next day, I related that story to my old friend Herbert Sax—a Swiss-born painter who had settled in Japan some 20 years before, and a keen observer of the local culture. He was not at all surprised. "They love perfection and will pursue this thing to the end," he said. "They want to get it right for the sake of getting it right, never mind the rewards." I loved that. Dennis Laurie, in *Yankee Samurai*, put that striving for perfection in more general terms:

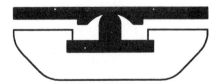

69 *A schematic drawing of the ball-and-socket arrangement*

Commitment—not to strategy but to mission and the immediate task at hand, in the form of patience, determination, and the willingness to allocate sometimes inordinate human and capital resources—is a basic quality of Japanese management style. Japanese firms rarely abandon a product line; there is shame in doing so. Rather, they tend to pursue *kaisen* (continual enhancement and improvement) until it finally succeeds, albeit in a final form perhaps different from that originally intended.

Towards the end of that second visit, we agreed to divide up the work. They would work on optimizing the distribution of ribs and cavities in the plastic-and-metal sandwich alternative. I would work on a new foot design, and possibly on a new metal-and-foam sandwich plate alternative. We all agreed that plate deflection needed to be reduced to a minimum if accuracy was to improve.

The negotiations on the license agreement were being pursued in parallel with the technical discussions, and they were brought to a satisfactory close by the end of that visit. I had to forego minimum royalties, and it mattered little to me because I no longer felt strongly about it. After some more tinkering with the language during a couple of meetings, we arrived at an amicable consensus on all the remaining issues. I typed the agreement myself at the business center of the Sunshine City Prince Hotel in Ikebukuro, I brought it back, and Tanida and I signed.

After we signed the agreement, Tanida sent me a handwritten note in Japanese. It said: "We would like to do our best to prevent competitors from entering the market once we start selling the scale. Kindly do your best to invent new flat load cells of different shapes and materials, as well as new plate structures that could compete with honeycombs."

I wished it were that simple. Once a patent was issued, there was nothing one could do to prevent others from circumventing it with slight modifications in the design that were not originally claimed in the patent. It was too late to make new claims by then, and slight modifications circumventing the patents could certainly come to torment us later. Yes, I already had a patent application drafted for a new load cell, but that was a different story. I chose not to bring it up yet. All in due time.

I left Tokyo a day earlier than planned, not wanting to impose on my hosts any further. Much as they were eager to collaborate and to make me feel at home, my presence there created havoc in their daily routines.

* * *

I came to Tokyo for the third time in early December of 1994, and this time I was not alone. I was accompanied by Lucinda, Adam, who was 13 at the time, and Daniella, who was 10. We were going to explore Japan and Thailand together and Tokyo was our first stop. The three of them were cruising the department stores at Ikebukuro, or visiting tourist sites accompanied by young Tanita staff members, while I sat in meetings with the engineers to compare our latest accomplishments.

This time I brought with me yet another new prototype, the most accurate one that Charlie and I had ever constructed. It attained a 50-gram (0.1-pound) accuracy on all the required tests, double the accuracy required on most of them. And this time it was not at all difficult to convince the R&D engineers that the accuracy was there. They were more than ready to acknowledge that it was.

The new prototype worked—as they indeed had predicted during my last visit—because (a) it incorporated the ball-and-socket arrangement; and (b) it reduced the deflection of the plate at full load to one-thirty-secondth of an inch—it was now no longer visible to the naked eye. Unfortunately, reducing deflection came at a price: we abandoned the Lexan-and-aluminum plate and adopted a steel-and-foam sandwich plate instead. The sandwich plate was now only six millimeters thick—slightly less than a quarter of an inch—but the steel skins on both sides weighed considerably more. The scale now weighed no less than two pounds, one pound more than my original goal.

On the second day of my visit, Tanida came to the R&D laboratory for a meeting to evaluate the steel-and-foam prototype. He was very happy with the new level of accuracy and thought is was a great improvement. He thought it still needed a plastic cover over the steel and expressed some concern over the added weight. He would like the scale to be lighter and thinner, he said.

He was telling us—in gentle yet not uncertain terms—that he wanted us to remain true to the original vision of the project, as well as to the mission of the corporation, a mission that included the motto *Kei Haku Tan Shou* (light, thin, short, small). Even though it was an indirect criticism of my latest prototype, it was good to be with someone who was keeping me honest and focused on my original goal. The thin-scale project was now in good hands, I felt. "They are finally on board, playing the game I want to play," I wrote in my notes. "I found some partners who want to play the same game. I am no longer alone in this venture."

On the morning of 11 December 1994, a fax arrived at Tanita headquarters. It was addressed to Lucinda. She had left the Tanita phone and fax numbers with her mother, in case there was an emergency, and now her mother wrote her to wish her a happy birthday. The fax was passed on to us, but it also caught the eye of the people in the office. They said nothing.

On that same evening, the top management of the corporation invited us all to an intimate Japanese dinner, this time a surprise birthday party for Lucinda. Tanida and his colleagues then spent the whole evening with us, serving us food, entertaining the children, and making us feel at home. It was a sweet gesture. Tanida, with a beautiful smile on his face, presented Lucinda with a single red rose and a small birthday present. Lucinda reciprocated with her own beautiful smile.

That evening Tanida informed me in passing that the manufacture of the thin scale could not start before Tanita could produce strain gages by itself. The cost of buying them outside was prohibitive, he said. That could mean a long delay, I thought. I asked him whether there was any way I could be of further assistance. He said that he thought that my job was now finished; the R&D engineers would take over from there. There were still some serious technical problems to be solved, he said, but the engineers would know how to finish the development and to prepare the scale for production.

He was very grateful to me, he said, for everything I had done. I was very grateful too, and I let him know it. My consulting assignment with Tanita came to an end that night. There was nothing for me to do now but wait. I felt strangely empty and more than a little disoriented, but the ensuing trip to the Japanese countryside with my little family proved a good palliative for that condition.

21

The Happy End Version of the Tale

So closes an eventful passage in the life of Luke Larkin. He has struggled upward from a boyhood of privation and self-denial into a youth and manhood of prosperity and honor. There has been some luck about it, I admit, but after all he is indebted for most of his good fortune to his own good qualities.

Horatio Alger Jr., *Struggling Upward*

———

Simply waiting on Tanita to get the thin scale ready for production was not an acceptable proposition. I was not yet willing to give up on the scale quest, to pass the baton, so to speak, to the next runner in the relay race to market. Surely, having the competent engineers at Tanita working on their own to complete the development of the thin bathroom scale was a great relief. But that did not mean that there was nothing left for me to do on the scale front.

There was still the new load cell, now nicknamed the owl face. Its patent was now pending, and it was time to take it off the back burner and do something with it.

Shortly after I returned from Tokyo in January 1995, I started to pay serious attention to this load cell. I now set myself yet a new goal: to bring it to the attention of commercial and industrial scale manufacturers with the prospect of a new licensing arrangement. I was now more confident than ever that I would obtain a strong patent for this load cell; that I could build highly accurate commercial and industrial scales that employed it; that these scales would be thinner than any made before; that they would not be more expensive than comparable scales; and, last but not least, that I knew what I was doing.

Surely, making thin commercial and industrial scales was not one of my original goals when I set out. Why was I pursuing it now? This was a difficult question to answer, and I did not really examine it closely at the time. I believe that my confidence was propelling me forward: I pursued the new goal simply because I now could pursue it.

But, come to think of it, it may also have been my need for acknowledgment —by those skilled in the art—that my inventions were indeed worthwhile. I had always assumed that, when it came to scales, thin was equivalent to good and useful, but I had no way of knowing if my inventions were a timely response to a real need. I was an outsider, after all. I now had to go into the field to find out if my inventions were indeed timely and relevant, and whether they had something to contribute to the dialogue currently taking place there.

Howard Gardner, in *Creating Minds,* suggests that the locus of creativity does not simply reside in the creative individual himself, but in his interaction with the domain in which he operates and with the culture that ultimately judges the value of his contributions: "The creative individual is a person who regularly solves problems, fashions products, or defines new questions in a domain in a way that is initially considered novel, but that ultimately becomes accepted in a particular cultural setting. . . . Nothing is, or is not, creative *in and of itself.* Creativity is inherently a communal or cultural judgment."

In other words, what is ultimately deemed creative can not be decided at the time that a creative act occurs, when a problem is solved, or when a new product is invented. Assessing the true creative value of any invention requires going beyond the novelty of the product itself to examine the impact it has on its domain.

The painter Georgia O'Keeffe, for example, had this to say about the relationship between her talent as a creative artist and her impact on her domain: "I can imagine myself to be a much better painter and nobody paying any attention to me at all. But it happens that things I've been doing were in touch with their time."

For now, I had no idea whether my new owl face load cell ("and scales incorporating it") was indeed in touch with the times. My plan, upon my return from Tokyo, was to find that out. The way I proposed to find out was to bring them to the attention of the scale industry; not the domestic appliances industry this time, but the scale industry.

The next annual convention of the International Society of Weighing and Measurement (ISWM) was scheduled to take place at the MGM Grand Hotel in Las Vegas in June of 1995. I resolved to come to the convention with a set of looks-like works-like commercial and industrial scale prototypes that employed the new load cell. Would I rent a booth at the convention hall to exhibit my wares, like the other vendors? No. I would rent a suite at the hotel and invite selected industry representatives to examine the prototypes in strict confidence. That, I already knew, was the way things were done when new products were involved.

Making the new prototype load cells and testing them was a breeze. I now had reliable (or at least predictable) suppliers and subcontractors for every step in the process. Charlie and I tested a series of load cells in close succession and they worked to our satisfaction. Soon enough, we had owl face load cells for a counter scale in the 20-pound range, for a bench scale in the 500-pound range (Fig. 70), and for a floor scale in the 1,000-pound range. They all performed well.

The bench and floor scales required adjustable, self-leveling feet, and I

70 *An owl face load cell for a 500-pound scale*

quickly completed a novel design for them and had some made. These self-leveling feet screwed directly into the load-receiving tongue of the load cell from below, and they had a built-in ball-and-socket arrangement that ensured that the load cells saw only point loads. They worked the first time we tried them. We were on a roll.

We then built three looks-like works-like scale prototypes. The nicest one of them—the 1,000-pound floor scale—was three-quarters of an inch thick, and its top was only 0.9 inches off the floor (Fig. 71). All three prototypes passed the basic tests with flying colors, attaining a level of accuracy of one part in 10,000, an accuracy that certainly gave them a good shot at obtaining an official Certificate of Conformance.

By the time I arrived in Las Vegas for the convention, my patent application for a "Mass-Produced Flat Multiple-Beam Load Cell and Scales Incorporating It" was already at an advanced stage. In the last "office action" by the patent examiner in Washington, all the main claims were deemed allowable. It would only be a matter of time before the examiner granted me a patent.

The MGM Grand was a tacky 5,000-room hotel-casino complex, desperately trying to transform itself into a family-oriented theme park. My suite at the hotel was almost suitable for my purposes, but not quite. As expected, its floor was covered with a thick, dark, wall-to-wall carpet, and there was no question that the floor scale would fail to retain its accuracy on such a carpet. I needed a piece of three-quarter-inch plywood to be brought to the room, four feet by four feet, and, if possible, clad in white Melamine plastic.

71 *The floor scale prototype*

I picked up the *Yellow Pages* from the bedside table. I soon found the phone number of a lumberyard that was more than happy to sell me a four-by-eight sheet of Melamine-clad plywood, cut it in half, and deliver one half of it to my hotel room in a matter of hours. They would keep the other half if I had no use for it. Las Vegas, without a doubt, was eager to please. At a price.

Once I set up the little show-and-tell in my suite, I went downstairs to mingle with the scale industry crowd. Oshima and some of his colleagues from Tokyo were there, of course. We exchanged pleasantries. They reported little progress on their development efforts, but let me understand that things were moving ahead according to schedule. Their own efforts at the convention focused mainly on making arrangements for as many golf games as they could fit in between dawn and dusk. There was really little for them to do on the convention floor. From what I could gather, no major innovations and not even minor ones were exhibited. This, as Stephen Lee had said to Amos and me in Taipei, was a mature technology.

I spotted some floor scales. They were bulky. They could only be mounted from two sides, and they had low, narrow walls on the remaining two sides in which load cells were installed. These miserable creations surely did not offer serious competition for my graceful floor scale upstairs. It was not at all difficult for me to arouse the interest of the major players. They were all there—presidents, heads of marketing, and heads of development—either hanging around their booths or walking along from one booth to the other to chitchat with their counterparts in other companies. After some inquiries, I introduced myself to the right people, inviting them one by one to come up to my suite for a demonstration.

Over the next few days, I held numerous discussions with the people from Mettler-Toledo, Cardinal-Detecto, Rice Lake Weighing Systems, and the Ohaus Corporation, to name a few. One after the other, they all readily acknowledged that my designs were new, innovative, and daring; and they complimented me profusely on my work. They were frustrated, they said, with the slow pace of innovation in the field, and they were happy to see some fresh load cell designs that were not simply trivial variations on tired themes.

Their genuine enthusiasm aside, they worried that there was still considerable product development work to be done on the new load cell. Apparently, over the preceding years, most of the effort devoted to the development of load cells had gone into making them immune to harsh environments—both indoors and outdoors—protecting them from humidity, dirt, corrosive chemicals, extreme temperatures, and other environmental hazards. The goal was to make them as rugged as possible while maintaining their accuracy. Slowly, as is often the case, production lines for more sensitive load cells were abandoned, and rugged load cells replaced sensitive ones even in applications where there was no call for ruggedness.

The new load cell I had shown them was still a very sensitive one, with exposed strain gages and wiring and little protection from environmental hazards of any kind. Making it into a rugged load cell, some of them said, would require a significant investment in product development that they were reluctant to make without further study. I had a strong sense that investment in product development in the scale industry was considered by one and all as risky as putting money on the roulette and blackjack tables nearby.

I invited the Tanita people to my suite too. They were impressed with the new load cell, they said, and they liked to see that I was moving into new territory. They could see that the new load cell would be more accurate than the cat face one, but they could also see that it would be more expensive because it had four strain gages instead of two. This would render it inappropriate for the thin-scale model we were developing together. Still, they asked me whether I would be willing to send a prototype of the bench scale to Tokyo for evaluation. They had other uses for it in mind, they said. I promised I would, as soon as I retrieved it from the people who were going to take it back with them for further study.

After the convention, the prototypes traveled to Rice Lake, Wisconsin, and then to Mettler-Toledo in both North Carolina and Ohio.

I did not get very far with the Rice Lake people. They pondered the load cell prototype for a while and then they sent it back, saying that according to their estimates, investing in preparing that load cell for manufacturing was not a feasible option for them.

The engineers at Mettler-Toledo in North Carolina put the counter scale through the test procedures required by the National Institute of Standards and Technology (NIST) and sent me a copy of the test results. I could not really understand the paperwork I received from them, and to this day I do not know how well that scale performed. My discussions with them did not lead anywhere. The Ohio Mettler-Toledo people kept the floor scale for a few months while maintaining a strict silence, and then sent it back without packing it properly, simply attaching it with steel bands to a rickety wooden skid. It was bent out of shape en route and I had to throw it away.

The signals I was receiving from my domain, so to speak, were quite clear: the scale industry had no real interest in my inventions. Pity. As Oscar Wilde once remarked, "The play was a great success but the audience was a failure." Well, at least I now had the answer to my question, and that answer did provide me with some sort of closure too. Unlike Georgia O'Keeffe, I was apparently not in touch with the time in the things I had been doing with commercial and industrial scales. By the end of 1995, my relatively short affair with the scale industry had come to an end. I had made a pass at it and it had rejected me. Some affairs do end like that.

* * *

It was time to move on. I had by and large exhausted my interest in the matter of thin scales, their invention, their design, and their development. I now had three patents to my name—the third one still pending but expected shortly—and my quarter-inch personal scale was soon to grace the shelves of stores everywhere.

In early February of 1996, at a large meeting at Tanita headquarters in Tokyo, President Tanida made known the production schedule of the thin scale: 50,000 units were to be produced and sold in 1997; 100,000 in 1998; and another 100,000 in 1999. I sat there quietly, trying to prevent too wide a grin from spreading across my face. At that rate, I would soon make my million dollars. I had now largely accomplished what I set out to do, and—as I could never have done it alone—I felt a deep sense of gratitude to all those I had encountered along the way. Finally, some nine years after I had started my quest, I could just sit back and watch it all happen.

So maybe the American Dream—the belief in the gospel of individual success—was still realizable after all? Maybe it was still possible in our day and age to eschew the corporate collar and to succeed on one's own? The myth, the lure, and the promise of becoming a self-made man was surely still alive. Social and economic facts to the contrary, the myth itself must have survived in some form—at least in my own mind—much along the lines of Horatio Alger's 135 "way to success" novels that fed the imaginations of Americans in the late nineteenth century. The ending of his book *Struggling Upward,* quoted at the beginning of this chapter, though sounding a bit too naïve for our time, is not altogether alien in spirit to the ending of my story.

* * *

Now that the scale was on its way to the market, my design energies turned away from thin scales into an altogether new venture. Lucinda and I were now searching for a plot of land in the Hamptons, the resort communities on the eastern edge of Long Island where affluent New Yorkers spend their summers. We wanted to design and build a house there, then sell it, then buy another plot and

72 *The timber frame for the Bridgehampton house*

build another house, and so on in close succession, until we had a half dozen beautiful houses to our name. We already knew that we enjoyed working together and building together, and we loved designing together.

At the beginning of 1996, we bought a one-acre plot in Bridgehampton—on a gentle slope facing the sunset at the edge of a forest—and started working together in a relaxed and unhurried pace on plans for a large new house. We sought to make a place that celebrated the expanse of the SoHo loft we lived in; that embodied the warm, earthy touch of the post-and-beam structures of country barns; and that inspired the awe and silence of Asian temples.

Gradually, our design ideas started to take shape. What eventually emerged from our drawing board was a large Palladian villa in timber, ordered by simple symmetries. A spacious loft-like atrium occupied its center, its high ceilings supported by great laminated arches that formed palmlike canopies above the central columns (Fig. 72).

We didn't design that house working in parallel. Rather, it felt as though any design problem we worked on pulled us toward itself, and the closer we got to it, the closer we got to each other. Occasionally, when we resolved an intricate spatial conflict together, our minds joined in a gentle cuddle. At some special times—when our designs reached elegance and came to a rest—that "sharp sense of joy" that Rollo May wrote about in *The Courage to Create*, the one "that comes when you find the particular form required by your creation," took on the character of a sublime embrace. And as we delved deeper and deeper into this new adventure, the scale gradually receded from my mind and let me be.

22

Either Things Go According to Plan or There Is a Story

You have a right to your actions, but never to your actions' fruits. Act for action's sake. And do not be attached to inaction. Self-possessed, resolute, act without any thought of results, open to success or failure. That equanimity is yoga.

Bhagavad Gita

———

Much as I would have preferred it, the tale of the scale simply refused to end peacefully, in the "happily ever after" tradition. There was still another chapter to be written.

Not long after the meeting with Tanida in Tokyo, Oshima called. He sounded agitated and his delivery was more staccato than usual. A Tanita delegation that had just returned from a home appliances exhibition in Europe, he said, saw a thin scale in the Tefal booth at the exhibition. It had four load cells that appeared to be similar to the cat face. The situation seemed very serious, Oshima went on to say, and the continuation of Tanita's development of the thin scale was now in jeopardy. He told me in no uncertain terms that Tanita expected me to stop the production and worldwide distribution of the offending scales soon. Once I composed myself, I promised him that I would get a Tefal scale and examine it to see if indeed there was an infringement of the patent, and that I would look into our legal options.

Tefal? This was the one European scale company that I had decided not to visit at the time I called on Krups and Soehnle in April of 1990, some six years earlier; I had had too much on my plate then. Tefal (sometimes marketed as T-fal) was a global brand name and a global market leader in small domestic appliances—from pots and pans to irons, pressure cookers, and scales. It was part of Groupe SEB, one of the largest manufacturers of small appliances in the world, with sales of some $1.5 billion in more than 100 countries in 1996, and on its way to becoming a global monopoly. Six years later, in early 2002, the French Monopolies Commission would authorize Groupe SEB's takeover of parts of Moulinex and Krups. Those people would be formidable adversaries, to say the least.

It took a while before I obtained a Tefal Slimmer scale from France, and it was late August already by the time Charlie and I got around to taking it apart and examining its innards. By that time, I had also received a copy of the French patent application on which the Tefal load cell was based. That application, filed in 1995, referred extensively to my patent in its discussion of prior art and sought to improve upon it. It proposed to do so by extending the outer arms of the cat face load cell until they met each other and formed a square (Fig. 73). That square, it was claimed, could simply rest in a cavity in the scale plate, without requiring rigid screw connections, thus making the scale simpler to manufacture.

I liked that. It was no doubt a marked improvement on the cat face—because it eliminated the screw connections altogether. Still, it did not fall outside the main claim of my patent. The wording of the main claim did not disclose any form of connection to the scale plate, let alone specific screw connections, even though the drawings did show holes that could possibly receive screws. The wording of the claim only required that the mounting element be fastenable to a rigid surface, but did not specify how. From a strictly legal standpoint, only the wording of the claim mattered, and, therefore, eliminating the screw holes did not distinguish the Tefal patent from mine at all. That much was clear.

Moreover, extending the two outer arms of the cat face load cell and connecting them so that they formed a square—or any other closed form, such as a circle or a hexagon—did not distinguish the Tefal embodiment from mine either, again, because my claim did not rule it out. My claim only specified that the two outer arms reach *beyond the midpoint* of the middle beam. How far they reached beyond that midpoint did not really matter. There was no special merit or advantage in actually connecting the two arms to each other anyway, and the Tefal application readily acknowledged it.

In addition, looking closely at the Tefal load cells, it became clear that they were stamped from a flat sheet of metal; the top edges of the vertical surfaces of the metal part were slightly rounded, while the bottom edges were angular— clear evidence of a stamping operation. On the face of it, this was an open and shut case. There was no question in my mind that Tefal was clearly infringing on my patent. Charlie concurred and so did Marc, my patent lawyer.

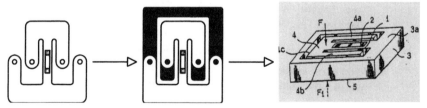

73 *The Tefal variation on the cat face load cell*

Marc put me in touch with a Parisian law firm specializing in patent law—the same law firm that had registered the cat face patent in France—and by early fall of 1996 we had started to exchange long faxes and letters. The lawyers handling my case—Jean Jacques and Dominic—made it clear to me that if I wanted to sue Tefal it had to be in France, and more specifically in the High Court in Lyon, which was the nearest court to the factory where the offending load cells were apparently being produced. That did not bode well. Not only was this shaping up as a David and Goliath contest, it now had to take place in Goliath's backyard.

Jean Jacques and Dominic laid out my options for me. The most aggressive one—and the one they recommended—involved sending a registered letter to the court demanding that Tefal cease and desist from infringing on my patent immediately. A judge might then order "the instant cessation of the alleged infringement, subject to funds from the Plaintiff as a guarantee against possible prejudice suffered by the Defendant." In other words, I could bring their scale production to a halt right now, but only if I deposited enough money in escrow so that, in the event that I lost the case, they could be fully compensated for their losses. The lawyers were of the opinion that this would give the court a strong signal: that I was so convinced I had a case that I was willing to back it up with my money. Appealing as this course of action was, I declined to take it, mostly for lack of sufficient depth in my pockets.

Otherwise, my Parisian counsels wrote, I could engage in normal infringement proceedings. They recommended that we start with the seizure of evidence at the Tefal factory, to be effected by a bailiff. They expected the seizure to turn up important evidence concerning the load cells: drawings, manufacturing information (especially proof that the load cells were indeed stamped from metal sheets), sales reports, and the like. Once the seizure was carried out, a barrister would be appointed to represent me at the Lyon court.

They estimated that a court decision would take 18 to 24 months and cost me some $75,000 in fees and expenses; that the decision would be appealed; that an appeal court would take 18 to 24 months and cost yet another $75,000; that the appeal court decision would be appealed too; that an appeal to the Supreme Court would take the same time and cost yet another $75,000. If I eventually lost the case, I would also have to pay damages, but these were not likely to exceed $25,000. In short, the total cost of the proceedings, over the next six years, could amount to some $250,000.

Did the lawyers think that I had a case? What were my chances of winning? On the face of it, they said—after having their expert examine the offending scale—the Tefal load cells did appear to infringe on my patent. But then they started to worry. My main claim included the phrase "the center beam bends under a load into a symmetrical S-shape," and their expert was not sure that the Tefal load cell behaved in that fashion. If it did not, they said, it would fall outside my patent and would not be infringing on it, even though its shape was similar. Our chances of winning the case would then be of the order of 25 percent, i.e., much lower than the chances offered at the roulette wheel in the casino.

Charlie and I then proceeded to examine the offending load cell more thoroughly. We carefully measured the strains in the two gages on the center beam of the Tefal load cell under different load conditions and came to the conclusion that sometimes the center beam bent into a symmetrical S-shape and sometimes it did not.

In their letter of 22 October 1996, the lawyers were now more confident. "We understand from the latest measurements that under some—but nevertheless realistic—load conditions, the pair of strain gages in the Tefal load cell produces opposite resistance variations. Accordingly, we believe that there is now a serious basis for starting an infringement action against Tefal." They upped my chances to 60 percent, still not great, but now considerably better than those offered at the roulette table.

My intermittent correspondence with Oshima on the matter made it clear to me that Tanita expected me to protect my patent from infringement by Tefal at my own expense; that it was willing to assume part of the expenses, but certainly only a part; that it worried about having to pay untold damages to Tefal in case we lost; and that it did not think that the chances of winning the case were all that great.

Oshima also said that the people in Tokyo felt that the French lawyers' approach was too aggressive. Maybe it would be possible to just send a letter to Tefal cautioning them against further infringement, to see how they react, like they do in Japan? I informed Oshima that, as far as I was given to understand, the French had their own way of handling infringements, and that they did not believe that sending a cautionary note was enough. They also believed in awarding only symbolic damages to the winner of the lawsuit, usually not exceeding $25,000; at least we did not have to worry about that.

I visited the Tanita headquarters in Tokyo at the beginning of April 1997, to discuss our joint legal strategy and to inquire about the progress made in preparation for starting production. At the meeting on the Tefal issue, I explained the case in detail, but I had the distinct feeling that my Tanita counterparts were not convinced we had a case. They wanted to be protected and they expected me to protect them, but they did not feel it was worth their while to invest in the lawsuit. I found myself in a difficult bind. I could see their point: there were dangers inherent in pursuing Tefal, and it could prove to be a costly affair. Yet, I could not simply walk away from these dangers. After all, I had sold Tanita patent protection, and I now felt personally obliged to protect it from infringement. These people had been generous with me, and it was only fair that I reciprocate. If they decided not to join me in suing Tefal, I would have to venture out on my own. I told them so in so many words. "I just want you to agree that you have no objection to my pursuing it myself," I said.

A long discussion ensued. What if I won the case against Tefal? What if Tefal asked me to allow it to continue production in exchange for paying me running royalties or one lump sum? Tanita would have to make the decision, because, as things stood, it held exclusive rights to my patent. That contingency was left open. They needed to think about it some more, they said. All in all, however, the consensus was that I was on my own. They would contribute half the costs I incurred, as long as I consulted them along the way. But they preferred to remain outside the affair altogether. That, I said, was fine with me. I was convinced I had a case, I said, and I was willing to prove it.

The meeting on progress made in getting the new scales to market was alarming, to say the least. They were seriously behind schedule. I was shown a plastic prototype that was nice and slick, but no longer very thin. They were now worried about the carpet problem too, and they said that they could not mass-produce the scale without solving it because if it lost its accuracy on carpets, they could not sell it overseas. They now hoped to begin mass production in the fall, nearly a year later than expected. I was not amused.

Tanida invited me out to dinner later that day. I was in a foul mood. He was intent on making me feel better. He explained to me that the delay in production was partly the result of their preoccupation with body-fat scales. Tanita was now set on becoming the world leader in body-fat scales, and no effort was spared on developing this new line of products.

Body-fat scales measured the percentage of fat in the body by sending a small and undetectable current from one foot to another. "Generally, the faster the current moves through the legs and midsection and the less resistance it encounters, the leaner the person is."

Tanida explained to me, rather apologetically, that Tanita was working feverishly on making body-fat scales available to ordinary consumers, and was putting all its R&D, production, and marketing energies into this effort. The development of the thin scale had suffered as a result, he acknowledged, and was now seriously behind schedule.

As we poured each other saké further into the night, I confessed to him that I now wanted out of the scale business altogether, that it no longer held any interest for me. I was now engaged in writing a book on housing policy and in building a beautiful house in the Hamptons with Lucinda. The scale problem that I had set for myself was solved, as far as I was concerned, and I had decided to move on.

He then asked me how much money I wanted as a one-time payment, in lieu of running royalties. He felt bad, he said, about having me wait on Tanita for my royalties. I told him that this required some thinking. Shortly after my return to New York, I wrote him: "I was happy to meet you in Tokyo during my last visit, and I apologize for being sad during our meeting. I had a dream—to produce the thinnest, lightest, and most accurate personal scale—and I was very happy to find you as a willing partner to share my dream. It is very difficult for me to give up hope. I am willing to wait and I am in no hurry."

* * *

The seizure at the Tefal plant took place on 11 April 1997. It did not require that I be present there. As I expected, the offending load cells were manufactured by a process known as *fine-blanking*, a variation on traditional stamping perfected by the Swiss. A document served by a bailiff on 24 April summoned Tefal to court, asking the court to prohibit Tefal from further infringement, under threat of a fine of $1,000 per infringement observed; to confiscate infringing products wherever they may be found and regardless of who may be in possession of them; to pay me $50,000 immediately as an advance on royalties on offending scales already sold; and to publish the court's decision in five journals of my choice.

Tefal countered immediately with its own lawsuit, requesting the court to declare my patent null and void; to affirm that the seizure was abusive and vexatious and to order me to pay Tefal $50,000 to cover the damages incurred during that seizure; and to make me responsible for any costs incurred by its lawyers in defending its case. The battle lines were now drawn.

* * *

On 7 May 1997, one month after my return from Japan, I received a letter from Oshima that paraphrased in English a letter he had received from Tokyo. President Tanida had received two reports, he wrote, one from the sales people and one from the R&D people.

The sales people "reported to him that they don't want to handle the thin scale because of its high price, around $150, at the stores. . . . They want to stop further development of the thin-scale project until the price comes down or different features are added."

Yabé's group at R&D could not get their latest prototype to pass the accuracy tests. They too wanted to suspend the project, and to "cool down." They were fatigued by their never-ending work, he wrote, and much distracted by the requirements placed upon them by the body-fat scales.

Originally, Oshima continued, Tanida had expected the thin scale to have many advantages over other scales, and many prospects in the future. Now he had received reports that were very discouraging to him, and that were making him feel very sorry for me as well. Still, Tanida felt that the thin-scale technology had some potential. He therefore proposed to pay me $150,000 for the patent rights, in lieu of running royalties.

In other words, Tanida had now decided to shelve the thin-scale project until further notice. The thin scale was not going to see the light of day anytime soon. It was not going to grace the shelves of stores anywhere, and it would not be displayed on the third floor of the Museum of Modern Art.

The prophet Moses, who walked through trials and tribulations in the desert for 40 years, got as far as seeing the Promised Land, but was not allowed to enter it. As it was said in the Book of Deuteronomy, "And Moses went up from the plains of Moab unto the mountain of Nebo . . . and the Lord said unto him, This is the land which I sware unto Abraham, unto Isaac, and unto Jacob, saying, I will give it unto thy seed: I have caused thee to see it with thine eyes, but thou shalt not go over thither."

I was no prophet and I was no Moses, but I too got as far as seeing the Promised Land without being allowed to enter it. Some trials and tribulations do end like that.

After some minimal negotiation, I agreed to assign all my patents—including the new patent for the owl face load cell—to Tanita for $250,000 and to forego any future royalties. We signed the assignment agreement in August 1997. All in all, Tanita paid me some $650,000 for my patents and know-how. It was more than enough to cover my costs and to pay for my living expenses while I played my never-ending thin-scale games. I never became fabulously rich.

* * *

I kept paying the French lawyers' fees over the next couple of years, unable to negotiate an out-of-court settlement and powerless to stop the proceedings as they dragged on. On 28 October 1999, the Lyon High Court issued its verdict. It found my French patent devoid of novelty because of the prior art disclosed in the Philips patent application of 1965, my claims to having differentiated it from the said application notwithstanding. Consequently, it ordered the French version of my patent cancelled, and it rejected my infringement claim. It also ruled that Tefal had suffered from the infringement seizure and the resulting uncertainty of its sales following the seizure, and instructed me to pay $10,000 in compensatory damages. I chose not to appeal.

A few months after that verdict was issued in France, on 20 April 2000, I received a letter from Soehnle's legal counsel in Germany. The counsel challenged my German load cell patent, given the above-mentioned Philips prior art, and advanced the opinion that Soenhle was now free to use the information disclosed in my patent, if and when it saw fit to do so (and certainly without the payment of any and all compensation).

With these corporate giants eager to exploit my patent, there was no question in my mind that my work was not all in vain, and that I had made some small contribution to the body of knowledge pertaining to personal scales. I felt like that small stream coming down from Eltz Castle, disappearing into the wide Mosel River below, losing its identity in something larger than itself as it started its final journey into the great sea.

* * *

Was I disappointed that, after all these years, nothing had come out of my untiring efforts? Surely, I was disappointed. But that painful disappointment had its bright side too. It made it possible for me to let go of my vision and to get on with the rest of my life.

I had had a vision of a new consumer product, after all. And the ultimate reality test for a consumer product—or for any product or service offered on the market, for that matter—is its profitability. "A business should quickly stand on its own," says Konosuke Matsushita, the founder of the Matsushita Electric Company, "based on the service it provides the society. Profits should not be a reflection of corporate greed but a vote of confidence from society that what is offered by the firm is valued. When a business fails to make profit it should die—it is a waste of resources to society." My vision of the thin scale did not pass that profitability test, and until it does, it will not have a place in the marketplace.

I had worked long and hard to bring that thin scale to market, and I had given it years of my best creative energies. But much as I had tried, and much as I had wanted to, I knew all along that I could not will it into being. In *The Bhagavad Gita*, the famous Indian epic poem, Krishna says to Arjuna: "You have a right to your actions, but never to your actions' fruits." In his commentary on *The Bhagavad Gita*, Mahatma Gandhi had this to say:

> This is the unmistakable teaching of the Gita. He who gives up action falls. He who gives up only the reward rises. But renunciation of fruit in no way means indifference to the result. In regard to every action one must know the result that is expected to follow, the means thereto, and the capacity for it. He, who, being thus equipped, is without desire for the result, and is yet wholly engrossed in the due fulfillment of the task before him, is said to have renounced the fruits of his action.

At the end of the day, the fruits of my actions were not to be mine. And that was fine. That essential insight offered at the beginning of this book—"Either things go according to plan or there is a story"—did not come to mean that the story is the consolation prize for people whose plans do not materialize, for people who do not reap the fruits of their actions. That would imply that it is preferable for things to go according to plan and to not produce a story. I, for one, do not harbor such a preference, and I am sure that my father's partner—the man who imparted this lesson to me when I was ten—did not either. I remember him as an avid storyteller, and in due time, as I grew up, I became one too.

And so, while I was pursuing the vision of the thin scale, my curiosity about my own story held the same power over me as did my intention to realize that vision, to carry out my plan, and to reap the fruits it promised. I was curious to know where the scale would lead me next, what I would do when I confronted the next monster on my path, and what lessons I would learn along the way that I could pass on to others. And while the vision of the thin scale compelled me towards its realization, I have to confess that my zeal for adventure—for getting deeper into the story—pulled me ahead with no less force.

It was the same force that has always driven storytellers. "The story-teller makes many a station," says Thomas Mann, "roving and relating, but pauses only tentwise, awaiting further directions, and soon feels his heart beating high, partly with desire, partly too from fear and anguish of the flesh, but in any case as a sign that he must take the road towards fresh adventures which are to be painstakingly lived through, down to their remotest details, according to the restless spirit's will."

Right from the start, in fact, I chose a plan that promised to set me free, a goal that would force me to climb hills from which I could see new landscapes that were not visible from the already trodden paths that I had taken before. I knew myself enough by then to understand that, much as I was interested in realizing life's higher truths, I was not cut out for silent contemplation and long hours of meditation in quiet mountain monasteries.

No, if there was a meditative practice that suited me it would have to be meditation in action, developing awareness and searching for higher levels of understanding while I embarked on a voyage of discovery that would take me all the way to the knowledge frontier, to the land where inventions are made, where our collective psyche rubs against the unknown. The teachings, I knew already, were everywhere.

What I wanted to accomplish on that journey was no less than to create myself anew as I created a new scale, to affect my transformation into a truly unique individual. "A true individual," writes Alexander Nehamas in *Nietzsche: Life as Literature*, "is precisely one who is different from the rest of the world, and there is no formula, no set of rules, no code of conduct that can possibly capture in informative terms what it is to be like that. . . . The very notion of the individual makes it impossible to say in informative terms how one could ever become that."

My approach to that creative challenge was to take on a small vision of little consequence and to pursue it to the four corners of the world, sparing no effort to realize it. True, I did not manage to realize that vision. But I did, in no small measure, manage to fashion a story that now defines me as an individual. Pursue your story, I say, and the story shall set you free.

Notes

Chapter 1:

5   Questions . . . religions: See discussion in De Botton, Alain, 2000, *The Consolations of Philosophy,* New York: Vintage Books, 106.

6   This . . . career: O'Connor, J. J., and E. F. Robertson, 1999, "William Thomson (Lord Kelvin)," School of Mathematics and Statistics, University of St. Andrews, Scotland, online at www-history.mcs.st-andrews.ac.uk/history/mathematicians/Thomson.html, updated July.

8   Science . . . rational: Feyerabend, Paul, 1988, *Against Method,* London and New York: Verso, 26.

9   Edison's . . . bamboo: Jerome and Dorothy Lemelson Center for the Study of Invention and Innovation, 1997, "The Electric Light," Washington D.C.: The Smithsonian Institution, online at www.si.edu/lemelson/edison/html/electric light bulb_html, updated 22 October.

9   New . . . perception: Quoted in Shah, Idries, 1970, *Tales of the Dervishes,* New York: E. P. Dutton, 197.

Chapter 2:

11   Weighing . . . 1250 B.C.: Budge, E. A. Wallis, editor, 1899, *The Egyptian Book of the Dead: Facsimiles of the Papyiri of Hunefer, Anhai, Kerāsher and Netchemet,* Chap. CXXV, British Museum.

16   No sooner . . . line: Shurkin, Joel, [1984] 1996, *Engines of the Mind: The Evolution of the Computer from Mainframes to Microprocessors,* New York and London: W. W. Norton, 48.

18   An unknown . . . to me: Doebelin, Ernest O., 1975, *Measurement Systems: Application and Design,* New York: McGraw Hill, 333.

Chapter 3:

21   There . . . *Knots*: Laing, R. D., 1970, *Knots,* New York: Pantheon Books, 56.

Chapter 4:

28   *Notes . . . Form*: Alexander, Christopher, 1964, *Notes on the Synthesis of Form,* Cambridge, Mass.: Harvard University Press.

29   We should . . . misfit: Alexander, 1964, 24.

29   The Magical . . . Information: Miller, George A., 1956, "The Magical Number Seven, Plus or Minus Two: Some Limits on Our Capacity for Processing Information, *The Psychological Review,* vol. 63, 81–97.

30   In the beginning . . . God: *The Gospel According to St. John,* 1:1.

30   Alexander . . . *Language*: Alexander, Christopher, Sara Ishikawa, Murray Silverstein, Max Jacobson, Ingrid Fiksdahl-King, and Shlomo Angel, 1977, *A Pattern Language: Towns, Buildings, Construction,* New York and Oxford: Oxford University Press.

30   Harry Jones: Not his real name. A few names of people, institutions, and places mentioned in the book have been changed, but the facts and stories pertaining to them have not.

31   Harry . . . inaccurate: House Committee on Government Operations, 1992, "Oversight Hearing on the Performance of the Patriot Missile in the Gulf War," One Hundred Second Congress, Washington D.C., April 7, 179.

31   When . . . them: Welch, Jack, 2001, *Jack: Straight from the Gut,* with John A. Byrne, New
      York: Warner Business Books, 40–41.

33   A still . . . compression: Hatschek, Emil, 1914, "Gestalt und Orientierung von Gesblasen in
      Gelen," *Kolloidzschrift* 15, 226–34, described in D'Arcy Wentworth Thompson, [1917] 1971,
      On Growth and Form, abridged edition edited by John Tyler Bonner, Cambridge: Cam-
      bridge University Press, 224.

34   When . . . kind: Quoted in MacHale, Desmond, 1993, *Comic Sections: A Book of Mathemati-
      cal Jokes, Humour, Wit and Wisdom*, Dublin: Boole Press, 145.

35   Peter . . . frustration: Stein, Peter K., 2001, "Strain Gage History and the End of the Twenti-
      eth Century," *Experimental Techniques*, March/April, 15.

37   Mortgages . . . affordable: Angel, Shlomo, *et al.*, 1987, *The Land and Housing Markets of
      Bangkok: Strategies for Public-Sector Participation*, Planning and Development Collabora-
      tive International (PADCO), Bangkok.

38   As far . . . countries: Hoffman, Michael, Barbara Haupt, and Raymond J. Struyk, 1992,
      International Housing Markets: What We Know; What We Need to Know, Washington, D.C.:
      Fannie Mae Office of Housing Policy Research.

Chapter 5:
39   In . . . *Bedazzled: Bedazzled*, a screenplay by Peter Cook, 1967.
41   For this . . . about it: Scale Diary, 17 September 1987.
41   In fact . . . Mousetrap: Statement by Jodie Bernstein, Director, Bureau of Consumer Pro-
      tection, Federal Trade Commission, press conference, 23 July 1997, online at
      www.ftc.gov/opa/1997/9707/mousejb.htm.

42   While . . . best efforts: MacCracken, Calvin D., 1983, *A Handbook for Inventors: How to Pro-
      tect, Patent, Finance, Develop, Manufacture, and Market Your Ideas*, New York: Charles
      Scribner's & Sons, 111.

42   All know-how . . . property of: See, for example, MacCracken, 1983, 110.

Chapter 6:
47   It was . . . structure: Hoff, N. J., and S. E. Mautner, 1944, "Sandwich Construction," *Aero-
      nautical Engineering Review*, vol. 3, August, 463.

47   The core . . . side: Gordon, J. E., 1978, *Structures, or Why Things Don't Fall Down*, Har-
      mondsworth and New York: Penguin Books, 296.

47   The core . . . construction: Vinson, Jack R., 2001, "Sandwich Structures," *Applied Mechanics
      Reviews*, vol. 54, no. 3, May, 203.

47   The main . . . weight: Vinson, 2001, 201.
47   A simple. . . . times: Vinson, 2001, 201–202.
48   And Pharaoh . . . themselves: Exod. 5:6–7.
50   A young . . . blaze: It was quickly rebuilt. The story of that monk is recounted by Yukio
      Mishima, [1956] 1994, *Temple of the Golden Pavilion*, translated by Ivan I. Morris, paper-
      back edition, New York: Random House.

Chapter 7:
52   Purity . . . 1846: Kierkegaard, Søren, [1846] 1956, *Purity of Heart is To Will One Thing*, trans-
      lated by Douglas V. Steere, New York: Harper & Row, 53.

54   But . . . details: Henri Poincaré, [1908] 1924, *The Foundations of Science*, translated by G. B.
      Halstead, New York and Garrison, N.Y.: Science Press. First published in 1908 as *Science et
      Méthode*, Paris: Flammarion. Reproduced in Vernon, P. E., 1970, *Creativity: Selected Read-
      ings*, Harmondsworth, Middlesex: Penguin Education, 84–85.

54   Under . . . aggregated (*coacervatio*): Kant, Immanuel, [1881] 1911, *Immanuel Kant's Critique
      of Pure Reason*, translated by F. Max Müller, revised second edition, New York: Macmillan,
      667–668.

Chapter 8:

59 During... territories: U.S. Patent and Trademark Office, 2000, *Century of American Invention*, a Patent and Trademark Office Review, Washington D.C., Table 8.

60 All in... engineering: A multiple regression model using the number of patents issued as a dependent variable and these three variables as independent variables shows that variations in these three variables explain 96 percent of the variation in the numbers of patents issued. All three were significant at the 1 percent level.

60 Of... Los Angeles: U.S. Patent and Trademark Office, 2001, Agent and Attorney Roster, online at www.uspto.gov/web/offices/dcom/olia/oed/roster/index.html.

63 To some... China: Morris, de Witt Clinton, and Rutherford, quoted in Mackay, Donald A, 1987, *The Building of Manhattan*, New York: Harper and Row, 20.

64 Many are... themselves: Mainstone, Rowland J., 1977, "Brunnelleschi's Dome," *Architectural Review*, September, 164, quoted in King, Ross, 2000, *Brunneleschi's Dome: How a Renaissance Genius Reinvented Architecture*, Harmondsworth: Penguin Books.

64 Brunelleschi... invention: Frumkin, Maximilian, 1947, "Early History of Patents for Invention," *Transactions of the Newcomen Society*, 26, 48.

64 In 1421... usual: Prager, Frank D., and Gustina Scaglia, 1970, *Brunneleschi: Studies of His Technology and Inventions*, Cambridge: MIT Press, 111.

64 The ship... inventor: King, 2000, 108–117.

64 We have... years: Quoted by Gilfillan, S.C., 1968, *Invention and the Patent System*, presented for consideration of the Joint Economic Committee, Congress of the United States, Washington D.C.: U.S. Government Printing Service, 11; after Mandich, G., 1948, "Venetian Patents 1450–1550," translated by F. D. Prager, *Journal of the Patent Office Society*, vol. 30, 166–224.

65 The king's grants... at large: Blackstone, William, 1768, *Commentaries on the Laws of England*, vol. 2, Oxford: Oxford University Press, 346.

66 The self-help... time: Pressman, David, 1985, *Patent it Yourself*, Berkeley, Calif.: Nolo Press.

68 A low-profile... shear: U.S. Patents and Trademark Office, 1989, "Portable Electronic Scale of Minimal Thickness and Weight," U.S. Patent No. 4,800,973, issued to S. Angel, 31 January, 10.59–11.8.

Chapter 9:

69 And then... made: Goldman, William, 1983, *Adventures in the Screen Trade: A Personal View of Hollywood and Screenwriting*, New York: Warner Books, 401.

70 A modest... City: *New York Times*, 1995, "The Oldest Drinking Establishment in New York," November 19, online at www.bridgecafe.citysearch.com.

72 The architect... old: Venturi, Robert, 1966, *Complexity and Contradiction in Architecture*, New York: The Museum of Modern Art, 43.

76 Design... praise: Dormer, Peter, 1990, *The Meanings of Modern Design: Towards the Twenty-First Century*, London: Thames and Hudson, 134.

77 If there... craft: Greenough, Horatio, [1852] 1947, *Form and Function: Remarks on Art by Horatio Greenough*, edited by Harold A. Small, Berkeley and Los Angeles: University of California Press, 118–121.

77 The laws... origin: Greenough, 1947, 116.

77 Not only... incompleteness: Greenough, 1947, 74.

77 That was... 1908: Loos, Adolf, [1908] 1998. *Ornament and Crime: Selected Essays*, Riverside, Calif.: Ariadne Press.

77 The turning point... corruption: Greenough, 1947, 125–126.

78 The simplest... spherical: Weyl, Herman, 1952, *Symmetry*, Princeton: Princeton University Press, 27.

79 The qualities... physical: Morris, Robert, 1968, "Notes on Sculpture," in Battock, Gregory, editor, *Minimal Art: A Critical Anthology*, New York: E. P. Dutton, 225.

79 Indeed... potent: Rudolph, Paul, 1961, *Perspecta: the Yale Architectural Journal*, 7, vol. 51, quoted in Venturi, 1966, 17.

80 Architects . . . bore: Venturi, 1966, 17.

82 An old . . . felt like: Dormer, 1990, 21–22.

83 Initially . . . unfamiliar: Caplan, Ralph, 1982, *By Design: Why There Are No Locks on the Bathroom Doors in the Hotel Louis XIV and Other Object Lessons*, New York: McGraw Hill, 116.

83 A steelyard . . . first century A.D.: Ciarallo, Annamaria, and Ernesto de Carolis, editors, 1999, *Pompeii: Life in a Roman Town*, Milan: Electa, Fig. 369, 299.

83 How . . . its use: Mitchell, C. Thomas, 1996, "Michael McCoy: Interpretive Design," an interview with Michael McCoy, in *New Thinking in Design: Conversations on Theory and Practice*, New York: Von Nostrand Reinhold, 6.

83 Posted . . . design: Mitchell, 1996, "Donald Norman: Cognitive Engineering," an interview with Donald Norman, 99.

83 That building . . . concealed: Ruskin, John, [1849] 1989, *The Seven Lamps of Architecture*, New York: Dover, 35.

86 Thinking . . . you are: Mitchell, 1996, "John Chris Jones: Of All So Many of Us," an interview with John Christopher Jones, 152.

86 Its designer . . . shoes: Quoted in Specter, Michael, 2001, "The Phone Guy: How Nokia Designed What May Be the Best-Selling Cellular Products on Earth," *New Yorker*, November 26, 67.

Chapter 10:

89 King David . . . [nail]: Klein, H. Arthur, 1974, *The World of Measurements*, New York: Simon and Schuster, 54.

97 A bathroom scale . . . tyrant: Moorhouse, Laurence E., and Leonard Gross, 1975, *Total fitness in 30 Minutes a Week*, New York: Simon and Schuster, 92–93.

Chapter 11:

105 This insensitivity . . . motions: Simon, Herbert A., [1969] 1981, *The Sciences of the Artificial*, second edition, Cambridge Mass.: MIT Press, 11–12.

107 The methods . . . critical: Gregotti, Vittorio, 1996, *Inside Architecture*, Cambridge, Mass.: MIT Press, 52.

108 In other . . . load: It also turns out that when the gages are lined exactly along the centerline of the beam, the arrangement is also insensitive to shifting the load in the direction parallel to the wall—one resistance increases, the other decreases by the same amount, and the difference between them remains the same.

Chapter 12:

111 The past . . . Society: Katona, George, 1964, *The Mass Consumption Society*, New York: McGraw Hill, 3.

112 A clever . . . in them: Count Helmuth von Moltke (1848–1916), quoted in Liddell Hart, Basil H., 1967, *Strategy*, New York: Signet Classics, xiii.

116 By the 1970s . . . (Fig. 34): Paraphrased form Durham, Ken, 1996, "History of Coin Operated Scales," online at www.GameRoomAntiques.com.

116 His most . . . perspiration: Van der Helden, Albert, 1995, "Santorio Santorio (1561–1636)," online at es.rice.edu/ES/humsoc/Galileo/People/santorio.html.

116 According . . . years: Katch, Frank I., William D. McArdle, and Victor L. Katch, 1997, "Santorio Santorio (1561–1636)," online at www.sportsci.org/news/history/2002/santorio.html.

117 The patient . . . or worse: Quoted from *Today in Technology History*, 2002, online at www.tecsoc.org/pubs/history/2002/feb22.html.

117 The chair . . . ridiculous: Sanctorius, 1676, *Medicina Statica: Or, Rules of Health in Eight Sections*, translated by J. D., London: John Starkey.

119 A patent . . . 1822: Kisch, Bruno, 1965, *Scales and Weights: a Historical Outline*, New Haven and London: Yale University Press, 76.

122 By the time . . . markup: Brzezinski, Matthew, 2002, "Re-Engineering the Drug Trade," *New York Times Magazine*, 23 June, 26.

122   The heroin ... $10: National Drug Intelligence Center, 2000, "Heroin Distribution in Three Cities," November, online at www.usdoj.gov/ndic/pubs/648/retail.html.

Chapter 13:

125   Here then ... *Things*: Petroski, Henry, 1992, *The Evolution of Useful Things*, New York: Alfred A. Knopf, 2.

125   The library ... *Pocus*: Vonnegut, Kurt, 1990, *Hocus Pocus*, New York: G. P. Putnam Sons, 41.

128   David Pye ... an impossibility: Pye, David, [1964] 1978, *The Nature and Aesthetics of Design*, New York: Van Nostrand Reinhold, 70.

129   Nothing ... design: Bucciarelli, Louis L., 1994, *Designing Engineers*, Cambridge, Mass.: MIT Press, 156–157 and 187.

129   For most ... flailing effort: Dickinson, Duo, 1996, *Expressive Details*, New York: McGraw Hill, xvii.

130   Design ... thing: Pugh, Stuart, 1990, *Total Design: Integrated Methods for Successful Product Engineering*, Wokingham: Addison Wesley, 136.

130   Eloquent ... simple: Gregotti, 1996, 83–84.

133   Problem solving ... error: Simon, 1981, 193–194.

133   We see ... eliminated: Simon, 1981, 195–196.

138   Cues signaling ... subassembly: Simon, 1981, 194.

138   The designer ... idea: French, Michael, 1994, *Invention and Evolution: Design in Nature and Engineering*, second edition, Cambridge, Mass.: Cambridge University Press, 251.

140   It is ... improvements: Petroski, Henry, 1994, *Design Paradigms: Case Histories of Error and Judgment in Engineering*, Cambridge, UK: Cambridge University Press, 94.

140   *Basics of ... Design*: Brendel, Albert E., *Basics of Successful Transducer Design*, 1981, unpublished, Hartford, Conn.: Sensor Development Inc.

141   The mind ... repertoire: French, 1994, 308.

Chapter 14:

143   Genius? ... Edison: Quoted in Petroski, 1992, 49.

143   For those ... *Words*: Canetti, Elias, [1965] 1979, "Dialogue with the Cruel Partner," in *The Conscience of Words*, New York: The Seabury Press, 52.

144   Often ... Ship it!: Kidder, Tracy, 1981, *The Soul of a New Machine*, Boston: Little, Brown, 120.

144   No ... design: Scale Diary, 11 March 1989.

145   When ... obituary: Bucciarelli, 1994, 195.

146   I have ... them: Scale Diary, 30 November 1989.

146   There is ... unkind: Scale Diary, 30 November 1989.

147   I ... last one: McKay, Harvey, 1990, *Beware the Naked Man Who Offers You His Shirt*, New York: William Morrow, 176.

147   I explained ... work: Scale Diary, 21 February 1989.

148   These forces ... unloaded: Scale Diary, 28 February 1989.

150   Every day ... too tight: Hirschmann, Jane, and Carol M. Munter, 1988, *Overcoming Overeating: Living Free in a World of Food*, New York: Addison-Wesley, 70–71.

151   Traditional ... injustice: Kula, Witold, 1986, *Measures and Men*, translated by R. Szreter, Princeton, N.J.: Princeton University Press, 123.

151   Among ... significance: Kula, 1986, 13.

151   By ... priority: Scale Diary, 7 December 1988.

152   The ... good or not: Papanek, Victor, 1992, *Design for the Real World: Human Ecology and Social Change*, second edition, Chicago: Academy Chicago Publishers, 55.

152   No longer ... himself: Papanek, 1992, 40.

154   At a dinner ... technologies: Scale Diary, 11 March 1989.

156   The moment ... in it: Eco, Umberto, 1989, *The Open Work*, 1989, Cambridge, Mass.: Harvard University Press, 126–130.

157   The availability ... essential: Eco, 1989, 134.

160   Hubert . . . *Let Go*: Benoit, Hubert, 1962, *Let Go*, London: George Allen and Unwin.

163   Designing . . . exchange: Bucciarelli, 1994, 159.

165   Creativity . . . failures: Simonton, D. K., 1995, "Creativity as Heroic: Risk, Failure, and Acclaim," in Ford, C. M., and D. A. Gioia, editors, *Creative Action in Organizations,* Thousand Oaks, Calif.: Sage, 88.

Chapter 15:

167   People think . . . yes: Fisher, Roger, and William Ury, 1981, *Getting to Yes: Negotiating Agreement Without Giving In,* New York: Houghton Mifflin, 106–108.

167   If money . . . *Friend:* Laut, Phil, [1978] 1989, *Money Is My Friend,* New York: Ballantine, 11 and 37.

168   It's probably . . . in: Quoted in *New York Times,* 31 October 1971.

171   The vital . . . separate: Papanek, 1984, 292–293.

177   Looks like . . . the market: Scale Diary, 24 February 1990.

177   That is . . . to accept: Fisher and Ury, 1981, 104.

183   Americans . . . basis: Karrass, Chester L., 1974, *Give and Take: The Complete Guide to Negotiating Strategies and Tactics,* New York: Thomas Y. Crowell, 142.

Chapter 16:

185   What you . . . *Dollars:* Kracke, Don, with Roger Honkanen, 1979, *How to Turn Your Idea Into a Million Dollars,* New York: Doubleday, 89–90.

185   *Grant of . . . Inventors:* MacCracken, Calvin, 1983, 190.

191   They still . . . time: U.S. Department of Labor data, quoted in Business Research Bureau, 1997, *South Dakota Business Review: December 1996,* "Table 5: Manufacturing Employment Shares in Selected Countries (Percent)," University of South Dakota, online at www.usd.edu/brbinfo/businessreviews/1996/ dc96tabs.html.

193   We see . . . Jahn said: Joedicke, Joachim Andreas, 1986, *Helmut Jahn: Design of a New Architecture,* New York: Nichols Publishing Company, 9–10.

197   The outcome . . . you: Scale Diary, 12 June 1990.

202   He really . . . *Success:* Floyd, Chris, 1997, *Managing Technology for Corporate Success,* Aldershot: Gower, 201.

204   I was . . . solve: Scale Diary, 20 October 1990.

204   Ziggy Zee: Not his real name.

Chapter 17:

205   I have . . . *Development:* Frand, Erwin A., 1989, *The Art of Product Development: From Concept to Market,* Homewood, Ill.: Dow Jones-Irwin, 4.

205   The conditions . . . *Postmodernity:* Harvey, David, 1989, *The Condition of Postmodernity,* Oxford: Blackwell, 101.

205   The company . . . Systems: In this chapter, the names of people, companies, their locations, as well as some of their identifying characteristics, have been changed.

207   A dominant . . . following: Narayanan, V. K., 2001, *Managing Technology and Innovation for Competitive Advantage,* Upper Saddle River, N.J.: Prentice Hall, 137.

208   A core . . . market: Burgelman, Robert A., Modesto A. Maidique, and Steven C. Wheelwright, 1996, *Strategic Management of Technology and Innovation,* second edition, Boston: Irwin/McGraw Hill, 137. Italics are mine.

209   Whirled . . . blind: Ungo (1580–1659), in Stryk, Lucien, editor, 1968, *World of the Buddha: An Introduction to Buddhist Literature,* New York: Grove Press, 354.

210   The acquisition . . . technology: Roberts, E. B., 1995, "Benchmarking the Strategic Management of Technology—I," *Research Technology Management,* January-February, Fig. 12, 55; quoted in Chiesa, Vittorio, 2001, *R&D Strategy and Organization: Managing Technical Change in Dynamic Contexts,* London: Imperial College Press, 235–236.

211   Outsourcing . . . high: Chiesa, 2001, 249.

214 They observed . . . it: Smith, Preston G., and Donald G. Reinersten, 1991, *Developing Products in Half the Time,* New York: Van Nostrand Reinhold, 43–46.

215 A characteristic . . . specific: Narayanan, 2001, 83.

215 Stigler . . . name to it: Stigler, Stephen M., 1999, *Statistics on the Table: The History of Statistical Concepts and Methods,* Cambridge, Mass.: Harvard University Press.

217 In . . . for success: Burgelman *et al.,* 1996, 657–659.

217 We . . . need more champions: Thomas E. Singer, quoted in Gruenwald, George, 1985, *New Product Development: What Really Works,* Chicago: Crane Books, 81.

219 He may . . . finisher: Paraphrasing a comment by Floyd, 1997, 185.

220 To play . . . obstacles: Suits, Bernard, 1990, *The Grasshopper: Games, Life and Utopia,* Boston: David R. Godine, 41.

223 The paper . . . "to Work": World Bank, 1993, *Housing: Enabling Markets to Work,* World Bank Policy Paper, Washington, D.C.: The World Bank.

223 The World . . . place: Gilbert, Alan, 2000, "Housing in Latin America," draft background paper, prepared for the Inter-American Development Bank, Washington, D.C., 30 November.

227 Am I . . . the ugly: Scale Diary, 14 October 1992.

Chapter 18:

228 That all . . . *Generalis:* Translated from the Latin by Daniella Gitlin.

228 The manufacture . . . *Weights:* Kisch, 1965, 211.

228 Abraham . . . silver: Gen. 23:15, King James Version.

228 Currencies . . . are examples: Kisch, 1965, 6 and 219.

232 But . . . ethical commerce: Kisch, 1965, 1.

232 Kisch . . . the object: Kisch, 1965, 3–4.

232 Tested in . . . the mint: Soloweitschik, Max, 1924/5, *Sekhiyot ha-Mikra: Otsar Temunot le-Khitve ha-Kodesh Ulekadmoniyotehem,* Berlin: Devir-Mikra, Fig. 152, 75.

Chapter 19:

237 There is . . . *Create:* May, Rollo, 1975, *The Courage to Create,* New York: W. W. Norton, 126–127.

238 Inspirations . . . spontaneously: Sinnott, Edmund W., [1959] 1970, *The Creativeness of Life;* reproduced in Vernon, P. E., 1970, *Creativity: Selected Readings,* Harmondsworth, Middlesex: Penguin Education, 110.

239 What are . . . smile at it: Henri Poincaré, [1908] 1924, 84–85.

240 The superior . . . connections: Carroll, J. T., and T. F. Bellinger, 1969, "Designing Reliability into Rubber and Plastic AC Motor Control Equipment," *IEEE Trans. Industry and General Applications,* vol. 5 no. 5, 455–464, quoted in Pugh, 1990, 134.

240 The term . . . originality: Koestler, Arthur, 1964, *The Act of Creation,* New York: Macmillan, 96.

244 There are . . . reversal: Alexander *et al.,* 1977, 518–519.

245 Like . . . scientific discovery: Briggs, John, 1988, *Fire in the Crucible: The Alchemy of Creative Genius,* New York: St. Martin's Press, 122.

Chapter 20:

247 There are . . . *Management:* Pascale, Richard Tanner, and Anthony G. Athos, 1981, *The Art of Japanese Management: Applications for American Executives,* New York: Simon and Schuster, 136–139.

253 In Japanese . . . performance: Laurie, Dennis, 1992, *Yankee Samurai: American Managers Speak Out About What It's Like to Work for Japanese Companies in the U.S.,* New York: Harper Business, 204.

257 Whereas . . . the role: Pascale and Athos, 1981, 126.

257 It is . . . his followers: Greenleaf, Robert K., 1996, *On Becoming a Servant-Leader,* edited by Don M. Frick and Larry C. Spears, San Francisco: Jossey-Bass, 171 and 334.

259   For every . . . scene: Laurie, 1992, 311.

261   Because . . . several statutes: Kirsh, 1965, 28.

261   According to . . . a minimum: Paraphrasing Chisholm, Henry William, 1877, *On the Science of Weighing and Measuring and Standards of Measure and Weight,* London: Macmillan, 135; quoted in Kisch, 1965, 32.

263   Commitment . . . intended: Laurie, 1992, 236.

Chapter 21:

266   So closes . . . *Upward*: Alger, Horatio, [1890] 1985, *Struggling Upward, or Luke Larkin's Luck,* in *Ragged Dick and Struggling Upward,* New York: Penguin Books, 280.

267   The creative . . . judgment: Gardner, Howard, *Creating Minds: An Anatomy of Creativity Seen Through the Lives of Freud, Einstein, Picasso, Stravinsky, Eliot, Graham, and Gandhi,* New York: Basic Books, 35–36.

267   I can imagine . . . time: Comment by Georgia O'Keeffe in *Georgia O'Keeffe,* 1977, a film produced and directed by Perry Miller Adato for WNET/13; quoted in Briggs, 1988, 132.

272   At some . . . embrace: May, 1975, 126–127.

Chapter 22:

273   You have . . . *Gita: Bhagavad Gita,* 2000, translated by Stephen Mitchell, New York: Harmony Books, 54–55.

273   Six years . . . and Krups: Groupe SEB, 2002, *Annual Report 2001,* 7, online at www.groupeseb.com/english/finance/pdf/doc/rapportannuel2001.pdf.

274   There was . . . acknowledged it: French Patent Application 2,734,050, page 6, line 35.

274   Fig. 73 . . . the cat face load cell: Drawing on the right is Fig. 1 in French Patent Application 2,734,050, *Capteur de Poids Autoporteur et Appareil de Pesage Compartant de tells Capteurs,* submitted by Anthoine, Pitaud, and Sarrazin on 9 May 1995 on behalf of SEB.

277   Generally . . . the person is: Bannan, Karen J., 2002, "No Calipers or Cringing: A Discreet Gauge of Body Fat," *New York Times,* 28 November, G5.

278   And Moses . . . over thither: Deut. 34:1–4.

280   A business . . . to society: Quoted in Pascale and Athos, 1981, 46.

280   This is . . . his action: Mohandas K. Gandhi, [1982] 1996, *The Words of Gandhi,* selected by Richard Attenborough, New York: Newmarket Press, 18.

280   The storyteller . . . spirit's will: Quoted by Ghiselin, Brewster, 1952, editor, *The Creative Process,* Berkeley and Los Angeles: University of California Press, 8.

281   A true individual . . . become that: Nehamas, Alexander, 1985, *Nietzsche: Life as Literature,* Cambridge, Mass.: Harvard University Press, 225.

Acknowledgments

Many friends helped me in the preparation of this book. I thank Lucy Gitlin and Itzhak (Koko) Kronzon for patiently reading each chapter after it was completed, and for giving me useful, detailed comments all along the way that kept my writing on course. I also thank Ralph Gakenheimer, Peter Swan, Murray Silverstein, and Alain Bertaud for reading the manuscript in its entirety and providing me with invaluable suggestions for improvement.

Several others read selected chapters and offered useful comments. I thank Jacob Enoch, Paul Minden, Lee Adamo, Daniella Gitlin, Terry Higgins, Ziva Kronzon, Joshua Neustein, Avi Nesher, Gideon Ofrat, Gershon Ben-Shakhar, Avraham Vachman, and Ziva Schwartz for their supportive encouragement and their constructive remarks. I am also grateful to Aharon Gluska for his sustaining optimism along the way.

I am grateful to Joyce Berry at Oxford University Press for giving me the opportunity to publish this book, and for my editor at the Press, Kirk Jensen, for his numerous suggestions for improvements and for advancing the book project along with enthusiasm and effectiveness.

I thank James Dee, Talia Cohen, Michael Gitlin, and Ariel Lifshitz for helping me prepare the manuscript for publication.

Finally, I would like to thank my little family—Lucy, Adam, and Daniella—who shared their enthusiasm, their love, and their patience with me, and helped release and sustain the good energies I needed to embark upon and finish this work.

Credits

The author drew the sketches accompanying the text. Several photographs used in the text were taken by the author or by his friends.

The following illustrations were reproduced by permission from the following persons and institutions: Fig. 3. Edison's patent for the electric lamp (page 9): U.S. Patent and Trademark Office; Fig. 6. A drawing of the Babbage difference engine (page 16): Science and Society Picture Library, London; Fig. 11. A column being stretched in a universal testing machine (page 32): photo of Zwick Model Z2.5/TN1S by Zwick/Roell AG; Fig. 15. Public housing overshadowed by illegal housing in Caracas (page 45): photo by Michael Menendez; Fig. 16. The Mosquito fighter-bomber (page 46): Model by Chris Wauchop, photographed by Brett Green; Fig. 22. The 1999 geographical distribution of patents (page 59): U.S. Patent and Trademark Office; Fig. 24. Brancusi's *Bird in Space*, 1924 (page 78): Philadelphia Museum of Art; Fig. 25. The Eishin School, Alexander and Associates (page 81): Artifice Inc.; Fig. 27. A steelyard scale found in Pompeii (page 83): Superintendency of Archaeology Napoli; Fig. 28. "Rose is Rose" cartoon (page 84): United Media; Fig. 34 A National Novelty coin-operated scale (page 116): photo by Jeff Storck, personal collection; Fig. 37. "Frank and Ernest" cartoon (page 120): United Media; Fig. 51. The United Airlines Terminal in Chicago, Helmut Jahn: (page 192): Artifice Inc. Fig. 53. A Filipino Jeepney (page 209: Photo by Jens Peters in his Philippines Travel Guide, 2001; Fig. 57. A Babylonian lion weight (page 232): The Dorot Jewish Division, New York Public Library; Fig. 63. A Caucasian Star Kazak rug (page 243): Antique Collectors' Club, Suffolk, England; Fig. 68. A Hittite relief showing a balance (page 262): the Louvre Museum, Paris.

The poem on page 21, from *Knots* by R. D. Laing, is reproduced by permission from Random House Inc.

Index